John Dorst

The Literary
Journalists

D0048525

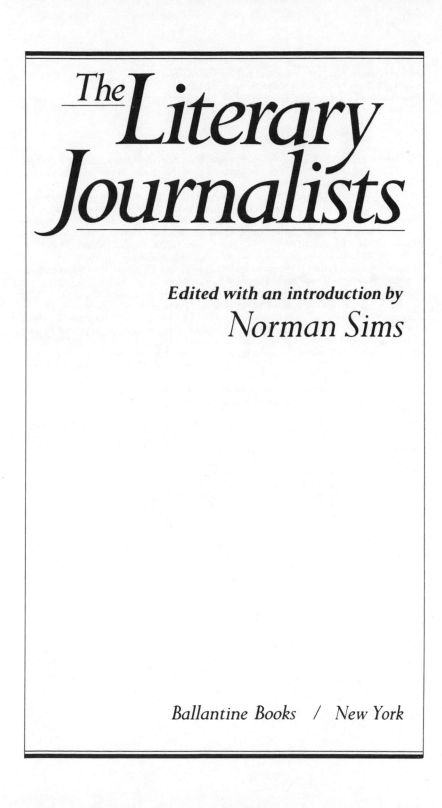

The Literary Journalists

Edited with an introduction by

Norman Sims

Ballantine Books / New York

Copyright © 1984 by Norman Sims

All rights reserved under International and Pan-American
Copyright Conventions. Published in the United States by
Ballantine Books, a division of Random House, Inc. New York,
and simultaneously in Canada by Random House of Canada Ltd.
Toronto.

"Travels in Georgia" by John McPhee is reprinted from *Pieces of the Frame*. Copyright © 1973,
1975 by John McPhee. This piece first appeared in *The New Yorker*. Reprinted by permission
of Farrar, Straus and Giroux, Inc.
"Salvador" by Joan Didion is reprinted from *Salvador*. Copyright © 1983 by Joan Didion. Reprinted by permission of Simon & Schuster, a division of Gulf & Western Corporation.
"The Angels" by Tom Wolfe appeared as Chapter 1 from *The Right Stuff*. Copyright © 1979
by Tom Wolfe. Reprinted by permission of Farrar, Straus and Giroux, Inc.
"Death All Day" by Richard Rhodes is reprinted from *The Inland Ground*. Copyright © 1969,
1970 by Richard Rhodes. Reprinted by permission of JCA Literary Agency, Inc.
"Cowboy" by Jane Kramer is excerpted from *The Last Cowboy*. Copyright © 1978 by Jane Kramer. Reprinted by permission of Harper & Row, Publishers, Inc.
"Invasive Procedures" by Mark Kramer is reprinted from *Invasive Procedures*. Copyright © 1979,
1983 by Mark Kramer. Reprinted by permission of Harper & Row, Publishers, Inc.
"Flying Upside Down" by Tracy Kidder is excerpted from *The Soul of a New Machine*. Copyright
© 1981 by John Tracy Kidder. This piece first appeared in *The Atlantic*. Reprinted by per-
mission of Little, Brown and Company in association with the Atlantic Monthly Press.
"Real Property" by Sara Davidson is reprinted from *Real Property*. Copyright © 1969, 1970,
1971, 1972, 1973, 1974, 1975, 1977, 1979 and 1980 by Sara Davidson. Reprinted by per-
mission of Doubleday & Company, Inc.
"The Power of '21' " by Richard West is reprinted from *New York* Magazine, October 5, 1981.
Copyright © 1981 by News Groups Publications, Inc. Reprinted by permission of *New York*
Magazine.
Illustrations for "The Power of 21," which originally appeared in *New York* Magazine, by New York
architect Robert Strong.
"Court Buff" by Mark Singer first appeared in *The New Yorker*. Copyright © 1980 by The New
Yorker Magazine, Inc. Reprinted by permission.
"Fisherman" and "Banderillero" by Barry Newman reprinted by permission of *The Wall Street
Journal*, where they first appeared, in slightly different form, on September 13, 1983, and
June 1, 1983. Copyright © 1983 by Dow Jones & Company, Inc.
"The Subterranean World of the Bomb" by Ron Rosenbaum originally appeared in *Harper's*.
Copyright © 1978 by Ron Rosenbaum. Reprinted by permission of The Sterling Lord
Agency.
"Magic" by Bill Barich is reprinted from *Laughing in the Hills*. Copyright © 1980 by Bill Barich.
Portions of this material originally appeared in *The New Yorker*. Reprinted by permission of
Viking Penguin, Inc.
Portions of "The Literary Journalists" by Norman Sims appeared in different form in *The Quill*,
July–August, 1982.

Cover design by Herbert Pretel

Designed by Ann Gold

Library of Congress Catalog Card Number: 84-90811

ISBN: 345-31081-0

Manufactured in the United States of America

First Edition: September 1984

10   9   8   7   6   5   4   3   2   1

Contents

Acknowledgments

I've wondered if a book can ever be the product of a single mind. So many editors, friends, and colleagues provide support that all books must be team projects. This one certainly was. Several people believed in it, made suggestions, and helped when they were needed. My thanks to Ron Dorfman, Laura Matthews, and Joëlle Delbourgo, whose faith made the project possible. Jim Boylan, David Eason, Jenny French, Lynn Kippax Jr., Mark Kramer, Sidney Kramer, Debbie Rubin, and Pamela Wood gave me their ideas and their assistance. My students at the University of Massachusetts provided insightful discussion. And I am especially grateful to the writers who took time away from their work to talk with me.

The Literary
Journalists

The Literary
Journalists

by Norman Sims

Things that are cheap and tawdry in fiction work beautifully in non-fiction because they are *true*. That's why you should be careful not to abridge it, because it's the fundamental power you're dealing with. You arrange it and present it. There's lots of artistry. But you don't make it up.

—John McPhee

For years, reporters have pursued their craft by sitting down near centers of power—the Pentagon, the White House, Wall Street. Like hounds by the dinner table, they have waited for scraps of information to fall from Washington, from New York and from their beats at the court house, city hall, and the police station.

Today, scraps of information don't satisfy the reader's desire to learn about people doing things. Readers deal in their private lives with psychological explanations for events around them. They may live in complex social worlds, amid advanced technologies, where "the facts" only begin to explain what's happening. The everyday stories that bring us inside the lives of our neighbors used to be found in the realm of the fiction writer, while nonfiction reporters brought us the news from far-off centers of power that hardly touched our lives.

Literary journalists unite the two forms. Reporting on the lives of people at work, in love, going about the normal rounds of life, they confirm that the crucial moments of everyday life contain great drama and substance. Rather than hanging around the edges of powerful institutions, literary journalists attempt to penetrate the cultures that make institutions work.

Literary journalists follow their own set of rules. Unlike standard journalism, literary journalism demands immersion in complex, difficult subjects. The voice of the writer surfaces to show readers that an author is at work. Authority shows through. Whether the

subject is a cowboy and his wife in the Texas Panhandle or a computer design team in an aggressive corporation, the dramatic details
yield only to persistent, competent, sympathetic reporters. Voice
brings the authors into our world. When Mark Kramer discovers
the smells in an operating room and cannot help thinking of steak,
"to my regret," his voice is as strong as a slap in the face. When John
McPhee asks for the gorp and his traveling companions in Georgia
discuss whether or not they should give any to "the little Yankee
bastard," his humble moment sets our mood.

Unlike fiction writers, literary journalists must be accurate.
Characters in literary journalism need to be brought to life on paper, just as in fiction, but their feelings and dramatic moments contain a special power because we know the stories are true. The
literary quality of these works comes from the collision of worlds,
from a confrontation with the symbols of another, real culture. Literary journalism draws on <u>immersion, voice, accuracy, and sym-
bolism</u> as essential forces.

Most readers are familiar with one brand of literary journalism, the New Journalism, which began in the 1960s and lasted
through the mid-1970s. Many of the New Journalists such as Tom
Wolfe and Joan Didion have continued to produce extraordinary
books. But literary journalists like George Orwell, Lillian Ross, and
Joseph Mitchell had been at work long before the New Journalists
arrived. And now there has appeared a younger generation of writers who don't necessarily think of themselves as New Journalists,
but do find immersion, voice, accuracy, and symbolism to be the
hallmarks of their work. For years I have collected and admired this
form of writing. Occasionally, magazine readers discover it in *Esquire, The Atlantic, The New Yorker, The Village Voice, New York,* some of
the better regional publications such as *Texas Monthly,* and even in
The New York Review of Books. Subscribers will recognize many of the
pieces collected in this book.

This form of writing has been called literary journalism and it
seems to me a term preferable to the other candidates: personal
journalism, the new journalism, and parajournalism. Some people in
my trade—I'm a journalism professor—argue it is nothing more
than a hybrid, combining the fiction writer's techniques with facts
gathered by a reporter. That may be. But the motion picture com-
bines voice recording with the photograph, yet the hybrid still deserves a name.

While trying to define the novel, Ian Watt found that the early novelists couldn't provide help. They hadn't labeled their books "novels" and were not working in a tradition. Literary journalism has been around just long enough to acquire a set of rules. The writers know where the boundaries lie. The "rules" of harmony in music have been derived from what successful composers do. The same method can help explain what successful writers have done in creating the genre of literary journalism. I asked several about their craft, and their answers fill most of this introduction. The form also has a respectable history; it didn't arrive full grown with the new journalists of the 1960s. A.J. Liebling, James Agee, George Orwell, John Hersey, Joseph Mitchell and Lillian Ross had discovered the power that could be released by the techniques of literary journalism long before Tom Wolfe proclaimed a "new journalism."

The new journalists of the 1960s called attention to their own voices; they self-consciously returned character, motivation, and voice to nonfiction writing. Standard reporters, and some fiction writers, were quick to criticize the new journalism. It was not always accurate, they claimed. It was flashy, self-serving, and it violated the journalistic rules of objectivity. But the best of it has endured. Today's literary journalists clearly understand the difference between fact and falsehood, but they don't buy into the traditional distinctions between literature and journalism. "Some people have a very clinical notion of what journalism is," Tracy Kidder told me in the study of his home in the New England Berkshires. "It's an antiseptic idea, the idea that you can't present a set of facts in an interesting way without tainting them. That's utter nonsense. That's the ultimate machine-like tendency." Kidder won both the Pulitzer Prize and the American Book Award in 1982 for *The Soul of a New Machine,* a book that followed a design team as it created a new computer. He constructs narrative with a voice that allows complexity and contradiction. His literary tools—a powerful story line and a personal voice—draw readers into something perhaps more recognizable as a real world than the "facts only" variety of reporting.

As a reader, I react differently to literary journalism than to short stories or standard reporting. Knowing *this really happened* changes my attitude while reading. Should I discover that a piece of literary journalism was made up like a short story, my disappointment would ruin whatever effect it had created as literature. At the same time, I sit down expecting literary journalism to raise emotions not evoked by standard reporting. Whether or not literary journalism equips me for living differently than other forms of literature, I read as if it might.

Literary journalists bring themselves into their stories to greater or lesser degrees and confess to human failings and emotions. Through their eyes, we watch ordinary people in crucial contexts. Mark Kramer watched during many cancer operations, while other people's lives were in jeopardy on the operating table. Crucial contexts, indeed, and more so when Kramer discovered a spot one day and feared that it meant cancer for him. In El Salvador, Joan Didion opened her handbag and heard, in response, "the clicking of metal on metal all up and down the street" as weapons were armed. At such moments we involuntarily take sides over social and personal issues. These authors understand and convey feeling and emotion, the inner dynamics of cultures. Like anthropologists and sociologists, literary reporters view cultural understanding as an end. But, unlike such academics, they are free to let dramatic action speak for itself. Bill Barich takes us to the horse races and brings alive the gambler's desire to control the seemingly magical forces of modern life; he aims to find the essences and mythologies of the track. By contrast, standard reporting presupposes less subtle cause and effect, built upon the events reported rather than on an understanding of everyday life. Whatever we name it, the form is indeed both literary and journalistic and it is more than the sum of its parts.

Two active generations of literary reporters are at work today. Both are represented in this book.

John McPhee, Tom Wolfe, Joan Didion, Richard Rhodes, and Jane Kramer found their voices during the "New Journalism" era from the mid-1960s to the mid-1970s. Wolfe's name summons visions of wild experimentation with language and punctuation. These pyrotechnics have diminished in his newer work. Through twenty years of steady production, Wolfe has proven the staying power of a literary approach to journalism.

Writers such as Wolfe, McPhee, Didion, Rhodes, and Jane Kramer have influenced a younger generation of literary journalists. I interviewed several of these younger writers. They told me they grew up on New Journalism and saw it as the model for their developing craft.

• Richard West, 43, who helped start *Texas Monthly,* and later wrote for *New York* and *Newsweek* magazines, remembers discovering, as a journalism student, the writing of Jimmy Breslin, Gay Talese, and Tom Wolfe. "Those guys were just wonderful writers. Stunning. It was like hearing rock 'n' roll rather than Patti Paige. It opened your eyes to new vistas if you wanted to be a nonfiction writer," West said.

• Mark Kramer, 40, author of *Invasive Procedures,* said George Orwell's work introduced him to literary journalism, especially *Down and Out in Paris and London* in which Orwell described his experiences as a tramp before World War II. The New Journalists were a more immediate role model for Kramer. "I read Tom Wolfe early," he said. "I'm second generation New Journalist. I read McPhee when I was just coming up. Ed Sanders' book on Manson, *The Family,* had a tremendous influence on me. He gave himself permission to speak. It was the first time I felt a reliable voice on the scene, rather than an institutional voice."

• Sara Davidson, 41, learned the routines of standard reporting in the late 1960s at the Columbia School of Journalism and *The Boston Globe.* "When I first started writing for magazines, Lillian Ross was my model," she said. "I was going to do what Lillian Ross had done. She never used the word 'I' and yet it was so clear there was an orienting consciousness guiding you." Later, Davidson discovered her stories needed the first person. The strong narrative voices of Joan Didion, Tom Wolfe and, recently, of Peter Matthiessen's *The Snow Leopard* have been her ideals.

• Tracy Kidder, 38, admired Orwell, Liebling, Capote, Mailer, Rhodes, Wolfe, and many others. But when I asked if one writer stood above the others in influencing Kidder's development, he quickly said, "McPhee has been my model. He's the most elegant of all the journalists writing today, I think."

• Mark Singer, at 33 the youngest in the group collected here, epitomizes the course of discovery traveled by the younger literary journalists. At Yale, he majored in English and simply read. "I think my models were journalists. I really studied journalists. I was very conscious of who was writing what. In the early 1970s journalists were starting to become stars. Only after I came to *The New Yorker* in 1974 did I get in touch with people like Liebling and John Bainbridge—he wrote *The Super Americans,* a brilliant book about Texas. He spent five years living in Texas. I went and read all of Bainbridge." Singer, who grew up in Oklahoma, was also influenced by Norman Mailer and *New Yorker* writers such as Lillian Ross, Calvin Trillin, and Joseph Mitchell. "This stuff has been written in every era by certain writers," he said. "People talk about Defoe or Henry Adams or whomever. Francis Parkman when he was writing *The Oregon Trail* was doing a kind of journalism as history. I think every era has those writers. I just happen to be shortsighted enough to focus upon my contemporaries."

During those months of visits with writers, they told me about the pleasures of their trade, about the difficulties they have encountered, about the essentials of literary journalism—the "rules of the game"—and about the boundaries of the form. Literary journalism wasn't defined by critics; the writers themselves have recognized that their craft requires immersion, structure, voice, and accuracy. Along with these terms, a sense of responsibility to their subjects and a search for the underlying meaning in the act of writing characterize contemporary literary journalism.

Immersion

I live in the Connecticut River valley of western Massachusetts, where a surprising number of novelists, freelance journalists, artists, and scholars make their homes. When I mentioned to some of my friends that I would soon be visiting John McPhee in Princeton, New Jersey, the reaction was always the same: "Ask him if he's read my books." They wanted me to mention their names. The writers, English professors, and avid readers I know respect him enormously.

At the same time, as a teacher of journalism history and reporting at the University of Massachusetts, I know that some of the old guard don't like him. Literary journalists are the heretics of the profession. An elder of the tribe of Old Journalists once wrote to inform me, using an oddly mixed metaphor, that "McPhee is a journalistic spellbinder, that's all . . . Mr. McPhee's journalistic warp and his literary woof make very thin cloth for any of us in the profession to use for patching our worn-out bromides." But the half dozen literary journalists I met before I interviewed McPhee were universally respectful. During the train ride to Princeton, I thought about Tracy Kidder's words—"McPhee has been my model"—and realized he had influenced many other young writers.

McPhee is a private man, friendly but guarded. Entering his office at Princeton University, I examined the mementos which testify to his immersion in subjects such as geology, canoeing, and the bears of New Jersey. On a bulletin board he has placed a warning sign:

DANGER

BEAR TRAP

DO NOT APPROACH

I took the message to heart. On the opposite wall he has a window-sized geologic map of the United States. He's pinned a piece of green nylon cord on the map from coast to coast. The cord cuts through the Appalachians, passes straight over the Plains and Rockies, then wavers in the province of the Basin and Range (the mountains and valleys of Utah and Nevada) where, McPhee said, the colored rock formations on the map "look like stretch marks." The green line clears the Sierra Nevada and ends at the Pacific Ocean. The nylon cord has followed Interstate 80 from coast to coast; it is the ribbon of narrative that binds together McPhee's two recent books on the geology of North America. The books started out as a single article about the road cuts around New York City. Then a geologist told him that North American geology is best represented by an east–west line, and McPhee's thoughts turned toward Interstate 80. "I developed a vaulting ambition," he said. "Why not go to California? Why not look at *all* the rocks?" Four years and two books later, he took a break from the subject, although he said it will take two more books to complete the journey.

"I discovered that you've got to understand a lot to write even a little bit. One thing leads to another. You've got to get into it in order to fit the pieces together," he said. That makes intuitive sense to most writers, but McPhee's seventeen books, produced in nineteen years, show an extraordinary staying power. He has fitted the pieces together to write about a designer of nuclear weapons, the history of the bark canoe, the technology of an experimental air-craft, environmental wars between Sierra Club director David Brower and developers hungry for wilderness land, the intricacies of tennis and basketball, the isolated cultures of both the New Jersey Pine Barrens and Scotland's Inner Hebrides, conflicts among the residents of Alaska, and the geology of North America. Today, no other nonfiction writer approaches McPhee's range of subject mat-ter.

For McPhee, and for most other literary journalists, under-standing begins with emotional connection, but quickly leads to im-mersion. In its simplest form, immersion means time spent on the job. McPhee drove 1,100 miles of southern roads with a field zo-ologist before writing "Travels in Georgia." He journeyed several times cross-country on I-80 with geologists for *Basin and Range* and *In Suspect Terrain.* Over a period of two years he made long journeys in Alaska, months at a time, in all seasons, collecting notes for *Coming Into the Country.*

Literary journalists gamble with their time. Their writerly im-pulses lead them toward immersion, toward trying to learn all there is about a subject. The risks are high. Not every young writer can stake two or three years on a writing project that might turn up snake-eyes. Bill Barich won his gamble. With five novels unpub-lished, he left home to live at the race track. His story of those weeks, *Laughing in the Hills,* won the attention of Robert Bingham and William Shawn, executive editor and editor of *The New Yorker.* Most literary journalists see immersion as a luxury that could not exist without the financial backing and editorial support of a mag-azine.

Tracy Kidder spent eight months inside a computer company before writing *The Soul of a New Machine.* Although he had written many articles for *The Atlantic,* as a freelance writer he could not count on a regular paycheck. An advance on the book released him from the constant need to produce articles during the two years it took to research and write.

Kidder's house rang with excitement when I first visited. Three days earlier the Pulitzer Prize committee had announced the winners for 1982. Kidder took the general nonfiction award. His cramped office just off the living room still showed signs of struggle. Decorations were sparse. Fishing poles, a net, and a battered straw hat hung in the corner near a small wood stove. Above the desk a photograph, taken while he was immersed in a piece about hobos, showed Kidder riding a flatbed railroad car somewhere in the Pacific Northwest. Haphazardly stacked notebooks lay around the typewriter. The place felt like a bar room where fights break out.

Kidder is physically imposing, built like a tight end. He looks like he would be as tough as an old-time city editor. But he doesn't drill holes through people with probing questions. "I don't know how to come barging in on people," he said. "I've never gotten anywhere with that technique. One of the ways you do good research is you really go and live with people. Once I feel I have the freedom to ask the unpleasant question, I'll do it. But I'm not very good at badgering people. I figure if they won't tell me now, they'll tell me later. I'll just keep coming back."

Mark Kramer gambled two years of his life writing *Three Farms: Making Milk, Meat and Money from the American Soil.* During those two years he received literary support from Richard Todd, the senior editor of *The Atlantic* who also saw Kidder through *Soul of a New Machine,* and survived on the slim finances of a small advance and a foundation grant. Again, the gamble paid off. The proceeds from *Three Farms* and another grant enabled him to write *Invasive Procedures.* He watched surgeons at work for nearly two years, until he was confident that he understood the operating room routine, could tell good techniques from bad, and could "translate the social byplay in the operating room."

"You have to stay around a long time before people will *let* you get to know them," Kramer said. "They're guarded the first time and second time and the first ten times. Then you get boring. They forget you're there. Or else they've had a chance to make you into something in their world. They make you into a surgical resident or they make you into a farmhand or a member of the family. And you let it happen."

Every writer I talked with told similar stories. Their work begins with immersion in a private world; this form of writing might well be called "the journalism of everyday life."

During a month of research, Richard West alternated day and night shifts while writing "The Power of '21' " for *New York* magazine. West's day schedule began at 6 A.M. in New York's famous restaurant "21." He followed the action of the restaurant upward, from the basement and the early morning prep crew, to the kitchen and the chefs, then at lunchtime out onto the floor with the bartenders and the maitre d'. His night shifts began around 4 P.M., when another crew arrived, and ended at 1 A.M. He inhaled the air of the kitchens, thick with steam and cooking aromas, and of the dining rooms, heavy with cigar smoke and status.

"It was a long day, but you had to be right there and they didn't throw any rules on me," West said. "You just become part of the woodwork until they open up and do things in front of you. You may get the surface details right, but you won't get the kind of emotions you're after—how people operate—until you disappear. Sometimes you never get that and your story falls flat on that point. It took a while, but they came to trust me and like me. So much of it is personality, it seems. If you are a person who likes people and respects people, and you genuinely show an interest, things come easily. You can't be arrogant. You can't be abrasive. That just won't work."

Mark Singer was only two years out of Yale when he came to *The New Yorker*. He had not yet discovered his voice as a writer. "I started traveling the city and I found it wasn't all Manhattan," he said. "I decided the people I wanted to write about were not famous people. Having grown up far away from New York City probably enabled me to see and write about things that I otherwise might have overlooked. I'm struck by ironies that a native might not notice."

I talked to Singer in his drab and noisy eighteenth floor cubicle at the *New Yorker* offices, which had once been McPhee's quarters. Singer's wife is a lawyer. She first mentioned the "buffs" at the courthouse in Brooklyn—spectators whose constant attendance at murder trials qualifies them as courtroom drama critics. "I started to hang out in the courthouse," Singer said. "For several months I would go a couple days a week. At the same time I was doing 'Talk of the Town' pieces. It took me something like sixteen months, going over there and just hanging out with them."

After all those months, the task shifted, as it always must, from reporting to writing. "I have to explain it to people who know only as much as I knew when I started out," Singer said.

Structure

John McPhee reached up to his bookshelf and pulled down a large, hardbound book, which contained his notes from 1976 in Alaska. "This is a hefty one," he said. These typewritten pages represented his passage from reporting to writing, from the field to the typewriter. Hidden inside those detailed notes, like a statue inside a block of granite, lies a structure that can animate the story for his readers.

"The piece of writing has a structure inside it," he said. "It begins, goes along somewhere, and ends in a manner that is thought out beforehand. I always know the last line of a story before I've written the first one. Going through all that creates the form and the shape of the thing. It also relieves the writer, once you know the structure, to concentrate each day on one thing. You know right where it fits."

Structure, in a longer piece of nonfiction writing, has more work to do than merely to organize, according to McPhee. "Structure," he said, "is the juxtaposition of parts, the way in which two parts of a piece of writing, merely by lying side-by-side, can comment on each other without a word spoken. The way in which the thing is assembled, you can get much said, which can be lying there in the structure of the piece rather than being spelled out by a writer."

McPhee rummaged around in a file cabinet for a moment and came up with a diagram of the structure in "Travels in Georgia." It looked like a lowercase "e."

"It's a simple structure, a reassembled chronology," McPhee explained. "I went there to write about a woman who, among other things, picks up dead animals off the road and eats them. There's an immediate problem when you begin to consider such material. The editor of *The New Yorker* is practically a vegetarian. I knew I was going to be presenting this story to William Shawn and that it would be pretty difficult to do so. That served a purpose, pondering what a general reader's reaction would be. When people think of animals killed on the road, there's an immediate putrid whiff that goes by them. The image is pretty automatic—smelly and repulsive. These animals we were picking up off the road were not repulsive. They had not been mangled up. They were not bloody. They'd been freshly killed. So I had to get this story off the ground without offending the sensibilities of the reader and the editor."

McPhee and his friends ate several animals during the journey, such as a weasel, a muskrat, and, somewhere well along in the trip, a snapping turtle. But the piece *begins* with the snapping turtle. Turtle soup offends less than roasted weasel. Then the story got away from the subject of road-kills by visiting a stream channelization project. That segment led into an extended digression, in which

McPhee told about Carol Ruckdeschel, who had cleaned the snapping turtle and had a house full of wounded and battered animals she was nursing back to health.

"After going through all that we *still* haven't had a weasel," McPhee said. "Now we're two-fifths of the way through the piece." He pointed to the back side of the "e" on his diagram.

"If you've read this far, now we can risk some of these animals. After all, this has either proved itself or not by now as a piece of writing. We then go back to the beginning of the journey—the journey that on page one we were in the middle of—and there's a fresh-killed weasel lying in the middle of the road. And the muskrat follows. When we come to the snapping turtle and the stream channelization project, we just jump over them and keep right on going in the form the journey had. The journey itself became the structure, broken up chronologically in this manner."

Chronological structure dominates most journalism, as McPhee learned when he worked at *Time* magazine. But chronological reporting does not always serve the writer best. McPhee restructured time in "Travels in Georgia" and in the first part of *Coming Into the Country*. Sometimes, chronology may give way to thematic structure. In *A Roomful of Hovings,* a profile of Thomas Hoving, former director of the Metropolitan Museum of Art, McPhee faced a peculiar problem. Hoving's life contained a series of themes: his scattered experiences learning to recognize art fakes, his work as parks commissioner in New York, his undistinguished early career as a student, his lifelong relationship with his father, and so on. McPhee told one tale at a time, one story following another in a structure McPhee compares to a capital "Y." The descending branches finally joined at a moment of an epiphany during Hoving's college career at Princeton, and then proceeded along the bottom stem in a single line. McPhee maintained time sequences within each episode, but the themes were arranged to set up their dramatic juxtaposition.

McPhee handed me a Xeroxed quotation. "Read this," he said. The passage quoted Albert Einstein, on the music of Shubert: "But in his larger works I am disturbed by a lack of architectonics." The term architectonics refers to structural design that gives order, balance, and unity to a work, the element of form that relates the parts to each other and to the whole.

I had previously heard the term architectonics from Richard Rhodes, who had said, "The kind of architectonic structures that you have to build, that nobody ever teaches or talks about, are crucial to writing and have little to do with verbal abilities. They have to do with pattern ability and administrative abilities—generalship, if you will. Writers don't talk about it much, unfortunately." They may not speak much of it, but good literary journalists are probably haunted by it.

Accuracy

In a society in which school children learn that there are two kinds of writing, fiction and nonfiction, and that the nonfiction is on the whole pretty flat prose, doing literary journalism is tricky business. We naturally assume that what reads like fiction must be fiction. A local editorial writer who set out to congratulate Tracy Kidder made one such revealing slip: "Tracy Kidder, a resident of Williamsburg, has won a Pulitzer Prize for his novel, *The Soul of a New Machine.*" Kidder read it and shook his head in disbelief. A *novel,* an invented narrative. It was a little irritating to him after he had practically lived in the basement of Data General Corporation for eight months, and spent two and a half years on the book. Kidder took great pains to get the quotations right, to catch all the details accurately.

A mandate for accuracy pervades literary journalism, according to its practitioners. McPhee, who finds an avuncular role uncomfortable, nevertheless has the right to make a few suggestions for those who find a model in his work. "Nobody's making rules that cover everybody," he said. "The nonfiction writer is communicating with the reader about real people in real places. So if those people talk, you say what those people said. You don't say what the writer decides they said. I get prickly if someone suggests there's dialogue in my pieces that I didn't get from the source. You don't make up dialogue. You don't make a composite character. Where I came from, a composite character was a fiction. So when somebody makes a nonfiction character out of three people who are real, that is a fictional character in my opinion. And you don't get inside their heads and think for them. You can't interview the dead. You could make a list of the things you don't do. Where writers abridge that, they hitchhike on the credibility of writers who don't.

"And they blur something that ought to be distinct. It's one thing to say nonfiction has been rising as an art. If that's what they mean by the line blurring between fiction and nonfiction, then I'd prefer another image. What I see in that image is that we don't know where fiction stops and fact begins. That violates a contract with the reader."

Part of the mandate for accuracy is good old-fashioned reporter's pride. Both Kramer and Rhodes mentioned the experience of reading, in their local papers or in national news magazines, stories they knew something about privately, and finding that the reports lacked accuracy. All reporters have a commitment to accuracy, but given time and immersion, it is not hard to improve on the record of ordinary news practice.

Accuracy can also insure the authority of the writer's voice, Kramer explained. "I'm constantly trying to accumulate authority in my writing, intersecting the reader's experience and judgment. I want to be able to make an observation and be trusted, so I have to show that I'm a good observer, that I'm savvy. I can do a lot of that with language, with sureness and informality. You can also blow your authority very quickly. One of the big motivations for getting all the details right—why I had farmers read my farm book in manuscript, and surgeons read the surgeons manuscript—is I don't want to lose authority. I don't want to get a single detail wrong."

Voice

The New Journalists of the 1960s and their critics never reached agreement on the use of the self in journalism. Sometimes New Journalists turned the spotlight on themselves in apparent violation of all the rules of objective reporting.

Much of the controversy over the self in journalism has been explicated by journalism professor David Eason, whose studies of New Journalism defined two groups. In the first camp, New Journalists were like ethnographers who provided an account of "what it is that's going on here." Tom Wolfe, Gay Talese, and Truman Capote, among others, removed themselves from their writing and concentrated on their subjects' realities.

The second group included writers such as Joan Didion, Norman Mailer, Hunter S. Thompson, and John Gregory Dunne. They saw life through their own filters, describing what it felt like to live in a world where shared public understandings about "the real world" and about culture and morals had fallen away. Without an external frame of reference, they focused more on their own reality. The authors in this second group were often a dominating presence in their works.

Either way, critics had a field day. Herbert Gold ripped holes in the personal journalism of Norman Mailer and others like him, calling it "epidemic first personism" in a 1971 article. Meanwhile, Tom Wolfe, who offered readers a mannered voice but never stood on center stage as Mailer did, suffered the reverse. Wilfrid Sheed said the distortion produced by Wolfe's interpretations was the source of our enjoyment. He should quit pretending to evoke a subject "as it really is," Sheed said. New Journalists, it seemed, either had too much of themselves in their writing, or not enough.

The younger literary journalists have calmed down. As I spoke with these younger writers, they seemed concerned with finding the right voice to express their material. "Every story contains inside it one, maybe two, right ways of telling it," Tracy Kidder said. "Your job as a journalist is to discover that." Richard Rhodes said he struggles to find the right voice, but that once he does, the story nearly tells itself. Literary journalists are no longer worried about "self," but they do care about tactics for effective telling, which may require the varying presence of an "I" from piece to piece.

The introduction of personal voice, according to Mark Kramer, allows the writer to play one world off against another, to toy with irony. "The writer can posture, say things not meant, imply things not said. When I find the right voice for a piece, it admits play, and that's a relief, an antidote to being pushed around by your own words," Kramer said. "Voice that admits 'self' can be a great gift to readers. It allows warmth, concern, compassion, flattery, shared imperfection—all the real stuff that, when it's missing, makes writing brittle and larger than life."

Kramer studied English at Brandeis and sociology at Columbia. For several years in the late 1960s, he wrote for the Liberation News Service in New York and for several Boston publications. He is quick to note irony. He flips conversations from one level to another, sometimes feigning ignorance, sometimes swiftly establishing his authority. He takes note of aggression or fragility in others.

"I think I create a different kind of architecture than most journalists," Kramer said. "I structure things so that I am commenting on the narrative, commenting on the reader's world, and on my world, and, also, I'm indicating that my style is self-conscious. I feel like a host at a semiformal party with clever guests, guests I care about."

Daily reporters subsume voice more often than they call attention to it, creating what Kramer calls an "institutional" voice. As I tell reporting students, whenever a newspaper writer makes a judgment or expresses an opinion, readers assume the newspaper itself has taken a stand. Without the newspaper standing behind them, literary journalists must discover how they belong in the story as private selves. Frequently, the writer's decision to use a personal voice grows from a feeling that publicly shared manners and morals can no longer be taken for granted.

"Once you don't have a common moral community for an audience," Kramer said, "if you want to go on talking about what's interesting, then it's useful to introduce the narrator. Even if there are a lot of different readers, they can all say, 'Oh, yeah, I know what sort of guy this is: a Jewish, New York, intellectual, left-liberal.' If the writer says who he is, and how he thinks about something, the reader knows a lot. But if he masks who he is, you're on your own. You have to look at other clues, his level of literacy and so on."

Personal voice can discomfit writers as well as readers, but that may be the point. The institutional voice of newspapers can carry nonfiction writing only so far. Beyond that, the reader needs a guide. Sara Davidson said her transition from the *Boston Globe* to literary journalism wasn't easy. "Anyone who has come up from a newspaper has a great deal of self-consciousness about even writing the word 'I.' I don't remember when I first used it, but it was just in one little paragraph, a trial balloon. The more I did it the easier it got and also I found I could do more with it. It enabled me to impose the storyteller on the material."

Responsibility

A writer's voice grows from experience. Sara Davidson's voice in "Real Property" developed while she kept a journal of her life. There are hazards in using the personal voice, however, some of which she explained to me.

Davidson lives in the hills of Los Angeles now. Stepping into her office, I was surprised to see a big, expensive, IBM word processor parked in the middle of the room like a Cadillac. The letters

I had received from her were handwritten. She composes longhand and later transcribes her manuscript pages, scrawled with lines and circles, onto the word processor for editing. The small room seemed filled with the high-speed printer, the computer, and a telephone answering machine. Davidson is a warm person, dedicated to the feelings of those she writes about. But she is an ambitious writer, willing to drive her writing hard and risk the consequences.

That spirit has a way of getting her into trouble. Davidson learned about responsibility after she wrote *Loose Change,* the story of three women's lives during the tumultuous years in the 1960s when America suffered through a social revolution. She was one of the three women in the book. In college at Berkeley they had lived in the same house. Later, they went their own ways, Davidson to New York and a journalism career, another to the radical political world of Berkeley, and the third to the big money art world. In the early 1970s, Davidson interviewed her former roommates and re-constructed their experiences for *Loose Change.* When she wrote it in the mid-1970s, two movements converged. First, she had learned that people responded best when her writing was personal, and she filled the book with intimate details of her life. Second, a confessional strain in the women's movement peaked at that time; many women were writing in the most direct terms about deep fears and personal relations.

"I think Freud said once that you owe yourself a certain discretion," Davidson told me. "You just don't go blabbing everything about yourself publicly. But that was not where the women were going. There was no discretion being practiced. Everything was permissible and I was caught up in the ideas. I wrote about my parents and my husband and all my old lovers, my career and my sister, affairs and abortion and sex—everything."

She showed drafts of the book to the two other women involved and to her husband. They participated in the revisions. But when the book was published, responsibility for these personal intimacies became the issue. Davidson had changed the names of many characters and the two women, but friends recognized them instantly. "Suddenly, something that was all right as a manuscript was not all right when it was being read widely and people were responding to it," Davidson said. "There's one scene where I had a fight with my husband and he slapped me. Well, he started getting crank calls from people who accused him of being a wife beater. It's true, he did slap me. But suddenly he was being vilified, publicly.

There were people who read it and thought he was a monster. One of the women would be walking down the street and someone would come up to her and say, 'My God, I didn't know you had an abortion in your father's office when you were 16!' Relatives of the family would call in horror that she had exposed this kind of thing about herself and her family. The man she had lived with for seven years thought it was a major violation of confidence and trust. He said, 'I wasn't living with you to have it become public knowledge. We weren't living our life as a research project.' " The other woman had a child old enough to be disturbed by Davidson's revelations of his mother's sex life, and her portrait of his father. The story did not fade away, like a magazine article. It was a selection of the Literary Guild, had a large paperback sale, and became a best seller. Later, there was a television production based on the book.

"They *turned* on me," Davidson said. "Quite understandably. They couldn't escape it. It didn't blow over. It's hard to describe their pain. It haunted them for two years. What bothered me was that I had caused pain to other people, to my husband, to the women, who went through hell."

After *Loose Change* was published, Davidson decided she would never write so intimately about her life again. Had she anticipated the results, Davidson said, she would have written a novel instead. "I would have written the exact same book. I would have said it was fiction. People say knowing it was about real people heightened their appreciation and relationship to it. They preferred that it was nonfiction. But I do know I would never, never write again so intimately about my life because I can't separate my life from the people who have been in it."

This conflict seems inherent in a form of writing where practitioners form friendships with their subjects. Davidson must surely have the right to draw on her own journal—her own life—and write however intimately she chooses about her experiences. The effect on others is another question.

"It's one thing if you decide to tell me, for print, about your marriage," she said. "But it's another thing for your wife. What do we owe her? Or your parents? Or your child? What do you morally owe to somebody in exposing things about them that aren't generally exposed?"

Other writers told me they use the role of the professional journalist to some advantage, but they have never written anything so intimate as *Loose Change*. McPhee said he takes the stance of the reporter with an open notebook. The people he interviews know he is writing for *The New Yorker*; they are responsible for their revelations. Reactions to McPhee's writing are unpredictable, he says, so he does not try to control or shape the reaction. During the two years he worked on *The Soul of a New Machine,* Tracy Kidder formed a friendship with Tom West, leader of the computer design team. Toward the end, Kidder showed West the manuscript. "He didn't talk to me for a while, but it was okay," Kidder said. "I don't like to do that. It's painful. If you're going to do a long piece you have to become friends with your subjects. You have to be pretty cold about it. Distance just comes naturally when you sit down at the typewriter." Many of the writers I talked with have their subjects sign releases at the beginning of projects. No one wants to spend time with someone who may later get cold feet. But the signature on a piece of paper is a legal release, not a moral one.

"Obviously, if you take a project, your assumption is you don't owe them anything," Davidson said. "Everything is for the record. Anything you observe is fair game. And that's how I've practiced it. All the women in *Loose Change* signed releases. They made it legal to give me this material. Emotionally and morally it's not always so clear cut."

The Masks of Men

Richard Rhodes sprawled on a couch, looking up and down a list of terms. He has an oval face and red hair. When he spoke, his eyes locked on mine. "These things are a seamless web," he said. "I'm such a primitive. I don't think much about writing, as writing." Rhodes has lived in Kansas City, Missouri, nearly all his 47 years. The twangy drawl I expected was not in his voice, however. The last couple years he has spent researching the history of nuclear weapons for his book, *Ultimate Powers.*

I had asked each writer to respond to several terms as descriptions of their own literary journalism. Rhodes ran his eyes down the list again:

historical sweep
attention to language
participation and immersion

symbolic realities
accuracy
sense of time and place
grounded observations
context
voice.

"Symbolic realities," Rhodes said. "My eye lights there every time I go down the page.

"That's been terribly important to me. The transcendentalist business of the universe showing forth, the sense that there are deep structures behind information, has been central to everything I've done in writing. Certainly it's central to writing about nuclear weapons, and I'm beginning to uncover some of those deep structures. We're talking not so much about nuclear weapons as that the twentieth century has perfected a total death machine. Making corpses is our highest technology.

"That's what I meant in the preface to *Looking for America* when I said I have looked for something else, 'The beast in the jungle, the masks of men.' I meant it all shows forth, shows forth for everybody. That's what I go after. It's not facile metaphor making. It's not drawing analogies to make a point. It's looking through, sifting through the information in the hope of seeing what's behind it."

More than any other writer I have met, Rhodes has reason to look through prose to the symbolic realities which lie beyond. "Symbolic realities" has two sides: the inner meaning writing may hold for a writer; and the "deep structures" Rhodes mentioned that lie behind the content of a piece of writing.

Rhodes spent his junior high and high school years in a boys' home near Independence, Missouri. His mother had committed suicide when he was a baby and his father, although remarried, had proved unable to raise a family of three sons. Rhodes went to Yale on a scholarship and returned to a job as a writer with Hallmark Cards in Kansas City. For ten years, he struggled. He edited house organs and then short books for Hallmark, and did occasional book reviews for *The New York Times* and the *Herald Tribune*. Encouraged by literary friends, he signed a contract for a book on the Midwest, *The Inland Ground.* After signing, he faced the horror of actually writing the book. He felt unprepared. Insecurity and writer's block plagued him. "I wrote two chapters, one about culture in Kansas City and one about a powerful foundation man. They didn't have any sparkle and unity," Rhodes said.

He signed on for a coyote hunt. "The violence of that experience broke everything open. I came back and got drunk and started writing that chapter. It came, almost without change, drunkenly, over a period of about a week of working at night while I worked the job all day." The chapter became "Death All Day," which is reprinted here.

"I had a sense of breaking out, of discharge. It was identical to the sort of thing that happens in anybody's psychoanalysis, where they suddenly just *let loose*. I have a friend who is a Kirkegaardian scholar. I was visiting him recently and we were talking late and he asked me a question about my life. I started telling him and he said, 'Ah, the story.' And he's right. At some point everyone finally reaches the point where he tells you his *story*.

"I keep repeating the same theme in everything I write—not consciously but apparently inevitably—of normal, good people suddenly confronted with diabolic evil or terrible disaster or tragedy and how they not only work through it but also, in a sense, *civilize* it, make rules around it, incorporate it into their lives. I'm not sure what that reworks for me, but my childhood was hair-raising enough."

Rhodes told me of a recurring nightmare he used to have, that he had murdered a baby and buried it somewhere. People were digging in the area and might expose it. He was the baby, he said. In "Death All Day," the piece in which he finally broke through to emotional material, Rhodes mentions that the hunted coyotes are "the size of young children."

"I had to spend an awful lot of time as a child not speaking. In fact, I remember a few times when my stepmother was preparing to educate my brother and me with some convenient artifact, a mophandle or a softball bat, when I found myself standing in a corner urgently straining to become *invisible*. I stored up a lifetime of observations out of experiences like that. A symbol of that anger for me clearly is the atomic bomb: the power to destroy the world, which children somehow think it's possible to do." Writing serves a purpose here, Rhodes says, not taking the place of therapy, but turning anger and passion to moral and social use.

Other writers avoided the phrase symbolic realities. Kidder absolutely recoiled. It sounded to him like a coat of paint on a piece of writing, added later to achieve academic respectability. Kidder found other terms to talk about the same thing. "I think of it in terms of resonance," Kidder said. "The conception of *Soul of a New Machine* was to convey something of the whole by looking at one of its parts, to let this team of computer designers stand for other teams. Usually the best works of literature have a close attachment to the particular. You pluck a guitar string and another one vibrates."

Like Kidder, John McPhee wanted to avoid placing his work in categories. It would be unfair, of course, to tie up any writer's work that way. Richard Rhodes does not write *only* about good people facing disasters. Finding that symbolism in a literary journalist's work does not characterize all the work. McPhee suggested such characterizations are the task of academics (he looked at me askance as he said it) but then he revealed one such secret about his own writing.

"There really are lots of ideas going by," McPhee said. "A huge stream of ideas. What makes somebody choose one over another? If you make a list of all the work I've ever done, and put a little mark beside things that relate to activities and interests I had before I was twenty, you'd have a little mark beside well over 90 percent of the pieces of writing. That is no accident.

"Paul Fussell said he wrote about the First World War as a way of expressing himself about his own experiences in the Second World War. That makes *complete* sense. Why did I write about tennis players? Why did I write about a basketball player? Why hold this person up for scrutiny and not that one? Because you've got some personal interest that relates to your own life. It's an important theme about anybody's writing."

After several months spent interviewing writers, dragging around my list of characteristics and concerns of literary journalism, the entries sounded mechanical. Just immerse yourself in a subject, find a good structure, maybe use some of Tom Wolfe's techniques for documenting "status life" and writing scenes, and then what? Will that be literary journalism?

I came to doubt that anything was so certain. Ultimately, everyone I spoke with circled around a difficult topic. Writers talk easily about techniques, but like all of us, they find it hard to explain their motivations. Sometimes we would get close enough for me to sense the artist behind the page. Sara Davidson was talking about creating strong narratives, where from the first paragraph the reader buys the ticket and has to take the trip. She stopped to consider for a moment, and said, "I'm not even sure how this is done. There are certain tricks but I don't think it's a matter of tricks. I think it has a lot to do with sensibility. I asked Philip Roth once if he thought he could create more sense of intimacy by using the first person. He said he thought it was the urgency and intensity with which he grabbed hold of the material, grasped it, and was able to pull the reader into his world. I think it has something to do with the author's sensibility."

A couple of years earlier, not long after I first met him, Mark Kramer had also tried to explain the heart of the differences between literary journalism and the standard forms of nonfiction. "I'm still excited about the form of literary journalism," he said. "It's like a Steinway piano. It's good enough for all the art I can put into it. You can put Glenn Gould on a Steinway and the Steinway is still better than Glenn Gould. It's good enough to hold *all* the art I can bring to it. And then some."

John McPhee

The finest qualities of John McPhee's work may be nowhere better represented than by "Travels in Georgia." The architecture of the piece depends on a skillfully designed looping flashback, entered through a smooth, nearly invisible transition. Through constant repetition, McPhee also creates a symbol of the term "D. O. R." (dead on the road) and drives it into the reader's world in a scene where he is stuck in traffic at the Newark airport. Many people feel McPhee is a writer's writer because of his careful craftsmanship and attention to structure.

At age 12, McPhee says, he held the simple notion that writers "talked through their fingers and made money." Six years later, he had developed a "well-formed desire to be a writer." He had some idea how difficult it would be—a piece of his writing had been rejected—and he knew he wanted to write for *The New Yorker*.

"I was eighteen when I decided to do that and thirty-two when *The New Yorker* finally published something of mine, after fifteen years of rejections. I submitted things all the time that were uniformly rejected. They kept the dialogue going but they had nothing to offer," McPhee said.

Born in 1931 in Princeton, New Jersey, he attended Princeton University as an undergraduate and then spent one year at Cambridge University. "Basketball and Beefeaters," a piece about touring England with the Cambridge basketball team, finally brought his work into *The New Yorker* in 1963. Two years later, following publication of McPhee's profile of basketball great Bill Bradley, *New Yorker* editor William Shawn hired him as a staff writer, fulfilling McPhee's dream and helping assure his career.

His production of books started in 1965 with *A Sense of Where You Are,* the long profile of Bradley, and continues through his recent works on Switzerland, *La Place de la Concorde Suisse* (1984), and on the geology of North America, *Basin and Range* (1981) and *In Suspect Terrain* (1983). He wrote *The Headmaster* (1966), *Oranges* (1967), *The Pine Barrens* (1968), *A Roomful of Hovings* (1968), *Levels of the Game* (1969), *The Crofter and the Laird*

(1970), *Encounters with the Archdruid* (1971), *The Deltoid Pumpkin Seed* (1973), *The Curve of Binding Energy* (1974), *Pieces of the Frame* (1975), *The Survival of the Bark Canoe* (1975), *Coming Into the Country* (1977), and *Giving Good Weight* (1979). A sampling of his best known works was collected by William L. Howarth in 1976 in *The John McPhee Reader*.

"In my case," McPhee said, "*The New Yorker* has been a superb seedbed. *The New Yorker* doesn't buy ideas and it doesn't assign ideas. Everything comes from the writer. It's the piece of writing that matters."

He writes in his office at Princeton University, where for eleven years he has occasionally instructed students in his brand of literary journalism.

Travels in Georgia

I asked for the gorp. Carol passed it to me. Breakfast had been heavy with cathead biscuits, sausage, boiled eggs, Familia, and chicory coffee, but that was an hour ago and I was again hungry. Sam said, "The little Yankee bastard wants the gorp, Carol. Shall we give him some?" Sam's voice was as soft as sphagnum, with inflections of piedmont Georgia.

"The little Yankee bastard can have all he wants this morning," Carol said. "It's such a beautiful day."

Although Sam was working for the state, he was driving his own Chevrolet. He was doing seventy. In a reverberation of rubber, he crossed Hunger and Hardship Creek and headed into the sun on the Swainsboro Road. I took a ration of gorp—soybeans, sunflower seeds, oats, pretzels, Wheat Chex, raisins, and kelp—and poured another ration into Carol's hand. At just about that moment, a snapping turtle was hit on the road a couple of miles ahead of us, who knows by what sort of vehicle, a car, a pickup; run over like a manhole cover, probably with much the same sound, and not crushed, but gravely wounded. It remained still. It appeared to be dead on the road.

Sam, as we approached, was the first to see it. "D. O. R.," he said. "Man, that is a big snapper." Carol and I both sat forward. Sam pressed hard on the brakes. Even so, he was going fifty when he passed the turtle.

Carol said, "He's not dead. He didn't look dead."

Sam reversed. He drove backward rapidly, fast as the car would go. He stopped on the shoulder, and we all got out. There was a pond beyond the turtle. The big, broad head was shining with blood, but there was, as yet, very little blood on the road. The big jaws struck as we came near, opened and closed bloodily—not the kind of strike that, minutes ago, could have cut off a finger, but still a strike with power. The turtle was about fourteen inches long and a shining hornbrown. The bright spots on its marginal scutes were like light bulbs around a mirror. The neck lunged out. Carol urged the turtle, with her foot, toward the side of the road. "I know, big man," she said to it. "I know it's bad. We're not tormenting you. Honest we're not." Sam asked her if she thought it had a chance to live and she said she was sure it had no chance at all. A car, coming west, braked down and stopped. The driver got out, with some effort and a big paunch. He looked at the turtle and said, "Fifty years old if he's a day." That was the whole of what the man had to say. He got into his car and drove on. Carol nudged the snapper, but it was too hurt to move. It could only strike the air. Now, in a screech of brakes, another car came onto the scene. It went by us, then spun around with squealing tires and pulled up on the far shoulder. It was a two-tone, high-speed, dome-lighted Ford, and in it was the sheriff of Laurens County. He got out and walked toward us, all Technicolor in his uniform, legs striped like a pine-barrens tree frog's, plastic plate on his chest, name of Wade.

"Good morning," Sam said to him.

"How y'all?" said Sheriff Wade.

Carol said, "Would you mind shooting this turtle for us, please?"

"Surely, Ma'am," said the sheriff, and he drew his .38. He extended his arm and took aim.

"Uh, Sheriff," I said. "If you don't mind . . ." And I asked him if he would kindly shoot the turtle over soil and not over concrete. The sheriff paused and looked slowly, with new interest, from one of us to another: a woman in her twenties, good-looking, with long tawny hair, no accent (that he could hear), barefoot, and wearing a gray sweatshirt and brown dungarees with a hunting knife in the belt; a man (Sam) around forty, in weathered khaki, also without an accent, and with a full black beard divided by a short white patch at the chin—an authentic, natural split beard; and then this incongruous little Yankee bastard telling him not to shoot the road. Carol picked up the turtle by its long, serrated tail and carried it, underside toward her leg, beyond the shoulder of the highway, where she set it down on a patch of grass. The sheriff followed with his .38. He again took aim. He steadied the muzzle of the pistol twelve inches from the turtle. He fired, and missed. The gun made an absurdly light sound, like a screen door shutting. He fired again. He missed. He fired again. The third shot killed the turtle. The pistol smoked. The sheriff blew the smoke away, and smiled, apparently at himself. He shook his head a little. "He should be good," he said, with a nod at the turtle. The sheriff crossed the road and got into his car. "Y'all be careful," he said. With a great screech of tires, he wheeled around and headed on west.

Carol guessed that the turtle was about ten years old. By the tail, she carried it down to the edge of the pond, like a heavy suitcase with a broken strap. Sam fetched plastic bags from the car. I found a long two-by-ten plank and carried it to the edge of the water. Carol placed the snapper upside down on the plank. Kneeling, she unsheathed her hunting knife and began, in a practiced and professional way, to slice around the crescents in the plastron, until the flesh of the legs—in thick steaks of red meat—came free. Her knife was very sharp. She put the steaks into a plastic bag. All the while, she talked to the dead turtle, soothingly, reassuringly, nurse to patient, doctor to child, and when she reached in under the plastron and found an ovary, she shifted genders with a grunt of surprise. She pulled out some globate yellow fat and tossed it into the pond. Hundreds of mosquito fish came darting through the water, sank their teeth, shook their heads, worried the fat. Carol began to remove eggs from the turtle's body. The eggs were like ping-pong balls in size, shape, and color, and how they all fitted into the turtle was more than I could comprehend, for there were fifty-six of them in there, fully finished, and a number that had not quite taken their ultimate form. "Look at those eggs. Aren't they beautiful?" Carol said. "Oh, that's sad. You were just about to do your thing, weren't you, girl?" That was why the snapper had gone out of the pond and up onto the road. She was going to bury her eggs in some place she knew, perhaps drawn by an atavistic attachment to the place where she herself had hatched out and where many generations of her forebears had been born when there was no road at all. The turtle twitched. It's neck moved. Its nerves were still working, though its life was gone. The nails on the ends of the claws were each an inch long. The turtle draped one of these talons over one of Carol's fingers. Carol withdrew more fat and threw a huge hunk into the pond."Wouldn't it be fun to analyze *that* for pesticides?" she said. "You're fat as a pig, Mama. You sure lived high off the hog." Finishing the job—it took forty minutes—Carol found frog bones in the turtle. She put more red meat into plastic sacks and divided the eggs. She kept half for us to eat. With her knife she carefully buried the remaining eggs, twenty-eight or so, in a sandbank, much as the mother turtle might have been doing at just that time. Carol picked away some leeches from between her fingers. The leeches had come off the turtle's shell. She tied the sacks and said, "All right. That's all we can say grace over. Let's send her back whence she came." Picking up the inedible parts—plastron, carapace, neck, claws—she heaved them into the pond. They hit with a slap and sank without bubbles.

As we moved east, pine trees kept giving us messages—small, hand-painted signs nailed into the loblollies. "HAVE YOU WHAT IT TAKES TO MEET JESUS WHEN HE RETURNS?" Sam said he was certain he did not. "JESUS WILL NEVER FAIL YOU." City limits, Adrian, Georgia. Swainsboro, Georgia. Portal, Georgia. Towns on the long, straight roads of the coastal plain. White-painted, tin-roofed bungalows. Awnings shading the fronts of stores—prepared for heat and glare. Red earth. Sand roads. Houses on short stilts. Sloping verandas. Unpainted boards.

"D.O.R.," said Carol.

"What do you suppose that was?"

"I don't know. I didn't see. It could have been a squirrel."

Sam backed up to the D.O.R. It was a brown thrasher. Carol looked it over, and felt it. Sam picked it up. "Throw him far off the road," Carol said. "So a possum won't get killed while eating him." Sam threw the bird far off the road. A stop for a D.O.R. always brought the landscape into detailed focus. Pitch coming out of a pine. Clustered sows behind a fence. An automobile wrapped in vines. A mailbox. "Donald Foskey." His home. Beyond the mailbox, a set of cinder blocks and on the cinder blocks a mobile home. As Sam regathered speed, Carol turned on the radio and moved the dial. If she could find some Johnny Cash, it would elevate her day. Some Johnny Cash was not hard to find in the airwaves of Georgia. There he was now, resonantly singing about his Mississippi Delta land, where, on a sharecropping farm, he grew up. Carol smiled and closed her eyes. In her ears—pierced ears—were gold maple leaves that seemed to move under the influence of the music.

"D.O.R. possum," Sam said, stopping again. "Two! A grown one and a baby." They had been killed probably ten minutes before. Carol carried the adult to the side of the road and left it there. She kept the baby. He was seven inches long. He was half tail. Although dead, he seemed virtually undamaged. We moved on. Carol had a clipboard she used for making occasional notes and sketches. She put the little possum on the clipboard and rested the clipboard on her knees. "Oh, you sweet little angel. How could anybody run over *you?*" she said. "Oh, I just love possums. I've raised so many of them. This is a great age. They are the neatest little animals. They love you so much. They crawl on your shoulder and hang in your hair. How people can dislike them I don't understand." Carol reached into the back seat and put the little opossum into a container of formaldehyde. After a while, she said, "What mystifies me is: that big possum back there was a male."

Bethel Primitive Baptist Church. Old Canoochee Primitive Baptist Church. "THE CHURCH HAS NO INDULGENCES." A town every ten miles, a church—so it seemed—every two. Carol said she frequently slept in church graveyards. They were, for one thing, quiet, and, for another, private. Graham Memorial Church of the Nazarene.

Sam and Carol both sat forward at the same moment, alert, excited. "D.O.R. Wow! That was something special. It had a long yellow belly and brown fur or feathers! Hurry, Sam. It's a good one." Sam backed up at forty miles an hour and strained the Chevrolet.

"What is it? What is it?"

"It's a piece of bark. Fell off a pulpwood truck."

The approach to Pembroke was made with a sense of infiltration—Pembroke, seat of Bryan County. "Remember, now, we're interested in frogs," Sam said, and we went up the steps of Bryan County Courthouse. "We understand there is a stream-channelization project going on near here. Could you tell us where? We're collecting frogs." It is hard to say what the clerks in the courthouse thought of this group—the spokesman with the black-and-white beard, the shoeless young woman, and their silent companion. They looked at us—they in their pumps and print dresses—from the other side of a distance. The last thing they might have imagined was that two of the three of us were representing the state government in Atlanta. The clerks did not know where the channelization was going on but they knew who might—a woman in town who knew everything. We went to see her. A chicken ran out of her house when she opened the screen door. No, she was not sure just where we should go, but try a man named Miller in Lanier. He'd know. He knew everything. Lanier was five miles down the track— literally so. The Seaboard Coast Line ran beside the road. Miller was a thickset man with unbelievably long, sharp fingernails, a driver of oil trucks. It seemed wonderful that he could get his hands around the wheel without cutting himself, that he could deliver oil without cutting the hose. He said, "Do you mind my asking why you're interested in stream channelization?"

"We're interested in frogs," Sam said. "Snakes and frogs. We thought the project might be stirring some up."

Miller said, "I don't mind the frog, but I want no part of the snake."

His directions were perfect—through pine forests, a right, two lefts, to where a dirt road crossed a tributary of the Ogeechee. A wooden bridge there had been replaced by a culvert. The stream now flowed through big pipes in the culvert. Upriver, far as the eye could see, a riparian swath had been cut by chain saws. Back from the banks, about fifty feet on each side, the overstory and the understory—every tree, bush, and sapling—had been cut down. The river was under revision. It had been freed of meanders. It was now two yards wide between vertical six-foot banks; and it was now as straight as a ditch. It had, in fact, become a ditch—in it a stream of thin mud, flowing. An immense yellow machine, slowly backing upstream, had in effect eaten this river. It was at work now, grunting and belching, two hundred yards from the culvert. We tried to walk toward it along the bank but sank to our shins in black ooze. The stumps of the cut trees were all but covered with mud from the bottom of the river. We crossed the ditch. The dredged mud was somewhat firmer on the other side. Sam and I walked there. Carol waded upcurrent in the stream. The machine was an American dragline crane. The word "American" stood out on its cab in letters more than a foot high. Its boom reached up a hundred feet. Its bucket took six-foot bites. As we approached, the bucket kept eating the riverbed, then swinging up and out of the channel and disgorging tons of mud to either side. Carol began to take pictures. She took more and more pictures as she waded on upstream. When she was fifty feet away from the dragline, its engine coughed down and stopped. The sudden serenity was oddly disturbing. The operator stepped out of the cab and onto the catwalk. One hand on the flank of his crane, he inclined his head somewhat forward and stared down at Carol. He was a stocky man with an open shirt and an open face, deeply tanned. He said, "Howdy."

"Howdy," said Carol.

"You're taking some pictures," he said.

"I sure am. I'm taking some pictures. I'm interested in the

range extension of river frogs, and the places they live. I bet you turn up some interesting things."

"I see some frogs," the man said. "I see lots of frogs."

"You sure know what you're doing with that machine," Carol said. The man shifted his weight. "That's a *big* thing," she went on. "How much does it weigh?"

"Eighty-two tons."

"Eighty-two *tons*?"

"Eighty-two tons."

"Wow! How far can you dig in one day?"

"Five hundred feet."

"A mile every ten days," Sam said, shaking his head with awe.

"Sometimes I do better than that."

"You live around here?"

"No. My home's near Baxley. I go where I'm sent. All over the state."

"Well, sorry. Didn't mean to interrupt you."

"Not 't all. Take all the pictures you want."

"Thanks. What did you say your name was?"

"Chap," he said. "Chap Causey."

We walked around the dragline, went upstream a short way, and sat down on the trunk of a large oak, felled by the chain saws, to eat our lunch—sardines, chocolate, crackers, and wine. Causey at work was the entertainment, pulling his levers, swinging his bucket, having at the stream.

If he had been at first wary, he no doubt had had experience that made him so. All over the United States, but particularly in the Southeast, his occupation had become a raw issue. He was working for the Soil Conservation Service, a subdivision of the United States Department of Agriculture, making a "water-resource channel improvement"—generally known as stream channelization, or reaming a river. Behind his dragline, despite the clear-cutting of the riverine trees, was a free-flowing natural stream, descending toward the Ogeechee in bends and eddies, riffles and deeps—in appearance somewhere between a trout stream and a bass river, and still handsomely so, even though it was shaved and ready for its operation. At the dragline, the recognizable river disappeared, and below the big machine was a kind of reverse irrigation ditch, engineered to remove water rapidly from the immediate watershed. "How could anyone even conceive of this idea?" Sam said. "Not just to do it, but even to *conceive* of it?"

The purpose of such projects was to anticipate and eliminate floods, to drain swamps, to increase cropland, to channel water toward freshly created reservoirs serving and attracting new industries and new housing developments. Water sports would flourish on the new reservoirs, hatchery fish would proliferate below the surface: new pulsations in the life of the rural South. The Soil Conservation Service was annually spending about fifteen million dollars on stream-channelization projects, providing, among other things, newly arable land to farmers who already had land in the Soil Bank. The Department of Agriculture could not do enough for the Southern farmer, whose only problem was bookkeeping. He got money for keeping his front forty idle. His bottomland went up in value when the swamps were drained, and then more money came for not farming the drained land. Years earlier, when a conservationist had been someone who plowed land along natural contours, the Soil Conservation Service had been the epicenter of the conservation movement, decorated for its victories over erosion of the land. Now, to a new generation that had discovered ecology, the S.C.S. was the enemy. Its drainage programs tampered with river mechanics, upsetting the relationships between bass and otter, frog and owl. The Soil Conservation Service had grown over the years into a bureau of fifteen thousand people, and all the way down at the working point, the cutting edge of things, was Chap Causey, in the cab of his American dragline, hearing nothing but the pounding of his big Jimmy diesel while he eliminated a river, eradicated a swamp.

After heaving up a half-dozen buckets of mud, Causey moved backward several feet. The broad steel shoes of the crane were resting on oak beams that were bound together in pairs with cables. There were twelve beams in all. Collectively, they were called "mats." Under the crane, they made a temporary bridge over the river. As Causey moved backward and off the front pair of beams, he would reach down out of the sky with a hook from his boom and snare a loop of the cable that held the beams. He snatched them up—they weighed at least half a ton—and whipped them around to the back. The beams dropped perfectly into place, adding a yard to Causey's platform on the upstream side. Near the tree line beyond one bank, he had a fuel tank large enough to bury under a gas station, and every so often he would reach out with his hook and his hundred-foot arm and, without groping, lift the tank and move it on in the direction he was going. With his levers, his cables, his bucket, and hook, he handled his mats and his tank and his hunks of the riverbed as if he were dribbling a basketball through his legs and behind his back. He was deft. He was world class. "I bet he could put on a baby's diapers with that thing," Sam said.

Carol said, "See that three-foot stump? I sure would like to see him pull *that* out." She gestured toward the rooted remains of a tree that must have stood, a week earlier, a hundred and fifty feet high. Causey, out of the corner of his eye, must have seen the gesture. Perhaps he just read her mind. He was much aware that he was being watched, and now he reached around behind him, grabbed the stump in his bucket, and ripped it out of the earth like a molar. He set it at Carol's feet. It towered over her.

After a modest interval, a few more buckets of streambed, Causey shut off the dragline and stopped for an adulation break. Carol told him he was fabulous. And she meant it. He was. She asked him what the name of the stream was. He said, "To tell you the truth, Ma'am, I don't rightly know."

Carol said, "Do you see many snakes?"

"Oh, yes, I see lots of snakes," Causey said, and he looked at her carefully.

"What kinds of snakes?"

"Moccasins, mainly. They climb up here on the mats. They don't run. They never run. They're not afraid. I got a canoe paddle in the cab there. I kill them with the paddle. One day, I killed thirty-five moccasins. People come along sometimes, like you, visitors, come up here curious to see the digging, and they see the dead snakes lying on the mats, and they freeze. They refuse to move. They refuse to walk back where they came from."

If Causey was trying to frighten Carol, to impress her by frightening her, he had picked the wrong person. He might have sent a shot or two of adrenalin through me, but not through Carol. I once saw her reach into a semi-submerged hollow stump in a man-made lake where she knew a water snake lived, and she had felt around in there, underwater, with her hands on the coils of the snake, trying to figure out which end was front. Standing thigh-deep in the water, she was wearing a two-piece bathing suit. Her appearance did not suggest old Roger Conant on a field trip. She was trim and supple and tan from a life in the open. Her hair, in a ponytail, had fallen across one shoulder, while her hands, down inside the stump, kept moving slowly, gently along the body of the snake. This snake was her friend, she said, and she wanted Sam and me to see him. "Easy there, fellow, it's only Carol. I sure wish I could find your head. Here we go. We're coming to the end. Oh, damn. I've got his tail." There was nothing to do but turn around. She felt her way all four feet to the other end. "At last," she said. "How are you, old fellow?" And she lifted her arms up out of the water. In them was something like a piece of television cable moving with great vigor. She held on tight and carried her friend out of the lake and onto the shore.

At Carol's house, Sam and I one night slept in sleeping bags on the floor of her study beside Zebra, her rattlesnake. He was an eastern diamondback, and he had light lines, parallel, on his dark face. He was young and less than three feet long. He lived among rocks and leaves in a big glass jar. "As a pet, he's ideal," Carol told us. "I've never had a diamondback like him before. Anytime you get uptight about anything, just look at him. He just sits there. He's so great. He doesn't complain. He just waits. It's as if he's saying, 'I've got all the time in the world. I'll outwait you, you son of a bitch.' "

"He shows you what patience is," Sam said. "He's like a deer. Deer will wait two hours before they move into a field to eat."

In Carol's kitchen was the skin of a mature diamondback, about six feet long, that Sam and Carol had eaten in southwest Georgia, roasting him on a stick like a big hot dog, beside the Muckalee Creek. The snake, when they came upon him, had just been hit and was still alive. The men who had mortally wounded the snake were standing over it, watching it die. A dump truck full of gravel was coming toward the scene, and Carol, imagining the truck running over and crushing the diamondback, ran up to the men standing over it and said, "Do you want it?" Surprised, they said no. "No, *Ma'am*!" So she picked up the stricken snake, carried it off the road and back to the car, where she coiled it on the floor between her feet. "Later, in a gas station, we didn't worry about leaving the car unlocked. Oh, that was funny. We do have some fun. We ate him that night."

"What did he taste like?" I asked her.

"Taste like? You know, like rattlesnake. Maybe a cross between a chicken and a squirrel."

Carol's house, in Atlanta, consisted of four small rooms, each about ten feet square—kitchen, study, storage room, bedroom. They were divided by walls of tongue-and-groove boards, nailed horizontally onto the studs. A bathroom and vestibule were more or less stuck onto one side of the building. She lived alone there. An oak with a three-foot bole stood over the house like an umbrella and was so close to it that it virtually blocked the front door. An old refrigerator sat on the stoop. Around it were the skulls of a porpoise, a horse, a cow, and a pig. White columns adorned the façade. They were made of two-inch iron pipe. Paint peeled from the clapboard. The front yard was hard red clay, and it had some vestigial grasses in it (someone having once tried a lawn) that had not been mowed for possibly a decade. Carol had set out some tomatoes among the weeds. The house stood on fairly steep ground that sloped through woods to a creek. The basement was completely above grade at the rear, and a door there led into a dim room where Carol's red-tailed hawk lived. He was high in one corner, standing on a pipe. I had never been in the immediate presence of a red-tailed hawk, and at sight of him I was not sure whether to run or to kneel. At any rate, I could not have taken one step nearer. He was two feet tall. His look was incendiary. Slowly, angrily, he lifted and spread his wings, reached out a yard and a half. His talons could have hooked tuna. His name was Big Man. His spread-winged posture revealed all there was to know about him: his beauty—the snowy chest, the rufous tail; his power; his affliction. One of his wings was broken. Carol had brought him back from near death. Now she walked over to him and stood by him and stroked his chest. "Come on, Big Man," she said. "It's not so bad. Come on, Big Man." Slowly, ever so slowly—over a period of a minute or two—the wide wings came down, folded together, while Carol stroked his chest. Fear departed, but nothing much changed in his eyes.

"What will he ever do?" I asked her.

She said, "Nothing, I guess. Just be someone's friend."

Outside the basement door was a covered pen that housed a rooster and a seagull. The rooster had been on his way to Colonel Sanders' when he fell off a truck and broke a drumstick. Someone called Carol, as people often do, and she took the rooster into her care. He was hard of moving, but she had hopes for him. He was so new there he did not even have a name. The seagull, on the other hand, had been with her for years. He had one wing. She had picked him up on a beach three hundred miles away. His name was Garbage Belly.

Carol had about fifteen ecosystems going on at once in her

twenty-by-twenty house. In the study, a colony of dermestid beetles was eating flesh off the pelvis of an alligator. The beetles lived in a big can that had once held forty pounds of mincemeat. Dermestids clean bones. They do thorough work. They all but simonize the bones. Carol had obtained her original colony from the Smithsonian Institution. One of her vaulting ambitions was to be able to identify on sight any bone that she happened to pick up. Also in the can were the skulls of a water turkey, a possum, and a coon.

The beetles ate and were eaten. Carol reached into the colony, pulled out a beetle, and gave it to her black-widow spider. The black widow lived in a commercial mayonnaise jar. Carol had found her in the basement while cleaning it up for Big Man. The spider's egg was getting ready to hatch, and when it did thousands like her would emerge into the jar. Efficiently, the black widow encased the beetle in filament gauze that flowed from her spinnerets.

Carol then fed dermestids to her turtles. She had three galvanized tubs full of cooters and sliders, under a sunlamp. "They need sun, you know. Vitamin D." She fed dermestids to her spotted salamander, and to her gray tree frog. Yellow spots, polka dots, on black, the salamander's coloring was so simple and contrasting that he appeared to be a knickknack from a gift shop, a salamander made in Japan. The tree frog lived in a giant brandy snifter, furnished with rocks and dry leaves. With his latex body and his webbed and gummy oversized hands, he could walk right up the inside of his brandy snifter, even after its shape began to tilt him backward, then lay a mitt over the rim and haul himself after and walk down the outside. He could walk straight up a wall; and he did that, while digesting his beetle. He had been with Carol three years. He was a star there in her house. No mayonnaise jar for him. He had the brandy snifter. It was all his and would be as long as he lived.

Notebooks were open on Carol's desk, a heavy, kneehole desk, covered with pens, Magic Markers, brushes, pencils, drawing materials. The notebooks had spiral bindings and were, in part, diaries.

17 April. Okefenokee. Caught two banded water snakes, one skink. . . .

18 April. To King's Landing. Set three line traps baited with peanut butter, caught a rather small moccasin AGKISTRODON coming from under shed. Put out ninety-five set hooks baited with

pork liner. To gator hole. Tried to use shocker, after putting up seines across exit. No luck!

    19 April. D.O.R. *Natrix rigida,* glossy water snake; *Farancia abacura,* mud snake; *Elaphe guttata guttata,* corn snake. . . .

    21 April. S. W. Georgia. D.O.R. vulture, ½ mi. E. Leary, Hwy 62, Calhoun County. Fresh. Possum D.O.R. nearby. . . .

The notebooks were also, in part, ledgers of her general interests.

Dissolve mouse in nitric acid and put him through spectrophotometer—can tell every element.

    A starving snake can gain weight on water.

    Gray whales are born with their bellies up and weigh a ton, and when they are grown they swim five thousand miles to breed in shallow lagoons and eat sand and stand on their tails and gravity-feed on pelagic crabs.

And the notebooks were, in part, filled with maps and sketches. Making a drawing of something—a mermaid weed, the hind foot of an opossum, the egg case of a spotted salamander, a cutaway of a deer's heart—was her way of printing it into her memory. The maps implied stories. They were of places too specific—too eccentric, wild, and minute—to show up as much of anything on other maps, including a topographical quadrangle. They were of places that Carol wanted to remember and, frequently enough, to find again.

12 May. Caught *Natrix erythrogaster flavigaster,* red-bellied water snake 9:30 A.M. Saw quite a large gator at 9:35. Ten feet. Swarm of honeybees 25 feet up cypress at edge of creek. Large—six-foot—gray rat snake in oak tree over water. *Elaphe obsoleta spiloides.* Tried unsuccessfully to knock it into canoe. Finally climbed tree but snake had gone into hole in limb. . . .

    26 June. Sleep on nest where loggerhead laid eggs Cumberland Island, to protect eggs from feral hogs. Return later find that hog has eaten eggs. Shoot hog. . . .

    27 August. Oconee River. Saw *Natrix* wrestling with a catfish in water. *Natrix* was trying to pull fish out on bank. Snake about 2½

feet. Fish 8 inches. Snake finally won. Didn't have heart to collect snake as he was so proud of fish and wouldn't let go even when touched. Camped by railroad bridge. Many trains. Found catfish on set hook, smoked him for supper. . . .

The rods of the vertebrate eye provide scotopic vision—sight in dim light. Nocturnal animals that also go out in daylight need slit eyes to protect the rods. Crocodiles. Seals. Rattlesnakes. Cottonmouths.

13 June. North Georgia. Oh, most glorious night. The fireflies are truly in competition with the stars! At the tops of the ridges it is impossible to tell them apart. As of old, I wished for a human companion. On the banks of a road, a round worm was glowing, giving off light. What a wonderful thing it is. It allows us to see in the darkness.

Above the desk, tacked to a wall, was the skin of a bobcat—D.O.R. two miles west of Baxley, Highway 341. "I was excited out of my mind when we found him," Carol said. "He was the best D.O.R. ever. It was late afternoon. January. He was stiff, but less than a day old. Bobcats move mostly at night. He was unbloody, three feet long, and weighed twenty-one pounds. I was amazed how small his testicles were. I skinned him here at home. I tanned his hide—salt, alum, then neat's-foot oil. He had a thigh like a goat's—so big, so much beautiful meat. I boiled him. He tasted good—you know, the wild taste. Strong. But not as strong as a strong coon."

Zebra lifted his head, flashed his fangs, and yawned a pink yawn. This was the first time in at least a day that Zebra had moved. Carol said the yawn meant he was hungry. Zebra had had his most recent meal seven weeks before. Carol went over to the gerbil bin to select a meal for Zebra. "Snakes just don't eat that much," she said, shaking her head in dismay over the exploding population of gerbils. She tossed one to a cat. She picked up another one, a small one, for Zebra. "Zebra eats every month or two," she went on. "That's all he needs. He doesn't do anything. He just sits there." She lifted the lid of Zebra's jar and dropped the gerbil inside. The gerbil stood still, among the dry leaves, looking. Zebra did not move. "I'm going to let him go soon. He's been a good friend. He really has. You sometimes forget they're deadly, you know. I've had my hand down inside the jar, cleaning it out, and suddenly realized, with cold sweat, that he's poisonous. Ordinarily, when you see a rattlesnake you are on guard immediately. But with him in the house all the time I tend to forget how deadly he is. The younger the snake, the more concentrated the venom."

The gerbil began to walk around the bottom of the big glass jar. Zebra, whose body was arranged in a loose coil, gave no sign that he was aware of the gerbil's presence. Under a leaf, over a rock, sniffing, the gerbil explored the periphery of Zebra's domain. Eventually, the gerbil stepped up onto Zebra's back. Still Zebra did not move. Zebra had been known to refuse a meal, and perhaps that would happen now. The gerbil walked along the snake's back, stepped down, and continued along the boundary of the base of the jar, still exploring. Another leaf, another stone, the strike came when the gerbil was perhaps eight inches from Zebra's head. The strike was so fast, the strike and the recovery, that it could not really be followed by the eye. Zebra lanced across the distance, hit the gerbil in the heart, and, all in the same instant, was back where he had started, same loose coil, head resting just where it had been resting before. The gerbil took three steps forward and fell dead, so dead it did not even quiver, tail out straight behind.

Sam had once told me how clumsy he thought rattlesnakes were, advising me never to walk through a palmetto stand third in a line, because a rattlesnake, said Sam, takes aim at the first person, strikes at the second, and hits the third. After watching Zebra, though, I decided to go tenth in line, if at all. Carol seemed thoughtful. "I've had copperheads," she said. "But I'm not really that much on snakes. I'm always worrying that someday I'll come home and find the jar turned over and several cats lying on the floor." That night, on the floor in my sleeping bag, I began to doze off and then imagined rolling over and knocking Zebra out of his jar. I spent most of the night with my chin in my hands, watching him through the glass.

There was a baby hawk in a box in the kitchen, and early in the morning he began to scream. Nothing was going to quiet him except food. Carol got up, took a rabbit out of the refrigerator, and cut it up with a pair of scissors. It had been a rabbit D.O.R. The rabbit was twice the size of the hawk, but the hawk ate most of the rabbit. There followed silence, bought and paid for. In the freezer, Carol had frogs' legs, trout, bream, nighthawk, possum, squirrel, quail, turtle, and what she called trash fish. The trash fish were for Garbage Belly. The destiny of the other items was indistinct. They were for the consumption of the various occupants of the house, the whole food chain—bird, amphibian, beast and beetle, reptile, arachnid, man. A sign over the kitchen sink said "EAT MORE POSSUM," black on Chinese red.

In the bedroom was a deerskin. "I saw blood on the trail," Carol said. "I knew a deer wouldn't go uphill shot, so I went down. I found it. It wasn't a spike buck, it was a slickhead. It had been poached. I poached it from the poacher." On the walls were watercolors and oils she had done of natural scenes, and three blown-up photographs of Johnny Cash. A half-finished papier-mâché head of Johnny Cash was in her bedroom as well, and other pieces of her sculpture, including "Earth Stars," a relief of mushrooms. Carol looked reverently at the photographs and said that whenever she had had depressing and difficult times she had turned to Johnny Cash, to the reassurances in the timbre of his voice, to the philosophy in his lyrics, to his approach to life. She said he had more than once pulled her through.

Carol grew up in Rochester, New York, until she was twelve, after that in Atlanta. Her father, Earl Ruckdeschel, worked for Eastman Kodak and managed the Atlanta processing plant. She was an only child. Animals were *non grata* at home, so she went to them. "You have to turn to something. There was a lot of comfort out there in those woods. Wild creatures were my brothers and sisters. That is why I'm more interested in mammals than anything else. They're warm-blooded. Fish are cold-blooded. You can't snuggle up with a fish." Her parents mortally feared snakes, but she never did. Her father once made her a snake stick. Her mother told her, many times a month and year, that it was not ladylike to be interested in snakes and toads. Carol went to Northside High in Atlanta. After high school, for five years, she worked at odd jobs—she fixed car radios, she wandered. Then she went to Georgia State University, studied biology, and married a biologist there. He was an authority on river swamps, an ecologist—a tall, prognathous, slow-speaking scientific man. His subspeciality was cottonmouths. He had found an island in the Gulf that had a cottonmouth under every palmetto, and he lived for a time among them. He weighed and measured them one by one. He was a lot older than Carol. She had taken his course in vertebrate zoology. The marriage did not really come apart. It evaporated. Carol kept going on field trips with him, and she stayed on at Georgia State as a biological researcher. The little house she moved into could not have been better: low rent, no class, high privacy, woods, a creek. And it was all her own. A cemetery was across the street. She could sleep there if she wanted to get out of the house. On Mother's Day, or whenever else she needed flowers, she collected bouquets from among the graves. From time to time, she wandered away. She had a white pickup truck and a German shepherd. His name was Catfish, and he was "all mouth and no brains." Carol and Catfish slept on a bale of hay in the back of the truck, and they went all over, from the mountains to the sea. They fished in the mountains, hunted in the sand hills, set traps in the Okefenokee Swamp. She began collecting specimens for the Georgia State University research collection. Most she found dead on the road. Occasionally, she brought new specimens into the collection, filling in gaps, but mainly she replenished exhausted supplies—worn-out pelts and skulls. There was always a need. An animal's skin has a better chance against a Goodyear tire than it does against the paws of a college student. She had no exclusive specialty. She wanted to do everything. Any plant or creature, dead or alive, attracted her eye.

She volunteered, as well, for service with the Georgia Natural Areas Council, a small office of the state government that had been established to take an inventory of wild places in Georgia worth preserving, proclaiming, and defending. While she travelled around Georgia picking up usable D.O.R.s for the university, she appraised the landscape for the state, detouring now and again into river swamps to check the range of frogs. Sam Candler, who also worked for the Natural Areas Council, generally went with her. Rarely, they flew in his plane. For the most part, they were on the road. Sam had a farm in Coweta County. He had also spent much of his life in the seclusion of Cumberland Island, off the Georgia coast. He was a great-grandson of the pharmacist who developed and at one time wholly owned the Coca-Cola Company, so he could have been a rampant lion in social Atlanta, but he would have preferred to wade blindfolded through an alligator swamp with chunks of horsemeat trussed to his legs. He wanted to live, as he put it, "close to the earth." He knew wilderness, he had been in it so much, and his own outlook on the world seemed to have been formed and directed by his observations of the creatures that ranged in wild places, some human, some not. Sam had no formal zoological or ecological training. What he brought to his work was mainly a sense of what he wanted for the region where he had lived his life. He had grown up around Atlanta, had gone to Druid Hills Grammar School and to Emory University and on into the Air Force. He had lived ever since

on the island and the farm. His wife and their four children seemed
to share with him a lack of interest in urban events. The Natural
Areas Council had been effective. It had the weight of the government behind it. Georgia was as advanced in this respect as say, In-
diana, Illinois, Iowa, and New Jersey, where important conservancy
work was also being accomplished on the state-government level,
and far more advanced than most other states. There was much to
evaluate. Georgia was, after all, the largest state east of the Mississippi River, and a great deal of it was still wild. Georgia forests,
mountains, swamps, islands, and rivers—a long list of sites of special
interest or value—had become Registered Natural Areas. Sam and
Carol had done the basic work—exploring the state, following
leads, assessing terrain, considering vegetation and wildlife, choosing sites, and persuading owners to register lands for preservation.

Sam had been a friend of mine for some years, and when he
wrote to say that he was now travelling around the state collecting
skulls and pelts, eating rattlesnakes, preserving natural areas, and
charting the ranges of river frogs, I could not wait until I could go
down there and see. I had to wait more than a year, though, while
finishing up some work. I live in Princeton, New Jersey, so I flew
from Newark when the day came, and I nearly missed the plane.
Automobiles that morning were backed up at least a mile from the
Newark Airport tollbooths (fourteen tollbooths, fourteen lanes),
and the jam was just as thick on the paid side as it was on the unpaid
side—thousands and thousands of murmuring cars, moving nowhere, nowhere to move, shaking, vibrating, stinking, rattling.
Homo sapiens D.O.R. I got out of my car and left it there, left it,
shamefully, with a high-school student who was accepting money
to drive it home, and began to make my way overland to the terminal. I climbed up on bumpers and over corrugated fences and
ducked under huge green signs. I went around tractor trailers and
in front of buses. Fortunately, Sam had told me to bring a backpack.
Carrying a suitcase through that milieu would have been like carrying a suitcase up the Matterhorn. Occasionally, I lost direction,
and once I had to crawl under a mastodonic truck, but I did get
through, and I ran down the cattle-pen corridors of the airport and,
with a minute to go, up the steps and into the plane—relieved beyond measure to be out of that ruck and off to high ground and
sweet air, taking my chances on the food. Sam and Carol met me,
and we went straight to the mountains, stopping all the way for
D.O.R.s. That night, we ate a weasel.

In a valley in north Georgia, Carol had a cabin that was made of peeled logs, had a stone fireplace, and stood beside a cold stream. We stayed there on the first night of a journey that eventually meandered through eleven hundred miles of the state—a great loop, down out of the river gorges and ravine forests of the mountains, across the granitic piedmont and over the sand hills and the red hills to the river swamps and pine flatwoods of the coastal plain. Sam had a canoe on the top of the car. We slept in swamps and beside a lake and streams. Made, in part, in the name of the government, it was a journey that tended to mock the idea of a state—as an unnatural subdivision of the globe, as a metaphor of the human ego sketched on paper and framed in straight lines and in riparian boundaries behind an unalterable coast. Georgia. A state? Really a core sample of a continent, a plug in the melon, a piece of North America. Pull it out and wildcats would spill off the high edges. Alligators off the low ones. The terrain was crisscrossed with geological boundaries, mammalian boundaries, amphibian boundaries— the range of the river frogs. The range of the wildcat was the wildcat's natural state, overlaying segments of tens of thousands of other states, one of which was Georgia. The State of Georgia. Governor Jimmy Carter in the mansion in Atlanta.

The first thing Sam and Carol wanted to assess on this trip was a sphagnum bog in Rabun County, off the north side of the Rabun Bald (4,696 feet). The place seemed marginal to me, full of muck and trout lilies, with swamp pinks in blossom under fringe trees and smooth alders, but Sam and Carol thought it ought to be registered, and they sought out the owner, a heavy woman, greatly slow of speech, with a Sears, Roebuck tape measure around her neck. She stood under a big white pine by the concrete front porch of her shingled house on a flinty mountain farm. Sam outlined the value of registering a natural area for preservation beyond one's years. She looked at him with no expression and said, "We treasure the bog." He gave her an application. ("Being aware of the high responsibility to the state that goes with the ownership and use of a property which has outstanding value in illustrating the natural history of Georgia, we morally agree to continue to protect and use this site for purposes consistent with the preservation of its natural integrity.") Perhaps she could consider it with her husband and his brothers and nephews when they came home. One day soon, he would stop back to talk again. She said,

"We likes to hunt arrowheads. We treasure the bog."

The D.O.R.s that first day included a fan belt Sam took for a blacksnake—jammed on his brakes, backed up to see—and a banana peel that Carol identified, at first glimpse, as a jumping mouse. Eager was the word for them. They were so much on the hunt. "It is rare for specimens to be collected this way," Carol said. "Most people are too lazy. Or they're hung up on just frogs or just salamanders, or whatever, and they don't care about other things. Watching for D.O.R.s makes travelling a lot more interesting. I mean, can you imagine just *going* down the road?"

We went around a bend in a mountain highway and the road presented Carol with the find of the day. "D.O.R.!" she said. "That was a good one. That was a *good* one! Sam, hurry back. That was a weasel!"

Sam hurried back. It was no banana peel. It was exactly what Carol said it was: *Mustela frenata,* the long-tailed weasel, dead on the road. It was fresh-killed, and—from the point of view of Georgia State University—in fine condition. Carol was so excited she jumped. The weasel was a handsome thing, minklike, his long body a tube roughly ten by two, his neck long and slender. His fur was white and yellow on the underside and dark brown on his back. "What a magnificent animal!" Carol said. "And hard as hell to trap. Smell his musk. The scent glands are back here by the tail." While backing up after seeing him, she had hoped against hope that he would be a least weasel—smallest of all carnivores. She had never seen one. The least weasel diets almost exclusively on tiny, selected mice. This one would have eaten almost anything warm, up to and including a rabbit twice his size. Carol put him in an iced cooler that was on the back seat. The cooler was not airtight. Musk permeated the interior of the car. It was not disturbing. It was merely powerful. Carol said they had once collected a skunk D.O.R. They had put it in a plastic bag within a plastic bag within four additional plastic bags. The perfume still came through.

Carol's valley resisted visitors. It was seven miles from a paved road. It was rimmed with mountains. It was the coldest valley in Georgia. A trout stream cascaded out of the south end. Ridges pressed in from east and west. The north was interrupted by a fifty-five-hundred-foot mountain called Standing Indian. Standing Indian stood in North Carolina, showing Georgia where to stop. The valley was prize enough. Its floor was flat and green with pastureland and shoots of new corn. Its brooks were clear. Now, in May, there would be frost across the fields in the morning, heavy and bright, but blossoms were appearing on the dogwoods and leaves on the big hardwoods—only so far up the mountains, though; it was still winter on Standing Indian, stick-figure forests to the top. Sam had flown over this whole area, minutely, in his Cessna—Mt. Oglethorpe to the Chattooga River, Black Rock Mountain to the Brasstown Bald. He said there was no valley in Georgia like this one in beauty or remoteness. It was about two miles long and a half mile wide. Its year-round population was twelve. Someone else, somewhere else, would have called it by another name, but not here. Lyrical in its effrontery to fact, the name of the valley was Tate City. On our way in, we stopped to see Arthur and Mammy Young, its senior residents. Their house, until recently, had had so many preserves stacked on boards among the rafters that the roof sagged. Their outhouse straddled a stream. Their house, made of logs, burned to the ground one day when they were in town, eighteen miles away. Now they lived in a cinderblock hut with a pickup truck outside, fragments of machinery lying on the ground, hound dogs barking. The Youngs were approaching old age, apparently with opposite metabolisms, he sinewy, she more than ample, after sixty years of cathead biscuits. Inside, Arthur rolled himself a cigarette and sat down to smoke it beside his wood-burning stove. Near him was a fiddle. Sam said that Arthur was a champion fiddler. Arthur went on smoking and did not reach for the fiddle. He exchanged news with Carol. Christ looked down on us from pictures on each wall. The room had two kerosene lanterns, and its windows were patched with tape. "I always wished I had power, so I could iron," Mammy said. "When I had kids. Now I don't care." Dusk was near and Carol wanted time in the light, so we left soon and went on up the valley, a mile or so, to her log cabin.

A wooden deck reached out from the cabin on stilts toward the stream. The place had been cut out of woods—hemlock, ironwood, oak, alder, dogwood, rhododendron. A golden birch was standing in a hole in the center of the deck. Carol got out the weasel and set him, paws up, on the deck. Sam unpacked his things and set a bottle of The Glenlivet near the weasel, with three silver cups. I added a bottle of Talisker. Sam was no bourbon colonel. He liked pure Highland malt Scotch whisky. Carol measured the weasel. She traced him on paper and fondled his ears. His skull and his skin

would go into the university's research collection. She broke a dou-
ble-edged Gillette blade in half the long way. "Weasels are hard to
come by, hard to scent, hard to bait," she said. "We've tried to trap
a least weasel. We don't even have one. I hate to catch animals,
though. With D.O.R.s, I feel great. We've got the specimen and
we're making use of it. The skull is the most important thing. The
study skin shows the color pattern."

   With a simple slice, she brought out a testicle; she placed it on
a sheet of paper and measured it. Three-quarters of an inch. Slicing
smoothly through the weasel's fur, she began to remove the pelt.
Surely, she worked the skin away from the long neck. The flesh inside the pelt looked like a segment of veal tenderloin. "I lived on
squirrel last winter," she said. "Every time you'd come to a turn in
the road, there was another squirrel. I stopped buying meat. I
haven't bought any meat in a year, except for some tongue. I do love
tongue." While she talked, the blade moved in light, definite
touches. "Isn't he in perfect shape?" she said. "He was hardly
touched. You really lose your orientation when you start skinning
an animal that's been run over by a Mack truck." From time to time,
she stopped for a taste of The Glenlivet, her hand, brown from sun
and flecked with patches of the weasel's blood, reaching for the silver cup. "You've got to be careful where you buy meat anyway.
They inject some animals with an enzyme, a meat tenderizer, before
they kill them. *That* isn't any good for you." Where the going was
difficult, she moistened the skin with water. At last it came away
entire, like a rubber glove. She now had the weasel disassembled,
laid out on the deck in cleanly dissected parts. "I used to love to
take clocks apart," she said. "To see how they were built. This is
the same thing. I like plants and animals and their relationship to
the land and us. I like the vertebrates especially." The weasel's tailbone was still in the skin. She tugged at it with her teeth. Pausing
for a sip, she said that sometimes you just had to use your mouth in
her line of work, as once when she was catching cricket frogs. She
had a frog in each hand and saw another frog, so she put one frog
into her mouth while she caught the third. Gradually, the weasel's
tailbone came free. She held it in her hand and admired it. "Some
bones are real neat," she said. "In the heart of a deer, there's a bone.
And not between the ventricles, where you'd expect it. Some animals have bones in their penises—raccoons, for example, and weasels." She removed the bone from the weasel's penis. It was long,
proportionately speaking, with a hook at the penetrating end. It was

called a baculum, she said, which meant "rod" in Latin. She would save it. Its dimensions were one way to tell the weasel's age. Baculums are also involved in keying differences in species. Sam said he kept a raccoon's baculum in his wallet because it made a great toothpick. Carol turned the pelt inside out and folded the forepaws in an X, standard procedure with a study skin. She covered it with a deep layer of salt and packed it away.

The dusk was deep then. Carol had finished working almost in the dark. The air was cold. It was on its way to thirty. Sam had a fire going, inside, already disintegrating into coals. The smell of burning oak was sweet. We went into the cabin. Carol put the weasel on the tines of a long fork and roasted it over the coals.

"How do you like your weasel?" Sam asked me.

"Extremely well done," I said.

Carol sniffed the aroma of the roast. "It has a wild odor," she said. "You *know* it's not cow. The first time I had bear, people said, 'Cut the fat off. That's where the bad taste is.' I did, and the bear tasted just like cow. The next bear, I left the fat on."

The taste of the weasel was strong and not unpleasant. It lingered in the mouth after dinner. The meat was fibrous and dark. "It just goes to show you how good everything is," said Carol. "People who only eat cows, pigs, sheep, chickens—boy, have those people got blinders on! Is that tunnelization! There's one poisonous mammal in the United States: the short-tailed shrew. And you can even eat that."

Sam built up the fire.

"How can you be sure that something is not too old?" I asked.

"My God, if you can't tell if it's bad, what's the difference?" said Carol.

Sam said, "If it tastes good, don't knock it."

"People don't make sense," Carol said. "They hunt squirrels, but they wouldn't consider eating a squirrel killed on the road. Only once have I ever had competition for a D.O.R. A man wanted a squirrel for his black servant, and we had a set-to in the road."

There were double-deck bunks in the corners of the room. The corners were cold. We pulled three mattresses off the bunks and put them down side by side before the fire. We unrolled our three sleeping bags. It had been a big day; we were tired, and slept without stirring. Sam dreamed in the night that he was eating his own beard.

With a load of honey and cathead biscuits, gifts of Mammy Young, we went down out of the valley in the morning, mile after mile on a dirt road that ran beside and frequently crossed the outlet stream, which was the beginnings of the Tallulah River. Some twenty miles on down, the river had cut a gorge, in hard quartzite, six hundred feet deep. Warner Brothers had chosen the gorge as the site for the filming of a scene from James Dickey's novel, *Deliverance.* This mountain land in general was referred to around the state as "*Deliverance* country." The novel seemed to have been the most elaborate literary event in Georgia since *Gone with the Wind. Deliverance* was so talked about that people had, for conversational convenience, labelled its every part ("the owl scene," "the banjo scene"). It was a gothic novel, a metaphysical terror novel, the structural center of which involved four men going through the rapids of a mountain river in canoes. They were attacked. The action climax occurred when one of the canoemen scaled the wall of a fantastically sheer gorge to establish an ambush and kill a mountain man. He killed him with a bow and arrow. Carol and Sam, like half the people in Atlanta and a couple of dozen in Hollywood, called this "the climb-out scene," and they took me to see where Warners would shoot. The six-hundred-foot gorge was a wonder indeed, clefting narrowly and giddily down through the quartzite to the bed of the river that had done the cutting. Remarkably, though, no river was there. A few still pools. A trickle of water. Graffiti adorned the rock walls beside the pools. There was a dam nearby, and, in 1913, the river had been detoured through a hydropower tunnel. Steel towers stood on opposite lips of the chasm, supported by guy wires. A cable connected the towers. They had been built for performances of wire walkers, the Flying Wallendas. Nearby was the Cliffhanger Café. A sign said, "Enjoy Coca-Cola. See it here, free. Tallulah Gorge. 1200 feet deep." The Georgia Natural Areas Council looked on. Too late to register that one. The eye of the Warner Brothers camera would, however, register just what it wanted to select and see, and it would move up that wall in an unfailing evocation of wilderness. I was awed by the power of Dickey. In writing his novel, he had assembled "*Deliverance* country" from such fragments, restored and heightened in the chambers of his imagination. The canoes in his novel dived at steep angles down breathtaking cataracts and shot like javelins through white torrents among blockading monoliths. If a canoe were ten inches long and had men in it three inches high, they might find such conditions in a trout stream, steeply inclined,

with cataracts and plunge pools and rushing bright water falling
over ledges and splaying through gardens of rock. Dickey must have
imagined something like that and then enlarged the picture until the
trout stream became a gothic nightmare for men in full-size canoes.
A geologically maturer, less V-shaped stream would not have
served. No actual river anywhere could have served his artistic purpose—not the Snake, not the Upper Hudson, not even the Colorado—and least of all a river in Georgia, whose wild Chattooga,
best of the state's white-water rivers, has comparatively modest
rapids. The people of the *Deliverance* mountains were malevolent,
opaque, and sinister. Arthur and Mammy Young.

There were records of the presence of isolated cottonmouths
on Dry Fork Creek, in wild, forested piedmont country east of Ath-
ens. Dry Fork Creek, a tributary of a tributary of the Savannah
River, was about halfway between Vesta and Rayle, the beginning
and the end of nowhere. We searched the woods along the creek.
It would not have been at all unusual had we found the highland
moccasin (the copperhead) there, for this was his terrain—*Agkistrodon contortrix contortrix.* What we were looking for, though, was the
water mocassin (the cottonmouth), inexplicably out of his range.
Cottonmouths belong in the coastal plain, in the rice fields, in the
slow-moving rivers—*Agkistrodon piscivorus piscivorus.* Seeing a cottonmouth in a place like this would be a rare experience, and Carol
fairly leaped into the woods. For my part, I regretted that I lacked
aluminum boots. Carol was wearing green tennis shoes. Sam's feet
were covered with moccasins. Carol rolled every log. She lifted anything that could have sheltered a newt, let alone a snake. By the
stream, she ran her eye over every flat rock and projecting branch.
Always disappointed, she quickly moved on. Sam sauntered beside
her. The flood plain was beautiful under big sycamores, water oaks,
maples: light filtering down in motes, wet leaves on the ground, cold
water moving quietly in the stream. But the variety of tracks she
found was disturbingly incomplete. "There, on that sandbar—those
are possum tracks. Possums and coons go together, but that's just
possum right there, no way about it. And that is not right. There
shouldn't be a bar like that with no coon tracks on it, even if the
water goes up and down every night. Possums can live anywhere.
Coons can't. Coon tracks signify a healthy place. I don't much like
this place. It's been cut over. There are no big dead trees." One big
dead tree with a cottonmouth under it would have changed that,
would have glorified Dry Fork Creek for Carol, coons or no

coons—*piscivorus piscivorus* caught poaching, out of his territory, off the edge of his map, beyond his range. I felt her disappointment and was sorry the snakes were not there. "Don't be disappointed," she said. "When we go down the Cemocheckobee, cottonmouths will show us the way."

Buffalo disappeared from Georgia in early Colonial time. William Bartram noted this when he visited the colony and wrote *Travels in Georgia and Florida, 1773–74.* Bartram, from Philadelphia, was the first naturalist to describe in detail the American subtropics. After his book reached London, sedentary English poets cribbed from his descriptions (Wordsworth, for example, and Coleridge). Ten miles south of Dry Fork Creek, Sam, Carol, and I crossed Bartram's path. In Bartram's words, "We came into an open Forest of Pines, Scrub white Oaks, Black Jacks, Plumb, Hicory, Grapes Vines, Rising a sort of Ridge, come to a flat levill Plain, and at the upper side of this, levell at the foot of the hills of the great Ridge, is the great Buffiloe Lick, which are vast Pits, licked in the Clay, formerly by the Buffiloes, and now kept smoothe and open by Cattle, deer, and horses, that resort here constantly to lick the clay, which is a greesey Marle of various colours, Red, Yellow & white, & has a sweetish taste, but nothing saltish that I could perceive." Bartram was describing what is now Philomath, Georgia 30659—a one-street town consisting of thirty houses and a buffalo lick. Philomath was established, early in the nineteenth century, as a seat of learning—hence the name. The town was the address of an academy whose students, in time, vanished like the buffalo. Now it was a place of preeminent silence under big oaks, and as we glided into town we were the only thing that moved. Ninety blacks, fifty whites lived there, but no one was out in the midday shade. The almost idling engine was the only sound. In an L-shaped elegant clapboard house, built in 1795, lived Dorothy Daniel Wright. Sam and Carol, having read Bartram's description and having determined that the buffalo lick was still intact, wanted to see it and, they hoped, to register it as a Georgia Natural Area. Miss Wright was the person to see. It was her lick. She was in her upper sixties. Her hair was white and swept upward, and crowned with a braided gold bun. Her welcome was warm. She showed us the lick. Cattle and deer had licked it slick all through her girlhood, she said. Now it was covered with grass, some hawthorn and sumac, and dominated by an immense, outreaching laurel oak. Carol squatted flat-footed, knees high, and dug with her hands for various colors of clay. She ate some blue clay, and handed pieces to me and Sam. It was sweet, bland, alkaline, slightly chewy. "My first thought was 'soapy,'" she said. "I expected it to get stronger, but it didn't. The final thought was 'sweetness.'" She put a bit more in her mouth and ate it contemplatively. There was, apparently, no sodium chloride in this ground. Phosphate, sodium, and calcium are what the buffalo licked. Where did they get their salt? "Twelve miles away there was salt," Miss Wright said. "Twelve miles is nothin' to a buffalo roamin' around. Between the two licks, they got all the minerals they needed for their bovine metabolism." Miss Wright had taught biology and chemistry in various high schools for forty-three years. She was eager to register the Great Buffalo Lick Natural Area, which had once been a boundary-line landmark separating the Georgia colony from the territory of the Creeks and Cherokees. She took us home to a lunch of salad and saltines. Into the salad went mushrooms, violets, and trout lilies that Carol had gathered in the mountains the day before.

Leaving Philomath, heading south, Sam commented how easy and pleasant that experience had been and how tense such encounters could sometimes be. He talked about a redneck peanut farmer in south Georgia, owner of a potential Natural Area. This redneck had taken one look at Sam's beard and had seemed ready to kill him then and there.

"What is a redneck, Sam?"

"You know what a redneck is, you little Yankee bastard."

"I want to hear your definition."

"A redneck is a fat slob in a pickup truck with a rifle across the back. He hates 'niggers.' He would rather have his kids ignorant than go to school with colored. I guess I don't like rednecks. I guess I've known some."

"Some of my best friends are rednecks," Carol said.

D.O.R. blacksnake, five miles south of Irwinton—old and bloated. "I'll just get it off the road, so its body won't be further humiliated," Carol said. Across a fence, a big sow was grunting. Carol carried the snake to the fence. She said, "Here, piggy-poo, look what I've got for you." She tossed the snake across the fence. The sow bit off the snake's head and ate it like an apple.

"Interesting," Carol said, "that we can feed a rotten snake to something we in turn will eat."

I said I would rather eat the buffalo lick.

Carol said, "I'll tell you the truth, I've had better clay."

We were out of the piedmont and down on the coastal plain,

into the north of south Georgia. The roadside ads were riddled with bullet holes. "PREPARE TO MEET JESUS CHRIST THE LORD." "WE WANT TO WIPE OUT CANCER IN YOUR LIFETIME." "WE CANNOT AC-CEPT TIRES THAT HAVE BEEN CAPPED AS TRADE-INS."

Johnny Cash was back. Indians were now his theme. He was singing about a dam that was going to flood Seneca land, although the Senecas had been promised title to their land "as long as the moon shall rise." Cash's voice was deeper than ever. He sounded as if he were smoking a peace pipe through an oboe. Carol hugged herself. "As long . . . as the moon . . . shall rise . . . As long . . . as the rivers . . . flow."

"DON'T LOSE YOUR SOUL BY THE MARK OF THE BEAST."

We ate muskrat that night in a campsite on flat ground beside Big Sandy Creek, in Wilkinson County, innermost Georgia—muskrat with beans, chili powder, onions, tomatoes, and kelp. "I have one terrible handicap," Carol said. "I cannot follow a recipe." The muskrat, though, was very good. Carol had parboiled it for twenty minutes and then put it through a meat grinder, medium grind. Firewood was scarce, because the area was much used by fishermen who were prone to build fires and fish all night. Carol went up a tall spruce pine, and when she was forty feet or so above the ground she began to break off dead limbs and throw them down. She had to throw them like spears to clear the living branches of the tree. Pine burns oily, but that would not matter tonight. The muskrat was in a pot. Sam and I built up the fire. He pitched a tent.

To pass time before dinner, I put the canoe into the river and paddled slowly downstream. Carol called to me from the tree, "Watch for snakes. They'll be overhead, in the limbs of trees." She was not warning me; she was trying to raise the pleasure of the ride. "If you don't see the snake, you can tell by the splash," she went on. "A frog splash is a concentrated splash. A snake splash is a long splat." Gliding, watching, I went a quarter of a mile without a splash or a splat. It was dusk. The water was growing dark. I heard the hoot of a barred owl. Going back against the current, I worked up an appetite for muskrat.

After dinner, in moonlight, Sam and Carol and I got into the canoe and went up the river. A bend to the left, a bend to the right, and we penetrated the intense darkness of a river swamp that seemed to reach out unendingly. We could only guess at its dimensions. Upland swamps occur in areas between streams. River swamps are in the flood plains of rivers, and nearly all the streams

in the Georgia coastal plain have them. They can be as much as six miles wide, and when the swamps of two or more big rivers connect, the result can be a vast and separate world. The darkness in there was so rich it felt warm. It was not total, for bars and slats of moonlight occasionally came through, touched a root or a patch of water. Essentially, however, everything was black: black water, black vegetation—water-standing maples, cypress—black on black. Columnar trunks were all around us, and we knew the channel only by the feel of the current, which sometimes seemed to be coming through from more than one direction. Here the black water sucked and bubbled, roiled by, splashed through the roots of the trees. Farther on, it was silent again. Silent ourselves, we pushed on into the black. Carol moved a flashlight beam among the roots of trees. She held the flashlight to her nose, because the eye can see much more if the line of sight is closely parallel to the beam. She inspected minutely the knobby waterlines of the trees. Something like a sonic boom cracked in our ears. "Jesus, what was that?"

"Beaver."

The next two slaps were even louder than the first. Carol ignored the beaver, and continued to move the light. It stopped. Out there in the obsidian was a single blue eye.

"A blue single eye is a spider," she said. "Two eyes is a frog. Two eyes almost touching is a snake. An alligator's eyes are blood red."

Two tiny coins now came up in her light. "Move in there," she said. "I want that one."

With a throw of her hand, she snatched up a frog. It was a leopard frog, and she let him go. He was much within his range. Carol was looking for river frogs, pig frogs, carpenter frogs, whose range peripheries we were stalking. She saw another pair of eyes. The canoe moved in. Her hand swept out unseen and made a perfect tackle, thighs to knees. This was a bronze frog, home on the range. Another pair of eyes, another catch, another disappointment—a bullfrog. Now another shattering slap on the water. Another. The beaver slapped only when the canoe was moving upstream. The frog chorus, filling the background, varied in pitch and intensity, rose and fell. Repeatedly came the hoot of the barred owl.

Sam dipped a cup and had a drink. "I feel better about drinking water out of swamps than out of most rivers," he said. "It's filtered. No one ever says a good word for a swamp. The whole feeling

up to now has been 'Fill it in—it's too wet to plow, too dry to fish.' Most people stay out of swamps. I love them. I like the water, the reptiles, the amphibians. There is so much life in a swamp. The sounds are so different. Frogs, owls, birds, beavers. Birds sound different in swamps."

"You see a coon in here and you realize it's his whole world," Carol said.

"It's a beautiful home with thousands of creatures," Sam said.

With all this ecological intoxication, I thought they were going to fall out of the canoe.

"Life came out of the swamps," Sam said. "And now swamps are among the last truly wild places left."

We went back downstream. Tobacco smoke was in the air over the river. Occasionally, on the bank, we saw an orange-red glow, momentarily illuminating a black face. Fishing lines, slanting into the stream, were visible against the light of small fires. The canoe moved soundlessly by, and on into the darkness. "The groids sure love to fish," Sam murmured. The moon was low. It was midnight.

Now, at noon, a hundred miles or so to the southeast and by another stream, we were sitting on the big felled oak, pouring out the last of the wine, with Chap Causey moving toward us a foot at a time in his American dragline crane. He swung a pair of mats around behind him and backed up a bit more, and as he went on gutting the streambed the oak began to tremble. It must have weighed two or three tons, but it was trembling and felt like an earthquake—time to move. Carol picked up a piece of dry otter scat. She bounced it in the palm of her hand and looked upcurrent at the unaltered stream and downcurrent into the new ditch. She said, "You can talk about coons' being able to go off into the woods and eat nuts and berries, because they're omnivores. But not this otter. He's finished." She broke open the scat. Inside it were fishbones and hair— hair of a mouse or hair of a young rabbit. There were fish otoliths as well, two of them, like small stones. She flung it all into the stream. "He's done for," she said, and waved goodbye to Chap Causey.

On down the dirt road from the stream-channelization project, we saw ahead a D.O.R.

"Looks like a bad one," Carol said.

Sam stopped. "Yes, it's a bad one," he said. "Canebrake. Do you want to eat him?"

Carol leaned over and looked. "He's too old. Throw him out of the road, the poor darlin'. What gets me is that some bastard is proud of having run over him. When I die, I don't want to be humiliated like that."

Sam threw the rattlesnake out of the road. Then we headed southwest through underdeveloped country, almost innocent of towns—Alma, Douglas, Adel, Moultrie, a hundred miles from Alma to Moultrie.

D.O.R. king snake, blue jay, sparrow hawk, wood thrush, raccoon, catbird, cotton rat. The poor darlin's. Threw them out of the road.

A.O.R. hobo—man with a dog. "Oh, there's a good guy," Carol said as we passed him. "He has a dog and a bedroll. What else do you need?"

D.O.R. opossum. Cook County. Three miles east of Adel. Carol spoke admiringly of the creature flexibility of the opossum. Among the oldest of mammals, the possum goes all the way back to Cretaceous time, she said, and, like people, it has never specialized, in a biological sense. "You can specialize yourself out of existence. Drain the home of the otter. The otter dies. The opossum, though, can walk away from an ecological disaster. So much for that. Try something else. He eats anything. He lives almost anywhere. That's why the possum is not extinct. That's why the possum has been so successful." One place this particular possum was never going to walk away from was Georgia Highway 76. Technology, for him the ultimate ecological disaster, had clouted him at seventy miles an hour.

Between Moultrie and Doerun, in the watershed of the Ochlockonee, was a lake in a pine grove surrounded by fifty acres of pitcher plants. They belonged to a couple named Barber, from Moultrie, who had read about the Natural Areas Council and had offered their pitcher plants to posterity. Sam and Carol, posterity, would accept. This was the largest colony of pitcher plants any of us was ever likely to see. Bright-green leaves, ruddy blooms, they glistened in the sun and nodded in the breeze and reached out from the lakeshore like tulips from a Dutch canal. Barber cut one off at the base and held up a leaf—folded upon itself like a narrow goblet, half full of water. The interior was lined with bristles, pointing downward. In the water were dozens of winged creatures, some still moving, most not. Barber had interrupted a handsome meal. His pitcher plants, in aggregate, could probably eat a ton of bugs a day. Sam said he sure was pleased to be able to make the pitcher plants a Georgia Natural Area. Carol saw a tiny water snake. She picked it up. It coiled in her hand and snapped at her. She talked gently to it until it settled down. "Are you going to be good now?" she said. She opened her hand, and the snake sat there, placidly, on her palm. The Barbers did not seem charmed. They said nothing and did not move. Carol set down the snake. It departed, and so did the Barbers. They went back to Moultrie in their air-conditioned car, leaving us their lake, their pines, their pitcher plants.

We jumped into the lake with a bar of soap and scrubbed ourselves up for dinner. In places, the lake was warm from the sun and in places cold from springs. We set up the tent and built a fire. The breeze was cool in the evening in the pines. Carol's stomach growled like a mastiff. She said that when she was hungry she could make her stomach growl on cue. It growled again. She had a tape recorder in the car. Sam got it and recorded the growls, which seemed marketable. He said they could scare away burglars. We fried beefsteaks and turtle steaks under a gibbous moon. We buried the fossils of pleasure: three cow bones and a bottle that had held The Glenlivet. Frogs were hooting. There were no owls. We slept like bears.

At six in the morning, we got into the canoe and moved slowly around the lake. Sam cast for bass. He could flick his lure seventy feet and drop it on a pine needle. He could lay it under stumps with the delicacy of an eyedropper, or drive it, if he wanted to, halfway down the lake. He caught two bass. One wrapped itself hopelessly into a big waterlogged multiple branch. We pulled the branch up out of the water. The bass had himself woven into it like a bird in a cage. Under the blue sky and star-burst clusters of longleaf pine— pitcher plants far as you could see, the lake blue and cool—we cooked the bass in butter and ate it with fried turtle eggs. Then we fried salt-risen bread in the bass butter with more turtle eggs and poured Tate City honey over the bread. Chicory coffee with milk and honey. Fish-crackling off the bottom of the pan.

The yolk of a turtle egg cooks readily to a soft, mushy yellow. The albumen, though, pops and bubbles and jumps around the pan, and will not congeal. No matter how blazing the heat beneath it may be, the white of the egg of the snapping turtle will not turn milky and set. It will jump like a frog and bounce and dance and skitter all over the pan until your patience snaps or the fire dies. So you give up trying to cook it. You swallow it hot and raw.

D.O.R. cat, D.O.R. dog. Near the Mitchell County line. Carol sighed, but no move was made to stop. We were heading west on 37 to check out a river that the Natural Areas Council had been told was like no other in Georgia. Florida was only forty miles away. The terrain was flat and serene between the quiet towns—Camilla, Newton, Elmodel. Cattle stood on light-green grassland under groves of dark pecans. Sometimes the road was a corridor walled with pines. Sometimes the margins opened out into farms, then closed down toward small cabins, more palisades of pine.

D.O.R. gray squirrel. "We could eat him," Carol said.

"We've got enough food," said Sam.

More pines, more pecans, more farms, a mild morning under a blue-and-white sky. Out of the sky came country music—the Carter Sisters, Johnny Cash, philosophy falling like hail: "It's not easy to be all alone, but time goes by and life goes on . . . for after night there comes a dawn. Yes, time goes by and life goes on."

D.O.R. fox squirrel. Baker County. He was as warm as in life, and he was in perfect shape. Kneeling in the road, Carol held out his long, feathery silver-gray tail so that it caught the sunlight. "There aren't many things prettier than that," she said. "Makes a human being sort of jealous not to have a pretty tail like that." Gently, she brushed the squirrel and daubed blood from his head. He looked alive in her hands. She put him in a plastic bag. The ice was low. We stopped at the next icehouse and bought twenty-five pounds.

D.O.R. nighthawk, fresh as the squirrel. Carol kept the hawk for a while in her lap, just to look at him. He could have been an Aztec emblem—wings half spread, head in profile, feathers patterned in blacks and browns and patches of white. Around the mouth were stiff bristles, fanned out like a radar screen, adapted for catching insects.

D.O.R. box turtle.

D.O.R. loggerhead shrike.

D.O.R. gas station. It was abandoned, its old pumps rusting; beside the pumps, a twenty-year-old Dodge with four flat tires.

D.O.R. cottonmouth. Three miles east of Bluffton. Clay County. Finding him there was exciting to Carol. We were nearing the Cemocheckobee, the river we had come to see, and the presence of one cottonmouth here on the road implied crowded colonies along the river. There was no traffic, no point in moving him immediately off the road. Carol knelt beside him. "He was getting ready to shed. He would have been a lot prettier when he had," she said. The skin was dull olive. Carol felt along the spine to a point about three-quarters of the way back and squeezed. The dead snake coiled. "That is what really frightens people," she said. She lifted the head and turned it so that we could see, between the mouth and the nostrils, the deep pits, sensory organs, through which the striking snake had homed on his targets. Slowly, Carol opened the creature's mouth. The manuals of herpetology tell you not to do that, tell you, in fact, not to touch a dead cottonmouth, because through reflex action a dead one can strike and kill a human being. Now a fang was visible—a short brown needle projecting down from the upper jaw. "You have to be very careful not to scratch your finger on one of those," Carol said. She pressed with her fingertips behind the eyes, directly on the poison sacs, and a drop of milky fluid fell onto a stick she held in her other hand. Four more drops followed, forming a dome of venom. "That amount could kill you," she said, and she pressed out another drop. "Did you know that this is where they got the idea for the hypodermic syringe?" Another drop. "It has to get into the bloodstream. You could drink all you want and it wouldn't hurt you." She placed the cottonmouth off the road. Carol once milked honeysuckle until she had about two ounces, which she then drank. The fluid was so concentratedly sweet it almost made her sick.

Carol's purse fell open as we got back into the car, and out of it spilled a .22-calibre revolver in a case that looked much like a compact. Also in the purse was a Big Brother tear-gas gun, flashlight bulbs, chapstick, shampoo, suntan lotion, and several headbands. Once, when she was off in a swamp frogging and salamandering, a state trooper came upon the car and—thinking it might be an abandoned vehicle—rummaged through it. He found the purse and opened it. He discovered the pistol, the chapstick, the shampoo, et cetera, and a pink garter belt and black net stockings. He might have sent out a five-state alert, but Carol just then emerged from the swamp. She was on her way, she told him, to make a call on Kimberly-Clark executives in an attempt to get them to register some forest and riverbank land with the Natural Areas Council, and for that mission the black net stockings would be as useful as the pistol might be in a swamp or the chapstick in a blistering sun. "Yes, Ma'am." The visit to the Kleenex people was successful, as it happened, and the result was the Griffin's Landing Registered Natural Area, fifty acres—a series of fossil beds on the Savannah River containing by the many thousands *Crassostrea gigantissima,* forty-million-year-old oysters, the largest that ever lived.

Down a dirt road, across a railroad track, and on through woods that scraped the car on both sides, Sam worked his way as far as he could toward the river's edge. We took down the canoe, and carried it to the water. The Cemocheckobee was a rejuvenated stream. Widening its valley, long ago, it had formed relaxed meanders, and now, apparently, the land was rising beneath it, and the river had speeded up and was cutting deeply into the meanders. The current was strong—nothing spectacular, nothing white, but forceful and swift. It ran beneath a jungle of overhanging trees. The river was compact and intimate. The distance from bank to bank was only about thirty feet, so there could be no getting away from the trees. "I'd venture to say we'll see our share of snakes today," Carol exulted. "Let's go! This is cottonmouth country!" Carol shoved up the sleeves of her sweatshirt over her elbows. Sam went to the car and got a snakebite kit.

I had thought I might be apprehensive about this part of the journey. I didn't see how I could help but be. Now I realized that I was having difficulty walking toward the river. "Sam," I said, "wouldn't you prefer that I paddle in the stern?" I had put in many more hours than he had in canoes on rivers, so it seemed only correct to me that Sam should sit up in the bow and fend off branches and cottonmouths while I guided the canoe from the commanding position in the rear.

"I'll go in the stern," said Sam. "Carol will go in the middle to collect snakes. You go in the bow." So much for that. It was his canoe. I got in and moved to the bow. They got in, and we shoved off.

The canoe found the current, accelerated, went downstream fifty feet, and smashed into a magnolia branch. I expected cottonmouths to strike me in both shoulders and the groin. But the magnolia proved to be snakeless. We shot on through and downriver. We could not avoid the overhanging branches. The current was too fast and there were too many of them. Once or twice a minute, we punched through the leafy twigs reaching down from a horizontal limb. But I began to settle down. There weren't any snakes, after all—not in the first mile, anyway. And things Carol was saying made a difference. She said, for example, that snakes plop off branches long before the canoe gets to them. She also said that cottonmouths rarely go out onto branches. They stay back at the river's edge and in the swamps. Snakes on branches are, in the main, as harmless as licorice. Bands of tension loosened and began to drop away. I looked ahead. At the next bend, the river was veiled in a curtain of water oak. I was actually hoping to see a snake hit the surface, but none did. We slipped through and into the clear.

This was heavy current for a river with no white water, and when we rested the river gave us a fast drift. Scenes quickly changed, within the steep banks, the incised meanders, against backgrounds of beech and laurel, white oak, spruce pine, Venus maidenhair, and resurrection fern. We came upon a young coon at the foot of a tree. He looked at us with no apparent fear. We pulled in to the bank. "Hey, there, you high-stepper, you," Carol said. "Get up that tree!" The coon put a paw on the tree and went up a foot or two and looked around. "Why aren't you afraid?" Carol went on. "Are you O.K., cooner?" The raccoon's trouble—probably—was that he had never seen a human. He was insufficiently afraid, and Carol began to worry about him. So she got out of the canoe and went after him. The coon moved up the tree fifteen feet. The tree was a slender maple. Carol started up it like a rope climber. The coon stayed where he was. Carol said, "I'm not climbing the tree to make him jump out. I'll just go high enough to let him know he ought to be afraid of people." When she got near him, the coon scrambled to the high branches, where he hung on to one and swayed. Carol stopped about twenty-five feet up. "Hey, coon! We're no good. Don't you know that?" she called to him. Then she slid on down. "Let that be a lesson to you!" she called from the bottom.

We moved on downstream, passing blue-tailed skinks and salamanders, animal tracks on every flat. A pair of beavers dived into the water and went around slapping the surface, firing blanks. Carol saw the mouth of their den, and she got out of the canoe, climbed the bank, and stuck her head inside. She regretted that she had not brought a flashlight with her. We moved on. We passed a banded snake sitting on a limb. He produced mild interest. Fear was gone from me. It had gone off with the flow of the river. There was a light splash to the right—as if from a slide, not a dive. No one saw what made it. "Otter," Carol said. "Pull in to the opposite bank—over there. Quickly!" We stopped the canoe, and held on to bush stems of the riverbank and waited. Nothing happened. The quiet grew. "The otter will come up and look at us," Carol said. We waited. Smooth, the river moved—never the same, always the same. No otter. "He is an extraordinarily intelligent and curious animal," Carol said. "He could go off somewhere, if he wanted to, just to breathe. But he wants to see us. He will not be able to stand it much longer. He will have to come up." Up came a face, chin on the water—dark bright eyes in a dark-brown head, small ears, wide snout: otter. His gaze was direct and unflinching. He looked at us until he had seen his fill; then he went back under. "Wouldn't you like to live in this creek?" Carol said. "You'd never get lonely. Wouldn't you like to play with the otter?"

A waterfall, about twelve feet high, poured into the river from the left. Two hundred yards downstream, another fall dropped into the river from the right. The feeder streams of the Cemocheckobee were not cutting down as fast as the river itself, and these hanging tributaries poured in from above, all the way down. We now moved through stands of royal fern under big sycamores and big beeches, and past another waterfall. "This is otter, beaver, coon heaven," Carol said. Her only disappointment was the unexpected scarcity of snakes. She said she had seen more than her share of "magnolia-leaf snakes" that day. Her imagination, charged with hope and anticipation, could, and frequently did, turn magnolia leaves into snakes, green upon the branches. I found myself feeling disappointed, too. Only one lousy banded snake. The day was incomplete.

Sam said the threat to this river was the lumber industry. Logging was going on in the forests on both sides, and he would try to persuade the lumbermen to register the river—and its marginal lands—before the day came when it would be too late. While he was speaking, I saw a snake on a log at the water's edge, and pointed to it, interrupting him.

"Is that a banded snake?"

"That is not a banded snake," Carol said.

"Is it a bad one?"

"It's a bad one, friend."

"Well, at last. Where have you been all day?"

He had been right there, of course, in his own shaft of sun, and the sight of a shining aluminum canoe with three figures in it was not going to cause him to move. Moving back was not in his character. He would stay where he was or go toward something that seemed to threaten him. Whatever else he might be, he was not afraid. He was a cottonmouth, a water moccasin. Carol was closer to him than I was, and I felt no fear at all. Sam, in the stern, was closest of all, because we were backing up toward the snake. I remember thinking, as we moved closer, that I preferred that they not bring the thing into the canoe, but that was the sum of my concern; we were ten miles downstream from where we had begun. The moccasin did not move. We were now right next to it. Sam reached toward it with his paddle.

"Rough him up a little to teach him to beware of humans," Carol said. "But don't hurt him."

Under the snake Sam slipped the paddle, and worked it a bit, like a spatula, so that the snake came up onto the blade. Sam lifted the cottonmouth into the air. Sam rocked the paddle. "Come on," he said. "Come on, there. Open your mouth so John can see the cotton."

"Isn't he magnificent?" Carol said. "Set him down, Sam. He isn't going to open his mouth."

Sam returned the moccasin to the log. The canoe moved on into a gorge. The walls of the gorge were a hundred feet high.

The Cemocheckobee was itself a feeder stream, ending in the Chattahoochee, there in southwestern Georgia, at the Alabama line. An appointment elsewhere with the Chattahoochee—a red-letter one for Sam and Carol—drew us back north. The Chattahoochee is Georgia's most prodigious river. Atlanta developed where railheads met the river. The Chattahoochee rises off the slopes of the Brasstown Bald, Georgia's highest mountain, seven miles from North Carolina, and flows to Florida, where its name changes at the frontier. It is thereafter called the Appalachicola. In all its four hundred Georgia miles, what seems most remarkable about this river is that it flows into Atlanta nearly wild. Through a series of rapids between high forested bluffs, it enters the city clear and clean. From parts of the Chattahoochee within the city of Atlanta, no structures are visible—just water, sky, and woodland. The circumstance is nostalgic, archaic, and unimaginable. It is as if an unbefouled Willamette were to flow wild into Portland—Charles into Boston, Missouri into Omaha, Hudson into New York, Delaware into Philadelphia, James into Richmond, Cuyahoga into Cleveland (the Cuyahoga caught fire one day, and fire engines had to come put out the blazing river). Atlanta deserves little credit for the clear Chattahoochee, though, because the Chattahoochee is killed before it leaves the city. It dies between Marietta Boulevard and South Cobb Drive, just below the Atlanta Water Intake, at the point where thirty-five million gallons of partially treated sewage and forty million gallons of raw sewage are poured into the river every day. A short distance below that stand two enormous power plants, whose effluent pipes raise the temperature of the river. A seven-pound brown trout was caught recently not far above the Water Intake. It is difficult to imagine what sort of fin-rotted, five-legged, uranium-gilled, web-mouthed monster could live in the river by Georgia Power. Seen from the air (Sam showed it to me once in his plane), the spoiling of the Chattahoochee is instant, from river-water blue to sewer ochre-brown, as if a pair of colored ribbons had been sewn together there by the city.

Now a sewer line was projected to run upstream beside the river to fresh subdivisions that would bloom beyond the city's perimeter highway. The sewer would not actually be in the water, but, unless it could be tunnelled or not built at all, it would cause the clear-cutting of every tree in a sixty-foot swath many miles long. A segment of the sewer was already under construction. The Georgia Natural Areas Council was among the leadership in an effort to put down this specific project and at the same time to urge a bill through the legislature that would protect permanently the river and its overview. Sam had asked Jimmy Carter to come get into a canoe and shoot the metropolitan rapids and see for himself the value and the vulnerability of the river. Carter was willing. So, in three canoes, six of us put in under the perimeter highway, I-285, and paddled into Atlanta.

Sam had Carter in his bow. Carter might be governor of Georgia but not of Sam's canoe. Carol and I had the second canoe. In the third was a state trooper, who had a pistol on his hip that could have sunk a frigate. In the stern was James Morrison, of the federal government, the Bureau of Outdoor Recreation's man in Atlanta. He wore wet-suit bootees and rubber kneepads and seemed to be ready to go down the Colorado in an acorn.

The current was strong. The canoes moved smartly downstream. Carter was a lithe man, an athletic man in his forties—at home, obviously enough, in boats. He was wearing a tan windbreaker, khaki trousers, and white basketball shoes. He had a shock of wind-tossed sandy hair. In the course of the day, he mentioned that he had grown up in Archery, Georgia, by a swamp of the Kinchafoonee and the Choctawhatchee. He and his friend A. D. Davis, who was black, had built a twelve-foot bateau. "When it rained and we couldn't work in the fields, we went down to the creek and set out set hooks for catfish and eels, and we drifted downstream in the bateau hunting ducks with a shotgun. We fished for bass and red-bellies, and we waded for jack. The bateau weighed eighty pounds. I could pick it up." Archery was three miles west of Plains, a cross-roads with a short row of stores and less than a thousand people. Sam, Carol, and I had passed through Plains—in fifteen seconds— on our way north. An enormous red-lettered sign over the stores said, "PLAINS, GEORGIA, HOME OF JIMMY CARTER." Carter had played basketball at Plains High School, had gone on to Annapolis and into nuclear submarines, and had come back to Plains in 1953 to farm peanuts and to market them for himself and others, busi-nesses he continued as he went on into the legislature and upward to become governor. The career of his boyhood friend had been quite different. The last Carter had heard of A. D. Davis, Davis was in jail for manslaughter.

Now, on the Chattahoochee, the Governor said, "We're lucky here in Georgia that the environment thing has risen nationally, be-cause Georgia is less developed than some states and still has much to save." With that, he and Sam went into the largest set of rapids in the city of Atlanta. The rip was about a hundred yards long, full of Vs confusing to the choice, broad ledges, haystacks, eddies, and tumbling water. They were good rapids, noisy and alive, and strong enough to flip a canoe that might hit a rock and swing broadside.

In the shadow of a two-hundred-foot bluff, we pulled out on a small island to survey the scene. Carol said the bluff was a gneiss and was full of garnets. The Governor had binoculars. With them, he discovered a muskrat far out in the river. The muskrat was gnaw-ing on a branch that had been stopped by a boulder. "He's sniffin' around that little old limb on top of that rock," Carter said. "Maybe he's eating the lichens off it. Look, there's another. Who owns the land here?"

"Various people," Morrison said. "Some are speculators. A lot of it is owned by Alfred Kennedy."

"Kennedy?"

"A director of the First National Bank," Carol said.

"Is he a good guy, so far as conservancy goes?"

"From what I hear, he's too busy making money."

"Sometimes it's better to slip up on people like that," Carter told her. "Rather than make an issue of it right away." He spoke in a low voice, almost shyly. There was a touch of melancholy in his face that disappeared, as it did frequently, when he grinned. A trillium caught his eye. He asked her what it was, and she told him. "And what's that?" he said.

"Dog hobble," Carol said. "*Leucothoë.* Look here." She pointed at the ground. "A coon track."

The canoes moved on, and the next stop was a visit with a fisherman who was casting from the bank. He was middle-aged and weathered, a classical, prototype fisherman, many years on the river. He was wreathed in smiles at sight of the Governor. I looked hard at Sam, but nothing in his face indicated that he had planted the man there. The fisherman, Ron Sturdevant, showed the Governor a Kodacolor print of a twenty-three-inch rainbow he had recently caught right here under this bluff. "I guess I'm glad I met you," Sturdevant said. "I'm glad you're taking this trip. I'm worried about the river."

"I hope we can keep it this way," Carter said.

We climbed from the river through a deep wood of oaks and big pines to a cave in which families of Cherokees had once lived. It was about a hundred feet up. The view swept the river, no structures visible. "Who owns this place?"

Sam said, "Alfred Kennedy."

"And he hasn't even slept here," said Carol.

"Have you slept here, Carol?" the Governor asked her.

"Many times," she told him. "With a dog named Catfish."

Morrison said, "There's gold here, around the Indian cave. It's never been mined."

"That would be a good way to keep this place undisturbed," Carter said. "To announce that there was gold up here."

Back on the river, he used his binoculars while Sam paddled. He saw four more muskrats and an automobile, upside down in the water, near the far bank. He also saw a turtle.

"What kind is it?" Carol asked him.

"If I knew what kind it was, I could tell you." He handed the binoculars across to her, too late.

"I've been down through here and seen fifteen turtles with bullet holes in their shells," Carol told him.

What kind?" Carter said.

"Cooters and sliders."

There was a racket of engines. Out of nowhere came two mo-

torcyclists riding *in* the river. A mile or so later, we took out, beside
an iron bridge. Carol said she had washed her hair any number of
times under that bridge.

The Governor invited us home for lunch. The mansion was
new—a million-dollar neo-Palladian Xanadu, formal as a wedding
cake, and exquisitely landscaped. Carol and Sam and I were ropy
from a thousand miles of mountains, rivers, and swamps. None of
us had changed clothes in nearly a week, but we would soon be eating grilled cheese sandwiches at a twenty-foot table under a crystal
chandelier. The Governor, for that matter, did not look laundered
anymore—mud on his trousers, mud on his basketball shoes. We
parked in back of the mansion. A backboard, hoop, and net were
mounted there. A ball sat on the pavement. Before going in, we shot
baskets for a while.

"The river is just great," the Governor said, laying one in.
"And it ought to be kept the way it is. It's almost heartbreaking to
feel that the river is in danger of destruction. I guess I'll write a letter to all the landowners and say, 'If you'll use some self-restraint,
it'll decrease the amount of legal restraint put on you in the future.'
I don't think people want to incur the permanent wrath of the governor or the legislature."

"I've tried to talk to property owners," Carol said. "To get
them to register their land with the Natural Areas Council. But they
wouldn't even talk to me."

The Governor said, "To be blunt about it, Carol, why would
they?"

The Governor had the ball and was dribbling in place, as if
contemplating a property owner in front of him, one-on-one. He
went to the basket, shot, and missed. Carol got the rebound and fed
the ball to Sam. He shot. He missed, too.

Joan Didion

Joan Didion's early articles and essays often interpreted her home state, California, as a land of end-of-the-continent nightmares rather than golden dreams. Born in Sacramento in 1934, Didion graduated from Berkeley in 1956 and began writing for *Vogue, The Saturday Evening Post, Holiday, Harper's,* and *National Review.*

Slouching Towards Bethlehem and *The White Album* collected her articles from the 1960s and 1970s. Her subjects included Haight-Ashbury and the hippie subculture, murder, John Wayne as a figure of popular mythology, self-respect, the governor's mansion built for Ronald Reagan, and the women's movement. She has written four novels, *Run River, Play It As It Lays, A Book of Common Prayer,* and *Democracy,* and has collaborated on several motion picture screenplays.

Salvador, from which this excerpt was drawn, was published in 1983, following a two-week stay in El Salvador. Ten years of experience and interest in Central America had taught Didion some of the meanings of Salvadoran institutions. Her detailed observations convey the feeling of this land where body dumps, death squads and fearful encounters are commonly met. Christopher Lehmann-Haupt said, in *The New York Times,* "She brings the country to life so that it ends up invading our flesh. To get rid of it then is as simple as shaking off leeches."

Salvador

*T*he three-year-old El Salvador International Airport is glassy and white and splendidly isolated, conceived during the waning of the Molina "National Transformation" as convenient less to the capital (San Salvador is forty miles away, until recently a drive of several hours) than to a central hallucination of the Molina and Romero regimes, the projected beach resorts, the Hyatt, the Pacific Paradise, tennis, golf, water-skiing, condos, *Costa del Sol;* the visionary invention of a tourist industry in yet another republic where the leading natural cause of death is gastrointestinal infection. In the general absence of tourists these hotels have since been abandoned, ghost resorts on the empty Pacific beaches, and to land at this airport built to service them is to plunge directly into a state in which no ground is solid, no depth of field reliable, no perception so definite that it might not dissolve into its reverse.

The only logic is that of acquiescence. Immigration is negotiated in a thicket of automatic weapons, but by whose authority the weapons are brandished (Army or National Guard or National Police or Customs Police or Treasury Police or one of a continuing proliferation of other shadowy and overlapping forces) is a blurred point. Eye contact is avoided. Documents are scrutinized upside down. Once clear of the airport, on the new highway that slices through green hills rendered phosphorescent by the cloud cover of the tropical rainy season, one sees mainly underfed cattle and mongrel dogs and armored vehicles, vans and trucks and Cherokee Chiefs fitted with reinforced steel and bulletproof Plexiglas an inch thick. Such vehicles are a fixed feature of local life, and are popularly associated with disappearance and death. There was the Cherokee Chief seen following the Dutch television crew killed in Chalatenango province in March of 1982. There was the red Toyota three-quarter-ton pickup sighted near the van driven by the four American Catholic workers on the night they were killed in 1980. There were, in the late spring and summer of 1982, the three Toyota panel truck, one yellow, one blue, and one green, none bearing plates, reported present at each of the mass detentions (a "detention" is another fixed feature of local life, and often precedes a "disappearance") in the Amatepec district of San Salvador. These are the details—the models and colors of armored vehicles, the makes and calibers of weapons, the particular methods of dismemberment and decapitation used in particular instances—on which the visitor to Salvador learns immediately to concentrate, to the exclusion of past or future concerns, as in a prolonged amnesiac fugue.

Terror is the given of the place. Black-and-white police cars cruise in pairs, each with the barrel of a rifle extruding from an open window. Roadblocks materialize at random, soldiers fanning out from trucks and taking positions, fingers always on triggers, safeties clicking on and off. Aim is taken as if to pass the time. Every morning *El Diario de Hoy* and *La Prensa Gráfica* carry cautionary stories. "*Una madre y sus dos hijos fueron asesinados con arma cortante (corvo) por ocho sujetos desconocidos el lunes en la noche*": A mother and her two sons hacked to death in their beds by eight *desconocidos,* unknown men. The same morning's paper: the unidentified body of a young man, strangled, found on the shoulder of a road. Same morning, different story: the unidentified bodies of three young men, found on another road, their faces partially destroyed by bayonets, one face carved to represent a cross.

It is largely from these reports in the newspapers that the United States embassy compiles its body counts, which are transmitted to Washington in a weekly dispatch referred to by embassy people as "the grim-gram." These counts are presented in a kind of tortured code that fails to obscure what is taken for granted in El Salvador, that government forces do most of the killing. In a January 15, 1982, memo to Washington, for example, the embassy issued a "guarded" breakdown on its count of 6,909 "reported" political murders between September 16, 1980, and September 15, 1981. Of these 6,909, according to the memo, 922 were "believed committed by security forces," 952 "believed committed by leftist terrorists," 136 "believed committed by rightist terrorists," and 4,889 "committed by unknown assailants," the famous *desconocidos* favored by those San Salvador newspapers still publishing. (The figures actually add up not to 6,909 but to 6,899, leaving ten in a kind of official limbo.) The memo continued:

"The uncertainty involved here can be seen in the fact that responsibility cannot be fixed in the majority of cases. We note, however, that it is generally believed in El Salvador that a large number of the unexplained killings are carried out by the security forces, officially or unofficially. The Embassy is aware of dramatic claims that have been made by one interest group or another in which the security forces figure as the primary agents of murder here. El Salvador's tangled web of attack and vengeance, traditional criminal violence and political mayhem make this an impossible charge to sustain. In saying this, however, we make no attempt to lighten the responsibility for the deaths of many hundreds, and perhaps thousands, which can be attributed to the security forces. . . ."

The body count kept by what is generally referred to in San Salvador as "the Human Rights Commission" is higher than the embassy's, and documented periodically by a photographer who goes out looking for bodies. These bodies he photographs are often broken into unnatural positions, and the faces to which the bodies are attached (when they are attached) are equally unnatural, sometimes unrecognizable as human faces, obliterated by acid or beaten to a mash of misplaced ears and teeth or slashed ear to ear and invaded by insects. *"Encontrado en Antiguo Cuscatlán el día 25 de Marzo 1982: camison de dormir celeste,"* the typed caption reads on one photograph: found in Antiguo Cuscatlán March 25, 1982, wearing a sky-blue nightshirt. The captions are laconic. Found in Soyapango May 21, 1982. Found in Mejicanos June 11, 1982. Found at El Playón May 30, 1982, white shirt, purple pants, black shoes.

The photograph accompanying that last caption shows a body with no eyes, because the vultures got to it before the photographer did. There is a special kind of practical information that the visitor to El Salvador acquires immediately, the way visitors to other places acquire information about the currency rates, the hours for the museums. In El Salvador one learns that vultures go first for the soft tissue, for the eyes, the exposed genitalia, the open mouth. One learns that an open mouth can be used to make a specific point, can be stuffed with something emblematic; stuffed, say, with a penis, or, if the point has to do with land title, stuffed with some of the dirt in question. One learns that hair deteriorates less rapidly than flesh, and that a skull surrounded by a perfect corona of hair is a not uncommon sight in the body dumps.

All forensic photographs induce in the viewer a certain protective numbness, but dissociation is more difficult here. In the first
place these are not, technically, "forensic" photographs, since the
evidence they document will never be presented in a court of law.
In the second place the disfigurement is too routine. The locations
are too near, the dates too recent. There is the presence of the relatives of the disappeared: the women who sit every day in this
cramped office on the grounds of the archdiocese, waiting to look
at the spiral-bound photo albums in which the photographs are
kept. These albums have plastic covers bearing soft-focus color photographs of young Americans in dating situations (strolling through
autumn foliage on one album, recumbent in a field of daisies on another), and the women, looking for the bodies of their husbands and
brothers and sisters and children, pass them from hand to hand
without comment or expression.

> "One of the more shadowy elements of the violent scene here [is]
> the death squad. Existence of these groups has long been disputed,
> but not by many Salvadorans. . . . Who constitutes the death squads
> is yet another difficult question. We do not believe that these squads
> exist as permanent formations but rather as ad hoc vigilante groups
> that coalesce according to perceived need. Membership is also un-
> certain, but in addition to civilians we believe that both on-and off-
> duty members of the security forces are participants. This was un-
> officially confirmed by right-wing spokesman Maj. Roberto D'Au-
> buisson who stated in an interview in early 1981 that security force
> members utilize the guise of the death squad when a potentially em-
> barrassing or odious task needs to be performed."
> —From the confidential but later declassified January 15, 1982, memo pre-
> viously cited, drafted for the State Department by the political section at the
> embassy in San Salvador.

The dead and pieces of the dead turn up in El Salvador everywhere, every day, as taken for granted as in a nightmare, or a horror
movie. Vultures of course suggest the presence of a body. A knot of
children on the street suggests the presence of a body. Bodies turn
up in the brush of vacant lots, in the garbage thrown down ravines
in the richest districts, in public rest rooms, in bus stations. Some
are dropped in Lake Ilopango, a few miles east of the city, and wash
up near the lakeside cottages and clubs frequented by what remains

in San Salvador of the sporting bourgeoisie. Some still turn up at El Playón, the lunar lava field of rotting human flesh visible at one time or another on every television screen in America but characterized in June of 1982 in the *El Salvador News Gazette,* an English-language weekly edited by an American named Mario Rosenthal, as an "uncorroborated story . . . dredged up from the files of leftist propaganda." Others turn up at Puerta del Diablo, above Parque Balboa, a national *Turicentro* described as recently as the April–July 1982 issue of *Aboard TACA,* the magazine provided passengers on the national airline of El Salvador, as "offering excellent subjects for color photography."

I drove up to Puerta del Diablo one morning in June of 1982, past the Casa Presidencial and the camouflaged watch towers and heavy concentrations of troops and arms south of town, on up a narrow road narrowed further by landslides and deep crevices in the roadbed, a drive so insistently premonitory that after a while I began to hope that I would pass Puerta del Diablo without knowing it, just miss it, write it off, turn around and go back. There was however no way of missing it. Puerta del Diablo is a "view site" in an older and distinctly literary tradition, nature as lesson, an immense cleft rock through which half of El Salvador seems framed, a site so romantic and "mystical," so theatrically sacrificial in aspect, that it might be a cosmic parody of nineteenth-century landscape painting. The place presents itself as pathetic fallacy: the sky "broods," the stones "weep," a constant seepage of water weighting the ferns and moss. The foliage is thick and slick with moisture. The only sound is a steady buzz, I believe of cicadas.

Body dumps are seen in El Salvador as a kind of visitors' must-do, difficult but worth the detour. "Of course you have seen El Playón," an aide to President Alvaro Magaña said to me one day, and proceeded to discuss the site geologically, as evidence of the country's geothermal resources. He made no mention of the bodies. I was unsure if he was sounding me out or simply found the geothermal aspect of overriding interest. One difference between El Playón and Puerta del Diablo is that most bodies at El Playón appear to have been killed somewhere else, and then dumped; at Puerta del Diablo the executions are believed to occur in place, at the top, and the bodies thrown over. Sometimes reporters will speak of wanting to spend the night at Puerta del Diablo, in order to document the actual execution, but at the time I was in Salvador no one had.

The aftermath, the daylight aspect, is well documented. "Nothing fresh today, I hear," an embassy officer said when I mentioned that I had visited Puerta del Diablo. "Were there any on top?" someone else asked. "There were supposed to have been three on top yesterday." The point about whether or not there had been any on top was that usually it was necessary to go down to see bodies. The way down is hard. Slabs of stone, slippery with moss, are set into the vertiginous cliff, and it is down this cliff that one begins the descent to the bodies, or what is left of the bodies, pecked and maggoty masses of flesh, bone, hair. On some days there have been helicopters circling, tracking those making the descent. Other days there have been militia at the top, in the clearing where the road seems to run out, but on the morning I was there the only people on top were a man and a woman and three small children, who played in the wet grass while the woman started and stopped a Toyota pickup. She appeared to be learning how to drive. She drove forward and then back toward the edge, apparently following the man's signals, over and over again.

We did not speak, and it was only later, down the mountain and back in the land of the provisionally living, that it occurred to me that there was a definite question about why a man and a woman might choose a well-known body dump for a driving lesson. This was one of a number of occasions, during the two weeks my husband and I spent in El Salvador, on which I came to understand, in a way I had not understood before, the exact mechanism of terror.

Whenever I had nothing to do in San Salvador I would walk up in the leafy stillness of the San Benito and Escalón districts, where the hush at midday is broken only by the occasional crackle of a walkie-talkie, the click of metal moving on a weapon. I recall a day in San Benito when I opened my bag to check an address, and heard the clicking of metal on metal all up and down the street. On the whole no one walks up here, and pools of blossoms lie undisturbed on the sidewalks. Most of the houses in San Benito are more recent than those in Escalón, less idiosyncratic and probably smarter, but the most striking architectural features in both districts are not the houses but their walls, walls built upon walls, walls stripped of the usual copa de oro and bougainvillea, walls that reflect successive generations of violence: the original stone, the additional five or six or ten feet of brick, and finally the barbed wire, sometimes concertina, sometimes electrified; walls with watch towers, gun ports, closed-circuit television cameras, walls now reaching twenty and thirty feet.

San Benito and Escalón appear on the embassy security maps as districts of relatively few "incidents," but they remain districts in which a certain oppressive uneasiness prevails. In the first place there are always "incidents"—detentions and deaths and disappearances—in the *barrancas,* the ravines lined with shanties that fall down behind the houses with the walls and the guards and the walkie-talkies; one day in Escalón I was introduced to a woman who kept the lean-to that served as a grocery in a *barranca* just above the Hotel Sheraton. She was sticking prices on bars of Camay and Johnson's baby soap, stopping occasionally to sell a plastic bag or two filled with crushed ice and Coca-Cola, and all the while she talked in a low voice about her fear, about her eighteen-year-old son, about the boys who had been taken out and shot on successive nights recently in a neighboring *barranca.*

In the second place there is, in Escalón, the presence of the Sheraton itself, a hotel that has figured rather too prominently in certain local stories involving the disappearance and death of Americans. The Sheraton always seems brighter and more mildly festive than either the Camino Real or the Presidente, with children in the pool and flowers and pretty women in pastel dresses, but there are usually several bulletproofed Cherokee Chiefs in the parking area, and the men drinking in the lobby often carry the little zippered purses that in San Salvador suggest not passports or credit cards but Browning 9-mm. pistols.

It was at the Sheraton that one of the few American *desaparecidos,* a young freelance writer named John Sullivan, was last seen, in December of 1980. It was also at the Sheraton, after eleven on the evening of January 3, 1981, that the two American advisers on agrarian reform, Michael Hammer and Mark Pearlman, were killed, along with the Salvadoran director of the Institute for Agrarian Transformation, José Rodolfo Viera. The three were drinking coffee in a dining room off the lobby, and whoever killed them used an Ingram MAC-10, without sound suppressor, and then walked out through the lobby, unapprehended. The Sheraton has even turned up in the investigation into the December 1980 deaths of the four American churchwomen, Sisters Ita Ford and Maura Clarke, the two Maryknoll nuns; Sister Dorothy Kazel, the Ursuline nun; and

Jean Donovan, the lay volunteer. In *Justice in El Salvador: A Case Study,* prepared and released in July of 1982 in New York by the Lawyers' Committee for International Human Rights, there appears this note:

> "On December 19, 1980, the [Duarte government's] Special Investigative Commission reported that 'a red Toyota ¾-ton pickup was seen leaving (the crime scene) at about 11:00 P.M. on December 2' and that 'a red splotch on the burned van' of the churchwomen was being checked to determine whether the paint splotch 'could be the result of a collision between that van and the red Toyota pickup.' By February 1981, the Maryknoll Sisters' Office of Social Concerns, which has been actively monitoring the investigation, received word from a source which it considered reliable that the FBI had matched the red splotch on the burned van with a red Toyota pickup belonging to the Sheraton hotel in San Salvador. . . . Subsequent to the FBI's alleged matching of the paint splotch and a Sheraton truck, the State Department has claimed, in a communication with the families of the churchwomen, that 'the FBI could not determine the source of the paint scraping.' "

There is also mention in this study of a young Salvadoran businessman named Hans Christ (his father was a German who arrived in El Salvador at the end of World War II), a part owner of the Sheraton. Hans Christ lives now in Miami, and that his name should have even come up in the Maryknoll investigation made many people uncomfortable, because it was Hans Christ, along with his brother-in-law, Ricardo Sol Meza, who, in April of 1981, was first charged with the murders of Michael Hammer and Mark Pearlman and José Rodolfo Viera at the Sheraton. These charges were later dropped, and were followed by a series of other charges, arrests, releases, expressions of "dismay" and "incredulity" from the American embassy, and even, in the fall of 1982, confessions to the killings from two former National Guard corporals, who testified that Hans Christ had led them through the lobby and pointed out the victims. Hans Christ and Ricardo Sol Meza have said that the dropped case against them was a government frame-up, and that they were only having drinks at the Sheraton the night of the killings, with a National Guard intelligence officer. It was logical for Hans Christ and Ricardo Sol Meza to have drinks at the Sheraton because they both had interests in the hotel, and Ricardo Sol Meza had just opened a roller disco, since closed, off the lobby into which the killers walked that night. The killers were described by witnesses as well dressed, their faces covered. The room from which they walked was at the time I was in San Salvador no longer a restaurant, but the marks left by the bullets were still visible, on the wall facing the door.

Whenever I had occasion to visit the Sheraton I was apprehensive, and this apprehension came to color the entire Escalón district for me, even its lower reaches, where there were people and movies and restaurants. I recall being struck by it on the canopied porch of a restaurant near the Mexican embassy, on an evening when rain or sabotage or habit had blacked out the city and I became abruptly aware, in the light cast by a passing car, of two human shadows, silhouettes illuminated by the headlights and then invisible again. One shadow sat behind the smoked glass windows of a Cherokee Chief parked at the curb in front of the restaurant; the other crouched between the pumps at the Esso station next door, carrying a rifle. It seemed to me unencouraging that my husband and I were the only people seated on the porch. In the absence of the headlights the candle on our table provided the only light, and I fought the impulse to blow it out. We continued talking, carefully. Nothing came of this, but I did not forget the sensation of having been in a single instant demoralized, undone, humiliated by fear, which is what I meant when I said that I came to understand in El Salvador the mechanism of terror.

The place brings everything into question. One afternoon when I had run out of the Halazone tablets I dropped every night in a pitcher of tap water (a demented *gringa* gesture, I knew even then, in a country where everyone not born there was at least mildly ill, including the nurse at the American embassy), I walked across the street from the Camino Real to the Metrocenter, which is referred to locally as "Central America's Largest Shopping Mall." I found no Halazone at the Metrocenter but became absorbed in making notes about the mall itself, about the Muzak playing "I Left My Heart in San Francisco" and "American Pie" ("... *singing this will be the day that I die* ...") although the record store featured a cassette called *Classics of Paraguay,* about the *pâté de foie gras* for sale in the supermarket, about the guard who did the weapons check on everyone who entered the supermarket, about the young matrons in tight

Sergio Valente jeans, trailing maids and babies behind them and buying towels, big beach towels printed with maps of Manhattan that featured Bloomingdale's; about the number of things for sale that seemed to suggest a fashion for "smart drinking," to evoke modish cocktail hours. There were bottles of Stolichnaya vodka packaged with glasses and mixer, there were ice buckets, there were bar carts of every conceivable design, displayed with sample bottles.

This was a shopping center that embodied the future for which El Salvador was presumably being saved, and I wrote it down dutifully, this being the kind of "color" I knew how to interpret, the kind of inductive irony, the detail that was supposed to illuminate the story. As I wrote it down I realized that I was no longer much interested in this kind of irony, that this was a story that would not be illuminated by such details, that this was a story that would perhaps not be illuminated at all, that this was perhaps even less a "story" than a true *noche obscura*. As I waited to cross back over the Boulevard de los Heroes to the Camino Real I noticed soldiers herding a young civilian into a van, their guns at the boy's back, and I walked straight ahead, not wanting to see anything at all.

In the absence of information (and the presence, often, of disinformation) even the most apparently straightforward event takes on, in El Salvador, elusive shadows, like a fragment of retrieved legend. On the afternoon that I was in San Francisco Gotera trying to see the commander of the garrison there, this *comandante,* Colonel Salvador Beltrán Luna, was killed, or was generally believed to have been killed, in the crash of a Hughes 500-D helicopter. The crash of a helicopter in a war zone would seem to lend itself to only a limited number of interpretations (the helicopter was shot down, or the helicopter suffered mechanical failure, are the two that come to mind), but the crash of this particular helicopter became, like everything else in Salvador, an occasion of rumor, doubt, suspicion, conflicting reports, and finally a kind of listless uneasiness.

The crash occurred either near the Honduran border in Morazán or, the speculation went, actually in Honduras. There were or were not four people aboard the helicopter: the pilot, a bodyguard, Colonel Beltrán Luna, and the assistant secretary of defense, Colonel Francisco Adolfo Castillo. At first all four were dead. A day later only three were dead: Radio Venceremos broadcast news of Colonel Castillo (followed a few days later by a voice resembling that of Colonel Castillo), not dead but a prisoner, or said to be a prisoner, or perhaps only claiming to be a prisoner. A day or so later another of the dead materialized, or appeared to: the pilot was, it seemed, neither dead nor a prisoner but hospitalized, incommunicado.

Questions about what actually happened to (or on, or after the crash of, or after the clandestine landing of) this helicopter provided table talk for days (one morning the newspapers emphasized that the Hughes 500-D had been *comprado en Guatemala,* bought in Guatemala, a detail so solid in this otherwise vaporous story that it suggested rumors yet unheard, intrigues yet unimagined), and remained unresolved at the time I left. At one point I asked President Magaña, who had talked to the pilot, what had happened. "They don't say," he said. Was Colonel Castillo a prisoner? "I read that in the paper, yes." Was Colonel Beltrán Luna dead? "I have that impression." Was the bodyguard dead? "Well, the pilot said he saw someone lying on the ground, either dead or unconscious, he doesn't know, but he believes it may have been Castillo's security man, yes." Where exactly had the helicopter crashed? "I didn't ask him." I looked at President Magaña, and he shrugged. "This is very delicate," he said. "I have a problem there. I'm supposed to be the commander-in-chief, so if I ask him, he should tell me. But he might say he's not going to tell me, then I would have to arrest him. So I don't ask." This is in many ways the standard development of a story in El Salvador, and is also illustrative of the position of the provisional president of El Salvador.

During the week before I flew down to El Salvador a Salvadoran woman who works for my husband and me in Los Angeles gave me repeated instructions about what we must and must not do. We must not go out at night. We must stay off the street whenever possible. We must never ride in buses or taxis, never leave the capital, never imagine that our passports would protect us. We must not even consider the hotel a safe place: people were killed in hotels. She spoke with considerable vehemence, because two of her brothers had been killed in Salvador in August of 1981, in their beds. The throats of both brothers had been slashed. Her father had been cut but stayed alive. Her mother had been beaten. Twelve of her other relatives, aunts and uncles and cousins, had been taken from their houses one night the same August, and their bodies had been found some time later, in a ditch. I assured her that we would remember, we would be careful, we would in fact be so careful that we would probably (trying for a light touch) spend all our time in church.

She became still more agitated, and I realized that I had spoken as a *norteamericana:* churches had not been to this woman the neutral ground they had been to me. I must remember: Archbishop Romero killed saying mass in the chapel of the Divine Providence Hospital in San Salvador. I must remember: more than thirty people killed at Archbishop Romero's funeral in the Metropolitan Cathedral in San Salvador. I must remember: more than twenty people killed before that on the steps of the Metropolitan Cathedral. CBS had filmed it. It had been on television, the bodies jerking, those still alive crawling over the dead as they tried to get out of range. I must understand: the Church was dangerous.

I told her that I understood, that I knew all that, and I did, abstractly, but the specific meaning of the Church she knew eluded me until I was actually there, at the Metropolitan Cathedral in San Salvador, one afternoon when rain sluiced down its corrugated plastic windows and puddled around the supports of the Sony and Phillips billboards near the steps. The effect of the Metropolitan Cathedral is immediate, and entirely literary. This is the cathedral that the late Archbishop Oscar Arnulfo Romero refused to finish, on the premise that the work of the Church took precedence over its display, and the high walls of raw concrete bristle with structural rods, rusting now, staining the concrete, sticking out at wrenched and violent angles. The wiring is exposed. Fluorescent tubes hang askew. The great high altar is backed by warped plyboard. The cross on the altar is of bare incandescent bulbs, but the bulbs, that afternoon, were unlit: there was in fact no light at all on the main altar, no light on the cross, no light on the globe of the world that showed the northern American continent in gray and the southern in white; no light on the dove above the globe, *Salvador del Mundo.* In this vast brutalist space that was the cathedral, the unlit altar seemed to offer a single ineluctable message: at this time and in this place the light of the world could be construed as out, off, extinguished.

In many ways the Metropolitan Cathedral is an authentic piece of political art, a statement for El Salvador as *Guernica* was for Spain. It is quite devoid of sentimental relief. There are no decorative or architectural references to familiar parables, in fact no stories at all, not even the Stations of the Cross. On the afternoon I was there the flowers laid on the altar were dead. There were no traces of normal parish activity. The doors were open to the barricaded main steps, and down the steps there was a spill of red paint, lest anyone forget the blood shed there. Here and there on the cheap linoleum inside the cathedral there was what seemed to be actual blood, dried in spots, the kind of spots dropped by a slow hemorrhage, or by a woman who does not know or does not care that she is menstruating.

There were several women in the cathedral during the hour or so I spent there, a young woman with a baby, an older woman in house slippers, a few others, all in black. One of the women walked the aisles as if by compulsion, up and down, across and back, crooning loudly as she walked. Another knelt without moving at the tomb of Archbishop Romero in the right transept. "LOOR A MONSENOR ROMERO," the crude needlepoint tapestry by the tomb read, "Praise to Monsignor Romero from the Mothers of the Imprisoned, the Disappeared, and the Murdered," the *Comité de Madres y Familiares de Presos, Desaparecidos, y Asesinados Politicos de El Salvador.*

The tomb itself was covered with offerings and petitions, notes decorated with motifs cut from greeting cards and cartoons. I recall one with figures cut from a Bugs Bunny strip, and another with a pencil drawing of a baby in a crib. The baby in this drawing seemed to be receiving medication or fluid or blood intravenously, through the IV line shown on its wrist. I studied the notes for a while and then went back and looked again at the unlit altar, and at the red paint on the main steps, from which it was possible to see the guardsmen on the balcony of the National Palace hunching back to avoid the rain. Many Salvadorans are offended by the Metropolitan Cathedral, which is as it should be, because the place remains perhaps the only unambiguous political statement in El Salvador, a metaphorical bomb in the ultimate power station.

That the texture of life in such a situation is essentially untranslatable became clear to me only recently, when I tried to describe to a friend in Los Angeles an incident that occurred some days before I left El Salvador. I had gone with my husband and another American to the San Salvador morgue, which, unlike most morgues in the United States, is easily accessible, through an open door on the ground floor around the back of the court building. We had been too late that morning to see the day's bodies (there is not much emphasis on embalming in El Salvador, or for that matter on identification, and bodies are dispatched fast for disposal), but the man in charge had opened his log to show us the morning's entries, seven bodies, all male, none identified, none believed older than twenty-five. Six had been certified dead by *arma de fuego,* firearms, and the seventh, who had also been shot, of shock. The slab on which the bodies had been received had already been washed down, and water stood on the floor. There were many flies, and an electric fan.

The other American with whom my husband and I had gone to the morgue that morning was a newspaper reporter, and since only seven unidentified bodies bearing evidence of *arma de fuego* did not in San Salvador in the summer of 1982 constitute a newspaper story worth pursuing, we left. Outside in the parking lot there were a number of wrecked or impounded cars, many of them shot up, upholstery chewed by bullets, windshield shattered, thick pastes of congealed blood on pearlized hoods, but this was also unremarkable, and it was not until we walked back around the building to the reporter's rented car that each of us began to sense the potentially remarkable.

Surrounding the car were three men in uniform, two on the sidewalk and the third, who was very young, sitting on his motorcycle in such a way as to block our leaving. A second motorcycle had been pulled up directly behind the car, and the space in front was occupied. The three had been joking among themselves, but the laughter stopped as we got into the car. The reporter turned the ignition on, and waited. No one moved. The two men on the sidewalk did not meet our eyes. The boy on the motorcycle stared directly, and caressed the G-3 propped between his thighs. The reporter asked in Spanish if one of the motorcycles could be moved so that we could get out. The men on the sidewalk said nothing, but smiled enigmatically. The boy only continued staring, and began twirling the flash suppressor on the barrel of his G-3.

This was a kind of impasse. It seemed clear that if we tried to leave and scraped either motorcycle the situation would deteriorate. It also seemed clear that if we did not try to leave the situation would deteriorate. I studied my hands. The reporter gunned the motor, forced the car up onto the curb far enough to provide a minimum space in which to maneuver, and managed to back out clean. Nothing more happened, and what did happen had been a common enough kind of incident in El Salvador, a pointless confrontation with aimless authority, but I have heard of no *solución* that precisely addresses this local vocation for terror.

Any situation can turn to terror. The most ordinary errand can go bad. Among Americans in El Salvador there is an endemic apprehension of danger in the apparently benign. I recall being told by a network anchor man that one night in his hotel room (it was at the time of the election, and because the Camino Real was full he had been put up at the Sheraton) he took the mattress off the bed and shoved it against the window. He happened to have with him several bullet-proof vests that he had brought from New York for the camera crew, and before going to the Sheraton lobby he put one on. Managers of American companies in El Salvador (Texas Instruments is still there, and Cargill, and some others) are replaced every several months, and their presence is kept secret. Some companies bury their managers in a number-two or number-three post. American embassy officers are driven in armored and unmarked vans (no eagle, no seal, no CD plates) by Salvadoran drivers and Salvadoran guards, because, I was told, "if someone gets blown away, obviously the State Department would prefer it done by a local security man, then you don't get headlines saying 'American Shoots Salvadoran Citizen.' " These local security men carry automatic weapons on their laps.

In such a climate the fact of being in El Salvador comes to seem a sentence of indeterminate length, and the prospect of leaving doubtful. On the night before I was due to leave I did not sleep, lay awake and listened to the music drifting up from a party at the Camino Real pool, heard the band play "Malaguena" at three and at four and again at five A.M., when the party seemed to end and light broke and I could get up. I was picked up to go to the airport that morning by one of the embassy vans, and a few blocks from the hotel I was seized by the conviction that this was not the most direct way to the airport, that this was not an embassy guard sitting in front with the Remington on his lap; that this was someone else. That the van turned out in fact to be the embassy van, detouring into San Benito to pick up an AID official, failed to relax me: once at the airport I sat without moving and averted my eyes from the soldiers patrolling the empty departure lounges.

When the nine A.M. TACA flight to Miami was announced I boarded without looking back, and sat rigid until the plane left the ground. I did not fasten my seat belt. I did not lean back.

Tom Wolfe

In 1962, while in his early 30s, Tom Wolfe began working for the "New York Magazine" supplement to the *Herald-Tribune*. Born in 1931 in Richmond, Virginia, Wolfe attended Washington & Lee University, then completed a Ph.D. in American Studies at Yale before taking up newspaper work. At the *Herald-Tribune* and later, at *New York* magazine and *Esquire,* Wolfe developed his distinctive style and voice. By the time his first three books were published—*The Kandy-Kolored Tangerine-Flake Streamline Baby* (1965), *The Pump House Gang* (1968), and *The Electric Kool-Aid Acid Test* (1968)—no doubt remained that he was an innovator among journalists.

Wolfe was one of the first to suggest that new journalists used the techniques of fiction and recorded the symbolic details of their subjects' "status lives." "Saturation Reporting," he said in *The New Journalism* (1973), permitted them to write nonfiction scenes filled with authentic dialogue, emotion and status.

In Wolfe's early work, punctuation ran wild. He imitated in print the sounds of hotrods and motorcycles, crashing into readers' minds with dots, dashes and exclamation points. His subjects were the trendy leaders of the 1960s—surfers, hotrod customizers, and pop art collectors. Some critics thought Wolfe's approach to journalism would fade as quickly as the subcultures he wrote about.

Wolfe's career has proved them wrong. Although he has given up on his experiments with punctuation, Wolfe has continued to examine the meanings of popular movements and styles in American life. His other books and collections of articles are *Radical Chic and Mau-Mauing the Flak Catchers* (1970), *The Painted Word* (1975), *Mauve Gloves and Madmen, Clutter and Vine* (1976), *The Right Stuff* (1979), *In Our Time* (1980), *From Bauhaus to Our House* (1981), and *The Purple Decades* (1982).

Wolfe opened *The Right Stuff,* his study of the social myths surrounding America's early astronauts, with this chapter on "The Angels." Here Wolfe displays his skill as a cultural reporter in describing the lives and experiences of the test pilots who were later chosen for the Mercury space program.

The Angels

Within five minutes, or ten minutes, no more than that, three of the others had called her on the telephone to ask her if she had heard that something had happened out there.

"Jane, this is Alice. Listen, I just got a call from Betty, and she said she heard something's happened out there. Have you heard anything?" That was the way they phrased it, call after call. She picked up the telephone and began relaying this same message to some of the others.

"Connie, this is Jane Conrad. Alice just called me, and she says something's happened . . ."

Something was part of the official Wife Lingo for tiptoeing blindfolded around the subject. Being barely twenty-one years old and new around here, Jane Conrad knew very little about this particular subject, since nobody ever talked about it. But the day was young! And what a setting she had for her imminent enlightenment! And what a picture she herself presented! Jane was tall and slender and had rich brown hair and high cheekbones and wide brown eyes. She looked a little like the actress Jean Simmons. Her father was a rancher in southwestern Texas. She had gone East to college, to Bryn Mawr, and had met her husband, Pete, at a debutante's party at the Gulf Mill Club in Philadelphia, when he was a senior at Princeton. Pete was a short, wiry, blond boy who joked around a lot. At any moment his face was likely to break into a wild grin revealing the gap between his front teeth. The Hickory Kid sort, he was; a Hickory Kid on the deb circuit, however. He had an air of energy, self-confidence, ambition, *joie de vivre.* Jane and Pete were married two days after he graduated from Princeton. And today, here in Florida, in Jacksonville, in the peaceful year 1955, the sun shines through the pines outside, and the very air takes on the sparkle of the ocean. The ocean and a great mica-white beach are less than a mile away. Anyone driving by will see Jane's little house gleaming like a dream house in the pines. It is a brick house, but Jane and Pete painted the bricks white, so that it gleams in the sun against a great green screen of pine trees with a thousand little places where the sun peeks through. They painted the shutters black, which makes the white walls look even more brilliant. The house has only eleven hundred square feet of floor space, but Jane and Pete designed it themselves and that more than makes up for the size. A friend of theirs was the builder and gave them every possible break, so that it cost only eleven thousand dollars. Outside, the sun shines, and inside, the fever rises by the minute as five, ten, fifteen, and, finally, nearly all twenty of the wives join the circuit, trying to find out what has happened, which, in fact, means: to whose husband.

After thirty minutes on such a circuit—this is not an unusual morning around here—a wife begins to feel that the telephone is no longer located on a table or on the kitchen wall. It is exploding in her solar plexus. Yet it would be far worse right now to hear the front doorbell. The protocol is strict on that point, although written down nowhere. No woman is supposed to deliver the final news, and certainly not on the telephone. The matter mustn't be bungled!—that's the idea. No, a man should bring the news when the time comes, a man with some official or moral authority, a clergyman or a comrade of the newly deceased. Furthermore, he should bring the bad news in person. He should turn up at the front door and ring the bell and be standing there like a pillar of coolness and competence, bearing the bad news on ice, like a fish. Therefore, all the telephone calls from the wives were the frantic and portentous beating of the wings of the death angels, as it were. When the final news came, there would be a ring at the front door—a wife in this situation finds herself staring at the front door as if she no longer owns it or controls it—and outside the door would be a man . . . come to inform her that unfortunately something has happened out there, and her husband's body now lies incinerated in the swamps or the pines or the palmetto grass, "burned beyond recognition," which anyone who had been around an air base for very long (fortunately Jane had not) realized was quite an artful euphemism to describe a human body that now looked like an enormous fowl that has burned up in a stove, burned a blackish brown all over, greasy and blistered, fried, in a word, with not only the entire face and all the hair and the ears burned off, not to mention all the clothing, but also the *hands* and *feet,* with what remains of the arms and legs bent at the knees and elbows and burned into absolutely rigid angles, burned a greasy blackish brown like the bursting body itself, so that this husband, father, officer, gentleman, this *ornamentum* of some mother's eye, His Majesty the Baby of just twenty-odd years back, has been reduced to a charred hulk with wings and shanks sticking out of it.

My own husband—how could this be what they were talking about? Jane had heard the young men, Pete among them, talk about other young men who had "bought it" or "augered in" or "crunched," but it had never been anyone they knew, no one in the squadron. And in any event, the way they talked about it, with such breezy, slangy terminology, was the same way they talked about sports. It was as if they were saying, "He was thrown out stealing second base." And that was all! Not one word, not in print, not in conversation—not in this amputated language!—about an incinerated corpse from which a young man's spirit has vanished in an instant, from which all smiles, gestures, moods, worries, laughter, wiles, shrugs, tenderness, and loving looks—*you, my love!*—have disappeared like a sigh, while the terror consumes a cottage in the woods, and a young woman, sizzling with the fever, awaits her confirmation as the new widow of the day.

The next series of calls greatly increased the possibility that it was Pete to whom something had happened. There were only twenty men in the squadron, and soon nine or ten had been accounted for . . . by the fluttering reports of the death angels. Knowing that the word was out that an accident had occurred, husbands who could get to a telephone were calling home to say *it didn't happen to me.* This news, of course, was immediately fed to the fever. Jane's telephone would ring once more, and one of the wives would be saying:

"Nancy just got a call from Jack. He's at the squadron and he says something's happened, but he doesn't know what. He said he saw Frank D————take off about ten minutes ago with Greg in back, so they're all right. What have you heard?"

But Jane has heard nothing except that other husbands, and not hers, are safe and accounted for. And thus, on a sunny day in Florida, outside of the Jacksonville Naval Air Station, in a little white cottage, a veritable dream house, another beautiful young woman was about to be apprised of the *quid pro quo* of her husband's line of work, of the trade-off, as one might say, the subparagraphs of a contract written in no visible form. Just as surely as if she had the entire roster in front of her, Jane now realized that only two men in the squadron were unaccounted for. One was a pilot named Bud Jennings; the other was Pete. She picked up the telephone and did something that was much frowned on in a time of emergency. She called the squadron office. The duty officer answered.

"I want to speak to Lieutenant Conrad," said Jane. "This is Mrs. Conrad."

"I'm sorry," the duty officer said—and then his voice cracked. "I'm sorry . . . I . . ." He couldn't find the words! He was about to cry! "I'm—that's—I mean . . . he can't come to the phone!"

He can't come to the phone!

"It's very important!" said Jane.

"I'm sorry—it's impossible—" The duty officer could hardly get the words out because he was so busy gulping back sobs. *Sobs!* "He can't come to the phone."

"Why not? Where is he?"

"I'm sorry—" More sighs, wheezes, snuffling gasps. "I can't tell you that. I—have to hang up now!"

And the duty officer's voice disappeared in a great surf of emotion and he hung up.

The duty officer! *The very sound of her voice was more than he could take!*

The world froze, congealed, in that moment. Jane could no longer calculate the interval before the front doorbell would ring and some competent long-faced figure would appear, some Friend of Widows and Orphans, who would inform her, officially, that Pete was dead.

Even out in the middle of the swamp, in this rot-bog of pine trunks, scum slicks, dead dodder vines, and mosquito eggs, even out in this great overripe sump, the smell of "burned beyond recognition" obliterated everything else. When airplane fuel exploded, it created a heat so intense that everything but the hardest metals not only *burned*—everything of rubber, plastic, celluloid, wood, leather, cloth, flesh, gristle, calcium, horn, hair, blood, and protoplasm—it not only burned, it gave up the ghost in the form of every stricken putrid gas known to chemistry. One could smell the horror. It came in through the nostrils and burned the rhinal cavities raw and penetrated the liver and permeated the bowels like a black gas until there was nothing in the universe, inside or out, except the stench of the char. As the helicopter came down between the pine trees and settled onto the bogs, the smell hit Pete Conrad even before the hatch was completely open, and they were not even close enough to see the wreckage yet. The rest of the way Conrad and the crewmen had to travel on foot. After a few steps the water was up to their knees, and then it was up to their armpits, and they kept wading through the water and the scum and the vines and the pine trunks, but it was nothing compared to the smell. Conrad, a twenty-five-year-old lieutenant junior grade, happened to be on duty as squadron safety officer that day and was supposed to make the on-site investigation of the crash. The fact was, however, that this squadron was the first duty assignment of his career, and he had never been at a crash site before and had never smelled any such revolting stench or seen anything like what awaited him.

When Conrad finally reached the plane, which was an SNJ, he found the fuselage burned and blistered and dug into the swamp with one wing sheared off and the cockpit canopy smashed. In the front seat was all that was left of his friend Bud Jennings. Bud Jennings, an amiable fellow, a promising young fighter pilot, was now a horrible roasted hulk—with no head. His head was completely gone, apparently torn off the spinal column like a pineapple off a stalk, except that it was nowhere to be found.

Conrad stood there soaking wet in the swamp bog, wondering what the hell to do. It was a struggle to move twenty feet in this freaking muck. Every time he looked up, he was looking into a delirium of limbs, vines, dappled shadows, and a chopped-up white light that came through the treetops—the ubiquitous screen of trees with a thousand little places where the sun peeked through. Nevertheless, he started wading back out into the muck and the scum, and the others followed. He kept looking up. Gradually he could make it out. Up in the treetops there was a pattern of broken limbs where the SNJ had come crashing through. It was like a tunnel through the treetops. Conrad and the others began splashing through the swamp, following the strange path ninety or a hundred feet above them. It took a sharp turn. That must have been where the wing broke off. The trail veered to one side and started downward. They kept looking up and wading through the muck. Then they stopped. There was a great green sap wound up there in the middle of a tree trunk. It was odd. Near the huge gash was . . . tree disease . . . some sort of brownish lumpy sac up in the branches, such as you see in trees infested by bagworms, and there were yellowish curds on the branches around it, as if the disease had caused the sap to ooze out and fester and congeal—except that it couldn't be sap because it was streaked with blood. In the next instant— Conrad didn't have to say a word. Each man could see it all. The lumpy sac was the cloth liner of a flight helmet, with the earphones attached to it. The curds were Bud Jennings's brains. The tree trunk had smashed through the cockpit canopy of the SNJ and knocked Bud Jennings's head to pieces like a melon.

In keeping with the protocol, the squadron commander was not going to release Bud Jennings's name until his widow, Loretta, had been located and a competent male death messenger had been dispatched to tell her. But Loretta Jennings was not at home and could not be found. Hence, a delay—and more than enough time for the other wives, the death angels, to burn with panic over the telephone lines. All the pilots were accounted for except the two who were in the woods, Bud Jennings and Pete Conrad. One chance in two, acey-deucy, one finger–two finger, and this was not an unusual day around here.

Loretta Jennings had been out at a shopping center. When she returned home, a certain figure was waiting outside, a man, a solemn Friend of Widows and Orphans, and it was Loretta Jennings who lost the game of odd and even, acey-deucy, and it was Loretta whose child (she was pregnant with a second) would have no father. It was this young woman who went through all the final horrors that Jane Conrad had imagined—*assumed!*—would be hers to endure forever. Yet this grim stroke of fortune brought Jane little relief.

On the day of Bud Jennings's funeral, Pete went into the back of the closet and brought out his bridge coat, per regulations. This was the most stylish item in the Navy officer's wardrobe. Pete had never had occasion to wear his before. It was a double-breasted coat made of navy-blue melton cloth and came down almost to the ankles. It must have weighed ten pounds. It had a double row of gold buttons down the front and loops for shoulder boards, big beautiful belly-cut collar and lapels, deep turnbacks on the sleeves, a tailored waist, and a center vent in back that ran from the waistline to the bottom of the coat. Never would Pete, or for that matter many other American males in the mid-twentieth century, have an article of clothing quite so impressive and aristocratic as that bridge coat. At the funeral the nineteen little Indians who were left—Navy boys!—lined up manfully in their bridge coats. They looked so young. Their pink, lineless faces with their absolutely clear, lean jawlines popped up bravely, correctly, out of the enormous belly-cut collars of the bridge coats. They sang an old Navy hymn, which slipped into a strange and lugubrious minor key here and there, and included a stanza added especially for aviators. It ended with: "O hear us when we lift our prayer for those in peril in the air."

Three months later another member of the squadron crashed and was burned beyond recognition and Pete hauled out the bridge coat again and Jane saw eighteen little Indians bravely going through the motions at the funeral. Not long after that, Pete was transferred from Jacksonville to the Patuxent River Naval Air Station in Maryland. Pete and Jane had barely settled in there when they got word that another member of the Jacksonville squadron, a close friend of theirs, someone they had over to dinner many times, had died trying to take off from the deck of a carrier in a routine practice session a few miles out in the Atlantic. The catapult that propelled aircraft off the deck lost pressure, and his ship just dribbled off the end of the deck, with its engine roaring vainly, and fell sixty feet into the ocean and sank like a brick, and he vanished, *just like that.*

Pete had been transferred to Patuxent River, which was known in Navy vernacular as Pax River, to enter the Navy's new test-pilot school. This was considered a major step up in the career of a young Navy aviator. Now that the Korean War was over and there was no combat flying, all the hot young pilots aimed for flight test. In the military they always said "flight test" and not "test flying." Jet aircraft had been in use for barely ten years at the time, and the Navy was testing new jet fighters continually. Pax River was the Navy's prime test center.

Jane liked the house they bought at Pax River. She didn't like it as much as the little house in Jacksonville, but then she and Pete hadn't designed this one. They lived in a community called North Town Creek, six miles from the base. North Town Creek, like the base, was on a scrub-pine peninsula that stuck out into Chesapeake Bay. They were tucked in amid the pine trees. (Once more!) All around were rhododendron bushes. Pete's classwork and his flying duties were very demanding. Everyone in his flight test class, Group 20, talked about how difficult it was—and obviously loved it, because in Navy flying this was the big league. The young men in Group 20 and their wives were Pete's and Jane's entire social world. They associated with no one else. They constantly invited each

other to dinner during the week; there was a Group party at someone's house practically every weekend; and they would go off on
outings to fish or waterski in Chesapeake Bay. In a way they could
not have associated with anyone else, at least not easily, because the
boys could talk only about one thing: their flying. One of the
phrases that kept running through the conversation was "pushing
the outside of the envelope." The "envelope" was a flight-test term
referring to the limits of a particular aircraft's performance, how
tight a turn it could make at such-and-such a speed, and so on.
"Pushing the outside," probing the outer limits, of the envelope
seemed to be the great challenge and satisfaction of flight test. At
first "pushing the outside of the envelope" was not a particularly
terrifying phrase to hear. It sounded once more as if the boys were
just talking about sports.

Then one sunny day a member of the Group, one of the happy
lads they always had dinner with and drank with and went water-
skiing with, was coming in for a landing at the base in an A3J fighter
plane. He came in too low before lowering his flaps, and the ship
stalled out, and he crashed and was burned beyond recognition. And
they brought out the bridge coats and sang about those in peril in
the air and put the bridge coats away, and the Indians who were left
talked about the accident after dinner one night. They shook their
heads and said it was a damned shame, but he should have known
better than to wait so long before lowering the flaps.

Barely a week had gone by before another member of the
Group was coming in for a landing in the same type of aircraft, the
A3J, trying to make a ninety-degree landing, which involves a sharp
turn, and something went wrong with the controls, and he ended
up with one rear stabilizer wing up and the other one down, and his
ship rolled in like a corkscrew from 800 feet up and crashed, and
he was burned beyond recognition. And the bridge coats came out
and they sang about those in peril in the air and then they put the
bridge coats away and after dinner one night they mentioned that
the departed had been a good man but was inexperienced, and
when the malfunction in the controls put him in that bad corner,
he didn't know how to get out of it.

Every wife wanted to cry out: "Well, my God! The *machine*
broke! What makes *any* of you think you would have come out of
it any better!" Yet intuitively Jane and the rest of them knew it
wasn't right even to suggest that. Pete never indicated for a moment
that he thought any such thing could possibly happen to him. It

seemed not only wrong but dangerous to challenge a young pilot's confidence by posing the question. And that, too, was part of the unofficial protocol for the Officer's Wife. From now on every time Pete was late coming in from the flight line, she would worry. She began to wonder if—no! *assume!*—he had found his way into one of those corners they all talked about so spiritedly, one of those little dead ends that so enlivened conversation around here.

Not long after that, another good friend of theirs went up in an F–4, the Navy's newest and hottest fighter plane, known as the Phantom. He reached twenty thousand feet and then nosed over and dove straight into Chesapeake Bay. It turned out that a hose connection was missing in his oxygen system and he had suffered hypoxia and passed out at the high altitude. And the bridge coats came out and they lifted a prayer about those in peril in the air and the bridge coats were put away and the little Indians were incredulous. How could anybody fail to check his hose connections? And how could anybody be in such poor condition as to pass out *that quickly* from hypoxia?

A couple of days later Jane was standing at the window of her house in North Town Creek. She saw some smoke rise above the pines from over in the direction of the flight line. Just that, a column of smoke; no explosion or sirens or any other sound. She went to another room, so as not to have to think about it but there was no explanation for the smoke. She went back to the window. In the yard of a house across the street she saw a group of people . . . standing there and looking at her house, as if trying to decide what to do. Jane looked away—but she couldn't keep from looking out again. She caught a glimpse of *a certain figure* coming up the walkway toward her front door. She knew exactly who it was. She had had nightmares like this. And yet this was no dream. She was wide awake and alert. Never more alert in her entire life! Frozen, completely defeated by the sight, she simply waited for the bell to ring. She waited, but there was not a sound. Finally she could stand it no more. In real life, unlike her dream life, Jane was both too self-possessed and too polite to scream through the door: "Go away!" So she opened it. There was no one there, no one at all. There was no group of people on the lawn across the way and no one to be seen for a hundred yards in any direction along the lawns and leafy rhododendron roads of North Town Creek.

Then began a cycle in which she had both the nightmares and the hallucinations, continually. Anything could touch off an hallu-

cination: a ball of smoke, a telephone ring that stopped before she
could answer it, the sound of a siren, even the sound of trucks starting up (crash trucks!). Then she would glance out the window, and
a certain figure would be coming up the walk, and she would wait
for the bell. The only difference between the dreams and the hallucinations was that the scene of the dreams was always the little
white house in Jacksonville. In both cases, the feeling that *this time
it has happened* was quite real.

   The star pilot in the class behind Pete's, a young man who was
the main rival of their good friend Al Bean, went up in a fighter to
do some power-dive tests. One of the most demanding disciplines
in flight test was to accustom yourself to making precise readings
from the control panel in the same moment that you were pushing
the outside of the envelope. This young man put his ship into the
test dive and was still reading out the figures, with diligence and
precision and great discipline, when he augered straight into the
oyster flats and was burned beyond recognition. And the bridge
coats came out and they sang about those in peril in the air and the
bridge coats were put away, and the little Indians remarked that the
departed was a swell guy and a brilliant student of flying; a little too
much of a student, in fact; he hadn't bothered to look out the window at the real world soon enough. Beano—Al Bean—wasn't quite
so brilliant; on the other hand, he was still here.

   Like many other wives in Group 20 Jane wanted to talk about
the whole situation, the incredible series of fatal accidents, with her
husband and the other members of the Group, to find out how they
were taking it. But somehow the unwritten protocol forbade dis-
cussions of this subject, which was the fear of death. Nor could Jane
or any of the rest of them talk, really *have a talk,* with anyone around
the base. You could talk to another wife about being worried. But
what good did it do? Who *wasn't* worried? You were likely to get a
look that said: "*Why dwell on it?*" Jane might have gotten away with
divulging the matter of the nightmares. But *hallucinations?* There was
no room in Navy life for any such anomalous tendency as that.

   By now that bad string had reached ten in all, and almost all
of the dead had been close friends of Pete and Jane, young men who
had been in their house many times, young men who had sat across
from Jane and chattered like the rest of them about the grand adventure of military flying. And the survivors still sat around *as before*—with the same inexplicable exhilaration! Jane kept watching

Pete for some sign that his spirit was cracking, but she saw none. He talked a mile a minute, kidded and joked, laughed with his Hickory Kid cackle. He always had. He still enjoyed the company of members of the group like Wally Schirra and Jim Lovell. Many young pilots were taciturn and cut loose with the strange fervor of this business only in the air. But Pete and Wally and Jim were not reticent; not in any situation. They loved to kid around. Pete called Jim Lovell "Shaky," because it was the last thing a pilot would want to be called. Wally Schirra was outgoing to the point of hearty; he loved practical jokes and dreadful puns, and so on. The three of them—*even in the midst of this bad string!*—would love to get on a subject such as accident-prone Mitch Johnson. Accident-prone Mitch Johnson, it seemed, was a Navy Pilot whose life was in the hands of two angels, one of them bad and the other one good. The bad angel would put him into accidents that would have annihilated any ordinary pilot, and the good angel would bring him out of them without a scratch. Just the other day—this was the sort of story Jane would hear them tell—Mitch Johnson was coming in to land on a carrier. But he came in short, missed the flight deck, and crashed into the fantail, below the deck. There was a tremendous explosion, and the rear half of the plane fell into the water in flames. Everyone on the flight deck said, "Poor Johnson. The good angel was off duty." They were still debating how to remove the debris and his mortal remains when a phone rang on the bridge. A somewhat dopey voice said, "This is Johnson. Say, listen, I'm down here in the supply hold and the hatch is locked and I can't find the lights and I can't see a goddamned thing and I tripped over a cable and I think I hurt my leg." The officer on the bridge slammed the phone down, then vowed to find out what morbid sonofabitch could pull a phone prank at a time like this. Then the phone rang again, and the man with the dopey voice managed to establish the fact that he was, indeed, Mitch Johnson. The good angel had not left his side. When he smashed into the fantail, he hit some empty ammunition drums, and they cushioned the impact, leaving him groggy but not seriously hurt. The fuselage had blown to pieces; so he just stepped out onto the fantail and opened a hatch that led into the supply hold. It was pitch black in there, and there were cables all across the floor, holding down spare aircraft engines. Accident-prone Mitch Johnson kept tripping over these cables until he found a telephone. Sure enough, the one injury he had was a bruised shin from tripping over a cable. The man was accident-prone! Pete and Wally and Jim absolutely cracked up over stories like this. It was amazing. Great sports yarns! Nothing more than that.

A few days later Jane was out shopping at the Pax River commissary on Saunders Road, near the main gate to the base. She heard the sirens go off at the field, and then she heard the engines of the crash trucks start up. This time Jane was determined to keep calm. Every instinct made her want to rush home, but she forced herself to stay in the commissary and continue shopping. For thirty minutes she went through the motions of completing her shopping list. Then she drove home to North Town Creek. As she reached the house, she saw a figure going up the sidewalk. It was a man. Even from the back there was no question as to who he was. He had on a black suit, and there was a white band around his neck. It was her minister, from the Episcopal Church. She stared, and this vision did not come and go. The figure kept on walking up the front walk. She was not asleep now, and she was not inside her house glancing out the front window. She was outside in her car in front of her house. She was not dreaming, and she was not hallucinating, and the figure kept walking up toward her front door.

The commotion at the field was over one of the most extraordinary things that even veteran pilots had ever seen at Pax River. And they had all seen it, because practically the entire flight line had gathered out on the field for it, as if it had been an air show.

Conrad's friend Ted Whelan had taken a fighter up, and on takeoff there had been a structural failure that caused a hydraulic leak. A red warning light showed up on Whelan's panel, and he had a talk with the ground. It was obvious that the leak would cripple the controls before he could get the ship back down to the field for a landing. He would have to bail out; the only question was where and when, and so they had a talk about that. They decided that he should jump at 8,100 feet at such-and-such a speed, directly over the field. The plane would crash into the Chesapeake Bay, and he would float down to the field. Just as coolly as anyone could have asked for it, Ted Whelan lined the ship up to come across the field at 8,100 feet precisely and he punched out, ejected.

Down on the field they all had their faces turned up to the sky. They saw Whelan pop out of the cockpit. With his Martin-Baker seat-parachute rig strapped on, he looked like a little black geometric lump a mile and a half up in the blue. They watched him as he started dropping. Everyone waited for the parachute to open. They waited a few more seconds, and then they waited some more. The little shape was getting bigger and bigger and picking up tremendous speed. Then there came an unspeakable instant at which everyone on the field who knew anything about parachute jumps knew what was going to happen. Yet even for them it was an unearthly feeling, for no one had ever seen any such thing happen so close up, from start to finish, from what amounted to a grandstand seat. Now the shape was going so fast and coming so close it began to play tricks on the eyes. It seemed to stretch out. It became much bigger and hurtled toward them at a terrific speed, until they couldn't make out its actual outlines at all. Finally there was just a streaking black blur before their eyes, followed by what seemed like an explosion. Except that it was not an explosion; it was the tremendous *crack* of Ted Whelan, his helmet, his pressure suit, and his seat-parachute rig smashing into the center of the runway, precisely on target, right in front of the crowd; an absolute bull's-eye. Ted Whelan had no doubt been alive until the instant of impact. He had had about thirty seconds to watch the Pax River base and the peninsula and Baltimore County and continental America and the entire comprehensible world rise up to smash him. When they lifted his body up off the concrete, it was like a sack of fertilizer.

Pete took out the bridge coat again and he and Jane and all the little Indians went to the funeral for Ted Whelan. That it hadn't been Pete was not solace enough for Jane. That the preacher had not, in fact, come to her front door as the Solemn Friend of Widows and Orphans, but merely for a church call ... had not brought peace and relief. That Pete still didn't show the slightest indication of thinking that any unkind fate awaited him no longer lent her even a moment's courage. The next dream and the next hallucination, and the next and next, merely seemed more real. For now she *knew*. She now knew the subject and the essence of this enterprise, even though not a word of it had passed anybody's lips. She even knew why Pete—the Princeton boy she met at a deb party at the Gulf Mill Club!—would never quit, never withdraw from this grim business, unless in a coffin. And God knew, and she knew, there was a coffin waiting for each little Indian.

Seven years later, when a reporter and a photographer from *Life* magazine actually stood near her in her living room and watched her face, while outside, on the lawn, a crowd of television crewmen and newspaper reporters waited for a word, an indication, anything—perhaps a glimpse through a part in a curtain!—waited for some sign of what she felt—when one and all asked with their ravenous eyes and, occasionally, in so many words: "How do you feel?" and "Are you scared?"—America wants to know!—it made Jane want to laugh, but in fact she couldn't even manage a smile.

"Why ask *now?*" she wanted to say. But they wouldn't have had the faintest notion of what she was talking about.

Richard Rhodes

Richard Rhodes, born July 4, 1937, grew up in Missouri. Much of his writing is set in the Midwest. "Death All Day," his first published work, debuted in *Esquire* and formed the centerpiece of his first book, *The Inland Ground*. His other nonfiction work includes *Looking for America* and *Ultimate Powers,* a narrative history of the development of the atomic and hydrogen bombs.

Violence marked Rhodes' childhood. His mother died, a suicide, when he was one. He moved with his father and brother from boarding house to boarding house and wandered city streets. He spent his adolescence at a boys' home outside Independence, Missouri, where he learned farming, including the slaughter of animals for food. A scholarship saw him through four years at Yale University.

Rhodes had difficulty finding his voice as a writer. Even after he began *The Inland Ground,* he says, he felt blocked from revealing the depths of his feelings, publicly, in prose. He was several chapters along before the violence of the coyote hunt, which he recounts in "Death All Day," finally released him. The words began to flow.

He has written for *Esquire, Harper's, Atlantic, American Heritage,* and *Playboy.* He was a contributing editor at *Harper's* and since 1974 has been an independent novelist and journalist. His novels include *The Ungodly, Holy Secrets, The Last Safari,* and *Sons of Earth.*

Death All Day

I suppose, from a modern moral point of view, that is, a Christian point of view, the whole bullfight is indefensible; there is certainly much cruelty, there is always danger, either sought or unlooked for, and there is always death, and I should not try to defend it now, only to tell honestly the things I have found true about it. To do this I must be altogether frank, or try to be, and if those who read this decide with disgust that it is written by some one who lacks their, the readers', fineness of feeling I can only plead that this may be true. But whoever reads this can only truly make such a judgment when he, or she, has seen the things that are spoken of and knows truly what their reactions to them would be.

Ernest Hemingway, DEATH IN THE AFTERNOON

*W*ho would have thought the old man to have had so much diffidence in him? He was a young man then, in 1932, and of course his apology to the high-toned Christians he despised is ironic. But the earnest apology is there too, the apology for enjoying a spectacle that expressed no sweat from the Anglo-Saxon brow nor added any treasure to the Anglo-Saxon glory vaults, as did the war he had survived a decade before. Other wars since have darkened that brow and emptied those vaults, wars so bloody and so relentlessly brutal that the gutting of horses in the *Plaza de Toros*—or the tearing of coyotes and cocks on the Kansas prairie—must seem antique entertainments. Today there is little need to apologize for killing merely animals. We have learned subtleties of husbandry unknown to Hemingway in 1932.

My own husbandry was developed during the six years I spent on a Missouri farm. For three of those years I butchered a steer every month and helped butcher a dozen hogs and several hundred chickens every quarter. Those with fineness of feeling may make of these facts what they will, but should consider that they eat the flesh of animals every day, only cutting meat from bone and with smaller knives. I left the farm for the city at eighteen, and would be as squeamish about butchering today as any other citizen, though I might sooner get on with it.

Portis, Kansas, I discover on my Standard Oil map, is located within forty miles of the geographical center of the forty-eight continental states. That makes it precisely the heart of America, or at least of America before Alaska and Hawaii joined the fun. Portis is a knot of pitch and wood in north central Kansas surrounded by wheatfields, a village of 200 souls that is not even listed on my map's index of Kansas communities. As in every small town in Kansas, its landmark is a grain elevator and adjacent grove of storage bins rising high above the one-story houses around it, the town's name printed in block capitals—PORTIS—on the side of the elevator.

Dodge City remembers its gunsmoked past, Holcomb its murders, and Abilene its Eisenhowers (the latest grave is fresh there as I write). Portis notches its years on the performance of its high-school basketball team. The children depart for the city as regularly as cattle go to market, leaving behind cooling scores and tarnishing trophies that recall years when their parents were young and their families united. Such memories the parents value. Portis used to support a population of 240, and as the children move out no new families move in, and those who live there know the town will go to ghosts soon enough.

Portis remembers basketball; its young people remember coyote hunting, a sport or art form less venerable than bullfighting, and less elegant, but hotter. Everyone who goes on a hunt, young or old, takes part; cruelty, if coyote hunting is cruel, is shared, and so is such excitement as a wild-assed chase at fifty miles an hour over broken ground can supply.

We are three in Kansas City preparing to leave for Portis on a Friday afternoon in April, late season for coyotes but the weather has been impossible all winter. Dan Cram, D.V.M., a Portis boy now settled in Kansas City as associate veterinarian at a dog-and-cat clinic, will be our guide. Leaving the clinic, he carries a lithe breakdown .22 rifle he will take along to side-hunt prairie dogs and not have occasion to use. Portis hunts coyotes with hounds, not with guns. One of Dan's patients, an enthusiastic cocker, passes him in the parking lot with a little girl holding its leash. "Mommy, what is that *gun* for?" the girl querulously asks her mother, meaning, "Is that how they put animals to sleep?" The clinic is longer on service than on public relations. Dan's boss, the owner, hangs animal pelts, including the pelt of a bear cub, in the office and hunts big game in Canada and the Pacific Northwest. A lady, says Dan as we begin the drive to Portis, brought her child's stool sample into the clinic last week to be checked for worms, and when a pet bites a child the clinic is as likely to be called as the family physician. Hunting, for Dan's boss and for Dan, may be a healthy response to the over-pressures of Kansas City pet lovers.

The other third of our party is Ron Nolan, an Ohio boy who overcame New York a few years back to homestead a two-room cabin in the woods outside Kansas City. His cabin contains an Italian racing motorcycle, a KLH20 + stereo, a wall of books, tennis rackets, board games, a hookah, rifles, pistols, a Beretta Golden Snipe .12-gauge over-and-under shotgun, a Pacific shotshell reloader, and outside a golden sand Jaguar XKE convertible and for short hauls an aging Morris Oxford station wagon, likely the only one in the Midwest. Ron is a bachelor.* He has lately acquired a faithful dog, Nolan's Irish Clancy, and currently pursues goose and duck and quail in season, trap-shooting on Wednesday nights. He is thinking of raising bees in the woods behind the cabin as a cash crop. For the trip to Portis he has left red Clancy at home to gnaw on the cabin siding, but brings along a guitar.

Eastern Kansas, through which we now drive, is an area of enclaves like those General Gavin proposed for sanity in South Vietnam. Lawrence, the first big town beyond Kansas City on the turnpike, encloses the University of Kansas, a respectable school with Oxonian pretentions. K.U. annually holds a festival of the arts which trucks in New York critics for what may be their once-in-a-lifetime glimpse of the Midwest. The school also boasts a Shakespearean scholar who capped his distinguished career recently by subjecting the First Folios to an exhaustive textual analysis using methods adapted from aerial photography. He discovered that the printer's devil couldn't spell and that one of the typesetters was a drunk. And established texts that approach Shakespeare's originals—not bad for a prairie man.

---

*Was. He has since married an intelligent, attractive, long-legged mathematician of a girl, and settles into prosperity with only an occasional huckleberry.

Topeka, on down the Kansas Turnpike, the state capital, embraces the Menninger Clinic, with more shrinks per capita than any other city in the world, a great place for cocktail hours and late dinners, plump with Viennese *Gemütlichkeit.* When Anna Freud came to visit, a decade ago, the entire establishment turned out, as if Mary Magdalene had returned to tell her tale of miracles and resurrections. I have heard of people who moved to Topeka just to be near the Menningers, and not as patients, either. Hemingway never visited Menningers', though an ill-advised staff member allowed, soon after the old man's death, that the Clinic could have saved his life and even set him writing again, and perhaps it could have. It has done as well with others. Across the street from the Clinic's front gate a solitary buffalo stalks the fence of the city zoo. Down the road a battalion of grain elevators marches west, aromatic of bran. Most of the Clinic's patients grow flowers. I wonder what variety Hemingway would have planted.

Beyond Topeka, big enclaves give way to small towns. Trees disappear except for scattered huddles of cottonwood, and the population thins in inverse proportion to the thickening of the wheatfields. It is a region most people fly over. Driving through it on an April evening, we count five jet contrails above us at the same time, the jets playing high, silent games of tag, racing each other for Kansas City, of all places, or seeming to collide head-on as they pass east and west at different altitudes. Farmers are burning off their pastures; in the dusk the fires glow like minor sunsets. The wheat is green in April, spraying in explosive tufts from holes drilled at precise intervals in the hard ground. The rest of the land is brown, the grass short and sere, the milo and cornfields kneehigh stubble. In one farmyard we pass we notice an old Chevy panel truck painted in psychedelic swirls, an April Easter egg nested against a weathered gray barn.

Junction City, where we leave the turnpike for a two-lane highway, feeds on Fort Riley, a military camp twice as large on the map as the shrunken Pottawatomie and Kickapoo Indian Reservations north of Topeka. Crowds cheered when Riley sent its Big Red One off to Vietnam in 1968, despite the loss of local revenue. The only movie house I find on Junction City's main street features *Animal Lusts of the Nights,* but there are no posters in the display cabinets to define which animal or whose lusts. That is Junction City's sort of compromise. In the black end of town, whores are no longer allowed to hook from street corners, but everyone knows they are still available. White whores, better camouflaged, man roadhouses staked out around the Fort. Junction City is hog heaven for the troops, its main drag a progress of beer bars. It preserves its country character with balloon-frame gothic houses jammed in among the store fronts and pungent assertions of skunk blowing through the streets.

In a Junction City diner where we stop to eat, a sunburned young farmer comforts his squirming son while his wife sips coffee and recalls the high-school prom. Ron orders pineapple pie, hoping its rich homemade goodness will set the tone for the trip, but the pie is store-bought. Through the window at my elbow the wooden scrollwork on the diner's marquee glows red and yellow, garish lights from a neon sign across the parking lot, and around and above the sign swells the vast Kansas sky, black as space. Dick Hickock and Perry Smith, diabolic engines with oddly ordered gearings and photocell eyes, also made this trip on a windy night. It is no wonder, under such a sky, that Perry killed, rived his gentleman's throat, narrowing the vastness into violence. The mantle of that violence must have covered him just long enough to get him safely back to Olathe. *The plains of Kansas are even lonelier than the sea,* a friend of mine once wrote, reviewing *In Cold Blood.* They are, and they would madden the battered children of our cities. What balances the people who live out here, most of them, is humility. They gird themselves in shyness and sleep well. And, when the loneliness echoes, fish and hunt.

Beyond Junction City, heading northeast now, we travel state highways, two-lane asphalt roads lit only by our headlights and the yardlights farmers leave on all night to keep the local kids away from the farm gas pump. And to say hello. Everyone hellos everyone in Kansas country, even with yardlights late at night. Ron breaks out his guitar and gives us ten verses of his favorite song:

> Every time I go to town,
> The boys keep kickin' my dog around,
> Makes no difference if he is a hound,
> They oughta quit kickin' my dog around

and falls asleep among the boots and the guns. Dan, wild farm boy turned dog doctor, drives on, pushing ninety, scanning his rearview mirror for the state patrol, confident that beyond the next hill or around the next curve no car will appear to destroy us at the desperate country hour of eleven o'clock.

We core the blackness with the tunnel vision of jet pilots, but start jackrabbits and possums on the ground. I am convinced Dan would hit one if it got in his way and drive right on. It would be an act without malice. He throws his beer bottles out the window too, as later, at the hunt lunch, we will leave our orange peels and bread wrappers on the roadside. Petty desecrations irritate me because I know how little of the country is left for us to litter, but for Dan, as for Portis' hunters, open land is the commonage of the people. It is also Kansas' most apparent natural asset, and perhaps there is irony in the littering of it: most of America spurns Kansas anyway as the Great American Desert, where the sedge is withered on the creek and no birds sing.

Dan's parents have waited up for us with Johnny Carson and Ed McMahon. Mrs. Cram appears to let us in—a slim, pleasant, dark-haired woman in a quilted robe, feminine without fluffiness, with delicate and graceful hands. She does not, as a farm woman might, leave the conversation to the men; as she asks her questions her eyes examine her son, assaying his health, his appetite, his state of mind. Married only ten months, Dan has not yet finally left home, and between his mother and his grandmother, in the next twenty-four hours, he will receive more attention than makes him comfortable, as befits a former Portis high-school basketball player. His father, Wendal, is an older and easier version of Dan, trim, built for endurance, a little shy, a World War II Navy man and small-town banker who will soon marry off his last child and only daughter.

The house is what we used to call "spick-and-span": landscapes painted by Mr. Cram on the walls, a bonsai sketched in wallpaper across the living room's west end, a nubby carpet on the floor. We sip instant iced tea and itemize the town's eccentrics. A lady down the street raises magpies for company and gives them the run of her speckled house. Old Les Wolters lost all his teeth twenty years ago and refuses to wear his plates—we will meet Les again on the hunt. A chauvinistic spectator made a Portis basketball referee so mad once that he kicked the spectator out of the gymnasium on a technical foul. And so to bed. Ron and I are offered, in frontier style, a double bed, which we find awkward: I haven't slept with a male since my brother left home; Ron hasn't slept near a male since Korea. We bed down uneasily. His snoring wakes me at six-thirty in the morning, and Mr. Cram is already boiling the coffee.

Harold and John Wolters, toothless Les's brother and nephew respectively, call for us at eight o'clock. The Wolters are a Portis legend. Harold is seventy-four, all sockets and wires, gold front teeth, a weathered hatchet of a face half hidden beneath a plaid cotton baseball cap that is several sizes too large and settled on his ears, bib overalls harnessed over a thick plaid shirt with its collar buttoned and turned up against the morning chill. He is a man completely at ease, patriarch of his clan and unofficial master of the hunt; a man who will drive all day and not appear to be tired, certainly not as tired as I will be; a man who hands down his cars and his farms to his sons and son-in-law as easily as younger parents hand down children's clothes. John, in his early thirties, is solid, honest, reliable, but otherwise his father's opposite: big-bellied, heavy-fleshed, stubby-handed, strong as an ox. John has laryngitis, and his voice is cloudy and uncertain. Harold's voice is clear, and after an hour on the road of uncanny *déjà vu* I place it: in pitch and cadence and dialect, and in a certain tendency to loquaciousness, Harold sounds exactly like Hubert Humphrey.

The Wolters pickup truck, a broad-beamed Ford, startles me with its sweet reek of cow manure rising up from a robe of beige carpeting laid over the seat cushion. Former butcher boy and cattle feeder, I had forgotten the smell. By the end of the day I feel at home.

We rendezvous at the Co-op filling station in Portis with three other trucks of hunters. We will acquire three more at Long Island, Kansas, another town that isn't on the map despite its portentous name. It is the largest hunt, Harold tells me, he has ever gathered together in fifty years of coyote chasing. The presence of two women among the trucks reduces the badinage on the two-way radios to awkward gossip and hurried speculations about the weather. From down around Lincoln, Kansas, someone named Harry overtakes us, and at our grocery-store rendezvous schemes with Harold to call the girls "fuzzy-tail." The scheme works for a while. "Guess he just doesn't want to catch that *fuzzy-tail,*" quips Harold over the radio when one of the party lags behind, and jabs a bawdy elbow in my ribs as old Harry cuts in over the radio with a guffaw. "Fuzzy-tail" gets forgotten in the excitement of the chase, except when we stop to relieve ourselves; then John scouts fuzzy-tail while Harold and I wet down the dust on the womanless side of the truck.

I ride between Harold and John in the middle of the wide seat, my legs hanging over John's side of the transmission hump. A riding crop coils on the dashboard; a hammer hangs in a loop of binder twine from the floor-mounted gearshift. The crop will discipline the dogs; the hammer will quiet the coyote.

The pickup has been stripped to its floorbed in back, and mounted on the floorbed is a box the size of a shipping crate. In two compartments, their heads stuck out through a narrow slot cut the length of the box, stand the dogs. They are greyhound, mostly, with some staghound mixed in for endurance. Names you would expect: Blue is blue-black, the color of gunmetal; Nig is night black; Ring sports a white ring of fur around his neck, the rest of him black; Red is red; collectively Harold calls them "you bastards," but treats their hunt wounds with care, dousing them from a plastic squeeze bottle of methylene blue. They are big dogs, nearly as big as a man on all fours would be, but light; Dan estimates their average weight at forty-five or fifty pounds, though they look seventy-five. Their mass is all long legs with sinewy muscles to move them and a deep barrel for wind, and even then the coyote, at thirty pounds, can outrun them if the chase goes anything over a mile. "I always say you can run a little faster if your life depends on it than if you're just doing it for fun," one of the hunters will answer my question as we drive back from the hunt.

Poking their long greyhound muzzles out of the head slot of their box, they are docile animals with soft eyes, expressions made downcast by their tough training and uncomfortable quarters. They must twist their heads to force them through the slot, and their necks rub uncomfortably against the bare plywood edges. Harold has carpeted the compartments in his dog box with pieces of an old Oriental, and the traps also are carpeted so that the dogs can spring onto them and into the box from the ground, a leap of five feet which they make with complete ease even when winded from the chase and the kill.

We arrive at the area where the hunt will begin, an hour northwest of Portis, and the trucks fan out around four sides of a mile-square section of land. The sport of coyote hunting, Portis style, is founded on the section, the basic division of land on the plains, 640 acres bounded on four sides by barbed-wire fences and usually divided inside with other fences into quarter-sections.

Dirt ruts along the half-mile lines inside—Harold calls them "by-roads," the old term—give access to each quarter-section, but the placing of gates is capricious; and more than once a hunter lost a coyote to a fence he couldn't find a way through. The land is bro-

ken up by copses of trees, by deep gullies and draws, by high contoured terraces, and by young wheatfields which the code of Kansas
hunting requires the farmer-hunters to avoid. The land's roughness
further complicates the chase—Harold buys a new pickup every
year, and ravages it in one winter's season of hunting. If there had
been no fences in the area we would have caught more coyotes, but
not in sport. For sport, the animal must have a reasonable chance
to escape; with fences and wheatfields it has that chance. Some Kan-
sans hunt coyotes with light planes or helicopters, driving the animals to the road, where they are shot by men in trucks: that is no
more sport than a Saturday-night rat shoot at the city dump would
be, and perhaps less. At least the rats have holes to hide in; with a
plane overhead, the coyotes do not.

Coyote hunting, Portis style, is coursing, the sport of czars and
kings, for which the greyhounds and borzois and staghounds of the
dog kingdom were bred long ago. It is a sport almost completely
unknown in the United States except in the western ranges of the
Middle West. The Duke of Norfolk first established its rules in the
days of Shakespeare's Elizabeth; England unfortunately lacking coyotes, the sport was practiced there on hares, which are not animals
renowned for their ferocity. Coursing differs from other types of
hunting with dogs in one important respect: coursing dogs hunt by
sight, not by smell, and the dead trophies—coyotes the size of
young children, looking like foxes on the bum, with narrow yellow
teeth bared in death as in life—may be slung from the top of the
dog boxes, out of sight but very much in smell. Coursing dogs do
not attend their noses. They are, like man, all eyes.

With the trucks deployed on four sides of a section, the first
we surrounded during the long day, Harold turns in at the south
gate, drives up a by-road, and heads through a field of milo stubble.
He extracts a nine-shot .22 revolver from the glove compartment
and fires into a long draw at the edge of the field. Nothing emerges.
John swings out of the cab onto the side of the dog box, which has
a length of water pipe bolted on at the top for a handhold. Through
territory that will throw me all over the cab, John holds on easily
to the outside of the truck. "You just kinda relax and bend your
knees," he explained later. Even inside the cab, I found that hard to
do.

A second gate at the "old mile road"—the half-mile by-road
in the middle of the section—lets us into the northeast quarter, and
in the first draw we start a pair of coyotes that divide, one heading

northeast in the same direction we are traveling, the other, the bitch as it turns out, heading southwest along the center fence. Ron and Les, alerted by Harold on the radio, head south along the west road outside the section to intercept the bitch; we accelerate to chase the dog coyote, Harold in second gear racing the engine up to a turbine-like whine, taking terraces at a sixty-degree angle that he jerks the truck out of as soon as the front wheels clear the top, throwing us back and forth in the cab, John still spotting the coyote as it runs through the stubble down to a brush-surrounded creek. We hit fifty miles an hour, dry weeds slapping the hood and filling the air with chaff; we brake abruptly and smash down a dropoff that jams me to the bottom of the seat, the coyote veering back southward to cut by us and escape, Harold slamming on the brakes full force and yelling to John to release the dogs, John pulling the release rod, the dogs out of the truck now, yelping and barking and closing on the coyote at the bottom of the contoured hill. I jump from the truck and run down the hill to find the dogs, five of them, all over the fighting coyote, biting at its neck and legs and groin. It is still alive; it locks one dog's ear in its jaws, its narrow yellow teeth bared. The dogs have it on its back, one is trying to clamp its neck and cut off its wind, another pulls on a hind leg, another clamps the neck from the opposite side, with yelps when the coyote manages a hit. It stares at John and me as we move to it with an expression in its eyes strangely detached for an animal being torn—"What the hell am I doing here?" John motions me back and works in toward the head. The coyote catches his leather glove and he pulls away just in time to avoid a bite, tearing the glove. He moves in again and pries the coyote's mouth off a dog's lower jaw, then maneuvers his boot onto the coyote's head and hits the skull with the hammer, the sound like driving a nail into hard oak, resonant but damped at the same time, tunk, tunk, tunk, tunk. Sensing the coyote slumping beneath them, the dogs relax, and John begins pulling them off. Their mouths drip with blood, their own and the coyote's; one has a hole the size of a quarter in its upper lip that I can see the sky through, another a deep gash on its neck, another a torn foreleg. Bloodthirsty as they have been—they showed the coyote no mercy once the braver dogs began the kill—they display no anger when John takes them off their catch, as even a house pet would if you pulled him off a bone. I hold two of them by the collar while John works at the others, and except for a slight straining away from me they are entirely docile.

By the time we get the dogs off, Harold has clambered down

the hill. He flips the coyote over and reaches between its legs, en-countering a small black bag. "Why, it's an old dog coyote," he says, and pulls back the lips to check the teeth. "Big one, too. Looks to be about four years old. We got us an old dog coyote. Them's the hardest kind to catch." He is obviously pleased with the first catch of the day.

Back in the truck, over the radio: "WE GOT US A OLD DOG COYOTE, 'BOUT FOUR YEARS OLD. YEP, IT'S A GOOD 'UN. ANYBODY SEE THAT OTHER ONE? WE STARTED TWO OF 'EM DOWN IN A DRAW." Les reports in: "WE'RE AFTER THAT ONE DOWN HERE IN THE NEXT SECTION SOUTH. HE'S RUNNIN' TOWARD A PATCH OF TREES. WE DROPPED OUR DOGS."

In the background I could hear the dogs yelping. Ron told me later they dropped the first box of dogs at the east fence to keep the coyote in sight while they raced to the south fence to find a gate. Halfway across the section, going west on its south road, they saw the coyote crossing the road in front of them with the dogs a hundred yards behind. They found an opening in the north fence of the next section south, which the coyote by then had entered, and turned through it into a stubble field, driving fast right through the dogs. Then they dropped their second box of dogs, which closed on the coyote just before it reached the copse. "If it gets to the trees, it'll get away," Les told Ron. The dogs stopped the coyote in the last seconds before it entered the trees. It was the bitch from the pair we had started almost two miles back.

The chase, Harold tells me later, requires two types of dogs—catchers and fighters. The best dogs will catch and fight both. "I'll pay $200 for a good coyote dog any time," he says. Coyote hunting is not an inexpensive sport.

Our first coyote turned out to be the only one we would catch that day, though we scouted as hard as anyone on the hunt. Les, canny operator that he was, usually waited out on the road for someone else to flush the coyotes his way, but even with that tactic he caught only two. Someone else got three. Old Harry, the wrong man in the wrong place at the wrong time, got none. The star of the day was a twenty-five-year-old county employee and novice coyote hunter named Johnny Wagonblast, who took Dan on as a rider—which means spotter and aimer and dog-dropper—and caught no fewer than five coyotes, his shy, sunburned grin stretching wider and wider as the day progressed.

We draw the trucks together on a north-south stretch of road and drop the dogs a box at a time to relieve themselves, which they do by finding a fencepost, strange habit for dogs of the treeless prairie. One even settles for a dry weed. Ron is grinning when we meet; so am I. The men look over Harold's catch, which we have thrown onto the top of the dog box with one of its hind legs hooked into a piece of bailing wire attached to the pipe rail. They seem to make a ritual of squeezing the dog's bag, but that may be a city fancy.

After the rest we search resolutely westward, as Thoreau advised. The remainder of the day's hunting will exercise Harold's and John's patience. We hunt hard but catch no more coyotes, though once we come close enough to release the dogs only to see them miss the coyote's sudden northward turn—they are coursing west behind it—and head for a pickup truck stationed opposite us. Good soldiers all, the dogs have only responded to their training, but with the perversity of field marshals we want them momentarily to forget training and think for themselves. The dogs' confusion makes John mad. "Goddamn it, Dad, if you'd released the dogs back in that wheatfield they could of headed that coyote off before he got to the brush. We'd of caught the son of a bitch"—which angers Harold enough that he tells his son, who outweighs him by at least a hundred pounds, to shut the hell up, which John, being a good son, does. Even lucky Johnny Wagonblast's dogs will miss an easy catch when the coyote they are chasing veers across a road and they, yelping like a neighborhood pack harassing its favorite garbage truck, home in on a passing car.

Before that time, most of us still fresh from other chases of the morning, we stop for lunch, and one of the hunters, a drugstore cowboy in Stetson, Western shirt, Levi's, and tooled black boots, announces that we are in Nebraska. We have hunted our way northwest over an area of fifty miles, and searched most of the one-mile sections along the way. We have seen no towns and only a few occupied farmhouses. That kind of range is possible with seven trucks. Harold's prediction that with so many hunters we would be "falling all over each other" has not come true. The large number of trucks simply makes it unlikely that the hunters who flush the game will get the kill.

We park on a gravel road, completely blocking it. Harold hauls out a brown cardboard box and sets it down by John on a ridge next to the road. In it are hamburger buns, lunch meats, American cheese, potato chips, bananas, oranges, and chocolate-covered fudge sandwiches. "Help yourself—just pile it on like you was at home," Harold tells me. Les sits down next to Harold, unpacks his own supplies with Ron, and is soon happily gumming a cold hotdog which he douses from time to time with ketchup. The ladies eat discreetly in the trucks. I make a sandwich with a little of everything at hand and peel an orange for fluid. Les brings out a thermos jug, swigs from the spout, and announces to Ron that it contains "Portis brew." The conversation swerves from reconstructions of the morning's chase to the problem of Nebraska coyote-hunting licenses. "The game warden stopped me up here one time," someone says. "I had two coyotes on the truck and he asked me if I'd caught them in Nebraska. I said I had, and he wanted to know if I had an out-of-state hunting license, since the truck has Kansas plates. I said I didn't, but I owned some acreage in Nebraska and caught the coyotes on it. He let me go that time."

"The warden down by Russell is a real hardnosed old bastard," someone else says. "He caught those Nebraska boys down there one time and fined them heavy."

The cowboy, who is in fact the owner of a sales barn in Mankato, northeast of Portis, suggests we turn the hunt southwestward after lunch to avoid the river to the north and to get back into Kansas. Soon we pack up our gear and start off.

While Johnny Wagonblast, with Dan beside him, sweeps up the afternoon honors, Harold and John and I dig into every gully and ditch and copse we can find. We buck down by-roads washed out by spring rains, thread around creek beds still soft enough to mire the truck, fire into milo fields and draws, and never see a coyote. We flush pheasant and quail and jackrabbits, which we leave alone. At one point we race up a forty-degree bluff, slip back down, gun up twice more, and finally make the top only to find our way barred by a fence. And all the while we listen to the cowboy come on over the radio like Red Barber announcing the Yankees as the other hunters rack up their coyotes for the afternoon: "THERE HE COMES, LES, OUT THAT SOUTH FENCE—GO SOUTH, LES! GO SOUTH, GO SOUTH, HE'S CROSSED THE ROAD, HE'S IN THAT SOIL BANK* IN

---

*A "soil bank" is not a ridge of soil but a plot of land set aside by the farmer in compliance with the Department of Agriculture's Soil Bank program, a self-denial for which the farmer has been amply rewarded over the years out of federal funds. The purpose of the program was to take wheat land out of production and thus reduce the wheat surplus which once plagued the United States. But farmers aren't fools, and the land they banked—fenced and left fallow—is the roughest and least productive land on their farms. It makes excellent cover for coyotes.

THE NEXT SECTION, BETTER GO WEST AND HEAD HIM OFF, LES, JOHNNY WAGONBLAST, WHERE ARE YOU? YOU OUT ON THE WEST ROAD? COME NORTH, JOHNNY, HE'S IN THE NORTHWEST QUARTER, COME NORTH," and Harold nudging me, Harold in love with his radio, "See, I told you he was a real good boy, regular sportscaster," and then the sound, sweet jealous sound now, of the dogs dropped from Johnny's truck, and cowboy back on the horn, "HE'S GOT HIM, JOHNNY WAGONBLAST'S GOT HIM, THEY GOT THE COYOTE!" John riding up on top without a word, Harold crashing his truck through the thumping stubble, coyotes anywhere but here. "There's days like that," Harold tells me. "That's what makes it such a sport. Some days a man can't do nothing wrong, other days he can hunt as hard as hell and still get no coyotes. I thought we'd see more out here, though. Don't know where they've all got to."

Then the near-miss when we dropped the dogs, and the flare of anger between father and son. John thought Harold spent too much time on the radio—"If you come out here to catch coyotes you got to *drive,* not talk on that damned radio all the time"—and more futile hunting. The afternoon sky has clouded over and the air cooled, but after our second and final dog-drop I can hear the animals raggedly panting, a torn, screeching pant that rips great chunks of air from the road to feed tissue completely used up in the chase. I have heard such a sound only once before, at the finish line of a two-mile cross-country race, the runners vomiting green bile and packing their lungs with air as if they might never breathe again.

We stop at a pond and John carries a number-ten can to the water and brings it back for the dogs. Harold holds it up to them, and they jam their muzzles two at a time into the muddy froth and drink. He moves quickly from dog to dog, allowing them only enough to wet their throats, avoiding the tanking that would cramp them. Their condition leaves me wondering how Johnny Wagonblast's dogs have lasted the afternoon, especially since he announced coyly at one of our rest stops that he almost missed the last coyote because he dropped his "cripples" instead of his good dogs. Almost.

A coyote hunt has no official end. Portis men, like country men everywhere, practice indirection in all matters of public behavior. Harold continues to search for coyotes until the light begins to fail, and so do the others, but the hunt turns from west to southeast, and without perceptible effort we find ourselves searching a section only a mile outside Long Island. We drive into that village to get gas for the pickup. Everyone else has had the same idea and we are soon swigging Coca-Cola at the filling station. Even then no one admits he has to get home to chores. The closest anyone comes to announcing his destination is a laconic "Guess I'll head on in." By this time old Harry has started to drink, someone says. He still wants his coyote—do the wives judge their husbands' *cojones* by the quantity of their kill?—and Harold senses his discomfort and offers to work over the hills outside Long Island on the way back to Portis. Harry agrees and we set off once more, all of us tired now and half-hearted. We fire into several promising draws, but no coyotes emerge even though Harold and John, who have phenomenal memories for past kills, recall having caught several coyotes there two years before. Finally we leave Harry to his own diversions and drive back to Portis. Together, all seven truckloads of us, we have caught thirteen coyotes.*

At dinner at the Crams', Ron entertains us with Wolters stories passed on to him by Les, a non-stop talker. The Wolters are a fighting family, he says, squabbling among themselves, but they turn a solid front to the world. They are regionally famous for their coyote hunts. They usually pile their entire winter's catch of coyotes in their front yards, or line them up along the road. Harold averages more than 150 coyotes every season. Someone once came by at night and snipped off all the ears of Les's collection, which made him furious. The ears are required to collect the two-dollar bounty the county still offers for coyotes, though the bounty is not enough money even to pay for the gas used on the hunt, much less to support each hunter's ten or fifteen dogs year-round. Les's dogs, Dan remembers, can be identified by a brown streak of tobacco juice across their muzzles. Les chews Red Man tobacco and spits the juice

---

*It was Harold's last hunt. His father rode out for buffalo; by the time Harold was old enough to hunt, the buffalo were gone, so he switched to coyotes. He caught more than 6,000 of the animals in his fifty years of hunting, raised a large and able family, and made himself and his sons into prosperous farmers. "The abler spirits of the pioneers," writes William Carlos Williams in "The American Background," "cut themselves off from the old at once and set to work with a will directly to know what was about them. It set out helter-skelter. And, by God, it was. Besides, it couldn't wait. Crudely authentic, the bulk of a real culture was being built up from that point. The direct attack they instituted [was] shown in many cases by no other results than the characters of the men and women themselves. . . ." Born on the 29th of April, 1894, Harold Wolters died of a heart attack on Friday, the 13th of June, 1969. *Sic transit gloria mundi.*

out the window; the wind carries it back across the dogs' heads as they stick out of their boxes behind the cab.

We are tired from the hunt, but Dan has described to us the Saturday-night chicken fights in the nearby town of Minneapolis, Kansas, and after supper we pack up and head east on Highway 24.

Dan says the town has held chicken fights on Saturday night for years. They are open to the public for a fee, and legal, according to a local handler, as the result of a test case brought by the A.S.P.C.A. and carried to the Supreme Court (of Kansas, presumably), which held that the Kansas statute concerning cruelty to animals did not apply to chickens since they are technically not animals but fowl. No record of such a judgment exists. According to the statutes, chicken fighting is illegal in Kansas only on Sunday, a day of rest for fowl.

We pull into the parking lot of the Minneapolis Pit, a converted auction barn, at nine-thirty in the evening and enter through a screen door into its small anteroom. Our tickets, $1.50 each, are white tags with the words "received," "ready," and "bundle" on them—laundry tags, probably—which we are supposed to hang onto a shirt button in plain view.

Inside the barn, an amphitheater full of smoke. I had expected to find men; instead I find men and women and boys and girls and little children, and not much animation among them. A few of the women look well-to-do, and none looks poor. The best seats, on the south wall above one long side of the pit, are filled; on the north side of the pit stands a line of men, some of them handlers, some there to take the crowd's bets. The main pit, painted white, is sunk into the center of the floor, an oval twelve feet wide and eighteen feet long with twenty-inch walls dropping to a sand base littered with short feathers and spattered with blood. Wooden steps lead up steep benches to a top loft near the ceiling.

Below, the lurid pit, a pygmy Colosseum floored in dirty sand; above, the sober crowd, pewed on gray, siding-faced benches that might have come from a Puritan meetinghouse or a medical-school lecture hall. The abrupt change in scale and lighting shocks, as if the pit were shrunken to obscure the brutality of the spectacle enacted there. Even the lights over the pit—a rectangular bank of fluorescent tubes—enforce the dislocation, the fluorescent light cold and narrow as the light in an autopsy room while the crowd above is warmed and enlivened with incandescent bulbs.

The birds themselves seldom weigh more than five pounds; dressed, they would hardly match a good boiling hen. They fan their neck feathers vainly to frighten their opponents, and admit their size by leaping easily over each other, a feat for lice and lizards and birds, not for men. Even their red and brown feathers conspire to diminish the bloodletting by masking, in their colorful profusion, the wounds. The birds predominantly white still sport a mingling of red feathers. But red and black were the colors of the evening: red of feathers, of fresh blood, of lung tissue coughed from a stricken bird's yellow beak; black of feathers also, of dried blood, and of the darkness at the height of the room.

The spurs—they are gaffs, not slashers, pointed miniature foils two and a half inches long—jut out of scale, cold manmade weapons that connect the two perspectives. No bird could grow such spurs, the length of a man's index finger slightly crooked, the tempered steel of scalpels and clamps and interrogation chambers. They penetrate so deep into the victimized bird that the cock cannot pull them out. The referee must stop the match and carefully, in a parody of concern, extract them as a claw or a fang is extracted. A man with a sword in his hand would not match the scale of those spurs.

The handlers carry their cocks to the edge of the pit. They cradle them in the nest of their arms like infants, talk to them, croon to them, baby them as soldiers baby their weapons in the seconds before battle begins. The referee jumps into the pit, absolute authority in cockfighting from whom there is no appeal. The handlers bring their cocks to the center line, jam the birds together to anger them and give them a taste of blood. No horses here. They warm up on each other. The birds click at red combs, sample an eye and a wattle, alert red instincts honed on a diet of cracked corn and pep pills.

Set down on their starting lines, they strain toward each other, held by their handlers by the tail. The referee signals and they go forward, flare their feathers, dance, circle, leap over each other, peck, jab, jibe, close, seeking the head, the eyes, the spurs an afterthought, and above them the crowd stares almost without sound until a plump woman in black pants with cash wadded in her fist yells, "Shoot 'em! Shoot 'em!"—shoot the spurs in. A spur stabs underneath the white cock: "Handle them!" says the referee, and he comes to the end of the pit to calculate the hit and extract the spur. Drawn back to its end of the main, the white cock appears dazed, flicking its reptilian inner eyelids. Its handler is a young man, thin, dark, breathing hard, new to cockfighting and intent on winning. He pinches the back of his bird's neck, draws out its beak, rises its tailfeathers and blows on its vent.

Matched again, the recovered white cock scores on the red, and after the spur is drawn the red reels. A florid man in an orange polo shirt, receding hairline, bulging eyes, bulging belly, handles the bird, sticks his finger down its throat and stretches out its neck to bring it back. He sends the red cock out again to fight the white, and again the red is hit and loses ground. The referee calls time and the two men pick up their cocks and leave the main. Two smaller pits—"drag pits"—have been laid out at right angles to the main in a side room that opens into the arena. The drag pits are smaller than the main because by the time the cocks reach them one of the birds is usually wounded and no longer has the strength to maneuver.

In the drag pit the slaughter continues, the red bird set on its feet at the starting line immediately falling over, the white cock with its furiously intense handler behind it advancing to tear at the red's head and eyes. Before the red cock dies, the white will peck out both its eyes.

> *Before the red cock dies*
> *The white will peck out both its eyes*

The white cock has already lost an eye.

The red flops onto its back, breathing in gasps, but the fight still continues, timed and counted out by the referee, who consults a stainless-steel watch and scolds its luminous sweep second hand. The boy blows on his bird's vent; the florid handler sweats with anger, working over his bird as if it were a mis-sighted rifle or a dull knife which exasperates him because it needs unavailable repair. At the edge of the drag pit stand two blonde college girls, sisters perhaps, attracted by the boy's passion but uninterested in the match. When a by-stander remarks the white cock's missing eye, one of the girls says casually, "Oh, he'll never fight again, that's too bad." Then the white spurs the red fatally and the red convulses, dead. The florid man picks it up by its claws, snips the waxed threads that hold on the spurs, and tosses it onto a pile of dead birds in the corner.

He wipes the spurs and returns them to their case, worn like a sliderule in a holster on his hip. The boy, tightly smiling, cradles his winning cock out a side door.

I glimpse the evening. Two boys, eight or nine years old, lying on a bench head to head before a window at the top of the stands, talking to each other and the moon. Fresh cocks in their narrow varnished pine boxes, with small screened windows in front, crowing as if at sunrise. A keeper raking a billow of pinfeathers out of the main. A mustached, bib-overalled, bereted handler coaching his cock in the moments before its match. A pretty, dark-eyed country girl with black hair falling down her back, in sandals and a poor-boy and pants, country hip, posing for such eyes as might find her. A sign on the wall advertising chicken feed. The florid handler's cleft butt squeezing out of his pants as he squats to eke another stand from his dying bird. A slumming college girl in a linen pantsuit leaving abruptly when a cock shoots its spurs. Wives gossiping easily at tables in the anteroom, waiting for their husbands as they might wait at a bowling alley. A white cock with both eyes torn out running in blind fear from the drag pit to be caught and brought back for another round, the fight finally conceded and the cock taken outside and its neck wrung. Dan's protective boredom, Ron's protective silence, my protective curiosity. The smell like a chickenhouse of dust and ammonia, the smoke like a hustled poker game stinging and blue. From the look of the spectators they might be conspiring a town orgy, sex in the pit, casual lays arranged in the stands, silent onlookers breathing hotly from their seats. But the children wouldn't be present at an orgy, whispering to each other of alliances and tomorrow. Sex is more private than death.

Enthusiasts, the books say, justify cockfighting for the gambling it generates, continuing through the main as the fortunes of the two birds change, and Ron brings me tales of Kansas City gamblers motoring out to Minneapolis for big stakes, but the bets I see at the fights are low, a dollar or two, seldom five, rarely ten, and they do not continue through the main. The Minneapolis fights are held not for gamblers but for kids and married couples, who watch with little apparent passion, as they might watch *Mission Impossible* on an easy Sunday night. "Chicken fights," they call them in Minneapolis, banally, and all of us who know the farm know the banality of chickens.

The schoolmasters of Victorian England judged their pupils'

cockfights to earn the dead birds for food; in prosperous Kansas the birds lie rotting in a corner, to be burned tomorrow with the trash. Conspicuous waste, the beer cans at roadside, the cocks in the corner: it is the American compulsion going back as far as the slaughter of the Indians, the slaughter of the buffalo, the littering of the Oregon Trail when the emigrants' wagons proved too heavy for the march with heirloom chests and Eastern frocks and family quilts and hopeful pianos. We have always littered the land, and pious folk have always deplored our littering, but it has measured our desperation, our determination to move on before we are found out. We have not needed to hoard, we say, the promise being rich before us. It is truer that we have understood the death the hoarder dies. We have moved west as a hounded people moves, fleeing the destruction of Sodoms. The Jews of Europe who could not litter—who could not leave house and home and position, walk out their doors for the west and not look back—lost everything. We have ever been a people who could litter.

And now, the oceans having bound us, we devour the land and each other. We thought we were peaceful, but a pair of coyotes sniffing rabbits in the brush are peaceful, cocks crowing pride at each other across a barnyard are peaceful, dogs rolling in the grass are peaceful. Guns are not; trucks across broken fields are not; lean sutured spurs are not, nor are we who devise them. "Ah! what a plastic little creature he is! so shifty, so adaptive! his body a chest of tools, and he making himself comfortable in every climate, in every condition."* We need not fear our machines. We become them on this late continent. We are the avant garde of our race, locked in continental sanctity, feeding on roots and carrion, stripping ores and oils down to the hot core of the earth, sparing not even the small fossil shells.

There is no darkness of nature so dark as the darkness of men. We observe with a cold agreement of brain cells that do not reproduce and feel no pain. We stare, unblinking eyes, at dying beasts and see only casual transformations. Corn grows, and we pluck it; wheat grows, and we cut it; coyotes run, and we tear them; cocks crow, and we murder them; men die, and we send others after them. We are nature's full circle, the end product of her millennial butchery of forms, form feeding on form unto the ends of the earth. We nest

*Emerson, in rare humor, mocking Hamlet.

as animals: we hunt as men. We huddle as animals: we murder as men. We are most extraordinary where we appear most common, as in a cockfight in central Kansas. We are backward and spare in our kindnesses, and even these will not abide.

Beyond Portis, now far behind, the land stretches west to the Rockies. Shallow hills blow barren of houses and men, fertile in wind and wheat and coyotes. Ghosts of Indians and buffalo wander the steppes, but the short grass preserves no mark of their passing or of ours. *The plains of Kansas are even lonelier than the sea.* They are lonely as men are lonely who seek, as we seek beyond all civility, blood to freshen us, wounds to warm our hands. Perry Smith's glowing mantle of violence is ours also, and only our flesh shrinks below that shelter. We would eat the moon and rape the sun if we could. Hemingway did well to apologize, but not to the Christians.

Out here in Kansas, I say now in impulsive justification, "having suffered myself and learned mercy,"* we murder animals more often than we murder men. We are the old primitives of the country set against the city's new.

And what is local of this? The surprising appropriateness of cockfighting in Union Kansas, spiritual home of John Brown. The earnest indifference of the handlers, who pit their birds for gain, not for love—some were exceptions, but most were not. The stolid audience of spectators, plainly watching murder with no English lust or Latin ardor. The penny-ante bets in a society which creates capital faster than it can destroy it. The human warmth of the Portis people, who seemed, plain truth or proud face, at home with themselves and with strangers, pleased to show their ways, comfortable in judgment and unwilling to judge. Their care with each other, pride meeting pride across politeness and indirection. The coyotes. The cocks. The yardlights. The wheat. The sky. The sky.

And Dan, and Ron? Ron went to Portis and to Minneapolis for a manhood ceremony, as he goes to all festivals, and passed the test of the coyote hunt by doing it better than a novice should, and passed the test of cockfighting by despising its brutality. Dan went and came home and kept his council; I saw him the following Sat-

---

*The English naturalist Charles Waterton, defending from slaughter the ghostly and superstitiously feared barn owls on his estate: "Having suffered myself and learned mercy, I broke in pieces the code of penal laws which the knavery of the gamekeeper and the lamentable ignorance of the other servants had hitherto put in force. . . ." Our mercy is not of that quality. Not yet.

urday cheerfully treating a clinic full of cats and dogs, and at the hunt and the fights and the clinic he wore the same honest face.

And I, since I am of this place and this time also? Old veteran of the knife and the noose and the capsule, I found nothing amiss. Did you?

Jane Kramer

Jane Kramer's "Letter from Europe" appears frequently in *The New Yorker,* where she has been a staff writer since 1964. Four of Kramer's family profiles, from that magazine, were collected in 1980 in *Unsettling Europe.* She has also written *Off Washington Square* (1963), *Allen Ginsberg in America* (1969), *Honor to the Bride* (1970), and *The Last Cowboy* (1978), from which this excerpt is drawn.

Kramer was born in 1938 in Providence, Rhode Island. She graduated from Vassar College in 1959 and received a master's degree in English and American literature from Columbia University two years later. Before joining *The New Yorker* staff, she wrote for *The Village Voice* and other publications. She lives in Paris.

Kramer went to Texas, as she explained in the introduction to *The Last Cowboy,* wishing to write about a cowboy, but not knowing where to start. Friends guided her toward the Panhandle. There she met the man she calls Henry Blanton, and his wife, who became the main characters in her profile. "There was something about him that moved me," she said. He seemed different. "He had settled into his life, but he could not seem to settle for it." The myth of the American cowboy had influenced Blanton's life. It was as inescapable as the Panhandle dust. Kramer began by showing the myth in action, complete with a foreshadowing of the problems it would bring for Blanton.

Cowboy

*H*enry Blanton turned forty on an April day when the first warm
winds of spring crossed the Texas Panhandle and the diamondback
rattlers, fresh and venomous from their winter sleep, came slipping
out from under the cap rock of the Canadian River breaks. It was a
day full of treachery and promise, the kind of day that Henry would
have expected for the showdown in a good Western. Henry was
particular about Westerns. When he was a boy and hired out in the
summer—for fifty cents a day and the privilege of keeping a local
rancher's thirsty cows from ambling downriver from their summer
pasture—he saved his pay in a rusty tin bank shaped like a bull and
planned a winter's worth of Westerns at Amarillo's movie houses.
At night, summers, with the covers pulled tight above his head,
Henry braved the moaning ghosts who rode the river breeze past
the old stone line camp where he slept alone—and the way he did
it was by fixing his thoughts on calm, courageous movie cowboys.
He never summoned up the image of his father, who once had been
as fine a cowboy as any man in the Panhandle, or the image of his
Grandaddy Abel, who had made the long cattle drive to Wyoming
back when Indians were still marauding and a rustler with a long
rope would as often as not shoot a trail boss who rode out looking
for his strays. Henry, deep in his bedroll, shoring up courage against
the river's dead, called on John Wayne, Gary Cooper, and Glenn
Ford. Especially Glenn Ford. He was convinced then that for "expressin' right," as he put it, there had never been a cowboy to equal
Glenn Ford—and he was still convinced of this at forty.

"Expressin' right" was important to the man I call Henry
Blanton. It was a gift that he had lost, and he did not know why and
was ashamed of himself anyway for wondering, since part of expressing right as a cowboy had to do with the kind of quiet certainty
that sustained a man when times were bad. Henry believed that
other men might talk to themselves too much, like women, or fret

and complain, but a proper cowboy did not. When he watched a Western now, on the big television console he had bought on credit the day the electric lines reached his house on the Willow Ranch, it was less for pleasure or amusement, or even courage, than to find a key to the composure that eluded him. Henry never doubted his abilities as a cowboy. He was the foreman of ninety thousand acres, and he ran them well, considering that he had to take his orders from a rancher who had moved to Eaton Square, in London, and that those orders came to him through a college-boy ranch manager who knew more about juggling account books than raising cattle and was so terrified of cows anyway that he did most of his managing from the driver's seat of a locked, air-conditioned Buick. Henry was a good rider and a fine roper. He could pull a calf with considerable skill, and when he had to he could cut a dogie from the belly of its dying mother. He could account for every one of the twenty-two hundred cows in his charge as if they were his own. He knew which cows delivered strong, healthy calves each spring, which cows needed help calving, which ones tended to miss a year or deliver stillborn. He knew by instinct when a fence was down or a pole had rotted. He could put his ear to the pump pipe of a windmill well that was drawing poorly and tell in minutes whether the checks were broken or the water, three hundred and fifty feet underground, was drying up. He had all those skills, but somehow he was not the sort of cowboy who inspired admiration or respect.

People regarded Henry with exasperation or indulgence. There was something unsettled about his character—something that made him restless and a little out of control. He could not quite manage that economy of gesture and person which was appropriate in a cowboy. Some frustration drove him to a kind of inept excess. He drank too much in town, and worked with a bottle of bourbon in his Ford pickup truck and another bottle in his saddlebag. His stunts were famous—people still talked about the time Henry and his brother, Tom, backed a wild mare into a Pampa funeral parlor— but lately they had turned ugly and immodest. He was hard on his wife, Betsy, and neighbors had begun to remark that he was getting hard on his animals, too. He moved his cows a little too fast for their placidity, drove his yearlings a little too fast for their daily gain. When he worked cattle these days, he was apt to forget to keep his knife sharpened. Sometimes, dehorning, he sawed too deep into a calf's horns, and the creature's lowing turned mad with pain.

Henry had lived on ranches where his camp was thirty or forty miles from a paved road; ranches where Betsy had to cart water from a spring to do the dishes or wash her babies' diapers; ranches where even the best cowboy was worth no more to his boss than a hundred and fifty dollars a month in wages, a shack for a home, and the meat from steers that were too scrawny to send to auction. He did not like to complain about his life now, in a neat prefabricated house with electricity and a telephone and running water—a house with a highway only twelve miles away down a negotiable dirt road. But a rancher could trust his foreman with ninety thousand or nine hundred thousand acres and still regard him as a kind of overgrown boy who was best protected from himself by a stern paternal hand guiding him through a life's indenture.

The movies Henry loved had told him that a good cowboy was a hero. They had told him that a cowboy lived by codes, not rules—codes of calm, solitude, and honor—and that a cowboy had a special arrangement with nature and, with his horse under him and the range spread out around him, knew a truth and a freedom and a satisfaction that ordinary men did not. Even the circuit preacher who came to town every second Sunday claimed that, while no one was really free, a man on a horse surely had a head start in the business of grace over Communists and New Yorkers and all the other sinners who lived by malice and greed. But the movies were changing—they were full of despair lately. The preacher himself had started making money giving I.Q. tests to the Baptists on his route for a rich Bible college that was running a study called God and Intellect. And Henry, turning forty, had little to show for his life as a cowboy except a hand-tooled saddle and a few horses. Betsy had baked a cake, but she was not speaking to him that birthday morning. His daughter Melinda, washing for school, had used up all the hot water. Henry began his forty-first year with a hangover and an icy shower, and, pulling on his boots, he brooded about the future. The West was full of fences and feedyards now. It was crowded with calf traders and futures brokers, college boys who didn't know a Hereford from an Angus, and ranchers who commuted from London or the South of France—and, whatever the movies once promised, there was not much chance, in a showdown, for a hero on a horse.

The road to Henry Blanton's house began as a narrow, rutted cowpath off a highway north of the town of Canadian, and the only thing that distinguished it from a hundred other cowpaths off that stretch of highway was the big, rusty Willow Ranch brand that swayed, suspended, from an arch above the ranch gate. The brand made a fine target for the high-school boys from town who liked to cruise the highway nights in their fathers' pickups, taking potshots. Henry had to keep a standing order with the local blacksmith for a new brand every other year, but all in all he took the damage philosophically. Everyone he knew owned guns and rifles, and liked to use them. Henry himself carried a .30–30 Winchester slung across the gun rack on his Ford pickup. He believed that hiding weapons was low and cowardly—that a man's right to arm himself against villainy was something sacred, and came straight from God. Lately, of course, there was not much villainy of the sort that Henry and his neighbors could take on with a rifle or a six-gun. They heard a lot about the criminals down in Amarillo, but Amarillo was almost a hundred and fifty miles away, and out in the country people had to content themselves with shooting rattlers and coyotes. The only criminals they were apt to meet were a few fast-talking cattle dealers who specialized in swindling widows and were always safely across the state line anyway by the time people started looking for them.

The land on either side of the Willow gate was flat, irrigated land, planted in wheat for winter grazing, and by April it was almost ready for harvesting. The path ran straight between those precious wheat fields, following a line of wire fence that carried a mean dose of electric current. But once the grassland started, the path began to dip and curve. It followed a fence here, circled a patch of burned-out mesquite there, and veered off toward a windmill somewhere else. The land turned vivid and surprising then. Old, gnarled cactus, tall as trees, sprouted delicate, obscene caps of yellow flowers. Tiny white blossoms sprinkled themselves like spun sugar over the fanning spikes of giant yucca plants. The short blue-grama grass of the pastures, moist and green for a month before the summer sun began to cure it, made strange patches on the clay soil. And cows blocked the path at every turning. They stood motionless in the mud while their calves suckled—stubborn, melancholy creatures, staring out over the scrubby land as if it puzzled and repelled them. For miles, the only sign of human life was an old bunkhouse where Henry's three Mexican hands lived, along with a simple drifter named Jerome, who had wandered onto the ranch a couple of years ago, and who cooked for the Mexicans now and did their wash in exchange for a share of the bunkhouse food, a bed, and the Mexicans' reluctant company. But the road wound on and on, tracing enormous curves across the pastures. Twelve miles in from the highway, it dipped behind a little rise shaded by hackberry trees and cottonwoods, and there it trailed off into a footpath to the Blantons' front door.

Henry's camp was the ranch headquarters. Henry could stand at his door and look across a dirt courtyard to a sheet-metal barn the size of an airplane hangar which held nearly all the supplies he needed to run the Willow. Over the nine years that Henry had worked the ranch, the barn had grown by sections. Just last year, sixty feet had been added, but Henry had seen to it that the things that pleased him most as a cowboy were still within sight of his courtyard. The little hill, with its grove of hackberries and cottonwoods. The shabby, solitary willow by the well. The pasture where his horses grazed. The wooden pens, off the barn, where the milk cows and the dogies fed from troughs, and where Melinda, at fourteen, scrubbed and curried and adored her new roan, Sugar. The old chuck wagon that Abel Blanton once used on roundups—Henry had rescued it for twenty dollars and a promise to haul it home when the Caliche Ranch, where his grandfather had worked for thirty years, was sold to an Eastern conglomerate. By now, all the paraphernalia of modern ranching was well hidden behind the barn, out of sight of the house and the courtyard. Henry worked there when he had to—when he and his hands were branding the little calves that arrived regularly, in truckloads, from farms in Mississippi and Louisiana. Henry had improvised a kind of outdoor assembly line behind the barn. It was a line of ramps and chutes and sprayers ending up at one of the huge iron clamps that cowboys refer to tenderly as "calf cradles" and that can flatten a struggling calf with the turn of a handle and tip it onto its side for the ordeal of castration, branding, and dehorning. The cradle at the Willow was only two years old, but thousands of head of the mangy southern calves—Mississipps or Okies, the cowboys called them—that Henry's rancher bought and grazed for quick profit had already been run through it. It was foul with a crust of blood and feces which no spring rain could wash away.

Sometimes, toward evening, Betsy climbed onto a rail of one of the rough pine cattle chutes, with her copy of *Woman's Day* and a glass of sweet iced tea, to watch the sunset. There was a fine view west, from the chutes, to the Canadian breaks, and Betsy had always loved that moment just before the sun dropped, when the cliffs lit up like a jagged slash of fire on the horizon. But she could never persuade Henry to sit and watch with her. *His* favorite place for sitting was the driver's seat of his Granddaddy Abel's chuck wagon, which he kept parked under the willow tree. Henry had restored the wagon and was proud of it. The job had taken the better part of three days and nights, with Henry living out of his pickup in a pasture on the Caliche Ranch, but he had been determined. By the time Betsy got worried and sent a state trooper out to find him, he had mended the rotting boards with scraps of barn siding, painted the chuck box, realigned the wheels, and was heading home. The trooper found him easily—driving up the highway with the ancient wagon rattling along behind his pickup and a pint of bourbon in his hand. There was a brief bad moment between them after the trooper suggested taking Henry into town for a breath test. Henry had to explain that he was hauling his granddaddy's chuck wagon home to the family, where it belonged, so that no son-of-a-bitch corporation college boys would ever get the opportunity to pretty it up like a dude-ranch buggy and show it off to their Wall Street friends on hunting-season picnics. Then, of course, the state trooper repented. He even joined Henry in the pickup for some reminiscing. They knew each other well enough for that—they were old antagonists, in the way that cowboys and lawmen were meant to be antagonists, and between them they could count up eight serious confrontations over fights and stunts. But, sitting together in the Ford pickup on the hot, dusty day that Henry brought his grandfather's chuck wagon home, they shared a momentary truce, mourning the West that was supposed to be—mourning, even, their old, useless animosity.

After that, Henry did his best to introduce the chuck wagon to the Willow. Once, for a spring roundup, he fitted the wagon out with pots and pans, a water keg, and bedrolls, and ordered one of his Mexican hands to practice making sourdough biscuits and coleslaw and rhubarb pie from Betsy's "Chuck Wagon Cookbook." He wanted his hands and all the neighbors who would be helping on the roundup to sleep out under the stars, the way cowboys used to do in Abel Blanton's time. And everybody did sleep out—the first night. Henry brought his harmonica, and Tom—who always neighbored for his brother, despite the fact that their ranchers had not spoken since a lawsuit over some gas-drilling rights five years earlier—brought his guitar. The men sang and drank and enjoyed their pie and managed to put away an entire side of spit-roasted grass-

fed beef. They had a splendid time, in fact, until the wind blew up
and the bugs, attracted by the campfires and the cooking smells,
started coming. By morning, they were grumpy and exhausted. And
by late afternoon, after roping and branding some three hundred
frisky calves, they had all mumbled apologies and were leading their
horses to their horse trailers and heading home to hot baths, kitchen
dinners, and dry beds. Henry spent that night in a pasture with the
woeful Mexican cook, who served him another fine chuck-wagon
supper and then went off to eat alone, because Henry did not really
approve of breaking bread with wetbacks. Henry still brought the
wagon out to roundups, but by now the gesture was more ceremonial than practical, and he always hauled it home after supper.
Summers, the local cowboys' children borrowed it for serving hot
dogs and Dr Pepper at their Peewee Rodeo, but mostly it stayed put
under the willow, where Henry could sit and daydream in the
morning while he waited for his hands.

Henry was up at six most spring and summer mornings—in
winter, when the days were short, he got up at five—and on school
days he helped Melinda with the barn chores, which were hard for
her to manage by herself, now that her three older sisters were
grown and gone. While Betsy was in the kitchen grilling the bacon
and eggs and making coffee, they fed the milk cows and groomed
the horses. Sometimes Melinda would lead the horses out to the
small pasture off the courtyard. More often lately Henry did it for
her, stopping on his way back to breakfast to fill his pickup at the
gas tank by the last barn door and to switch off the two-way radio
that Lester Hill, the Willow ranch manager, had insisted on installing in the truck a couple of years ago. The radio, set to a base station
at Lester's house, shamed Henry. He kept it on when he was touring
the ranch alone or doing the chores at headquarters, but when he
imagined Lester, mornings, loafing in pajamas by the swimming
pool of his fancy new house on the edge of town, the picture convinced him that no ranch manager would ever get the chance to
challenge his authority when he was with his hands.

Henry valued his authority. He hurried through breakfast so
that he could always greet his men with the day's orders looking
relaxed and confident. He liked to sit on the wagon, waiting, with
his scratch pad in his hand and a pencil behind his ear, and he made
it a point to be properly dressed for the morning's work in his black
boots, a pair of clean black jeans, and his old black hat and jacket.

Henry liked wearing black. The Virginian, he had heard, wore black, and so had Gary Cooper in the movie "High Noon," and now Henry wore it with a kind of innocent pride, as if the color carried respect and a hero's stern, elegant qualities. Once, Betsy discovered him at the bathroom mirror dressed in his black gear, his eyes narrowed and his right hand poised over an imaginary holster. She teased him about it then—at least, until he got so mad that he stayed out half the night in town drinking—but a few weeks later she took a snapshot of him in that same gear and sent it to the Philip Morris company, with a note saying that in her opinion Henry Blanton was much more impressive as a cowboy than the people they used to advertise their Marlboro cigarettes. Henry was, in fact, a handsome man. He was tall and rugged, and ranch life had seasoned the smooth, round face that grinned, embarrassed, in the tinted wedding picture that Betsy kept on the upright piano in her parlor. There was a fine-lined, weathered look about Henry at forty. Too much bourbon and beer had put a gut on him, but his gray eyes were clear and quick most days, and often humorous, and his sandy hair had got thick and wiry as it grayed—a little rumpled and overgrown, because he hated haircuts, though never long enough to cause comment in a cowboy bar. He had a fine, solemn swagger. Saturday nights at the country-and-Western dance in Pampa, he thumped around the floor, serious and sweating, and the women liked to watch him—there was something boyish and charming about his grave self-consciousness. When he was younger, he used to laugh and bow and shake hands with everybody after a good polka. Now, more often than not, he blinked and looked around, suddenly embarrassed, and his laugh was loud and nervous, and made the women who had been watching him uncomfortable.

Betsy attributed the change in Henry to disappointment and drinking. She did not really approve of drinking. She did not want liquor in her house—none of the cowboys' wives she knew did—and even Henry agreed that there was something a little indecent about a bottle of bourbon on display in a Christian living room. Henry drank with guile—the guile of a schoolboy waiting to be caught and punished. It gave an edge to his pleasure, and turned his evasions of the household rules into an artful and immensely satisfying pastime. Besides the bottles in his pickup and his saddlebag, he kept a fifth of Jim Beam hidden behind some old cereal boxes on the top shelf of a kitchen cabinet and another stashed underneath the chuck-wagon seat. He liked to have a drink in the mornings with his white cowhands, but he was careful never to bring the wagon bottle out until his daughter and his wife were gone.

Usually, Melinda left first, careening down the cowpath in an old ranch jeep that Henry had overhauled years earlier to get his daughters to the Willow gate, where the school bus stopped at seven-thirty and, again, late in the afternoon. Then Betsy followed in the family Chevrolet. Betsy worked as an invoice clerk in a grain-sorghum dealer's warehouse thirty miles down the highway. Given the condition of the cowpath and the Panhandle weather, she had to spend some two and a half hours every day commuting, and in spring and summer, with tornado warnings out so often, there were nights when she had to stay in town and sleep at a cousin's house. The drive tired her, and the job had begun to bore her, but she kept working, because the family depended on the money that she made. She liked to say that the ranch took care of everything they needed except a decent income. The ranch provided their house, paid their electric bill, and kept their freezer full of beef. Two ranch steers went to Henry every year—he chose them himself, when they were coming off winter wheat, and then he turned them back to pasture, because, like most cowboys, he preferred the lean, sinewy meat of a range-fat steer to the rich, marbled meat of an animal fattened in a feedyard.

Still, Henry made only seven hundred dollars a month running the Willow, and most of that went out on payday just for bills and taxes. His monthly pickup allowance from the ranch gave him two hundred dollars more, but his pickup costs, for gas and bank payments, came to three hundred, and he had to add fifty dollars to meet the loan for the family car. Every winter, too, the pickup needed new tires, and they cost more than three hundred dollars. Then, there was the expense of keeping horses. The price of a colt, in a private deal, was over two hundred dollars, while a two-year-old quarter horse with some training could cost as much as seven hundred. A good saddle for that horse was another seven hundred lately; the bridle to go with it cost a hundred more, and the price of a nylon rope for roping and dragging calves was up to twenty dollars. And Henry was expected to provide the horses that he rode and to carry his own gear and saddle, just as he was expected to own the pickup that he drove. Every rancher he had ever worked for had made the assumption that cowboys took better care of their own property than somebody else's, and Henry agreed—in practice, if not in principle, his own assumption being that ranch gear was bound to be shoddy and unsafe and that ranch horses were untrustworthy. He had heard of a ranch hand down near Amarillo who had ridden out one day with a ranch bridle and suffered the rest of his life for it. The bridle was old and worn, but none of the cowboys on the ranch knew that the bit had snapped once and been welded. It snapped again that day, and the hand was thrown and trampled. Now, fourteen years and as many operations later, he was still paralyzed.

Henry had ordered his last saddle from the Stockman's Saddle Shop, in Amarillo, as a kind of compensation when Betsy started working, five years ago. His monthly pay then was only five hundred and fifty dollars, and there was never enough money to buy the groceries, keep the girls in school clothes, settle Henry's debts at the package store, and meet Betsy's Christmas Club payments at the bank. All four Blanton girls were still at home then. They wanted their own horses, and Betsy thought it would be nice if they had music lessons with the new piano teacher over in Perryton—the one who had been doing so well on the concert stage in Oklahoma City until she happened to start a conversation with a handsome cowboy in front of a statue at the National Cowboy Hall of Fame and abandoned her career for a ranch wife's life. As Betsy saw the problem, she had no choice but to take a job, and she took the first one that she was offered. Henry shouted a lot about it, and then he sulked, and finally he left the ranch one morning in the middle of work and drove straight to the sorghum dealer's office. He had been thinking, he said later, about his brother Tom, whose wife, Lisa Lou, had got herself a job in a bakery, and how humiliating it was for Tom to have to stay in the kitchen cooking lunch for everybody when he and the other hands at the Circle Y Ranch were working cattle near his camp. Henry told Betsy's boss that a cowboy's wife had her duty to her husband and to the ranch that paid him. He was eloquent. A foreman's house, he said, was a kind of command post, and a foreman's wife was like a general—well, maybe not a general but the general's secretary—whose job it was to stay at that post taking messages, relaying messages, keeping track of everybody on the ranch, sending help in an emergency. He talked about the time that winter that he had had a flat tire far from home, in a freezing and remote pasture. He said that he might have died waiting out there in the cold all night if Betsy had not been home to miss him—to call the hands from their supper and tell them where to search.

But the sorghum dealer was stubborn. Betsy could type and knew some shorthand, and she looked to him, he said, like a respectable woman—not like one of those town women, with their false eyelashes and skimpy skirts, who thought of a job as the free use of somebody else's telephone. Eventually, he and Henry arrived at a compromise: Betsy would work most days, but whenever Henry was working cattle at headquarters she would stay home and cook the hands a proper branding lunch.

The arrangement was fine with Betsy, whose only interest in a job anyway had been the money she would earn. That year, she gave the girls their horses, arranged for their music lessons, and bought herself a velvet pants suit with a lacy blouse for the Christmas holidays, and now, after two raises, she was making three dollars and sixty-five cents an hour and could afford a standing Saturday appointment with the hairdresser in Pampa. Still, Betsy was looking tired lately. All the cowboys' wives said so. She looked as if her life had hurt her and worn her out. Years ago, when Henry began to court her, she was the prettiest girl in her class at the district high school—a slender girl with wide blue eyes and a dimpled smile and wavy yellow hair that flipped in the wind when she went riding and was the envy of her friends. Now there was a tension— a kind of tightness—about her. Her face had hardened under the bright, careful pouf of hair that her hairdresser said was just the thing for softening the features of tall, thin women. She was getting sallow, the way people who spend their youth outdoors turn sallow when they are shut up in closed cars and offices. And there was an anxious, bewildered look in her blue eyes when she left the house mornings and passed her husband at the chuck wagon, his black boot tapping on the spot where she suspected that his bourbon was hidden. There was something shy and tentative about those morning partings. If Henry watched the Chevrolet disappear down the cowpath and started thinking about a wife who had to go to work and shame her husband, he was apt to be edgy and dispirited by supper. He would eat too fast then, and retreat to the parlor with a copy of *TV Guide,* looking for a Western to watch on television. But if he spent the day with his head full of dreams and schemes about the future, he sat down to supper exuberant and overwrought, and then he was ready for a night in town—just like one of his Granddaddy Abel's hands on the first payday after four months out on a spring roundup.

On the evening of his fortieth birthday, Henry picked Tom up at the Circle Y Ranch and the brothers drove to Pampa. Henry was in a celebrating mood, because he had just made a birthday resolution. "It's like this, Tom," he said after they had driven in silence for half an hour, passing Henry's pickup bottle back and forth. "Here I'm getting a certain age, and I find I ain't accumulated nothing. I find . . ."

Tom nodded.

"I mean, it was different with Daddy," Henry said. "Those old men like Daddy—they turned forty and they was just glad if they had a job. But nowadays, you turn forty—you figure you got ten, fifteen years left to really do something." Henry thought for a while. "So that's what I'm figuring to do," he said finally. "Do something."

"Shoot, Henry, we're just peons, you and me," Tom said. Tom was known for his way of putting things. He was nearly thirty-seven, but he was still all bones and joints and bashful blushes, like a boy, and when he talked, with his Adam's apple jumping around above his T-shirt collar, even his brother half expected that his voice would crack.

"Peons," Tom repeated. It was his favorite word for himself, and he liked to stretch it out in a long drawl—"peeeeons." But the fact was that Tom had been thinking about doing something, too. He had just bought an old jukebox for twenty-five dollars, and he was planning to fix it up, sell it, and, with his profit, buy two old jukeboxes, and then four, until he had bought and sold his way to a used-jukebox fortune.

When he and Henry got to town, Henry bought the first round in honor of Tom's jukebox, and Tom the next in honor of Henry's birthday resolution. They drank their bourbon and swapped stories about their best stunts. Tom played his guitar. Henry sang his favorite gospel song—"Love Lifted Me"—to anybody who would listen. And they agreed that the West was still a fine, promising place for a cowboy. They had such a good time celebrating, in fact, that when they left the bar they drove straight to a package store, with the idea of continuing in a pasture on the way home. An hour later, Henry appeared at the kitchen door of a big adobe house near Canadian, where a young ranching couple by the name of Robinson lived. His left eye was swollen shut, and he was holding Tom, who was barely conscious, in his arms.

Henry often ended up at Bay and John Robinson's house when he got into trouble. His own rancher didn't bother to keep a house in the Panhandle any longer, and Tom worked for an oilman whose wife did not like cowboys coming to her house. But the Robinsons were known to be in residence—a condition that had less to do with their living on their ranch than with a kind of patron's jurisdiction. Henry admired John Robinson because John was the nearest thing he knew to the old cattle barons in the movies that he liked so much—someone on the order of, say, John Wayne in "McClintock." John Robinson was just a boy, really, who had come home from studying Greek in Cambridge, Massachusetts, to take over the family ranch from an ailing father. But John understood his duty to the whole mythic enterprise of the West, and that meant he could be counted on to shield a cowboy, speak up for a cowboy, and use his extraordinary influence, as the owner of a piece of property the size of a French province, to settle a problem quickly and quietly for a cowboy, calling on his armamentarium of doctors, lawyers, friendly policemen, and obliging judges, so that a cowboy in trouble was spared the humiliation and confusion of accounting for himself. John had taken Henry on, the way a mama cow takes on a dogie, because Henry was without a rancher of his own in residence to stand up to a sheriff or an angry wife and say, "My cowboy, right or wrong"—even when that cowboy had been in the kind of fight that left his little brother with knife slashes on his back and the skin of his right hand in shreds from plunging through the glass door of a package store.

Henry waited outside the Robinsons' kitchen, with a light spring rain pattering on his black hat, until Bay Robinson looked up from the table, where she was writing out the morning's marketing list, and noticed him. Bay had been raised in Dallas, and she wore long dresses and perfume and huge pale-purple sunglasses around her house, and kept her red hair straight and shiny, like a schoolgirl's. When John first brought her to his ranch, the cowboys figured that she was one of those fluffy, fragile city girls whom ranchers' sons were fond of marrying, but Bay turned out to be a natural cowman's wife. The look that she gave Henry at the kitchen door was shrewd and maternal and amused. She helped him deposit Tom in a chair at the table, poured two drinks from a bottle of wine on the counter, and left for her library to start making phone calls. Henry sat and waited for her in the kitchen, turning his wet hat over and over in his hands and staring down at the designs on Bay's fancy Spanish floor tiles, trying to avoid the stares of the children, who came running in from their bedrooms to see what was going on.

Tom, who was beginning to revive, hung his head, stuffed his tattered hand discreetly in his jacket pocket, and began hiccupping.

"Oh, no," Tom told the children. "Ain't nothing wrong with old Tom here. Just the drizzles. The drizzles plus the hiccups."

"Come on, Tom, you been up to something," Bay said, coming back in and sitting down between the brothers. She had already called her husband, who was in Oklahoma buying a supermarket chain, as well as their lawyer, their ranch manager, and one of John's business partners with clout at police headquarters. And by the time the men drove out from town for a kitchen conference she had managed to coax a look at Tom's hand, send him down the hall to change into one of John's shirts, scrub the trail of blood off her floor tiles, and produce a platter of barbecued ribs for her visitors.

Henry did not talk to the three men who came to help him. He acknowledged them with a nod, and followed their hurried conversation about police and doctors less by listening than by a kind of furtive appraisal of the scene itself. He accepted an ice pack for his swollen eye, and with his other eye he watched the men, in their immaculately faded jeans and expensive Western shirts, talk about "Tom's troubles" while Tom himself sat patiently beside them, smiling bashfully and trying to eat his barbecued ribs with his left hand. From time to time, the men looked over at Henry, about to ask a question, but something about the way he stared back at them made them stop short. John's lawyer and the partner from town had been cultivating fine mustaches. They had let their hair grow long, nearly to their shoulders, and hair like that was a strong subject among Panhandle cowboys. When youngsters with long hair hitch-hiked across the Panhandle in the summer on their way to communes in New Mexico, a lot of cowboys took it as a duty to pick those youngsters up, drive them off onto a lonely cowpath, and remove their hair with a razor or a knife. Henry himself had taken a few hippie scalps, as he put it. He had a lot of contempt for the people he called hippies, and now he counted John Robinson's lawyer and partner among them. Actually, he had never talked with any real hippies except a couple of ranchers' sons and the Pampa and Amarillo boys who drifted into town every now and then to pick up a few days' work at the local feedyard. But he associated hippies and their long hair with some insidious Eastern effeminacy that had infected the moral landscape of the West and left a man like him nearly helpless in his outrage. Tonight in the package store, when two long-haired strangers dressed in boots and hats and flashy

Western suits took their time comparing bourbons, Henry had nudged Tom, and the two of them had taken up an old familiar litany.

"Seems like we're getting a lot of hats in this here store, Tom," Henry had started off politely.

"Yup, Henry, I'd say four hats—counting us, of course." Tom spoke so sweetly, and his smile was so shy and friendly, that one of the strangers smiled back.

"And how many hands, do you suppose, Tom?" Henry had asked him.

"Well, shoot, Henry, seems to me it takes more than a hat to make a hand."

"Now, Tom, I do believe you got a point there," Henry had said. Then he motioned toward the strangers. "I imagine our two new friends over here might just want to take them hats off."

No one had moved then except the clerk, who backed away from the counter.

"Second thought, Tom," Henry went on, "let's you and me be real nice and give these boys a hand taking off them hats."

The fight was over quickly. One of the strangers swung at Henry with a bottle. Henry kicked him back across the counter. Then the other stranger flicked open a switchblade knife, and Tom went wild. He charged blindly, leaping and kicking and butting, and the strangers fled. They took off down the street on a pair of orange motorcycles while Tom crashed through the glass door in pursuit and the clerk cried into his telephone, pleading with the lady on his party line to interrupt her nightly conversation with her married daughter so that he could call the police. Henry ran out of the store to get Tom off the sidewalk and start the pickup, but Tom was already feeling sorry about the blood and the broken bottles, and he wanted to go back in and apologize. He wanted to explain to the clerk that no one pulled a knife on Henry Blanton while Henry's little brother Tom was around. Henry had to drag him to the pickup, kicking and shouting, but finally they made their getaway. For a while, they cruised the highway, discussing what to do. There was no point in taking Tom to the hospital, where someone was sure to recognize the knife wounds on his back and report the fight to police headquarters. Then, too, Tom was modest. He would rather bleed to death than get undressed in front of a nurse, and, in fact, the last time a fight put him in the hospital he had made a fuss and insisted on sleeping in his hat and boots. There was no point in taking Tom home, either, until he was cleaned up and had a good story ready. So, a few miles past Canadian, with Tom getting weaker, Henry had turned in at the gate of the Robinsons' house. In a week or two, when Tom's hand healed, the fight tonight might enter Henry's repertoire of stories—he might brag about it then, embellishing some, until it made a dazzling stunt. But tonight Henry just sat, silent, in Bay Robinson's kitchen, looking as if he had done his duty to his brother and did not know why, suddenly, his duty seemed so humiliating to him. He waited while the men made their phone calls and Bay, setting a pan of water and some peroxide on the kitchen table, went to work cleaning Tom's hand. But when Bay noticed fresh blood seeping through the back of her husband's shirt and tried to talk Tom into taking the shirt off and letting her clean his back, too, Henry spoke up for the first time and said, "I wouldn't insist, Ma'am, if I was you."

Henry left then. He simply stood up and announced that it was time he and Tom were heading home.

Bay helped him steer Tom to the door. "Come on now, Henry," she whispered. "What were you boys up to?"

"Just celebrating, Ma'am," Henry said.

Mark Kramer

Access to the surgical theater can be gained several ways. You can be a worker in that arena, a doctor or nurse. Or you can be a patient, unconscious and unaware. As Mark Kramer explained in his third book, *Invasive Procedures,* writers are normally excluded. It is possible to submit your credentials to a hospital committee, respectfully requesting permission to watch surgery in progress, and after due consultation, be turned down. Kramer observed over one hundred operations by simply getting the permission of the surgeons doing the work. He watched them work, sat in their offices as they examined patients, and talked to their staffs and colleagues.

This excerpt gives a rare look inside the world of one of those surgeons by someone who is not a patient or physician. Kramer acts as our guide in this strange world. By revealing his own fears of cancer, he brings the subject into our world—if even our friendly guide can be afflicted, can we dare be complacent?

Kramer spent three years writing *Invasive Procedures,* of which eighteen months were devoted to field research. That kind of commitment had characterized his second book as well. While preparing *Three Farms: Making Milk, Meat, and Money from the American Soil* he spent a total of two years, part of the time living with the people on a New England dairy, a Midwest corn and hog operation, and a huge California corporate farm. Born in Brooklyn in 1944, Kramer went to Brandeis University and completed a master's degree in sociology at Columbia University. He began writing for the Liberation News Service and in 1969 moved to a rural area of western Massachusetts where his interest in farming ignited. His first book was *Mother Walter and the Pig Tragedy,* a collection of columns written about the country.

Kramer contributes articles to *The Atlantic, The New York Times Magazine,* and other magazines. He teaches a class on writing about American social issues at Smith College in Northampton, Massachusetts.

Invasive Procedures

Russell Stearne sees cancer all the time. He's used to it and he's even proud of his ability to defy the terror of it. "I think, my partner and I must have more cured cancer patients running around town," he says one day in early winter, "than any other surgical practice around here does." I feel trapped by the boast. I will have to see what he sees if I stick around. I've seen enough already: uncles, aunts, grandmothers, friends, and my very nice ex-mother-in-law.

I stick around. Every week a few cancer patients, some cured, visit Stearne's office. Then one week he announces, "I have an interesting series of appointments. There's a professor from the law school—came in through the HMO. He's had a five-year battle with cancer. They took out a perforated colon cancer to begin with, then more and more surgery, including some heroic surgery. He was working in spite of his disease for most of that time. Now he has a resurgence all over. Nothing to do for him anymore.

"Also, I have down a plastics engineer. A rare bile-duct cancer. May be job-related. It's hard to tell in these cases. He won't make it, either.

"And then there's a schoolteacher—she has cancer too. Stomach cancer. Knows what's going on. Her internist doesn't usually send me patients. But he's one of those people who does send me patients he cares for especially."

"Did the internist diagnose her?"

"She came in to me thinking she had a stomach ulcer."

"Does she have a chance?"

"About zero. That's what the long-term studies show. But some recent studies show that chemotherapy may possibly do some good. I'm going to discuss it with her."

"Will it really help?"

"Some, perhaps—for a while. But who knows? She may be a first. There's also a boy with Hodgkin's disease. He's number one on the list for this afternoon."

"You must look at these difficult visits with some dread?" I ask.

"I'm not to blame," he exclaims, quite intently. "I'm not the one who gave them cancer. I've done them good, in fact. Kept them alive. I feel good to see them, knowing there's a chance that I can help."

A giant of a teenager walks into the office, as big around as the trunk of an old maple. He's wearing gray sweat pants and sweat shirt, as if he's just come from doing roadwork.

"How's the truckdriving business?" Stearne asks as the boy opens the office door.

"Good, I guess," he answers slowly. His face, broad and red, stays expressionless. He's beyond reach of Stearne's professional manner.

"He has a couple of rocks in his neck," Stearne explains. The boy sits down. Stearne wheels his office chair forward a yard and feels the right side of the boy's neck, confirming his memory of the condition. "Remember," he asks, addressing the boy, "the last time, I told you there was a possibility that you had Hodgkin's disease? Hodgkin's has changed"—it doesn't appear to me that the boy understands, nor that the doctor is speaking to be understood—"and I think the probability is that you do have Hodgkin's disease. Now, eighty-five percent of the people who we see who get it, get over it completely, through X-rays, and medicine—"

A ringing phone interrupts the presentation. I wonder how Stearne, with a hundred or so cancer patients in various stages of learning their fates, fighting, raging, accepting, keeps track of the delicate progress of these hundred relentless narratives. Stearne remains on the phone for a full five minutes, arguing with some bureaucratically powerful nurse. The boy stares out the window and doesn't twitch a muscle. It seems Stearne has dictated yesterday's incoming-patient reports after the closing time stipulated by hospital regulation for new admissions. The nurse wishes to remove the name of a patient from the next day's surgery roster. Stearne is polite, claiming that he was on hold, awaiting his turn to dictate the admitting information, at three minutes before deadline, and that he appreciates the nurse's help in keeping things just as they are. He finally hangs up, assured that, just this once, she will make an exception for him.

"—and a bit of tissue from your neck, I think, and that hard gland under your arm there, would make it diagnostic. Also, the further you get from the source, into the armpit, the more your symptoms tend to be diagnostic—"

The patient still looks uncomprehending, unshaken, inert. Stearne notices. "You have a treatable cancer," he says. "Cancer of the lymph glands, I suspect. We need to get you in for a biopsy. The nurse can schedule it out there for you." He points out into the hallway.

"O.K.," says the boy, getting up. He grips the office door, then, holding on to it, asks, "You want this door shut or leave it open?"

Why can't he slam it, trap the bad news inside? I admire his defenses. This is the moment he hears that fate has turned on him. I ask Stearne about his own feelings: Does it bother him, telling the boy that kind of news?

"I tell maybe fifty patients a year that they have cancer—usually breast or colon. I didn't give it to him. It doesn't have emotional impact on me. I probably cure more than I don't. The patients get more of a charge out of it than I do."

"What if you were in the patient's shoes, and another doctor were giving you the news that *you* had cancer?"

"I don't know how I'd feel. Probably about the same as I feel telling them they have it."

Can it be that to be professionalized is to lose touch with all fear, all sense of the desperate sweetness of life? Can one become so mechanistic in comprehending one's own somaticism that one might actually *have* cancer dispassionately? And how long might the dispassion endure? Past the first ten pounds of weight loss? Twenty? Fifty? It's as if you might live on and on if only you can keep from noticing. For a few years, a late senior partner of Stearne's assisted in operations upon cancer patients, all the while keeping his own prostate cancer in check with hormonal treatments. The partner's insularity, like Stearne's, was awesome.

The law professor is in next, quickly seated in the armchair by the window. He and the truckdriver must have passed each other in the corridor, both lost in their own concerns. Did either notice the other? The professor is stooped, gray-haired and gray-skinned, curled in on himself in the bright-green chair—a garden snail on a leaf. He looks up at Stearne through groggy eyes, only half engaged by this late chapter of an old ordeal. There's nothing more to do. The questions that come from Stearne are kindly ones, about how he's doing, and if he's comfortable, and does he need or wish anything. "You can call me anytime," Stearne says. The professor just nods, and then he's gone, out through the open door, dying on his own now.

The receptionist says the plastics engineer has rescheduled for tomorrow. I'm glad. One fewer.

Later, the teacher with stomach cancer comes in. Rather, she slips in sideways, as if entering a lecture late, hoping not to be noticed while things go on normally, as they must have before her illness. She is powerful, imploding with the force of new terror. She returns nothing to the outer world as she moves in slowly, wide-eyed and stoop-necked. Stearne studies her appearance, and who knows what he thinks. My thoughts fly out toward her and fragment, gone. She's very thin. She says, quietly, "Can't keep food down." She makes an apologetic shrug. It's the only thing she says. She folds into the easy chair.

Her husband has walked in behind her, a big, sandy-haired man, a fireman. He doesn't touch her or look at her. He sits across the room and squints. "I traded time with someone so I could make it after all," he says. They have two kids. "Kluzko," he says, introducing himself, wrapping a hand like a rolled roast around the doctor's.

On Stearne's desk is a letter from a surgeon in Boston:

> I saw your nice young patient, Bea Kluzko, in consultation on Wednesday. She and her husband are certainly most delightful and pleasant people, and it is sad to see such a terrible problem thrust upon them. . . . The diagnosis is poorly differentiated adenocarcinoma of the stomach.

The cancer is gone now, along with the rest of the stomach. Stearne has told me that after removing the mass, he searched and found no visible metastases—"no macroscopic spread," is how he put it— but that he had taken little reassurance from that fact, because of the sort of tumor he found. "The numbers aren't good," he said to me. "They give us little reason to hope."

What he tells her now, however, is that a five-year study of adjuvant chemotherapy in gastrointestinal cancer has "given good evidence that we benefit people by giving this chemotherapy." He tells her she's fortunate, because an oncologist, a tumor expert, who helped in that very study lives in a city just half an hour away.

She doesn't ask him about the therapy; she doesn't even ask what he means by "benefit people." She's doing battle with the real issue. She nods a nod of assent so slight it might have been just an isolated tremor. Stearne says, "I'll have the oncologist's office call tomorrow to schedule a first visit," and she slips back out of the office, followed by her husband.

Then Stearne calls the oncologist. He carefully describes the patient and her disease, then stresses her youth, her children, her career, her happy marriage, and he tells the oncologist he plans to suggest chemotherapy to her. The oncologist may be resisting the idea that he can help, because Stearne says, "What else can we do?" The oncologist must finally be persuaded. "Then you'll call her tomorrow? Good."

Stearne dictates his record of her visit at once. It ends with the curious sentence: "Prognosis is, of course, guarded." The prognosis is, of course, death. And what is actually guarded is Stearne.

Still later, I follow Stearne into an examining room. He sees a man who got kicked by a horse. He sees a newlywed, examines her breasts and tells her that the lumps she has felt there do not alarm him.

My ear alarms me. I have thought about it now and then for a month or two, and it scares me, right now. I have a small disturbance of the skin, right on the upper tip of the left ear. It looks pearly in the mirror, like a spot of acne twenty years behind the times. Since I first noticed it, it has gotten slightly larger, birthed a tiny calf next to it, and it hurts when I sleep on it, although not very much. I've planned vaguely to mention it to the family doctor sooner or later.

Now, in the middle of Stearne's dreadful series of patients, I touch my ear, remember my anxiety, and violate a rule of work I have long followed: I stop being whatever Stearne makes of me and become a patient. May I steal a minute of your time too? Yes. Would you look at my ear? Certainly. He points to the stool under the strong lamp, and as I sit, starts to dial the telephone. He holds a receiver in one hand and tugs at my ear with the other, aligning my head so he can see well.

"Yup, cancer. You got cancer," he says. "Hello, dear," he says into the phone. He chats on the phone while I wait, about when it would be convenient to admit some patient to the hospital. He flirts with the "dear" on the other end. I start to write down what he says so I can show how he flirts. Instead I write down how I feel just then, because the first moment of detachment passes, and I know it's me who has cancer. The hair on the back of my neck stands straight out; I feel it rising. My notes:

1. Dissociation. Oh, he's just making another comment.
2. Numbness.
3. Go bugeyed, start breathing heavily, and panic.

The panic is firmly installed by the time Stearne hangs up the phone and grabs the ear again. I'm a patient now; he addresses not me but the attending nurse. "Classic. Basal cell. Wrong age, wrong place, for squamous. See the pearl color, the teardrop shape? And it's in a location that is subject to these lesions from sunlight. Classic."

"So that's what it looks like?" I hear the nurse remark to him.

"Tell me something reassuring," I say. I laugh nervously, to show him I'm a sport. I'm still looking nearly directly into the hot, bright examining lamp.

Dr. Stearne lets go of my ear. I turn toward him. "I'm ashamed of you," he says to me. "You really are neurotic. I thought you were a medical insider now. Don't you know the body's just a machine and it breaks down every once in a while?"

"This is *my* body breaking. You've just told me I have cancer."

"Skin cancer. Nobody dies from skin cancer."

"What do I do?"

"Come into the office tomorrow, when I have more time, and I'll take a biopsy, just to confirm it. I'm pretty sure it is. Next week you'll have an answer—we'll get the results on Monday or Tuesday. Then we'll cut it out. Just a little spot. Then maybe we'll need to freeze it, or electrocauterize the area too."

"It doesn't spread?"

"Not basal cell. It's probably basal cell. Your age, the location. Squamous looks the same. That one sometimes spreads."

I say nothing. I feel foggy, far off, askew from the body sitting bolt upright in the chair by the light and the examining table.

The next patient comes in. My notes say:

Tall, gangly, red-haired male student. Friendly. Has boil on sinewy leg. Treated topically. Surgeon shows restraint.

After the boy leaves, I come to my senses. I decide (as patient advocates recommend nowadays) to take control of the situation. "Russ Stearne," I say, "I want you to do me a favor. You've known me for over a year, and you'd have to call me an anxious sort, probably, insider or not. I want you to take the biopsy now. I want you to put it in a specimen jar, and I'll take it over to the hospital lab myself. I want you to mark it 'Rush,' and I'll hope to get an answer tomorrow, and not to have to wait through the weekend."

Stearne shrugs the sort of shrug I've seen him use on old persons too thick to understand the obvious. Like them, I ignore it. He shakes his head, and his palms rise. "I know what it is already. Don't you trust your doctor?" He's teasing me about the shift in roles. I regret it already. "It's just skin cancer. Don't worry about it." I still look worried about it. He shrugs again, this time a shrug of consent.

"Here, sit down on this table. Put your legs up. Now lie on your right side." I've heard these mechanical orders often, and have watched impassively while patients' bodies have moved into position for examination. He swings the harsh lamp back over to the burning ear.

"It's not anything I'd worry about," he says. After the line-up of cancer patients, and Stearne's dispassionate reception of them, I take little comfort in knowing what he wouldn't worry about. I think of saying so, but suddenly feel docile, whipped. I elect politeness. *I* know the diplomacy of survival.

"I'm not cutting you," he says, coming at me with a syringe of novocaine, and then with a pair of scissors. Oh, he remembers all our old chats. "This may sting." I've heard it before. He injects. It doesn't sting much. I think of writing this passage, and wonder if I will write it in the midst of a struggle against dying.

He cuts. "I fix people," he says as he cuts, still quoting himself. I hear the sound of gristle dividing against the edge of the blade. He readjusts the light. It's stronger in my closed eye. I feel only a tugging at the ear. I hear the cutting sound again.

I feel elated at being treated. I feel elated.

"I took them both right away. In the jar." I unsquint my eyes and sit up. He's writing on the tag attached to a squat jar. The tag says Rush.

I'm too bleary to rush. I climb down slowly from the table, as Stearne's patients do. I touch gauze and tape on the ear, and smell the fresh adhesive smell. In the jar the devil looks tiny, curled in on itself, afloat, drowned succubus. I walk out, thanking him, jar in hand, through a waiting room filled with more patients. I'd rather be carrying a fecal sample in Macy's parade.

I drop the jar, tied round with its label, at the lab. I have become the loathed thing. The test may come back tomorrow, they tell me there, and then again it may take the weekend. We are busy here. I drive home. Yesterday I felt the false pride of being the doctor's pal. Today I know the score; I'm nobody special. Cancer comes like the common cold. One breath away from health, achoo, and the ordeal, the long ordeal, is started. It's as easy as a sneeze.

I don't mind the death part. What scares me is the process of hopelessness, of having no prospects, of progressive incapability frustrating ambition. I repent my every wasted moment. I eat supper without tasting, and make life hard for everyone around. I phone the family doctor and she confirms that I'm "overdramatizing"—that even if it proves to be cancer, it is indeed almost certainly basal cell, and, indeed, she's never heard of anyone dying from it who has caught it this early, or even much later.

I can't desist, though. I dream awful dreams in spite of strong drink and kind words. By now I'm not mourning just the particulars of my case, but the awful prospect of cancer; it's a burden of modern times, the internal equivalent of nuclear war. The first skirmish has started. Cancer kills one in four, I read. One man in eighteen loses a lung. One woman in fourteen, a breast. Colons go, stomach, bladders, testes, the blood, pancreases, livers, ears. Death stew.

By the light of day, I listen to reason. I calm down. Stearne calls with a mean temptation. While we talk I'm aware that I'm jealous of him because he's growing wholesome cells only. He says, "I've got a lung to do first thing tomorrow morning." I say I'll be there; I've never seen chest surgery. I'll just hang on to my hat and go right back to work, I think.

Then it's later and I'm on my way, blank, detached, wary. In the hospital corridor, the hospice posters mean me, not my ex-wife's poor mother. I feel as if I'm visiting surgery for the first time and not the hundredth.

"It's bloody, going into chests," Stearne says. "On the way in there's well-vascularized tissue." The patient lies on her side, knocked out, with a table of tools swung out right over her head. She's sunk in anesthesia, buried in green cotton. A teardrop section of rib cage shows through the draping, swabbed the familiar Betadine orange. Stearne has begun below the woman's breast, cutting a sweeping curve along the contour of a rib, ending halfway down the left side of her back.

He cuts not with a knife but with the electric scalpel that cauterizes as it cuts. The room, to my regret, soon smells of steak. "This makes things neater until we get through the area here filled with all these small blood vessels—they tend to be a little messy," Stearne says over the sparking of the device. "There, now we're going through the latissimus dorsi, the wide muscles of the back . . ." He puts two rubber-clad fingers under the wide muscles of the back, draws the muscles up away from the underlying surface, and cuts through them. As blood oozes, he clamps and stitches the cut vessels. He looks around. His gaze settles on the tamest, oldest nurse.

"Charlene, how long does pulmonary surgery usually take?" He asks the question with a baby-faced grin.

Charlene shrugs. Other nurses, caught in his gaze in turn, shrug. His partner, Ted Culver, shrugs satirically. Even the anesthesiologist, staying out of trouble up at the end of the table, shrugs. Another shrug fest. Stearne is meeting with resistance.

"Three hours, frequently, doesn't it?" he asks the nurse.

"I suppose. It depends on the kind of pulmonary surgery, Doctor." Her answer will have to do.

"Well, this is going to take an hour and half." He dissects inward, buzzing, stitching, deepening the smile he's drawn across the absent patient.

"This is the rhomboid muscle, attached to the scapula," Stearne mutters. After a while he moves to the other end of the incision, ". . . and this is the serratus muscle." He again forces his gloved left hand under muscle, then halves the separated fascia with the cautery. "My partners and I have a lot of patients walking around town cured of cancer," he says.

"Yesterday was her birthday," says the anesthesiologist, looking up from his charts. I imagine the wistful comments that must have been exchanged in her hospital room last night.

"We usually take a rib out to do this. In this case"—Stearne pauses and counts ribs—"it's the fifth rib." With a sculptor's tool, a long-handled blunt chisel, he strips flesh from the candidate rib. Three firm slides of the tool and it's clean white bone. He works the chisel through the cartilage at the rib's chest end. He holds the rib up.

"Spare rib," he says, laying it on the specimen cart.

"There isn't much meat on it," the anesthesiologist says, cheerily. I remember the ability of anesthetized patients to register what is said in the operating room.

With the rib out, her lung shows, pale purple, like the skin of a boiled tongue, and as shiny as if it had been waxed and buffed.

Stearne lays down the chisel and the cautery, and reaches his hand, knuckles up, through the slot into the chest. He slides his fingers far up along the inside of the chest wall, toward whatever has made the shadow on the X-ray that hangs on the wall across the room.

Then, in a flat voice, a tone laden with disappointment and guardedness, he says, "Ooh, boy. This tumor has gone up into the chest wall."

It's a verdict. The prisoner shows no emotion. She is fitted with a rib spreader. It resembles a large woodworker's clamp, F-shaped and a foot long. A crank and gearing are built into the middle intersection, and prongs come out from the extremities of each crosspiece, like the legs of a trivet. Stearne fits the prongs of one crosspiece against the fourth rib, and the prongs of the other against the sixth rib. He cranks. The jaws spread, and the opening in her body, mail-slot sized, doubles in width. An elegant tool. It's easy to see more lung now, and easier to take stock. He reaches back up to feel the tumor again.

"This may not be operable at all," he says. "You got blood?" he asks the anesthesiologist. "If I take it out, it might be bloody. It comes right over to the aorta." He's feeling, reporting, working his hand in, feeling farther in. He shakes his head, draws his hand out, and sighs.

On the face of the upper lobe of the exposed lung, I see hundreds of black dots, as if someone had dabbed a fountain pen again and again against purple blotting paper. I ask about them.

"Carbon particles."

"That's not the cancer?"

"No, anyone who smokes has lungs like this. Also anyone who lives near a factory, or beside a busy road. Anyone who works in smoky areas, or where there's carbon dust. Anyone who lives in a city. Environmental pollution looks like this."

I look closely at the black spots. I wonder if the goals of environmental preservation would be more easily accomplished were we all transparent, like tropical fish—if our purple lungs showed their every foul soot spot right through glassy skin.

Stearne's partner, Culver, reaches in and feels the tumor. Stearne feels the tumor more, and describes what he finds for Culver's verification: "The tumor surrounds the upper lobe and impinges on the artery there. Also on the aorta. Also on the chest wall. The inter-lobar fissure is complete." Culver nods. Stearne thinks, and says decisively, "I am going to take the bulk of it out. If the arteries and veins are encased in tumor, you can't. At least in her case the artery isn't."

"I'm starting a unit of blood," the anesthesiologist says, "and, let's see, pressure reading, one-ten."

Stearne cuts, deep in the wound. He begins the resection in earnest. He's focused, civil, at his tamest when in action. He talks constantly to Culver as he works. "I can get a tie around here. . . . Yes. . . . This will be a palliative operation. She'll have radiation too. . . . Let's see if I can get a little more, distally . . . a clip for there. . . . I think there's a big patch under there . . . yes. . . . Maybe it'll be better using this. . . . Artery's good around here. . . . I've got to find the other branch now. . . . Theoretically, without this lobe she'll stand X-ray therapy better because there'll be less broken-down flesh for the body to cart away. . . . I can get to the end of that. . . ."

Culver, who has been assisting inside the wound, snipping sutures, probing and shoving tissue in order to display work better for Stearne, interrupts the monologue. "It's a total loss," he says. "Too much tumor." It's the first time he's spoken.

Stearne backs up and pauses. He looks over at the nurse who wouldn't tell him how long pulmonary surgery takes, and asks her a new question: "How are you, Charlene?"

"Fine."

"That's good, because if you weren't, it would ruin my day."

He has the lung freed of most of its attachments. He folds it up out of the wound and invites me to inspect, gesturing into the cleared opening, like a host leading a guest into the parlor, graciously. The incision now is a foot and a half long, half a foot wide, and a foot deep. In past the frame of the F-clamp, the gauze-cloaked sidewalls slope toward a pink, pulsing floor.

"That's the pericardium at the bottom, with the heart just inside it, making it bounce."

The pericardium shakes with sharp, healthy pulses. It is veined, like a leaf. Its rhythm matches the peeps of the anesthesiologist's heart monitor. The abstracted sound I've heard on every hospital visit for a year signals this throbbing flesh. I back away, listening.

"It's a very normal beat," the anesthesiologist says, and sings along: "Ta-deet, ta-deet, ta-deet." According to the clock on the wall, we are an hour into the operation. According to Stearne, we have half an hour to go.

He takes up his monologue again: "Now then, this *is* one large branch going down there. . . . Do you have a fine stitch to put into the pulmonary artery? . . . There, you're O.K., yes. . . . We control all arteries to the lower lobes, then the veins. . . . Over here the lobes aren't connected together by tumor . . . yes, they're not. . . . That's easier than when they're stuck together by lung cancer. In a case like that, though, a surgical stapler can quickly develop a fissure between the lobes. That's one good use for it. . . . O.K., let's flip the lobe over. . . ." The tumorous lobe, dangling from a tongs, comes up out of the incision further.

I see the cancer.

It's smog yellow, and it lurks just under the surface of the lung, smeared around in patches, like skin-covered cottage cheese. Stearne clips in around the strands of tissue that still tie the lobe into the lung, right down at the edge of the pericardium. In a moment, the lobe is attached by only one thin strip of tissue. He draws the lobe well clear of the wound. I can see across the arch of the chest interior to the far wall of the rib cage. The surgical lamps glow down through the skin. The view across the interior is like looking up at the arches and spokes of a pink beach umbrella.

Stearne points to the strand of lung running into the wound from the nearly severed lobe. "Is this anything important, Charlene?" he asks. "Is it O.K. if I tie and cut this thing here when I don't know what it is?" He cuts. "Have you any 3–0, Charlene?"

Charlene passes along 3–0. Stearne stitches. Charlene gingerly lifts the detached lobe of lung with a tongs and drops it into a stainless steel pan. She carries the pan away from the operating table, to the small cart by the door. I walk over to look. The lobe sits next to the rib. As I watch, it hisses, like a cut tire, sagging, losing life.

The same noise seeps from the severed bronchus, inside the patient, where the lobe joined the next lobe down. Stearne closes the breach with more 3–0, and says to the anesthesiologist, "O.K., hyperventilate the patient." He spills a gallon jug of warmed saline solution into the patched chest cavity and stands watching the pooled water, alert for bubbles that would indicate leakage of air. When he's sure she's airtight, he drains the chest with an aspirator, then closes.

Stearne relaxes. His shoulders unhunch. "Many people don't have too much pain from this operation," he says, "but it's variable."

"Official name of operation for the form?" a nurse asks. Behind her, two other nurses count sponges, then needles.

"Left upper lobectomy." The incision, stitched up, looks like two enormous pursed lips, beaming at the surgeon. He says, to no one in particular, "Taking out the tumor won't affect the length of survival. It may make her more comfortable. It will stop her from being short of breath; tumor infiltrated the lobe we removed, so that blood pumped in there didn't oxygenate. Now all the lung she has will oxygenate blood for a while. Lung cancer is very bad."

Charlene is crawling around the floor at Stearne's feet. "I dropped a needle," she says. She finds it, by a leg of the table. She groans getting back on her feet, and sighs, "I'm getting old."

Unburied from the draping, the patient is eased from table to cart. Her rib and lung leave the room on their own cart, draped now as if the cargo were a whole tiny cadaver. We follow in a line as the patient is wheeled down the hall to the recovery room. New nurses—among those in the hospital with the greatest opportunity to exercise their skill freely—flurry around the bed as it rolls in to the recovery room. Stearne hands one the intravenous jars he's held aloft during the short journey. The patient awakens quickly, and must, somewhere in her filling mind, hear a nurse, a big, sweating, red-haired nurse, talking quietly into her ear: "We're going to be all around you, honey. You want your blanket pulled up? Is your hand hurting? There's tubes in it is all."

A while later, Stearne meets me in the hospital parking lot. "Guess what?" he says. "You don't have cancer. I've been to pathology."

Once again it takes half a minute for me to know it's really me he's talking about. I invite friends in for supper and celebrate with champagne. I smile for three days running. But things are changed; I feel the logic of the full-time healers' armor. It makes more sense. To remain raw to the chanciness of life is to remain in mourning. After a week of doubt, my life is recreated. A toast to the doers.

Stearne offers more cancer surgery. I'm eager to go, and when I do, the room seems less exotic, and more humdrum than it ever has before. Today it's a workshop with good tools, with craft going on. Wheel in the job, check the work order that comes along with it, fix things as well as they can be fixed, and on to the next. The jokes seem mild, a handy way to relieve the pressures of a long workday. Old guy who's rich asks young girl to marry him. What about sex? she says. In-frequently, he says. That one word or two? she says. On the table, another incision develops, getting down to more business.

The patient is a mild, gray-haired man not yet sixty. He appeared trim and pleasant when I met him the previous evening. His X-ray now hangs in a lightbox behind the table. The shadow of the real thing, on film, leaves the malice of the disease unannounced. Only the gross trouble shows, and the patient's fate depends on details, on millimeters' difference of location, on the timing of the accident of discovery.

Stearne returned to the hospital after office hours yesterday to study this film. He visited with the radiologist, then went upstairs to see the patient. The man's head and hands shook as Stearne talked about what the films show. "As we mentioned in the office, it is a tumor, it is in the lower bowel, and it is about a foot above the anus. From this new X-ray, it does look small and easy to remove. We'll take six inches of intestine on either side of it, and join the remaining bowel together—you'll still have a colon, just it'll be a little shorter. If things are as they appear to be, no colostomy. You'll never miss that section. Looks good."

"I can't understand it," Stearne said once we were out in the corridor. "I don't know why he shook like that after I told him it looked O.K. I still don't think I'd react like that." This time, I believe him. He's got it all stored away, maybe for keeps. The patient and I are sentient apples; Stearne's a sentient orange. Takes all types. Judge not. He gets the job done.

In the operating room, Stearne has dissected down to the site of the shadow. He grabs hold of the loop of gut harboring the offending tumor and feels it.

"It's contained," he announces. "This feels favorable." He works it with his fingers. "It's easy to mobilize. There are no attachments. It isn't through the wall of the intestine. I can't see it now, and that's a *very* good sign." He reaches up, then, under the intestines, and feels the lobes of the liver, where bowel cancer usually migrates, where bad news might still announce itself. He searches the liver with his fingers, and as he searches, he glances up over his shoulder, catching the eye of one of the younger nurses, one he knows cares especially about the fate of patients, and he says, "There appear to be no metastases present, left lobe, and . . . none present, right lobe. It's clean." No sighs of relief, but everyone smiles. The eyes of masked faces do look nice.

A life is being saved. A newcomer might not see the rejoicing, but the procedure becomes downright festive. Nobody dances in place and kicks up heels. It looks like yesterday and last week, except that the laughter sounds less strained. The staff and the surgeon have reason to feel useful and not helpless. To be on the job now justifies much other labor amid hopelessness. The cleaned end of the severed gut, clamped off half an inch back by duck-billed hemostats, is fat, roseate, like a baby's pout after feeding. Stearne praises a prompt surgical technician straightforwardly, saying, "She's good. She's very good," and even when he repeats the line every now and then until its meaning changes, he draws a chuckle or two.

As he jokes, he works, more gymnastically than he must during most operations. The surgical field is deep in the patient, diagonally in from the navel, between and below the iliac arch, and on down into the funnel of space inside the pelvic cradle. He sews with curved needles held in long-handled clamps. He is bent over, and under his gown, his hips rotate as he stitches, tests stitches, and stitches again. "She's very good." His voice echoes out of the damp abdomen. His surgical fields always end up looking splendid. A lattice of clamps suspends the site of his stitching in Fulleresque tension. "She's very good." He hands the severed foot of gut over to a nurse, for transportation to the pathology lab. He inserts a machine that looks like a caulking gun and is in fact a colon stapler into the patient's anus, from the outside, slides it up the stub of gut still extending inward, then slides the free end of the man's colon down onto the machine's tip from the inside, trims and tucks until all tissue is nicely placed, and then fires off a ring of stainless staples.

Sealed, clean, cancer-free, the patient is again topologically identical to healthy persons, a torus, a doughnut, a solid with a hole through it, blood brother once more to every living thing further evolved than a paramecium. Into this patient, too, Stearne dumps a gallon of warm saline, as matter-of-factly as he might fill up a washbasin. No bubbles. Job done. He closes quickly. He sutures the scar with monofiliment. He helps the very good technician undrape the patient. When he comes to the penis, he pauses and regards it. It's pointed chinward, taped, a catheter emerging from its tip.

"You want to see an example of passive aggression?" he asks.

He yanks the adhesive off the penis, perhaps more forcefully than is necessary.

"There," he says. "Now I don't have to go home and kick the dog."

Another week or two go by and I chat with Stearne by phone. I'm planning to write about my brief experience as a patient facing the prospect of having cancer. Could he tell me again what mild thing the laboratory report said I actually had, and how to spell it?

"What if I tell you I was lying and you have six months to live?" he asks.

Somewhere I realize even at this moment that the guarded man is chiding me for making much of a minor complaint—and at that, one that turned out to be even more minor than he'd predicted. But my will, so recently strengthened, to interpret his comments with due allowance for his rough trade once again deserts me. "First off," I answer, "I'd tell you that was a sadistic answer—then I'd ask you if it's true."

"It's not true. I wasn't lying. No cancer. You'll live a long time."

When I hang up I go hunting for the dog.

Tracy Kidder

Tracy Kidder's Pulitzer Prize-winning *The Soul of a New Machine* traces an engineering team during the creation of a new model of computer at Data General Corporation near Boston. "Flying Upside Down" was drawn from the book.

The everyday lives of ordinary people at work have often attracted literary journalists. George Orwell, for example, wrote of the workers in a Paris restaurant. Kidder's success depended upon gaining complete access to the working world of the computer design team. Just as importantly, he found metaphors to explain what they were doing.

Winning the Pulitzer Prize and the American Book Award capped a long and difficult ten years as an independent journalist. Born in 1945, Kidder attended Harvard as an English major and, after graduation in 1967, went into the Army. In the early 1970s, he held a teaching fellowship at the Iowa Writer's Workshop. His first book, *The Road to Yuba City,* covered the Juan Corona murder trial. Corona, a California farm labor contractor, was accused of killing twenty-five migrant farm workers. Kidder tried to uncover the lives of the dead men, many of them hobos who rode the rails and worked the harvests in the West. Kidder hopped freights and followed the routines of the diffuse hobo community, but to his dismay, their world was largely impenetrable. The particular hobos he wanted to learn about could no longer speak and they left behind few records.

Over the following ten years Kidder wrote a dozen major articles and two short stories for *The Atlantic.* His topics included nuclear power, Washington politics, the mistreatment of disabled Vietnam veterans, solar energy, the development of Long Island real estate, and the trouble with American trains. *The Soul of a New Machine* began as another magazine article, but quickly expanded into a book. Kidder spent two-and-one-half years writing it, including eight months practically living with the engineering team. In 1982 he was named a contributing editor to *The Atlantic.*

Kidder continues writing articles for *The Atlantic* and other magazines. Two book projects consume most of his time. The first, which will be called *The Air,* brings together a series of reports on the atmosphere. For the second book, Kidder watched a group of carpenters build a house. He found that the carpenters, while building a physical frame for the life of a family, were also framing issues of social class, forms of economic organization, and metaphors that touch all our lives.

Flying Upside Down

One holiday morning in 1978, Tom West traveled to a city that was situated, he would later say guardedly, "somewhere in America." He entered a building as though he belonged there, strolled down a hallway, and let himself quietly into a windowless room. Just inside the door, he stopped.

The floor was torn up; a shallow trench filled with fat power cables traversed it. Along the far wall, at the end of the trench, enclosed in three large, cream-colored steel cabinets, stood a VAX 11/780, the most important of a new class of computers called "32-bit superminis." To West's surprise, one of the cabinets was open and a man with tools was standing in front of it. A technician, still installing the machine, West figured.

Although West's designs weren't illegal, they were sly, and he had no intention of embarrassing the friend who had told him he could visit this room. If the technician had asked West to identify himself, West wouldn't have lied and he wouldn't have answered the question, either. But the moment went by. The technician didn't inquire. West stood around and watched him work, and in a little while the technician packed up his tools and left.

Then West closed the door and walked back across the room to the computer, which was now all but fully assembled. He began to take it apart.

West was the leader of a team of computer engineers at a company called Data General. The machine that he was disassembling was produced by a rival firm, Digital Equipment Corporation, or DEC. A VAX and a modest amount of adjunctive equipment sold for something like $200,000, and as West liked to say, DEC was beginning to sell VAXes "like jellybeans." West had traveled to this room to find out for himself just how good this computer was, compared with the one that his team was building.

West spent the morning removing the VAX's twenty-seven

printed circuit boards. He'd take one out, study it, make a few notes, and then put it back. These boards were flat plates, each about the size of a shirt cardboard. In regular columns across their surfaces lay small rectangular boxes. Each of these boxes enclosed an integrated circuit, or "chip"; if bared and examined under a microscope, the chips would look like mazes—imagine the wiring diagram of an office building inscribed on a fingernail. It's possible to get inside the chips, inside the littlest boxes inside the boxes that constitute the central works of a modern computer, and, bringing back the details, to create a functionally equivalent copy of a machine. "Reverse engineering" is the name for that art, and it takes time and equipment. West called such engineering "knock-off copy work." He had a simpler purpose. He was not going to imitate VAX; he just wanted to size it up.

Looking into the VAX, West felt that he saw a diagram of DEC's corporate organization. He found the VAX "too complicated." He did not like, for instance, the system by which various parts of the machine communicated with each other; for his taste, there was too much protocol involved. The machine expressed DEC's cautious, bureaucratic style. West was pleased with this idea.

His hands in the machine, West was also studying and counting parts; many of the chips had numbers on their housings that were like names familiar to him. When he was all done, he added everything up and decided that it probably cost $22,500 to manufacture the essential hardware of a VAX. He left the machine exactly as he had found it.

"I'd been living in fear of VAX for a year," West said one evening afterward, while driving along Route 495 in central Massachusetts. "I wasn't really into G-2. VAX was in the public domain, and I wanted to see how bad the damage was. I think I got a high when I looked at it and saw how complex and expensive it was. It made me feel good about some of the decisions we've made."

West was forty but looked younger. He was thin and had a long narrow face and a mane of brown hair that spilled over the back of his collar. These days he went to work in freshly laundered blue jeans or pressed khakis, in leather moccasins, and in solid-colored long-sleeved shirts, with the sleeves rolled up in precise folds, like the pages of a letter, well above his bony elbows. He expostulated with his hands. When dismissing someone or some idea or both, he made a fist and then exploded it, fingers splaying wide. The gesture was well known to those engineers who worked for him.

Long index fingers inserted under either side of the bridge of his glasses signified thought, and when accompanied by a long "*Ummmmmmmmmh*" warned that some emphatic statement was near. Indeed, West made few statements that were not emphatic. Seen at the wheel of his shiny red Saab, he made a picture of impatience. His jaw was set; he had a forward lean. Sometimes he briefly wore a mysterious smile. He was a man on a mission.

"With VAX, DEC was trying to minimize the risk," West said, as he swerved around another car. "We're trying to maximize the win . . ."

In the early 1960s, several companies began to manufacture computers that were much less powerful but also much smaller and cheaper than the machines then in existence. These new devices were called minicomputers. By 1978, the increasingly imprecise term "minicomputer company" could be applied to about fifty corporations. Minicomputer sales had grown from about $1.5 million worth of shipments in 1968 to about $3.5 billion in 1978, and most interested parties believed that the business would continue to grow by about 30 percent a year.

DEC was one of the first minicomputer companies, and it was the largest corporation in this segment of the computer industry: the IBM of minis. In 1968, three young computer engineers who left DEC and a salesman from another company founded Data General. Minicomputer companies were known for playing rough; Data General had acquired a reputation as one of the roughest of them all. "The Darth Vader of the computer industry" was the way one trade journalist described the company. Meanwhile, Data General thrived. It made good computers inexpensively and it managed its business adroitly. By 1978, Data General was taking in about half a billion dollars a year. It was only ten years old, and its name had just been added to the list of the nation's 500 largest industrial corporations. Moreover, for most of its history Data General had maintained the highest profit margins in the computer industry, after IBM.

Making computers is a risky enterprise. Young, successful computer companies often get into serious trouble, largely because success in their business means rapid, stressful growth. Data General grew by more than 30 percent a year for a decade, and all the while the technology of computers was changing.

At some computer companies, it has fallen mainly to engi-

neers, working below decks, as it were, to make the first decisions
about new products. Data General was such a company, and one
often heard that its president, Edson deCastro, himself a very successful computer engineer, liked "self-starters." By 1978, though
the company's balance sheet had never looked better, it was becoming apparent that Data General had need of initiative from its engineers. Into the world of the minicomputer had come a new kind
of machine—the 32-bit supermini. DEC's VAX was the best-
known example of such a machine, and several other of Data General's rivals had also produced superminis. Data General, meanwhile, had yet to offer one of its own. "A disaster," Tom West said
of this situation.

The most important characteristic of the 32-bit mini was its
system of storage. Storage in a computer resembles a telephone system, in the sense that every piece of information in storage is assigned a unique number, so that it can be readily found. If the
standard length of a phone number is seven digits, then enough
unique numbers can be generated to serve the needs of New York
City; but if a three-digit area code is added, every telephone customer in America can have a unique number. The 32-bit supermini
was a computer with an area code. Since the advent of Data General, most minis had been "16-bit" machines. The standard length
of the numbers that such a machine assigns to items in its storage is
16 bits, 16 binary digits. A 16-bit machine can directly generate only
about 65,000 unique numbers for its storage system. A 32-bit machine, however, can directly generate some 4.3 *billion* different
numbers.

All interested parties agreed that the demand for superminis
would be huge; the market might be worth several billion dollars by
the 1980s, some said. If Data General failed to produce a 32-bit machine or something equivalent, it could expect to lose some old customers, and, perhaps more important, it would forfeit one of the
next decade's best opportunities for gaining new business. The company could not now be the first to enter this new market, but that
was all right; sometimes it was better not to be first. However, Data
General had to field a suitable machine fairly soon, because customers get married to computer companies in intricate ways, and
once they've married elsewhere they're often gone for good. Time
was running out, Tom West maintained. "We're gonna get
schmeared if we don't react to VAX," he said.

Data General's headquarters stand near the intersection of two superhighways some thirty miles west of Boston. It is a low-lying brick building with TV cameras mounted on the corners of its roof, and all in all looks like a fort. Its official name is Building 14 A/B. Inside, it is essentially divided into an upstairs and a downstairs. The executives work upstairs. The lower level of Building 14, subterranean in front and at ground level in back, is another country. It belongs mainly to engineers.

West led the way down into this region one evening in the late fall of 1978, through confusing corridors and past mysterious doors that were locked up and bearing signs that read "RESTRICTED AREA." Then the hallways ended, and all around, under fluorescent light, lay fields of cubicles without doors. Their walls stood too low for privacy. Most contained a desk with a computer terminal on it. In many, there was a green houseplant. Green plants poked their heads, like periscopes, above the cubicles' walls. "The great statement," said West, gesturing at the foliage and smiling faintly. "It's basically a cattle yard."

By day, the basement held a homogeneous-looking throng, made up largely of young white males wearing jeans and corduroys and hiking boots; few wore neckties, but neat grooming was the rule. Now and then a visitor might catch a glimpse of a fellow with wild hair, dressed in Army-surplus clothes, but such figures were rare.

West's team specialized in the design and development of the hardware of new computers. It was only one of several such teams at Data General, and it was not the largest or, in the fall of 1978, the most prestigious. It was named the Eclipse Group, after the current generation of 16-bit Data General computers. The Eclipse Group, which numbered about thirty then, occupied a portion of a field of cubicles and a few narrow, windowless offices, one of which belonged to West. No sign announced that this was the group's territory. At night, it did seem that more lamps burned on in the Eclipse Group's offices and cubicles than in many other parts of the basement. At some moments during the day, the area had the atmosphere of a commuter train, and at others it reminded one of a college library on the eve of exams: silent and intent youngsters leafing through thick documents and peering into the screens of computer terminals. Conversation, especially the speech of the senior engineers, contained words and phrases such as these: a *canard* was anything false, usually a wrongheaded notion entertained by some other engineering group or other company; things could be done in ways that created *no muss, no fuss,* that were *quick and dirty,* that were *clean. Fundamentals* were the source of all right thinking, and weighty sentences often began with the adverb *fundamentally,* while *realistically* prefaced many flights of fancy. There was talk of *wars, shootouts, hired guns,* and people who *shot from the hip. The win* was the object of all this sport, and *the big win* was something that could be achieved by *maximizing* the lesser one. From the vocabulary alone, one could have guessed that West had been there and that these engineers were up to something special.

In fact, they were building their own 32-bit supermini, a machine that West fervently hoped would be a worthy rival to DEC's VAX and maybe the basis for Data General's ascent in the Fortune 500. Oddly, though, West and some of the senior engineers on his team expressed the paradoxical feeling that they were building a machine absolutely essential to the company but were doing it largely on their own. "I think we're doing it in spite of Data General," said one of West's lieutenants in the middle of the project.

Setting up intramural competition among various parts of a company is an old strategy of management. Many firms in the computer industry, most notably IBM, have used it; they deliberately establish internal competition, partly on the theory that it's a useful prelude to competition with other companies. At Data General, such internal struggle had the name "competition for resources." An engineering team such as the Eclipse Group sometimes had to vie with other engineering groups for the right to produce a new computer. A year or so before, some members of the Eclipse Group had found themselves in such a competition, against a much larger team of Data General engineers, situated in North Carolina. The Eclipse Group had been competing with the team in North Carolina essentially for the right to produce Data General's supermini, what West would later call "the answer to VAX." The Eclipse Group's project had been scrapped. There had been an intramural competition for resources, and the Eclipse Group had lost. But West had decided not to abide by the decision. He had launched the Eclipse Group on another big project, one that would rival North Carolina's. Doing so had taken him some months. It had also required that he pursue some indirect measures.

West had believed that whatever its other virtues, the machine that the company engineers in North Carolina were building did not represent a timely solution to the problem that DEC's VAX posed for Data General. West also wanted to save the Eclipse Group and himself from the fate of working only on small projects. So he had borrowed ideas from anyone who had some to share, and by the very early spring of 1978 he had settled on a new plan. The Eclipse Group would build a schizophrenic computer, one that would work as both a 16-bit Eclipse and a 32-bit supermini. The proposed machine was nicknamed "Eagle."

The production of software, the programs that tell computers what to do, costs customers time and money and sometimes entails awful administrative problems. Eagle would protect old customers' substantial investments in 16-bit Eclipse software and would offer prospective buyers at least the possibility of savings in software development. At the same time, this machine would fulfill Data General's need for a computer with enlarged "logical address space." And West thought that the front office was likely to let the Eclipse Group build this computer, if it was presented correctly.

"You gotta distinguish between the internal promotion to the actual workers and the promoting we did to other parts of the company," West later explained. "Outside the group, I tried to low-key the thing. I tried to dull the impression that this was a competing project with North Carolina. I tried to sell it externally as not much of a threat. I was selling insurance; this would be there if something went wrong in North Carolina. It was just gonna be a fast, Eclipse-like machine. This was the only way it was gonna live. We had to get the resources quietly, without creating a big brouhaha."

And so, when he proposed the idea to people outside his group, West made Eagle appear to be a modest project, and he got permission to go ahead. But when he proselytized engineers who might help build this machine, it was clear that West's intentions weren't modest at all.

From the point of view of a purist ("technology bigot" is the usual term), Eagle in its vague outlines looked messy. Indeed, some engineers called the plan "a kludge," computer jargon for any ill-conceived thing. West varied his pitch to suit his audience. His general remarks ran as follows: Eagle might not look it from the outside, but in fact it was going to be a new, a fast, a "sexy" machine. It would be software-compatible with 16-bit Eclipses, not because it was going to be just another Eclipse, but because that feature would make it a "big win" commercially. They were going to build Eagle in record time, working "flat out by definition," because the company needed this machine desperately. And when they suc-

ceeded and Eagle went out the door with their names on it, as West
put it, and started selling like jellybeans, then they would all be
heroes.

Once in a while West and some members of his staff asked
themselves whether the company's president, deCastro, might not
have orchestrated everything, including their feeling that they were
on their own. Whatever its origin, though, that feeling was evidently invigorating. "Anytime you do anything on the sly, it's always
more interesting than if you do it up front," one of West's lieutenants remarked. West said, wearing his wry smile, "We're building
what I thought we could get away with."

By the spring of 1978, West had gathered a cadre of fairly experienced engineers. But to build Eagle, it was soon clear, more engineers were needed. West conferred with an old colleague named
Carl Alsing. Alsing was in his mid-thirties, a veteran, and a practitioner of an abstruse but essential craft called microcoding. He was
soft-spoken. He had a mischievous air and—in all matters, it
seemed—an aversion to the blunt approach. Alsing had joined the
Eagle project without any coaxing, and was the only one of West's
three lieutenants to do so. West regarded Alsing as one of the few
people around Building 14 in whom he could confide, and for his
part, Alsing, who was something of a watcher—a moviegoer—was
fascinated by West, especially at the onset of the project.

"We need more bodies, Alsing," West said that spring. "Shall
we hire kids?"

A famous computer engineer had remarked that he liked to
hire inexperienced engineers fresh from college, because they did
not usually know what was supposed to be impossible. West had
heard the remark. He liked the sound of it. He figured, too, that
"kids" would be relatively inexpensive to hire. Moreover, this could
be another way of disguising his true intentions: who would imagine
that a bunch of recruits could build an important new computer?
To Alsing, the idea was vintage West. It looked risky and compel-
ling. Alsing became the Eclipse Group's chief recruiter.

West and Alsing agreed that they would have to hire the very
best of that year's college graduates, even though, they told each
other, they might be hiring their own replacements, their own "as-
sassins." That was all very well, but the demand for young computer
engineers far exceeded the supply. What enticement could the

Eclipse Group offer that companies such as IBM could not? Clearly, it had to be the Eagle project itself. It was thought to be a fine thing in the fraternity of hardware engineers to be a builder of new computers—in the local idiom, it was the "sexy" job—and, Alsing knew, most big companies just didn't offer recruits the opportunity to be such a person right away. So they had what West called "a high-energy story."

But the new recruits were going to be asked to work at a feverish pace almost at once, and they'd have no time to learn the true meaning of the Eclipse Group's mysterious rite of initiation, which was known as "signing up." In the Eclipse Group, when you signed up, you agreed to do whatever was necessary for success and to forsake time with family, hobbies, and friends—if you had any of those left, and you might not, if you had signed up for too many projects before. In effect, a person who signed up declared, "I want to do this job and I'll give it my heart and soul." Formal declarations weren't called for. A simple "Yeah, I'll do that" could constitute signing up. But only veterans knew what such a statement might entail.

The Eclipse Group solicited applications. One candidate listed "family life" as his main avocation. Alsing and another of West's lieutenants were skeptical when they saw that entry. Not that they wanted to exclude family men, being such men themselves. But Alsing thought: "He seems to be saying he doesn't want to sign up." The other lieutenant pondered the application. "I don't think he'd be happy here," he said to himself.

Any likely-looking candidate was invited to Building 14, and the elders of the group would interview the young man; it was usually a young man, for female engineers specializing in the hardware of computers were still quite scarce. If the recruit was a potential microcoder, his interview with Alsing was crucial. And a successful interview with Alsing constituted signing up.

Alsing would ask the young engineer, "What do you want to do?"

If the recruit seemed to say, "Well, I'm just out of grad school and I'm not really sure," then Alsing would usually find a polite way to abbreviate the conversation. But if the recruit said, for instance, "I'm really interested in computer design," then Alsing would press on. The ideal interview would proceed in this fashion:

"What interests you about computer design?"

"I want to build one," says the recruit.

"What makes you think you can build a new computer?"

"Hey," says the recruit, "no offense, but I've used some of the machines you guys have built. I think I can do a better job."

"Well, we're building this machine that's way out in front in technology," says Alsing. "We're gonna design all new hardware and tools. Do you like the sound of that?"

"Oh, yeah," says the recruit.

"It's gonna be tough," says Alsing. "If we hired you, you'd be working with a bunch of cynics and egotists and it'd be hard to keep up with them."

"That doesn't scare me," says the recruit.

"There's a lot of fast people in this group," Alsing goes on. "It's gonna be a real hard job with a lot of long hours. And I mean *long* hours."

"No," says the recruit. "That's what I want to do, get in on the ground floor of a new architecture. I want to do a big machine. I want to be where the action is."

"Well," says Alsing, pulling a long face. "We can only let in the best of this year's graduates. We've already let in some awfully fast people. We'll have to let you know."

"We tell him that we only let in the best—then we let him in," Alsing said, after it was all done. "I don't know. It was kind of like recruiting for a suicide mission. You're gonna die, but you're gonna die in glory."

Getting a machine out the door may have been the object of the team's labors. But the main source of motivation lay elsewhere. One day an old hand (old in a relative sense, since most in the team were very young) reflected on his job: "I said, 'I will do this. I want to do it. I recognize from the beginning it's gonna be a tough job. I'll have to work hard, and if we do a good job . . . we get to do it again.' " West called this "pinball." "You win one game, you get to play another."

Salaries within the Eclipse Group were respectable. At the start of the project, in 1978, a "kid" earned about $20,000 a year. But engineers are regarded, and regard themselves, as professionals; therefore, they'd get no extra pay for overtime, no matter how many hours they worked. For previous jobs, old hands had received some stock options, and there was talk that the team's members might get options if Eagle was a success. No one in authority actually stated that promise, it seemed. "But it sure as hell was suggested!" said one of the recruits. No one in the team said he expected to receive large amounts of stock, however. Most insisted that they weren't working on Eagle for money. When they talked about rewards, they spoke mainly of pinball.

By the fall of 1978, the preliminaries were complete. The kids—about a dozen of them—were hired, the general sign-up had been performed, and at least one possible reward, the Sisyphean one, had been clearly established. They had already begun to design the computer.

Eagle took its first material form in paper, in bound books as large as atlases, which contained the intricate geometric depictions of the circuits (the "schematics"), and in a fat volume of pages filled up with line after line of 0's and 1's—the microcode, the synaptic language that would fuse the physical machine with the programs that would tell it what to do. One could think of this small library of microcode and schematics as the engineers' collected but not wholly refined thoughts on a variety of subjects. The language was esoteric, but many of the subjects were as familiar as multiplication.

Chips, the product of the era of microelectronics, took most of the pure physics and plain electrician's work from the engineers' endeavor. Some circuit designers likened the chips to a collection of children's building blocks, which they had to assemble. Some referred to the entire realm of chip design and manufacture as "technology," as if to say that putting those chips together to make a computer was something else.

Many of the chips that Eagle's circuit designers used came ready-made to perform certain operations, such as addition. Others weren't completely ready-made, but in all cases one of the routine parts of the engineers' job was transferring their ideas to silicon and wire. The hardest part was concocting those ideas. Creating Eagle's hardware was primarily a matter of constructing long skeins of logical thought. Some indication of the complexity of the job lies in the fact that Eagle would contain thousands of chips. The designers had to figure out what each of those chips should do and how to connect it to the others so that Eagle could perform all the operations in its "instruction set," and some of those operations were very tricky ones. That was only half of the job. The microcode had to be written, too. Each operation in Eagle's repertoire would be performed at the direction of a "microprogram"; each microprogram would consist of one or more (usually more) "microinstructions"; and each microinstruction would consist of seventy-five discrete electrical signals. Thus, in order to equip Eagle to perform just one of its roughly 400 basic operations, the engineers had to plan in complete detail the passage of hundreds, sometimes thousands, of signals through the circuitry. They had to ensure, of course, that there was an absolute marriage between those signals and the circuits. And they had to be sure that the performance of one operation did not foul up the performance of another. Possibilities for creating internal contradictions were numerous. The engineers had to try to anticipate all of them, and the difficulty of doing so was exacerbated by the fact that more than twenty people were creating this design in a hurry.

A brief description of the physical engine they were making could have been set to the music of "Dry Bones." This device was connected to that device, and so on. There was the microsequencer, which managed the microcode, sending it out to other parts of the engine on command from the instruction processor, or IP, which made assumptions about what basic chores the machine would be asked to perform in the future. There was the input/output controller, the IOC, which mediated between user and machine. The system cache was full of fast memory circuits and kept tabs on the IP. The address translation unit, ATU, kept track of the machine's main storage, and the control console (C/C), among other roles, acted as Eagle's therapist, by monitoring certain parts of the engine for problems and flaws, which are also known as "crocks." Practically every device relied upon the powers of the arithmetic and logic unit (the ALU), or "number cruncher," the heart of any computer; it did Eagle's math. There was also a clock, which ticked every 220 billionths of a second, telling all the rest of the machine that one microinstruction had ended and another had begun.

A great deal of the designing took place in silence, while engineers sat in their cubicles and paced in hallways and stood in their showers at home. It was the sort of work that was hard to escape, some said. One starts to imagine that trees and roads embody block diagrams and microprograms; this was the banal sensation that a member of the team had in mind when he said that it took three days for him to get Eagle out of his mind. During this time, West spent many hours in his office, staring at the team's designs of the circuitry. Usually, he drove away from Building 14 at high speed. "I can't talk about the machine," he said one evening, as he bent forward over the wheel. "I've gotta keep life and computers separate, or else I'm gonna go mad."

Some of the young engineers were assigned to work on microcode; they were called, and called themselves, "the Microkids." Those who went to work on the hardware, the actual circuitry, were known as "the Hardy Boys." This was the first real job for most of them. For some, at least, it was a strange beginning. Eager to make a good impression, and thinking it was the proper thing to do, one of the Hardy Boys set out, when he arrived, to meet his new team's leader. He went into West's office, extended his hand, and said, "Hi, I'm Dave." He would never forget that experience. "West just sat there and stared at me. After a few seconds I decided I'd better get out of there."

For a Microkid named Jon Blau, the first months on the job seemed relatively serene. After Blau was assigned his cubicle, Alsing and the group's chief secretary helped him to find his way around the in-house computing system. Then Chuck Holland, a submanager under Alsing, drew for him a clear picture of the entire microcoding job. Holland had divided the overall task into several smaller ones, and he let Blau choose one from among them. Blau decided that he would like to write the code that would tell Eagle how to perform a lot of its arithmetic. He had always liked math, and he felt that this job would help him understand it in new, insightful ways. He spent most of his first months reading, in order to prepare himself. All in all, life in the Eclipse Group did not seem very different from life at his alma mater, MIT.

Then one day in the fall of 1978, Blau was sitting in his cubicle studying Booth's Algorithm, a procedure for doing multiplication, and he was thinking to himself, "This is pretty slick," when Alsing poked his head around the partition and said, "There's a meeting."

Blau trooped into a conference room with most of the other new members of the team, joking and feeling a little nervous. There waiting for them were the brass: the vice president of engineering, another lower-level but probably important executive, and West, sitting in a corner, chewing on a toothpick. The speeches were brief. Listening intently, Blau heard all about the history of 32-bit minicomputers. They were really catching on, and the word was that DEC would probably introduce a new model of VAX in about nine months. Eagle was already late. It had to be designed and made ready for market by April, in just six months. That wouldn't be easy, but if any engineers could do it this group could, the bosses said.

Blau felt proud of himself and pleased about this first real job of his when he left that meeting. He went right back to his cubicle, and picked up Booth's Algorithm. Then, suddenly, he felt it, like a little trickle of sweat down his back. "I've gotta hurry," he said to himself. "I've gotta get this code written today. This is just one little detail. There's a hundred of these . . ."

Practically the next time he looked around him it was midnight, but he had done what he'd set out to do. He left the basement thinking, "This is life. Accomplishment. Challenges. I'm in control of a crucial part of this big machine." He looked back from his car at the blank, brick, monolithic back of Building 14 and said to himself, "What a great place to work." Tomorrow he would have to start encoding an instruction called FFAS. He told himself that this wouldn't be too hard. When he woke up the next morning, however, FFAS was upon him. "Oh, my God! FFAS. They need that code next week. I'd better hurry."

"The pressure," Blau later recalled. "I felt it from inside of me."

Around this time, a Hardy boy named Dave Epstein was dreaming up the circuits of the device called the microsequencer. No other parts of Eagle could begin to function without it, so the manager of the Hardy Boys, Ed Rasala, wanted it designed quickly. "How long will it take you?" Rasala asked Epstein.

Epstein replied, "About two months."

"Two months?" Rasala said. "Oh, come on."

"Okay," said Epstein. "Six weeks."

"I just wrote my own death warrant," Epstein thought. Six weeks didn't look like enough time. He took to staying at his desk half the night, and the microsequencer took shape more quickly than he had expected. He felt so happy that he went down the hall and told Rasala, "Hey, Ed, I think I'm gonna do it in four weeks."

"Oh, good," Rasala said.

Epstein returned to his cubicle. Then he realized what had happened. "I just signed up to do it in four weeks."

Afterward, Epstein remarked, "I don't know if I'm complaining, though. I don't think I am. I work well under pressure."

Not everyone was stimulated. One newcomer was astonished at the way the team was being managed. Hardy Boys and Microkids were making deals, saying to each other, in effect, "I'll do this function in microcode if you'll do this one in hardware." He was a little older than the other newcomers and had some experience in computer design, and he had never seen it done this way. "There's no grand design," he said. "People are just reaching out in the dark, touching hands." He was having some problems with his own part of the design and he felt sure that he could solve them properly if the managers would simply give him time. But they kept saying there was no time. No one seemed to be in control. Nothing was ever explained. The team's leader rarely even said hello to his troops. Make a mistake, however, and the managers came at you from all sides.

"The whole management structure . . ." said this young engineer. "Anyone in Harvard Business School would have barfed."

If West had heard that remark, he might have taken it as a compliment. Carl Alsing had often heard West use the phrase "flying upside down." The inspiration for it evidently came from a friend of West's who used to do that very thing in his airplane. By the term, West seemed to mean the assumption of large risks, and the ways in which he applied it left Alsing in no doubt that flying upside down was supposed to be a desirable activity, the very stuff of a vigorous life.

Ed Rasala acknowledged that West made a project more dramatic, "definitely more dramatic" than it had to be. Rasala smiled at the thought, however, and he did believe it when West said that they had to fly upside down in order to ship Eagle on time. As for Alsing, he admired West's style: "I screamed and hollered over NAND gates and microinstructions when we built the first Eclipse, but I'm too old to feel that way about computers now. This would be crashingly dull if I was doing it for someone else. West is interesting. He's the main reason why I do what I do."

First coaxing, then threatening, saying, "If you don't do this, your job description is inoperative," West had persuaded a senior engineer named Steve Wallach to work on Eagle. Wallach was a combative engineer, in his thirties. West called him "a walking dictionary and encyclopedia of computers." Wallach had not liked the looks of this machine; he had called it "a wart on a wart on a wart" and "a bag on the side of the Eclipse." But as he got deeply involved, he began to like the looks of Eagle. He was the machine's chief architect. One can think of a computer's architecture as a description of what the machine will do; it leaves out the intricate de-

tails of the computer's construction. But Wallach, who was doing a
fine job, in West's opinion, wasn't really finished before West had
the team designing printed circuit boards. Before the team could
clean up its designs, West was ordering prototype boards. Before
the prototype boards could possibly be perfected, West was ar-
ranging for the construction of final, etched boards. And long before
they could know whether Eagle would ever become a functioning
computer, West had the designers stand in front of a camera and
describe the various parts of the machine. The result of this last act
of hubris (there were many others) was a videotape some twenty
hours long. West planned to use it, when the right time came, as a
tool for spreading the news of Eagle all around Building 14. "Pretty
gutsy," he said, gesturing at the canisters of videotape in his book-
case.

West maintained that the team had to show quick and constant progress, whether or not any progress was being made, in order to get the various arms of the company interested in helping
out—in order, that is, to compete successfully for resources. One
evening he offered an additional explanation. "I'm flat out by definition. I'm a mess. It's terrible," he said. He paused, and added, "It's
a lot of fun."

Others echoed that remark. The team was working long hours
now, often twelve a day, and usually they put in six days a week.
They spoke about the harsh effects of such labor, but there was relish in their voices. One day Jon Blau said, "I've had difficulty forming sentences lately. . . . Pieces of your life get dribbled away. I'm
growing up, having all those experiences, and I don't want to shut
them out for the sake of Data General or this big project." But he
said that on the whole he was happy. He added, "That's the big kick,
that the guys with the purse strings are trusting a bunch of kids to
come up with the answer to VAX. That's what bowls me over, that
they haven't just put us in a corner somewhere, doing nothing."

Altogether, it took them about six months to dream up Eagle. By
January of 1979, two partially assembled prototypes were sitting in
the basement, behind the locked doors of a small lab. But Eagle was
not yet the equal of a hand-held calculator. The team had to make
the computer work. They had to test it, and find, identify, and repair the flaws in its design. They called this part of the project "debugging."

Eagle had been designed too quickly for prudence, and at the

onset of the debugging the question arose, in West's mind especially, whether "fatal" flaws in the design were about to be revealed.
Pursuing what he called "what's-the-earliest-date-by-which-you-
can't-prove-you-won't-be-finished scheduling," West had promised his bosses that Eagle would be debugged and brought to life by
April. Of course, one can't ever know how long a debugging will
take; the debugger delves into uncertainty. West was very nervous.
He had Rasala make up a debugging schedule that would bring the
machine in by April. Rasala put the Hardy Boys on two shifts in the
lab. They made some progress right away, and West felt relieved.
Then progress all but ceased. In the local idioms, they were moving
"three steps forward, two steps back" and the debugging schedule
was "slipping a week a week."

Right around the time when West was brooding over these
discouraging reports from the lab, he got word from his boss upstairs that the company team in North Carolina was going to miss
its deadline by a considerable margin. This was momentous news.
West had always maintained that Eagle was crucial to the company.
Now he was being proved right. He did not feel like celebrating,
though. At the moment, he was afraid that Eagle might never get
debugged, and yet he was being told that it had to be done within
four months. Everyone in the company was depending on the
Eclipse Group now; that was the message West thought he received
from upstairs. Carl Alsing thought it might be the message that
West decided to receive. "If you say you're gonna do it in a year
and you don't take it seriously, then it'll take you three years," Alsing explained. "The game of crazy scheduling is in the category of
games that you play on yourself, in order to get yourself to move."

An Englishman of the nineteenth century named Charles Babbage,
who is best known as the father of the modern computer, was one
of the first to express the principle that the way to get a job done
cheaply is to divide it into small parts that require relatively un-
skilled and therefore inexpensive labor. This is a basic principle of
modern industrial organization. The general problem that it causes,
one that has kept many consultants and psychologists busy over the
years, is that when jobs are reduced to tasks so small and simple that
the people performing them scarcely have to think, then work becomes boring and workers alienated. Most jobs were boring, in the
computer industry and elsewhere, Alsing suspected, and he'd heard
of systems of management that made even the building of a new

computer sound dull. West, by contrast, had an exalted notion of what it meant to build a new machine; he spoke of "getting way out on the edge of what your mind can comprehend." He said, "It's for the kind of guy who likes to climb up mountains." According to the theory that West expressed to Alsing, computer engineers—the "winners" among them, anyway—would motivate themselves and work passionately, their only reward pinball, if they were given real responsibility for creating a new machine. That was how Eagle was being managed.

In West's lexicon, these ideas were subsumed in the word "trust." He'd added the term to his vocabulary that fall, and the ways in which he used the word made Alsing wonder if either of them had ever heard it before. "Trust is risk, and risk-avoidance is the name of the game in business," West said in praise of trust. Although he scarcely seemed to notice them, West often bragged about the engineers on his team behind their backs, and he could draw convincing portraits of most. He believed that they were bound together by webs of mutual *trust.* They'd signed up to do a job for him, and he in turn *trusted* them to get it done. He did not attempt to keep complete control, by breaking every task into meaningless fragments.

But the debugging wasn't going well, and in the circumstances, watching from his lair of an office was strenuous work for West. Alsing had known West back in the days when West was an engineer and not a manager. In Alsing's opinion, West had been just a competent circuit designer, but he was a very adept debugger. West wanted to be a debugger again. He wanted to go into the lab and will that machine into life, Alsing thought. But if West barged in there now, he would be admitting that he didn't really trust his team. The magic would be lost. So West was staying away from the lab and worrying instead.

Almost every morning now, West called Alsing into his office, closed the door, and asked, "What's really going on in the lab, Alsing?"

Alsing made soothing replies. Consoling the boss, it seemed to him, had become part of his job, and not necessarily the easiest part.

The tension among the recruits seemed palpable. Alsing could feel it in the air, he said. One day, early in the debugging, in a cubicle right outside West's door, a couple of Microkids began to laugh—first one, then the other, then both of them, more and more raucously. Alsing was sitting nearby, in his own cubicle. He heard the laughter. In the midst of it, his phone rang.

It was West. "If you don't shut those guys up I'm gonna kill 'em!"

Alsing went out and asked the offending Microkids to do their laughing elsewhere. "It was awful," he said afterward. "I felt so embarrassed. I felt like one of those old supervisors from the 1800s who used to hire children and work them eighteen hours a day."

West took a day off and drove to the seacoast, to look at sailboats.

In the evenings, West would usually call a halt to flying upside down and climb out of the role of the tough, mean manager. He would leave his office door ajar, as an invitation, and, leaning back, his hands fallen still, he would entertain almost any visitor. But on the evening when West heard the news about North Carolina, nightfall seemed to bring him no relief. West had a wild air, as if his office were a cage. He talked on and on. He had grown perceptibly thinner in the past few months, and his hands looked outsized. As he spoke, he pushed his hair back, he drove his index fingers up under the bridge of his glasses, he made fists and exploded his fingers outward. His hands, one imagined, had primitive will; they wanted to get into the prototype Eagles.

West said that he had been told the company would be "in a lot of trouble" if Eagle weren't debugged by April. "Suppose I quit?" he asked. "I could just say, 'The hell with it,' and go . . ." Maybe he would buy a boat and sail away from Data General. No, he wouldn't do that yet. He'd see this project through, but only this project. "I'm not gonna do the next machine. I'm gonna give somebody else the chance to fail. I'm gonna get totally out of computers."

Saying he would quit was for West the equivalent of saying that he sometimes felt like quitting, and the statement was a substitute for the act itself.

The lab was borrowed space, a corner of a larger lab, sealed off by a thin steel partition. It was no bigger than most suburban living rooms and more crowded than most. Along one cinder-block wall stood the source of anxiety, a pair of Eagles. They were two bare metal frames, their tops about shoulder-high. Inside each frame, exposed to view (computers in this state are said to have their "skins" off), was a shelf full of boards. Small flat cables ran among the boards, and further inside, below the shelves, were many bundles of multicolored wire. Eagle was a tangle of wire. A system console, which looked like a large typewriter, attended each prototype, and a magnetic tape drive stood next to one. The tape drive is often shown on TV and in movies, in order to signify the presence of a working computer. Probably it is chosen because the reels of tape spin rapidly and thus prove that something is going on. In fact, though, tape drives are among the slowest parts of a computing system. The real action takes place inside and between the boards. To get a look at it, one needs special tools—boxy little machines, covered with switches, called "logic analyzers." They sat on low, wheeled carts. Each analyzer had a small screen. In essence, one engineer explained, the analyzers were cameras. They took pictures of what happened inside the computer. Eagle would do a cycle of work every 220 nanoseconds, or billionths of a second. Hooked up to some part of the machine, an analyzer could take pictures of what happened there in each of 256 cycles and play those pictures back on command. "It's funny," said Ed Rasala. "I feel very comfortable talking in nanoseconds. I sit at one of these analyzers and nanoseconds are *wide*. I mean, you can see them go by. 'Jesus,' I say, 'that signal takes twelve nanoseconds to get from there to there.' Those are real big things to me when I'm building a computer. Yet when I think about it, how much longer it takes to snap your fingers, I've lost track of what a nanosecond really means." He paused. "Time in a computer is an interesting concept."

One evening, when the lab was very still, everyone there bent to some task, one young engineer fiddled with a prototype Eagle. He was having a problem with the board he had designed. The machine, he said, kept "going to never-never land" whenever he asked it to add, and he was trying to take a picture with an analyzer of what was going wrong inside.

A straight white line ran horizontally across the analyzer's small blue screen. Nibbling his nails absentmindedly, the engineer made some arrangements around the prototype Eagle. Then, his nails still at his lips, he turned to the analyzer.

Something had happened. The straight white line on the screen had rearranged itself into a jagged shape. The young engineer stared at this picture. Slowly, he rotated his hand and took most of his knuckles in his teeth.

The jagged line on the screen was a picture of an electronic event that had taken place, in infinitesimal time, just a moment before. Though it was a common sort of picture in the lab, all of a sudden it looked dreadful.

This young engineer was, as it happened, one of those who did not enjoy flying upside down. He was capable, a Microkid said, of coming up with remarkable insights about the innards of a computer; there was no doubting his abilities. But he'd had trouble with the team's top managers and with his piece of Eagle's hardware. Many of the recruits felt that they were being given substantial freedoms. Clearly, though, time to revise was not one of them. This engineer was unhappy because he had been denied the right to fix the problem in his board in the way he thought was proper. In addition, he felt he had been insulted on a number of occasions. Perhaps most important, he felt worn out.

As the debugging continued, he felt under extreme pressure, which collected in his stomach. It hurt every day. This sort of work, even the occasional bad stomach, used to be fun. "Part of the fascination," he said, "is just little boys who never grew up, playing with erector sets. Engineers just don't lose that, and if you do lose it, you can't be an engineer anymore." He went on, "When you burn out, you lose enthusiasm. I always loved computers. All of a sudden I didn't care. It was all of a sudden a job."

One weekend some time before, he had visited what he called "a *very* liberal arts college" in Vermont. He was strolling across the campus when a young woman, bare to the waist, walked by. "She was a miracle of biological engineering," he said. "I was so stunned that I walked into the door of a geodesic dome. Although blood was pouring down the bridge of my nose, I was completely oblivious to it."

Back at Data General, one day during the debugging, his weariness focused on the logic analyzers and the small catastrophes that come from trying to build a machine that operates in billionths of a second. He went away from the basement of Building 14 that day, and left this note in his cubicle, on top of his computer terminal: "I'm going to a commune in Vermont and will deal with no unit of time shorter than a season."

Sara Davidson

Paul Fussell once noted that James Boswell's lifelong work was his journal, out of which he carved a new genre. His *Life of Johnson* became the model for "the excessively full literary biography." But Boswell's preeminent activity, *keeping a journal,* was not new. The journal dates from the ship's captain's log and was also the root of journalism. The daily account of the unexceptional begat the evening news.

The intervening years saw reporting move away from accounts of our common lives in favor of the extraordinary moments. Journalism focuses on the lives of leaders, to the extent that some might question whether an account such as "Real Property" is journalism at all. Sara Davidson returns journalism to its roots. "Real Property" grew directly from the journals she kept while living in Venice, California. She began keeping the journals in 1967 and they remain the raw material of her writing, both her fiction and nonfiction.

Davidson was born in California in 1943. She went to Berkeley and later the Columbia School of Journalism. She reported for *The Boston Globe,* and by the age of 26 was a successful freelance magazine writer. Her first book, *Loose Change,* told the story of her life and the lives of two friends from Berkeley during the late 1960s and early 1970s. Her articles have appeared in *Esquire, Harper's, Rolling Stone, Ms., The New York Times Magazine,* and *Ramparts.* Also, many were collected in the book entitled *Real Property.*

Davidson's articles have now reappeared in *Esquire* after a three-year pause during which she wrote her first novel, *Friends of the Opposite Sex.*

Real Property

What marijuana was to the sixties, real estate is to the seventies.
—Ron Koslow

"Who is the rich man?" asks the Talmud. The question has never seemed more relevant. The answer of the sages is: "He who is satisfied with what he has."

I live in a house by the ocean with an outdoor Jacuzzi. I owned, until an embarrassing little accident, a pair of roller skates. I still own a volleyball, Frisbee, tennis racket, backpack, hiking boots, running shoes, a Mercedes 240 Diesel and a home burglar alarm system. But I cannot say that I am satisfied.

I live in Venice, California. Venice is the closest place to downtown Los Angeles where it is possible to live by the water. Because of the breezes, it is relatively free of smog. It is also the only place in Los Angeles where there is street life: you are guaranteed to see people outside their cars.

A boardwalk, an asphalt path called Ocean Front Walk, runs the length of the beach. Alongside the boardwalk is a bike path, and beside it, the sand and sea. On the other side of the boardwalk are crumbling houses, new apartments, and condominiums packed tightly together. A real estate boom of such proportions has swept through here in the last five years that anyone who bought the most miserable shack for thirty thousand dollars could sell it a few years later for a quarter of a million. And the boom goes on.

Living in Venice is like living in a camp for semi-demented adults. At every hour, day and night, there are people playing volleyball, running, rolling on skates, riding bikes, skateboards, surfboards, flying kites, drinking milk, eating quiche lorraine. Old people sit under umbrellas playing checkers. Body builders work out in a sandy pen, and crowds line up three deep to perform on the paddle tennis courts. When do these people work? I used to wonder.

The residents of Venice fall into two groups: those who work, and those who don't. The latter includes senior citizens, drifters, drug addicts, hopeful moviemakers and aging hippies and surfers who have made a cult of idleness and pleasure. The other group includes lawyers, dentists, real estate brokers, accountants. Many are workaholics, attached to their jobs as they are to nothing else. They work nights and weekends, eat fast food while driving to and from their work and live alone, longing, in the silence before falling asleep, for connection.

Everyone comes together on the boardwalk. The natives own their own skates and the tourists rent them from places like "Cheapskates" and "United Skates of America." Those who have been at it a while can dance and twirl to music piped in their ears from radio headphones with antennae. The girls are dressed up in costumes like circus performers: sequined tube tops, feathers in their hair and leotards so skimpy that the nipples show and the cheeks of the buttocks hang out. The men wear shorts and vinyl racing jackets unzipped to the waist.

"Hey, that's radical," they call.

"Badass!"

Who are these people? Brown-skinned and lax, they sit around the floors of apartments, eating salads, walking out on balconies to smile and shake their towels. They are waging some kind of sexual competition through T-shirts and bumper stickers:

"I'm ripe—eat me."

"Sit on my face and I'll guess your weight."

"Skin divers do it deeper."

"Body builders pump harder."

"Plumbers have bigger tools."

"Worm fishermen have stiffer rods."

A high school cruising mentality prevails. A girl skates by wearing nothing but a body stocking and a silver g-string, but when two men stop and say, "That's some outfit. Where's the party?" her face turns to ice and she skates away.

Rolling, rolling. The wind is blowing, the palms are blowing and people are blowing every which way. I cannot walk on the boardwalk these days without feeling it in my stomach: something is wrong. There are too many people on wheels. The skaters will fall, the bikers will crash, they will fly out of control and there is nothing to hold onto.

I retreat to my house and remain indoors all weekend. This place is so odd, unique, and yet I see among the crowds on the boardwalk an exaggeration of common symptoms: the worship of wealth; the insatiable partying; the loss of commitment and ideals; the cult of the body; the wanderings of children in a sexual wilderness.

What does it mean, I ask myself, to be dressed as a strip tease artist on skates?

What does it mean to pay half a million dollars for a tacky, two-bedroom condo on the sand?

What does it mean that everyone I know is looking to make some kind of "killing"?

It means, I think, that we are in far deeper than we know.

In 1904, Abbot Kinney, who had made a fortune on Sweet Caporal cigarettes, traveled to Venice, Italy, and so loved what he saw that he conceived of building a replica in Southern California. Kinney raised the money to build canals, lagoons, bathhouses and bridges with fake Italian design, roller coasters and cottages with docks so people could visit each other by gondola. The idea caught on: "Venice of America" became a fashionable resort. Douglas Fairbanks and Mary Pickford, Charlie Chaplin and Paulette Goddard kept hideaways on Ocean Front Walk.

In time, the novelty wore off and the resort fell to seed. The canals turned stagnant and the unheated cottages became substandard housing for the poor. In the Sixties, Venice was the one place in Los Angeles where numbers of hippies and radicals lived. It was an outlaw gulch, a haven for draft resisters, struggling artists and drug addicts. At the same time, a real estate development was under way that threatened to permanently alter the character of Venice.

The new development was Marina del Rey, which means the King's Boat Basin. The Marina, just to the south of Venice, is a modern reworking of Abbot Kinney's dream. The Marina is the largest harbor for small pleasure boats in the world: a system of man-made channels and piers, on which there are restaurants, bars, discos, shops and acres of condominiums. The twenty-six streets leading to

the oceanfront have nautical names from A to Z: Anchorage, Buc-
caneer, Catamaran, Driftwood, Eastwind, Fleet . . . When I first
moved to Venice, I used to put myself to sleep by memorizing the
streets in the Marina.

Once completed, the Marina became one of the fastest-appre-
ciating real estate markets in Los Angeles. Everyone wanted to live
by the sea and still be close to work. The Marina was especially popular with the newly divorced. It was a playland: almost every condo
had a wet bar, a gas barbecue, a waterbed, and a fireplace that
sprang on at the push of a button. The tenants could use a community sauna, Jacuzzi, pool and gym. People filled their apartments
with fish tanks and telescopes and oars and shells and hammocks
and in the bathroom, stacks of flying magazines.

Those who could not afford the rents in the Marina began
spilling over into Venice. Prices jumped overnight. Speculators
bought up shacks, remodeled them and sold them for triple what
they had paid. Plans were announced to "clean up the canals," and
Venice became a "neighborhood in transition." The poor and the
hippies who could not adjust were forced to move east.

I arrived in Venice in 1974, with my own dream. I wanted to do
what Don Juan had advised Castaneda to do: erase personal history.
I was a refugee from the East, from a tumultuous marriage and the
revolutions of the Sixties. I wanted to begin life again in a place with
good weather, a place where I could work, and I wanted to find, if
such a creature existed, an unscarred man.

It was not long before I met such a person in Venice. His name
was Bruce; he was twenty-six, and chief of research at a botanical
laboratory. He loved his work but he also loved to be outdoors, to
dance and listen to rock 'n' roll. Even his handwriting was happy—
he drew little circles over his i's. He cooked and kept his house
clean. He had no sexual problems. He had made love with his last
girlfriend every day, "at least once," for four years, and he promised
to do the same with me, "as long as we love each other."

Being with Bruce was like a happy retrogression to teen-age
years. We drove around in his car with the top down, ate ham-
burgers and milk shakes, watched Kung Fu movies and spent all
weekend at the beach. There was a volleyball net by Bruce's house
and every weekend the same crowd appeared. The men reminded
me of fraternity boys who had never grown up. They had their own

businesses now, things like parking lots and vending machines, but they still drank beer and made jokes about fags and big boobs, jokes at which Bruce, to my relief, did not laugh.

The people on the beach played two-man volleyball—a different game entirely from the social volleyball I had played through the years. This volleyball was hard-core stuff. There were two people on a side, they played fast and savagely and were constantly diving in the sand. Bruce showed me the basic hits—bump, set and spike—but as a beginner, I could not keep up with their games. I was walking on the beach by myself one day when I spotted one of the regulars. This man was unforgettable: he had a head shaped like a pineapple. He must have been working out with weights, for the muscles on his arms and legs popped out and he even had small breasts. I told him, hopefully, how much I wanted to learn to play volleyball and how nice it would be if I could find someone who would play with me . . .

"You got a problem," he said in a dunce-like voice. "The good people want to play with other good people. What you should do is take a class."

"A volleyball class?"

"Yeah."

"Where am I supposed to find a volleyball class?"

"At the junior college."

Oh. I found out that Santa Monica College indeed had a volleyball class, and for the rest of the summer, my life had a wonderful rhythm. I would wake up, put on a pair of orange shorts that said "S.M.C.," drive to school and play volleyball. Then I would come home, work, go for a swim, work some more, run on the beach, work again, fix dinner with Bruce and go to sleep.

We were the only couple to reappear together at the volleyball net, week after week. The others were constantly shifting partners, and as one player said, five days with the same woman was "the same as five years." I thought Bruce and I were an island of sanity on this beach, but as the summer progressed, I began to understand why he was not scarred. He had very little compassion for people in trouble. "There's nothing in life that's worth being unhappy about," he used to say. "You choose to feel pain. You can choose, just as easily, not to feel it."

"What if someone dies?" I said.

"I wouldn't mind dying. And I wouldn't be sad if you died."

He did not want to hear about frustration. He did not want to know about writer's block. He did not think I should feel jealous if he dated other women, and he did not believe a relationship should be work.

"I think we do too much talking," he said.

"That's funny. I think we don't do enough."

In the fall, I went to New York and in my absence, Bruce took est and fell in love with one of the women at the volleyball net. When I returned, he told me it was time for us to break up because there was "no more cheese in the relationship."

I moved to a different part of the beach. A month later, I ran into Bruce with still another woman, whom he introduced as "the love of my life."

So much for that dream.

My mother sells real estate in Los Angeles. So do my aunt and three of my mother's closest friends. This business has always been appealing to women because there are no prerequisites, except passing a test; you can start at any point in life; you can set your own hours; and you have the potential to earn far more than was possible for women, until recently, in other fields.

My sister and I grew up with an aversion to the words "real estate." It meant my mother was never around on Sunday because she was "sitting on a house." It meant violent swings in her mood and our fortunes. Often, she would dash out of the house on a moment's notice to show property, canceling a date to take us to the movies. We never knew if she would return in a terrible mood or exultant, "I made my deal!"

At seventeen, I left Los Angeles and did not return until I was thirty. During the interim years, I grew to have contempt for people who spent money on houses and furniture, expensive cars and first-class airline tickets. I thought it was more interesting and adventurous to travel second class, if not to hitchhike. I visited and wrote about communes where "free land" was the ideology. It sounded right: no one should be able to own the land, any more than people could own the sky or the sea. One of my friends refused to buy a country house offered to him at a very low price, because, he said, "Owning property is theft, and in any case, it would put us in the camp of the ruling class." Another friend gave away her fifty-thousand-dollar inheritance. She believed that God would provide.

My sister, after college, became a gym teacher and lived communally in the San Fernando Valley. She ate only vegetables, practiced yoga, made God's-eyes out of yarn and sticks and rode long distances to march in peace demonstrations. She found, very quickly, that she didn't like teaching—being in a position of authority over children. So she quit her job, sold all her belongings and bought a one-way ticket to the South Seas.

In 1978, my sister began selling real estate in Hawaii. Her guru was a Chinese broker who gave her a life plan: use the commissions you make on sales to acquire one piece of property a year for ten years; then sell half the properties, pay off the mortgages on the rest, retire and live off the income. In her study at home, in what used to be a sewing and pottery room, was a sign:

Y.C.S.A.S.O.Y.A.

"What does that mean?" I said.
"You can't sell anything sitting on your ass."
We spent half of our vacation time driving around Oahu, looking at homes. The irony was so overpowering that we did not speak about it.

My own interest in real estate had begun the year I moved to Venice. In the previous twelve months, I had moved nine times. I was recently divorced, writing a book and free to live anywhere. I tried Bridgehampton, Santa Fe, Berkeley, Mill Valley, the Hollywood Hills, until the cycle of searching for perfect places, packing, moving, unpacking, installing phones and setting up bank accounts became so cumulatively unbearable that I didn't care where I landed, so long as I didn't have to move again.

The way to ensure such rootedness, I thought, was to buy a house of my own. For a year, I walked up and down the lanes of Venice. I, who had always disparaged the acquisition of property, was spending days with a broker named Milt, who was twenty-six, had a coarse mustache and little higher education but a winner's instinct for beach real estate.

Everything we looked at was old, dark, cramped, in terrible condition and ridiculously expensive. The same houses, if not so close to the beach, would have been considered uninhabitable. I was about to give up when I went to see a two-story Victorian house, and the minute I stepped in the living room, my heart began to race. Sunlight was pouring in through a wall of many-paned windows. The house had a Franklin stove, hardwood floors that needed refinishing, a large kitchen that needed remodeling, two primitive bathrooms and three eccentric bedrooms. I looked at Milt and said, "I want it."

"Keep your pants on," he said.

We made an offer, which was rejected. We made another offer—also rejected. "We got no deal," Milt said. "I won't let you pay a dollar more. It's not worth it." For the next two days I was miserable. Every time I drove past the house I felt a stab of longing and regret. It was a year since I had broken up with Bruce, and I was involved with a ballet dancer named Tommy, who had little money himself but whose father owned casinos and land in Las Vegas. When Tommy saw what was happening, he sat me down and said: "Pay the owner what he wants. Next year, it'll be worth even more."

I instructed Milt to make a third offer, which was accepted. "I bought a house!" I told friends, but everyone except Tommy thought I was crazy.

My lawyer said, "I'd never pay so much for that piece of junk."

My mother said, "You lost your senses. You got so excited, you couldn't see." She began to call me every few hours with new objections. "How will you fit your bed in the bedroom? Why should you have to pay for the termite repairs? The seller should pay."

By the time the escrow papers arrived, my enthusiasm had reversed itself and I was in a panic. I was sinking my life savings into an old, broken down house half eaten by bugs, and I would have to rent out the upstairs to meet the payments. What if the real estate market fell through? What if the house needed massive repairs? How would it hold up in an earthquake? What if I couldn't find a tenant and couldn't pay the mortgage? Hadn't my parents seen their friends dispossessed in the Great Depression?

At night I lay in bed and shook. Tommy said I was having "buyer's remorse." So there was a name for it. I found that comforting. I knew the panic was unrealistic but I was helpless to stop it. More was at stake than the purchase of a house. It was a statement about myself.

"He used to be a radical leader. Now he's an actor in soap operas."
    *"She tried to burn down the Bank of America at Isla Vista. Now she's
a vice president at Universal."*

It is a cliché, a joke, something we are past feeling anguished about,
but the fact is that a considerable number of people have passed
through a door and come out wearing different clothes, and this
transformation has taken place almost without comment. People
who, in the flowering of the Sixties, gave their children names like
Blackberry and Veda-Rama have changed them to Suzy and John.
The parents are "getting our money trip together." If they are successful, they are buying homes, Calvin Klein suits and Porsches and
sending their kids to private schools to avoid busing.

     Not all have come through the door, of course. There are still
groups of New Age people in places like Berkeley, Oregon, Hawaii
and Vermont. They are still dedicated to social change, still wearing
beards and flowing shawls, still holding symposiums where they talk
about holistic health care, living closer to the earth and creating
communities where people can love each other and share and co-
operate. But their numbers are dwindling and few young recruits
come along.

     Those who have crossed the line cannot help but feel some
irony and bafflement about "the people we've become." They retain
an awareness, however faintly it is pulsing, that the acquisition of
material wealth does not necessarily bring satisfaction, but that
awareness is fading rapidly into unconsciousness.

On a Sunday in May, 1979, I am walking on the boardwalk in Venice
with a friend, Andy, who is, in fact, a former radical student now
an actor in soap operas. Andy lives next door with his girlfriend,
Sue, who works as an accountant while Andy tries to find parts in
television. In 1969, Andy had stood in the front lines, arms locked
together with others who were occupying University Hall at Harvard. Today, he could pose for a life insurance ad, but ten years ago,
he wore a mustache, a torn leather jacket and a headband over thick
black hair that fell to his shoulder blades.

     On that night in 1969, when police broke down the doors of
University Hall with a battering ram, Andy was clubbed and carried
off in a paddy wagon. The next day, head wrapped in bandages, he
joined the strike that shut down the school. In June, his parents
took time off from their jobs in Cocoa, Florida, to drive up North

to see their son graduate from Harvard. But ten minutes into the ceremony, Andy walked out with about three hundred others, to protest the racist imperialist policies of Harvard University.

In the years that followed, Andy founded an alternative high school in the Roxbury ghetto, lived in a therapeutic community for chronic schizophrenics, worked on an organic farm, ran an assembly district for George McGovern and joined a commune of twelve who were sailing around the world.

Somewhere down the line he took an acting workshop, and decided to settle in Los Angeles. By stages, his appearance and then his values began to change. When I met him, in 1976, he was getting ready to break down and buy a suit—a custom-made suit from a tailor on Rodeo Drive, not from Good Will. He had decided he wanted to star in movies that would "alter the culture." He had also decided he wanted to be richly rewarded by the culture.

"Sometimes I lie in bed and think about how I've changed," Andy says. "I wouldn't want to live in, or even walk through a ghetto today. And I've become a racist about Arabs. Their oil money flooding in here is driving up the prices of everything—houses, gas. Did we think we wouldn't have to worry about such things?"

I feel myself sinking. "I suppose our commitment wasn't that sincere."

Andy disagrees. "Mine was. I gave up years of my life working to make society better. Those were years I could have been earning money and advancing in a career."

We notice a commotion on the mall in front of the Venice Pavilion. The usual crowds are skating and wheeling, but in the center, twenty people are standing in a circle, holding signs. "Stop Nuclear Power." The leader of the group is on skates and has bloody knees. He starts a chant, "Hell no, we won't glow," but the voices barely carry over the roller disco music.

A lone TV cameraman is photographing the group. Some of the spectators are laughing and calling insults. "Smoke a joint, guys, and mellow out." I feel embarrassed, the demonstrators look so silly and ineffectual, and yet I know that this is how things begin.

Andy says, "What is the point, who are they reaching here?"

We turn and walk away in troubled silence.

I am invited to speak at colleges about the "Sixties in America" and the "Changing Roles of Women." I am not invited to places like

Harvard and Yale. I go to Florida State University and Spokane Falls
Community College. The staff in charge of scheduling speakers at
these colleges are usually "Sixties people" who want to keep the
flame alive. The main reason I accept the engagements is that they
give me a chance to spend time with students. I have often thought
that the spirit of an era is most clearly expressed by those in college
at the time.

This particular generation, who were students in the Seventies, never managed to acquire an identity. No one figure, like the
Beatles, Elvis Presley or Sinatra, emerged to galvanize and articulate
their sensibility. No one was king, and no one was hanged in effigy.
The students seemed too bland, even, to merit a name. At best, they
were thought of as "the careerists," an ambitious, uninspired flock
who trotted as quickly as they could down paths they hoped would
lead to good jobs and success.

A speaker's visit to a college has a set choreography. I am met
at the airport by two or three nervous undergraduates, who want
to make a contact with the outside world. On the ride in, I cannot
bear the twitchy silence, so I ask about their school. "What do students here talk about and think about?"

The question throws them—they are not used to anyone caring. One young woman in Florida says, after a moment of blankness,
"Just themselves."

During the lecture, I try to paint a picture of what it was like
to be young in the Sixties. If the speech works, the students sit rapt.
They were born in 1960, or later, and the decade sounds as fan-
tastical and remote to them as the Roaring Twenties did to me.
After the speech, we go to a local restaurant, and the same students
who were tongue-tied before are now impatient to give their opinions. Some feel frustrated at having been born too late. "We waited
for our turn, and it never came," an eighteen-year-old in Boston
said. She was angry at my generation for failing her. "How can you
blame us for not running with the ball?" she said. "It's you who disappeared, left nothing behind and went into real estate."

A larger proportion of the students I met, however, responded
with some variation of: "Yuk. Who'd want to do that?" A premed
student at Wisconsin said, "I could never take off my clothes in
public and pop pills, like you did at Woodstock." His friends agreed.
"All that running in the street sounds ridiculous."

They said they were raised in a time of chaos and want order restored. They want assignments, reading lists, grades. What impressed me was that going to college these days is not a lot of fun. For one thing, it's hard financially. Everything is expensive—tuition, rent. Many have to work full time and, to conserve money, live at home.

From the moment they enroll as freshmen, they are pressured to make a career choice. They are told they must sacrifice their personal interests for "marketability." They must learn to think about what will "look good on the résumé." To change majors in midstream is disastrous—"You won't graduate in four years."

For women, there no longer seems to be the option of biding one's time until marriage. A student in California told me, "What I'd really like to do when I graduate is get married and have kids, but my sorority sisters would give me so much heat! They say you have to work or you have no identity." She gave a shrug. "So I'm applying to law school."

Of all the visits to colleges, the one I remember as most poignant and unsettling took place at a private co-ed school in Oregon. After the lecture, I went to a pizza restaurant with three women students and two women professors. The students sat on one side of the booth, the working women on the other. The three of us on one side were in our thirties, unattached and without children. One professor taught English, the other psychology. We were aware, and not entirely comfortable with the knowledge, that the students were looking at us, hoping to assay their own future.

The three students were attractive, graceful, obviously talented and hard-working. But they were worried they would not be able to find jobs. Pam, who had long red hair which she kept pushing behind her ears, said, "I'm afraid of not being able to make enough money to survive. I'm afraid of starving."

I tried to reassure her. "Nobody I know has ever come close to starving—not even free-lance writers."

"I realize that," Pam said. "But somehow it scares me. I've had to live on popcorn and pancakes because I've run out of grocery money."

The students talked about how much they wanted to be successful: to be paid well, rise to an important position in a corporation and have influence, prestige, power.

"Does love figure in this picture?" I asked.

Pam rested her chin in her hand. "I can't imagine that I would ever meet a man I would want to spend my life with. I think you would grow in different directions."

The three on my side of the table exchanged looks of surprise. Among us, we had been through five marriages and five divorces, and we still believed it would be possible to find a mate who would endure.

"What about children?" I asked the young women.

Rebecca, a brunette who wore oversized horn-rimmed glasses, said, "I'm afraid that if I have a child, my ambition will disappear. Somehow, magically, I'll be transformed into a woman like my mother—a housewife, trying at forty to figure out what she's doing with her life."

Lucy, the third student, said, "I'm not willing to give up years of my career for the sake of children. Men won't do it."

Once again, the three on my side were surprised. Deanne, the psychology professor, said, "I used to feel that way, but as I've gotten older, I realize the price I've paid for my independence. I feel deprived that I don't have a family. I see a whole generation of women I know getting stuck without children, and it's sad."

Pam twirled a strand of hair around her finger. "We may not feel that way." As the hours passed, I learned that all three students live alone—something the three of us would never have considered when we were in college. I asked about the young men they know. Pam: "The guys at this school have a lot of charm, but they're jocks. The women are more intellectual."

"Those types are not exactly made for each other," I said.

The young women laughed. "Yeah. The three of us are celibate."

"Don't you get lonely?" Deanne said.

Pam shook her head. "We have too much work."

The window of my study in Venice looks out on a building of single apartments. The average tenant stays six months, and I can tell where he or she is in the cycle by the state of the front yard. If there is a new resident in the building, the yard is full of young plants. They are carefully watered and begin to flower and then overnight everything turns brown. Weeds spring up, until the ground is so dry that nothing will grow on it and people throw beer cans and trash on the lot. The old tenants leave without saying good-by, and new ones arrive and begin to clean up. I watch them installing stereos, hanging wind chimes and putting out lawn furniture. Home at last: the good life by the beach.

One of the tenants this year was a man of thirty, Don, who taught phys. ed. in junior high school. After weeks of nodding to each other across the lane, we struck up an acquaintance. Sometimes we would sit on the beach together, or have a quick dinner on the Venice pier. Don was exceedingly attractive in a California way: blond hair, blue eyes, a pleasingly symmetrical if not terribly interesting face, and a body kept in wondrous shape. Every so often, preteen girls who had followed him home from school would tiptoe up to his door, ring the bell and, squealing with laughter, run away.

I liked to hear Don talk about teaching. He said the seventh-graders need to be disciplined, "or else it's *Lord of the Flies.* The kids are confused and can't keep things organized. They're always losing stuff. After a seventh-grade period, we have to go through the locker room and collect their junk in boxes." The eighth-graders, he said, are gaining confidence and want to test their limits. "They need to be smashed down." The ninth-graders "know what they can get away with, and you can actually teach them stuff."

A few months went by that I didn't see Don, until he appeared one Sunday night with a bottle of tequila. "I'm glad you were home," he said.

"Why?"

"I've been alone all week. I went skiing by myself. Every night I just sat and read, or daydreamed. I drove back today, and I thought I'd stop at Death Valley and take pictures of wild flowers, but there weren't any. So I came on in." He was staring at his lap. "I didn't want to be alone."

"I know what you mean."

"Do you?" He looked surprised.

I nodded.

"I'm in pain. Do you believe me?"

I realized, from the question, that people do not tend to take very seriously the pain of a blond gym teacher. "Yes," I said. "You want a close relationship with someone and you can't have it."

He let out a sigh.

I said, "It's been six months or so since I was close with any-one."

Don said, "It's been three or four years for me. And I have this fantasy—of having a home, a wife and kids. It's very strong. But it's not happening."

I said it seems puzzling: he's so attractive, warm and good humored. He meets and dates so many women.

He shrugged. "I could say the same about you."

Being unattached these days can be such a maddening business. You will have what feels to be the most intimate encounter: there is dazzling promise, blunt truth spoken, laughter and wonderful communication and you will never see the person again. Sometimes it lasts a few weeks, then one or the other calls in sick. I have observed the pattern in myself: infatuation turns suddenly and without warning to aversion. A friend said it comes over her in waves. "I hate the way he walks, the way he chews. I can't wait to be alone, but in a few days I'll get lonely again." It is nothing short of a disease, and those who have it tend to gravitate toward others with the same affliction.

On a weekend in July, I sat out by the lifeguard tower with Don, the gym teacher, and two of his friends. All three had been married and divorced, and every week, they would get together and recount their little disaster stories.

David, who is a doctor, described spending the night with a woman who turned out to have silicone breasts. "When she lay down on her back, the breasts didn't move. They felt like silly putty. It stopped me cold, man. It was like making love to a goddamned lamp or something."

The others howled with laughter.

Don reported that a teacher he'd been dating had just told him she wouldn't be seeing him as often. She was starting a new job and giving first priority to her career. Don said, "I grew up thinking my wife would cook while I was out running the school district. It's sad to think I probably won't have kids now."

"What makes you so sure?" I said.

"Who's going to raise them?"

I said there must be women who would want to stay home with children, at least part of the time. But Don disagreed. "Women who are interested in raising kids are dogshit."

I looked at the other men. Was this serious? Allan, a lawyer with an Afro, did not seem to be listening.

"Hey Al," Don said. "Where are ya?"

Allan said he had been thinking about a woman he'd met at a

dinner party. "At first I didn't think much of her, but as the evening progressed, she became more beautiful. She had a real nice smile, which turns me on. There was a gentleness about her. I liked her voice, and I liked what she was doing. I've been thinking about her all day."

"You gonna call her?" Don said.

Allan thought a moment. To my surprise, he said, "No."

"Why wouldn't you call her?" I said.

He tipped his head from side to side. "Just because I like someone doesn't mean I want to get into a scene."

I had a fleeting urge to have at him. What is wrong with these men? But David and Don seemed to empathize with their friend. David, the doctor, said, "You can't satisfy the women out there. No point trying. Anything you do will be criticized."

Once, while I was doing research for a film, I spent a day with David on his rounds at the hospital. He has a sensitive face, blue eyes and dark hair that looks black against the white doctor's coat. David treats very sick people—many are terminally ill—with kindness and concern. He is always overscheduled and yet remains cheerful. Every case requires him to make decisions that will prolong or curtail life. He works grueling shifts with no relief, and often goes home and falls asleep in his clothes with the lights on.

In his free time, he is adept at one-night stands. When we sat by the lifeguard tower, he described his operating procedure at singles bars. "The first thing is the preening—you've got to do everything you can to make yourself look great. Because it's real competitive. Make sure you smell good. Blow your hair dry. Your clothes should be casual but stylish."

"How long does it take you to get ready?" I said.

"About an hour. That includes shaving. I have to put in my contact lenses. Take a shower. Powder my balls."

"Come on."

"I have to—Johnson's baby powder—otherwise I get a rash from my bikini underwear."

When he leaves the house, he takes a leather shaving kit in which he has packed:

razor
contact lens solution
K-Y jelly
aspirin

rubber ("in case the bubblehead forgot to take her pill")
address book

"You always go to her place, if you can. Then you control when you leave. You don't get stuck with her all weekend." He said the first moves in the bar are most important. "You have to feel the woman out, learn what her fantasies are. The best approach is to ask a lot of personal questions, without giving her a chance to know that much about you. Let her talk about her problems and nod understandingly. Because really, people love to talk about themselves."

Don said, "What if she starts to get upset about her problems?"

David: "At this point, it's a good idea to commiserate; either share, or manufacture some sort of similar experience."

"You're good at this, aren't you?" I said.

David: "I'm pretty good at being very understanding."

"Do you ever make it clear you just want to fuck?"

"Not really, no."

"Why?"

"It's never worked for me. My basic assumption is that women don't want one-night stands. They want an emotional experience. So I make her feel like she's the most fascinating and unique person I've ever met."

"What if she is a fascinating person," I said. "What do you do then?"

"Either fall in love. Or run."

Don and Allan started hooting and slapping their legs. "Run like hell!"

> *Now you rich people listen to me,*
> *Weep and wail over the miseries*
> *That are coming, coming up on you . . .*
> *Your life here on earth has been filled*
> *With luxury and pleasure,*
> *You have made yourself fat*
> *For the day of slaughter.*
>
>   *"Warning Warning," by Max Romeo*

The only music I follow with any excitement these days is reggae from Jamaica. I cannot abide the monotony of disco, and I'm tired of listening to albums from the Sixties. Reggae music is alive; it has melody, wit, a hypnotic jungle beat and lyrics that burn with righteous fire.

Most reggae singers are Rastafarians—members of a mystic religion; they smoke ganja, worship Haile Selassie and believe that they are the lost Children of Israel who will one day return to Zion. On that day, the rich will eat each other alive and the blessed will survive. The Rastafarians sing about Jerusalem lost, and the temptations of dwelling in Babylon. The imagery seems relevant to me, and became even more relevant after I visited the actual Jerusalem in 1976.

In recent years, I have traveled to Israel so often that people have begun to think me odd. I keep returning for many reasons, one of which is that I find in Israel a sense of belonging to a family— the ancient family of Jews. To achieve this feeling in America, I would probably have to join a synagogue and come to some decision about observing the Orthodox laws. But in Israel, all one has to do is be present. Hebrew is spoken. Everywhere one is reminded of the biblical past. The week has a rhythm emanating from the Torah given to Moses at Sinai. On Friday afternoon, a quiet descends on the cities. Buses stop running, shops close. No newspaper comes out. Nobody works. Everyone, even the most irreligious person, has to be aware that the Sabbath has arrived and that this day will be different.

Life in Israel is in diametric contrast to life in Southern California. Israelis who are my age have fought and survived two wars. They still serve in the reserves. They know how to handle a gun, fix a jeep, find water in the desert and apply first aid to someone with a chest wound. Most of them were married in their early twenties, had at least two children and stayed married. To remain single after a certain age would make them an oddity.

In 1978, I spent a summer at Mishkenot Sha-ananim, a magnificent residence for artists and writers run by the city of Jerusalem. For two months, I did not hear a single remark about diet or jogging. I found great conversation—Israelis love to talk and laugh—about ideas, politics, history, "the conflict," music, art, books. But there was an absence of personal revelation.

I spent one Sabbath with a couple who lived in a farmhouse outside Jerusalem. The husband was German and the wife a sabra. Every Saturday, their closest friends would come by with their children to swim and eat a potluck meal. The day I was there, four couples sat around the table in the garden, eating roast chicken. I asked our hosts, the German and the Israeli, how they had met. The husband told a story, and I noticed that all other conversation at the table stopped. When the husband had finished, one of his friends said, "We never knew about that." For years, they had been going on trips and celebrating holidays and taking care of each other's children, and they had never asked one another how their marriages began.

Israel is beset with internal problems and in no way a paradise, but life there has an intensity and meaning, derived from having a common enemy and a sense of purpose in history. The most radical critics of the government will have no qualms about serving as officers in the reserves. There is no contradiction in being a left-wing pacifist and a soldier, because if people fight, it is to protect their homes and friends.

Israelis are reminded, almost daily, that human life is transient and relationships are not replaceable. Having a family becomes a matter of critical importance. I never ceased to be moved by the sight of muscular Israeli men playing with their children. One I knew, Gidon, was a commando in the navy and drove heavy machinery on his kibbutz. He had spent a year in New York, and told me he was puzzled by the attitude of people there. "All the men and women are interested only in their own careers," he said. "They don't want children." Gidon, who is twenty-eight, has two daughters and a newborn son. "Who says children take away your freedom? I have my family, and my work, and tell me, what is a career"—he held up his baby son—"compared to this?"

HAVE A GOOD TOMORROW,
BUY REAL ESTATE TODAY.

—a billboard in Marina del Rey

Six months after I moved into my house in Venice—the house for which everyone thought I had paid too much—realtors began to knock on the door and ask if I wanted to sell. The longer I stayed, the more they offered. After a year, the price of the house had doubled and after two years, I had earned more money just by living there than I had in my entire writing career.

It was phenomenal. The money was insurance for the future and I wanted more. I began looking in the Marina Peninsula at condominiums on the sand. My house was a short walk from the beach, but as Bruce Jay Friedman wrote about such homes: "It's either on the beach or it isn't . . . The fella who is 'a short jog away' is in the same boat as someone who has to be brought in by Concorde."

What I saw on the Marina Peninsula was shocking. The condominiums had been built with no concern for aesthetics or quality. They were like shoe boxes, long and narrow, with thin walls and sprayed acoustic ceilings aptly called "cottage cheese." The selling feature, of course, was that the front windows opened onto the surf. If you faced the ocean and forgot about the apartment, it was fine; but the apartments themselves were abysmal.

The price of one of these two-bedroom boxes was four hundred thousand dollars and up—the price you would pay for a nine-room house with a pool and tennis court in another part of the city. The realtors insisted, however, that the prices, outrageous as they were, would only go up. "Beach property is better than gold. They can mine more gold, but they're never going to make any more oceanfront."

I saw nothing that I would not have been embarrassed to own, and in any case I came to the conclusion that I could not afford to move. That is the Catch-22 about real estate: your house has gone up, but if you sell it, where are you going to live? If you buy another house, it will cost far more than what you received for your old house, the interest rate will be higher and you'll be stuck with a whopping overhead. So people tend to stay where they are and remodel. But they cannot stand being left out of the game, so they refinance their homes and use the cash to purchase income units, or join limited partnerships or get together with three friends and buy a house for speculation.

What has resulted is a feeding frenzy. Policemen, plumbers, film directors—everyone is making more in real estate than in the profession he was trained for. When a new "for sale" sign is posted on Pacific Avenue, cars screech to a halt. I am no less guilty than the others: I am tempted to quit work, cancel dates and run out if a broker calls to tell me about a "great deal." What is fueling this madness is anxiety about the future, and the wish for tangible security. Marriages may not last, political movements come and go, even money loses its value but the land gains. A woman I know, who recently quit her job as a public defender to become a realtor, put it this way: "I'm looking for something in real estate: freedom." The only problem with this kind of freedom, of course, is that you can never have enough.

"I think there's going to have to be a reorientation of what people value in their lives."
— Jimmy Carter, Camp David Summit, 1979

"I just made a major purchase," Andy told me on the phone. "Roller skates."

"You didn't."

"Ninety-five dollars." He laughed sheepishly. "Now I can float along with the rest of the flakes."

Once Andy had succumbed, it was only weeks before I followed. I had seen beginning skaters hobbling along the bike path and falling into trash cans, but I figured they had never skated before. When I was eight, I had lived with a skate key around my neck, and had been particularly skilled at taking the steep driveways on our block. But a long time had elapsed since I was eight.

I rented a pair, laced them on, stood up and rolled away. Just like that. I could not do tricks but I could move right along. I thought I had discovered a new and delightful way to keep in shape, and promptly bought myself some Road Skates.

The next Saturday, Andy and I left our homes in the morning and rolled a mile down the bike path. Despite the claims we had heard that skating is good for the legs, I did not find it strenuous. Andy agreed, "I'm not even sweating." The sensation was more of dawdling: mindless, effortless. It was pleasant, with the surf shooting in the air and gulls flapping overhead. We decided to skate back to Venice and have lunch at the Meatless Mess Hall.

The crowds on Ocean Front Walk were thicker than I had ever seen. People were skating down slalom tracks made of beer cans. A man crashed into a tree. A girl on a bike hit a boy on a skateboard. Bums and shopping-cart people were rummaging through the trash cans. A woman in a powder blue Mercedes had ignored the "Motor Vehicles Prohibited" signs and pulled onto the boardwalk. The license plate on her car said, "Moist 1." A policeman was giving her a ticket. He wore his beach uniform: shorts, a holster with a .38 and a T-shirt that said "L.A.P.D."

I saw two women I knew from the movie business, Sandy, a producer, and Lois, the token female vice president at a studio. Both are paid more than sixty thousand dollars a year. Sandy was wearing shorts, platform shoes and a blouse so low-cut that her breasts were spilling out. She said to me, "How's your life. Are you in love?"

"No, are you?"

"Are you kidding? I can't even get laid."

Lois said, "Forget it, you can't get laid in this town. I go to parties and take home phone numbers of women. I may have a guy for you, though, Sandy. He's an old friend."

"Yeah?"

"He's not that smart."

Sandy: "Can he move it in and out?"

Lois made a so-so gesture.

"Fuck it," Sandy said. "If this goes on much longer, I'll die of vaginal atrophy. Give me his number."

We said good-by, laughing, and I looked around for Andy. He was talking with a tall redhead, whom he introduced as Carl—"We used to be roommates at Harvard."

Carl was saying, "I'm playing the game of the Seventies: corporate executive."

Andy laughed. Carl explained that he had formed a production company and just finished shooting a movie for television.

"Great," Andy said, sounding not all that happy.

Carl: "I'm going to Cannes next week."

"That is fantastic," Andy said, but the word "Cannes" had struck him like a body blow.

Carl said, "Look, I spent ten years starving. Now I want to get even."

Andy: "I know the feeling."

Carl said, "Hey, let's have lunch. Keep in touch."

"Sure," Andy said. "And, uh . . . congratulations on your success."

As we began to skate away, I could tell Andy was upset. He was racing, making quick turns and plowing through people who were idly talking. I let him move ahead. Just before the Meatless Mess Hall, I saw a bump in the asphalt. I thought I could take it the way you take a wave in water skiing. I rolled up the rise but at the top, my skates continued flying upward instead of down the other side. Before I could think, my feet were in the air and my back hit the concrete, four feet down, smack! I blacked out for a second, and when I came to, I could feel the impact in my chest, head, teeth.

"Are you all right?" someone was asking.

"I don't know." I had no wind. I was afraid to move, afraid I had crippled myself. Was this dumb, I thought. What a price you're going to pay. Andy had to half-carry me home and drive me to the emergency room, but the X-rays showed nothing broken. I had bruised and badly swollen tissue, but with ice packs, followed by heat, I was told, I would recover.

For the next two weeks, I minced around painfully, unable to stand upright. I began to notice people on the boardwalk wearing casts on their arms and legs. One retired surfer on our block took a terrible spill and dislocated his shoulder. Still he went skating, wearing a brace. "Why?" I said. "Anytime you fall, you hit concrete." He shrugged. "What else is there to do?"

Every day, there was at least one call for an ambulance and somebody was carried off on a stretcher. Then in June, an eighty-six-year-old woman, Ann Gerber, was killed on the boardwalk when she was run over by a twenty-five-year-old bicyclist, who explained later, "She got in my way."

An emergency meeting was called of the Los Angeles City Council. On the boardwalk, it was war on wheels: shouting and pushing erupted between skaters and bicyclists and joggers and senior citizens over who had the right of way. The skaters had the numbers, and were gaining each day. People were skating to the bank, to the laundromat, to restaurants, to walk their dogs.

The City Council voted to ban skating on parts of the boardwalk, but people disobeyed.

"No skating on the boardwalk!"

"Up yours, ya jerk!"

A ninety-two-year-old woman struck a skater with her cane when he cut in front of her. "I'm living here twenty-five years," she shouted. "You should be ashamed."

I was driving home from the doctor's. I stopped at the light on Venice Boulevard and Pacific Avenue. A girl was waiting for the bus—an Oriental girl wearing a leopard skin bikini and thin high heels. She was carrying two electric guitars. Where could she be going on the bus? The light changed. As I started to move, a man who had a beard on one side of his face and was clean-shaven on the other, stepped off the curb. I hit the brakes. I nearly ran him over. You're going to have to be more alert, I thought. There are crazy people, and wouldn't it be terrible to hit someone. I saw a picture in my mind of the man lying under my car. If it had happened, if he was actually under the car, I thought, what should I do? Drive forward, or backward, or leave it there and try to jack it up? My thoughts drifted on, and soon it was time to pull into my carport.

The space is narrow, so I made a wide arc, glided through the turn and was coming to a stop when, clunkety clunk, I felt the car roll over something that sounded like a metal trash can. What was it? Why hadn't I seen it?

I stepped out of the car and got down on my knees. A man was lying under the car. A wino, flat on his back, dressed in a green plaid shirt and a woolen cap and brown shoes. I screamed. Should I drive forward, or backward . . . His legs were behind the rear wheels, extending out across the driveway. I had to have driven over his legs. I looked for blood.

"Are you all right?" My voice was high, like a shriek. "Did I hurt you?"

"No," he said fuzzily. He seemed to have been in a drunken sleep.

"You must be hurt."

"No I'm not."

"But my car . . ."

"Nahhh," he said in the slurred, combative manner of drunks. "If I was hurt, I'd know it."

He was struggling to raise himself. "I wanted to sit down here . . . think about shit."

Suddenly he jumped to his feet. I jumped back and screamed.

Andy, who had heard the commotion from next door, came running over.

The wino said, "What do you know goddamnit! I been in Venice longer 'n you. This is my home."

Andy said, sounding friendly, "You like it here, huh?"

"Yeah. I got shit on my mind, I wanna sit down, nobody's gonna stop me."

I said, "I'm just glad you weren't hurt. It scared the . . . life out of me."

The drunk swayed in my direction. "Awww, I'm sorry, miss, I didn't mean to bother you."

An urge to laugh came over me. This made the drunk laugh too.

"What's your name?" he said.

Pause. "Sharon," I lied.

"Okay, Sherry. Take it easy." He pulled his cap down and started to walk away, without apparent limp or pain.

"How could this be?" I said to Andy.

"I don't know."

"I must have driven over him."

"You did. I saw it from my window."

The drunk reached the corner, turned and disappeared. As I stood there, I realized that I was thirty-five and I was still waiting, expecting I would soon wake up from all of this.

Richard West

The self-contained world of a famous New York restaurant serves as the arena for Richard West's "The Power of '21.'" But this is no restaurant review. West followed the workers and owners of the restaurant day and night until he learned how they produce a status world that captivates the wealthy patrons of "21."

West's career has grown from his origins in Texas like waves spreading outward. Born in 1941, West grew up in an upper-middle-class Dallas suburb. His father was an editorial writer and political reporter. After studying government and journalism at the University of Texas, West took his first reporting job, at the *Longview Daily News,* in the heart of the East Texas oil country. In 1973, West helped found *Texas Monthly* magazine. He originated the "Texas Monthly Reporter" column, a roving assignment that filled a dozen magazine pages each month. The circle widened. West traveled Texas in a VW camper with a typewriter on the table in the back. Distances were so enormous that he returned to the office in Austin only once a month, turned in his copy, and hit the road again.

That kind of intensity and drive shows in his book, *Richard West's Texas*, published in 1981. Beginning in 1977, he moved successively to seven different parts of Texas, living in each area for months before writing about it. The areas included the Barrio in San Antonio, the Houston ghetto, the Piney Woods area of East Texas, the Panhandle and Marfa in West Texas. "If you're going to learn about a place, it's the only thing to do," West said. "The idea was to thrust myself into each community right away, from the bars to the banks and weddings and funerals."

The book completed, West thrust himself into a very different community, New York. He wrote for *New York* magazine, where his study of "21" was published. Later the circle grew again. He took a position as national correspondent at *Newsweek.* West is now a New York-based freelance writer, with the nation as his new beat.

The Power of "21"

S tanding at the curb absentmindedly rubbing his gold apple lapel pin and craning his neck down West 52nd Street, Fred Diel, the "21" Club's doorman, finally spotted the outline of Marvin Davis through the rear window of his limousine as it inched through noon-hour traffic. Quickly passing through the two sets of doors and into the lobby, Fred alerted "The Rope," Harry Lavin, who is in charge of the reception desk, this era's more benign version of the Cyclopean hole in the door used in the restaurant's speakeasy days. Harry whispered to Freddie Porcelli, one of the two escorts standing by the cloakroom (the same Freddie who played the head-waiter at the Le Château restaurant on *All My Children*), who scurried into the bar to pass the message along the employee grapevine: Get the chair.

Marvin still reached for door handles (he had bought Twentieth Century–Fox only four months before), but Fred was there first. Looking into the limo, he saw that Marvin was frowning, his brow creased and knotted, tension flickering up like summer lightning. Stepping out, Marvin Davis paused for an instant in front of the black wrought-iron grillwork, the two American flags, the white lanterns with their red "21"s, beneath the eternal gaze of the 25 cast-iron jockey statues. It was a scene he had known all his life, from the times after World War II when his father, Jack Davis of Seventh Avenue, would bring him to the famous Jack and Charlie's "21," when New York was the imperial city of the world and Jack Kriendler and Charlie Berns didn't need to have a chain running between the jockeys' legs.

By the time Marvin had walked through the opened sets of doors and stood in the lobby, his features had softened. The frown was gone, the bluster of importance had ebbed away and been left at the curb. He felt the old magic welling up, the pleasure of the expected: Nothing had changed; "21" represented the New York he remembered and loved—not a place of fictional grandeur but the real thing, strictly class, no vulgar rubbish, but personable, resolute, rich, a place people would go to even if the cook had just died of smallpox in the kitchen. Gliding up from nowhere, Sheldon Tannen (executive vice-president, one-fourth owner, nephew of co-founder Jack Kriendler) gripped Marvin's arm and unleashed a barrage of salutations and compliments—Did he need tickets to tennis matches, horse races, football games? How was his daughter Patty?—and slipping in, by the way, the fact that Herb Siegel (the Chris-Craft chairman and Fox shareholder, who had profited handsomely by Davis's takeover) was dining at Table 3.

Walter Weiss, headwaiter for 35 years, one of "21" 's many fixtures, watched the Davis-Tannen chat from the bar, dressed as always in one of his five $200 Palm Beach tuxedos, and, as always, wearing his overserious expression, grave with information and responsibility. As Davis, who is well over six feet and weighs hundreds of pounds, walked toward the bar, filling the narrow entrance like a solar eclipse, Walter once more glanced back at Table 15, Marvin's favorite, the corporate-star table nearest the kitchen, practical for a gourmand like Davis. It was in place, one of the sturdy upstairs-dining-room straight-backs called in to substitute for the flimsier first-string bentwoods. After shaking hands with Siegel, who was waiting at the center corporate-star table, No. 14, for John De Lorean of the gull-wing doors and stainless-steel bodies, Marvin settled in, his regular drink on the way, feeling not just welcomed but . . . cherished.

The nice young couple had been in the advancing and receding wave of patrons that had followed in the wake of Marvin Davis. Now they stood before Harry the Rope and looked into his perfect possible-impossible expression. "Reservations for two. Anderson, 12:30. We asked for the bar." Harry knew well this air of invented expectations, nice people who had said yes to folly so they could say back home they had had the $13.50 "21" burger. Some were prepared to look humiliation full in the face, and some weren't. Mrs. Anderson looked scared. (*Why didn't they back away? Why didn't they walk backward down Fifth Avenue past St. Patrick's Cathedral and the guy holding up the world, across the street, still walking backward as fast as they could until they grew vague and faded into the mist at South Ferry? Too late now.*) Never heartless candor from Harry Lavin, always a show of civilities. "Yes, Anderson. Right here. Please have a seat in the lounge.

We'll call you. Feel free to order a cocktail." The Andersons settled near another nice young couple on one of the leather sofas by the fireplace, all in a holding pattern, coming in on a wing and a prayer, thinking, *"Lord, Lord, give us clearance."* From time to time they received a glance from Harry that was neither sullen nor encouraging, merely attentive.

Sheldon Tannen rejoined Walter at the bar entrance and studied the clipboard holding the day's reservations. Tannen is in charge of daily VIP placement and table geography, a master at "dressing the room," spreading out the beautiful and well-known, diluting the gray clumps of businessmen, half-burying the loutish and unfortunately dressed ("John, you're wearing your sport coat. Guess you're still on vacation"). There was Bill Levitt (home builder) at Table 2, next to the sleek and Palm Springs-tanned Molly Berns, widow of co-founder Charlie, lunching with Mary McDonough Phillips (*Town & Country* magazine), across from Felix Rohatyn (Big Mac), who sipped his usual Bass ale waiting for Walter Wriston (Citibank), who, when he arrived, slid in next to Ray Stark (film producer), who had attended Rutgers with the late Bob Kriendler in the mid-thirties. Phil Hughes (Plaza Hotel managing director) sat across from Greg Dillon (Hilton executive vice-president for corporate properties), not far from Morton Downey (crooner) and his wife, Anne. Marvin Davis smiled at Orin Atkins (Ashland Oil), who sat beneath his company's truck, one of hundreds of customer-commercial stalactites hanging from the ceiling.

All these diners sat in the bar's first section, called "21," after the original brownstone's address. The midsection is "19," after the brownstone bought in 1935, and the far-eastern third, "17," for the address of the third property, bought a decade later. More often it was called the "Richard Bennett Room," after the tailor shop next door, Siberia to some, a sanctuary for others, such as Frank Polk and Richard Cass, regulars who preferred the section's last tables. Sheldon Tannen noticed that two tables in the sought-after "21" section remained vacant. One was for young, long-legged Howard Johnson. But who was slated for Table 10 today?

Sitting in the lounge under *How Order Number 6 Went Through,* part of the club's million-dollar collection of Frederic Remington paintings, was a small older woman with champagne-colored hair and dressed in red who seemed more like a piece of china in a bull shop in this masculine room with its rich, dark woods, western art,

Jack Kriendler's $10,000 silver saddle in a case topped by a TV showing stock quotations to pin-striped businessmen puffing on cigars. This lively little Meissen figure was Ruth Nash Bliss (automobiles), one of the richest women in the country. As usual, she wore pinned to her dress a diamond-and-ruby-and-emerald replica of her 112-foot yacht, the *Maid Marian,* in which she used to migrate from Palm Springs to Sag Habor. Albert Giannelli, Freddie's colleague, had once encountered the *Maid Marian* in his tiny runabout on Long Island Sound. "Up next to it with those uniformed guys it looked like a high rise," Albert said. Ruth Nash Bliss had recognized Albert and called out a hello. Last night at her favorite table, in the upstairs dining room, she and six friends had celebrated her birthday and played liar's poker with $1 bills. Today she waited for her luncheon guests, Mrs. Mary Roebling (Brooklyn Bridge, banking) and two others, Richard and Pat Nixon, all destined for Table 10.

The Secret Service men entered first, just as they had two nights before, when Jerry and Betty Ford had had a late dinner at Table 14 after *Amadeus.* Jerry had requested the ketchup for his "21" burger, and the captain had brought it over like a $200 bottle of wine. Betty had chicken hash Calcutta. There were two agents this time instead of Ford's six. Pat Nixon followed, looking healthy, her hair shade almost exactly matching Ruth Bliss's, and, behind her, the former president. His polite but formal attitude matched his austere upright posture as he shook hands with Jerry Berns (vice-president, secretary, one-fourth owner, brother of co-founder Charlie Berns), Sheldon Tannen, and his guests. "And how's the *Maid Marian?*" asked Nixon, smiling down at Ruth Nash Bliss, who beamed up at the famous jowls. The Andersons stared at the lobby scene in disbelief.

RICHARD MILHOUS NIXON, PRESIDENT'S TABLE, read the gold plaque above Table 8, where Nixon had eaten dinner while president, the only chief executive to visit the club while in office. Now he preferred the secluded Table 10, below the Uniroyal sign, his back to the corner wall, where he could gaze out at the crowd. Although Table 14 was his for the asking, it is not his style to be on display. Nixon greeted Walter Weiss fondly and discussed with the Austrian head-waiter his recent trip to Vienna. Did he know "21" had called ahead and spoken to the owner and maître d' of the Drei Husaren, the "21" of Vienna, to ensure personal treatment? After ten minutes of adagio chitchat, the Nixon-Bliss party ordered three of chef Anthony Pedretti's specialties: an omelette "21" for Pat, bay scallops for her husband. Ruth Bliss had her usual fish and asparagus "21."

Flanking Richard Nixon at Tables 9 and 11 sat two men who represented the quintessential "21" patron, the foundation of the restaurant's greatness, men of indeterminate date and style, older, wealthy—above all, loyal. H. Huber Boscowitz ("Mr. B.") had lunched at "21" since Prohibition days, in his more active business life upstairs in the quieter, deal-oriented, more elegant dining room. Then, one day, he unexpectedly showed up at Table 9 and has remained there since. Mr. B. always has a fluffy Bloody Mary, well blended to produce a thick layer of foam, before his fillet of sole and creamed spinach, or cherrystone clams and no creamed spinach. In the autumn, he switches from sole to bay scallops. Today, he lunched with his old friend and "21" regular Robert Sarnoff. At Table 11, just inside the entrance, Jim Gillon ("Mr. G."), another 45-year veteran, a retired executive of American Home Products married to the daughter of John Philip Sousa. Mr. G. always chooses one of three items—pea soup, a chicken sandwich, or Welsh rabbit—except on Mondays (corned beef). Gillon mysteriously switched a few years ago from grapefruit to orange juice. Never alcohol.

It is this continuity—unchanging, unaltered, faithful to its code—that has made the "21" Club the most powerful and famous restaurant in the country, a place of refuge and glory for the rich, the influential, the celebrated. Now in its fifty-first year, it has not been worn down by obsession but has been tested and strengthened by endurance. Like many of its older, loyal patrons, it is experiencing with undiminished esprit a second life better than the first. No matter that this American institution is scarcely democratic, that Lenin's famous division of the world into those who do and those to whom it is done could serve as the guiding principle of this bastion of the boardroom, this castle of capitalism. It has not foundered on any reefs of fad, finance, or philosphy but has stuck to its own course of public privacy from the beginning, take it or leave it.

If there is one reason above all others that "21" has survived, it is that the restaurant's operation has remained the obsession of its founding families since Jack Kriendler and Charlie Berns opened the Red Head in Greenwich Village in 1922. It has been true of New York City restaurants from that day in the eighteenth century when Sam Fraunces opened the Queen's Head Tavern: John Delmonico,

Louis Sherry (Sherry's), George Rector (Rector's), Gene Cavallero (Colony Club), Vincent Sardi, Sherman Billingsley (Stork Club), Toots Shor, John Perona (El Morocco)—men or families whose whole existence was "the joint." At "21," the man who carries this tradition forward is H. Peter Kriendler, 76, the club's president, brother of Jack, the premier restaurateur in the country. Like Sam Fraunces he is a connoisseur, extrovert, autocrat. And obsessed with rooting out whatever he sees as treasonous to "21" principles.

Pete Kriendler looked splendid coming down the stairs from the dining room to the lobby, a red carnation in the buttonhole of his dark suit. He spotted someone he didn't know leaving with an old friend.

In a gravelly voice that suggested he gargles with carpet tacks he said, "How are ya? I'm Pete Kriendler and I'm the boss. Did ya enjoy the meal? Was everything all right in the saloon?" One of the most coveted eating areas in America is still a saloon to Kriendler, who served glasses of beer for 10 cents, a nickel more than the competition, at the Red Head. He talked a while longer, gradually bringing the conversation around to his second obsession—western art. For years he has raised money and served as trustee for the Buffalo Bill Historical Center, in Cody, Wyoming, and for the Muscum of the American Indian, in New York, and has continued the acquisition of Remingtons begun by brother Jack. After saying good-bye, Pete Kriendler went on the prowl to assure himself the ship was in good shape.

Entering the saloon, Pete quickly paid his respects to the former president; Mr. G. and Mr. B.; *New Yorker* heavies Peter Fleischmann and George Green, asking the dapper Green if he got the shrimp cocktail without dill, as he had ordered. He lamented to another the temporary closing of La Scala, his favorite Italian restaurant, and waved to Freddy Woolworth, who likes the first bar section if he has a date, "19," the midsection, if alone. He checked the two warming tables in each section—Sterno burners and "21" Sauce Maison jars on top, silverware in the middle, napkins and saucers on bottom—before asking the captain to see if Doubleday chairman John Sargent and his companion, Constance Mellon, were ready for dessert. "Get Mr. Schoenfeld a phone, will ya, Walter?," Pete rasped after chatting with the Shubert Organization chairman. "And, Walter, tell that busboy we don't slide chairs here. We pick them up." "Yes, Mr. Pete," said Walter Weiss. Everyone at "21," from dishwasher to president, is called "Mister" followed by his

first name, a practice that grew out of the years when four Krien-
dlers stalked the floors. Particularly happy about the reversal of this
form of address was the club's steward, Costantinos Fragogiano-
poulos.

Working the middle bar section, Pete said hello to a special
customer, Lou Russek (Health-Tex), who sat at his usual table, No.
21, marked by the plaque MAXWELL'S TABLE OF HAPPY MEMORIES,
in memory of Lou's old friend Mac Kriendler. Directly across from
Russek was regular Bob Altman, at Table 30, near the BOGIE'S COR-
NER sign. Bogart loved "21" but hated the fans waiting for him outside the gates. "Commit insecticide," he snarled at the faithful and
true as he left one night. Mr. Pete watched his waiters for protocol:
Serve counterclockwise, clear clockwise; guest of honor to the right
of the host; host facing the door if possible.

One unvarying Kriendler law: no freebies. "What ya give
away, ya can't sell. When your bank gives you a buck, that's when
I'll give ya a buck" is how The Boss puts it. Sitting at Table 28, all
hair and teeth, Joe Kennedy III, unwittingly illustrating another
Kriendler canon: Don't put the attractive youngsters in the sacred
first section too soon. "What do they have to look forward to in 30
years?" asked The Boss.

There are more formal rules of the house: coats and knotted
ties required (but shoes without socks permitted); dark suits after
six encouraged; photograph taking forbidden; children in the bar
after six discouraged; seating requests for up or downstairs permitted; tables never promised, except to a select few. Pete Kriendler
could break all the above. He felt more comfortable with Louis
Sherry's philosophy—"*Never* disappoint a customer!"—rather than
George Rector's "The guest is right, right or wrong." During the
1930s, he waived the no-women-in-pants rule for Katharine Hep-
burn but no one else. Rudolf Nureyev was the first to be served
without a tie. Marc Chagall is welcomed in slacks and shirt if he
sketches his menu order and leaves it in lieu of payment. The same
applies to Joan Miró, who prefers sketching and paying. But there
are three creeds carved in stone subject to no man's whims:

- Insulting employees is not tolerated.
- Drunks are ejected but welcomed the next day, if sober. Forgotten is forgiven. ("I'm not in the grudge business. I'm a
  host.")
- Tables are not for sale.

Satisfied, Pete Kriendler left the far-eastern Richard Bennett Room after nodding to regular Polk at Table 53. All three sections of the bar were filled, the air charged with the thick smell of tarragon sauce and cigar smoke. It was a noisy crowd of businessmen, coupon clippers with the air of perpetual leisure, and sleek women with summer-colored skin, slender wrists, and slim legs—all a display of expensive, imported health. Prospective diners and drinkers-only stood two-deep along the mahogany bar, which curves the length of the room, munching Charles Chips pretzels (less salt) from five silver bowls and sipping $3 ginger ales and more costly Bloody Marys mixed by silver-haired Henry Zbikiewicz, bartender since 1939 (his only job).

Coming through the entrance was Otto Preminger. Walter greeted the elderly film director in German before showing him to Table 3 (BENCHLEY'S CORNER), not far from where he sat fifteen years ago, when his bald head was cut by a glass thrown by literary agent Swifty Lazar in a battle over the film rights to *In Cold Blood*. Otto waved across to Freddie de Cordova, Johnny Carson's producer, who had replaced Felix Rohatyn. Pete Kriendler was trying to leave the bar to take his prowl elsewhere but now was grateful for the delay. Striding in came the beautiful model Christina Ferrara De Lorean to join her handsome husband. Tall, swathed in red, with long, undulating black hair, Christina swept in past the other women who had turned out this day to air their egos only to be left in her perfumed wake. Seated behind the De Loreans, blond Mrs. Donald Trump, a former model herself, continued an intense discussion with her father.

After the De Lorean amenities, Pete darted out of the entrance to the bar, asked Phillip Lutton, behind the tobacco counter, about his vacation, swung through the door across from the cloakroom with the SERGEANT medallion on the front to spruce up in the Gents' and see if the soap was properly placed on the blue sponges. The man his friends call "The Electric Jackrabbit" visited with Harry the Rope about "OTW" 's (on-the-way's), and headed upstairs to greet the 200 guests eating in the more formal dining areas. The only thing the president of "21" missed was an empty Binaca-mouth-spray dispenser on the floor of the telephone booth.

The "21" Club's main dining room stretches across the front of the three converted brownstones, one floor above West 52nd Street, to the right as you come up the green-carpeted stairs. A large

serving room occupies the center of the floor at the top of the stair-
way, and to the left of the stairs, toward the rear of the building,
the small Tapestry (Tables 105 through 114) and Bottle (200
through 211) Rooms, the latter displaying eleven champagne-bottle
sizes of a 1928 Louis Roederer from the one-fourth-bottle split to
the giant twenty-bottle Nebuchadnezzar. Two nickel-plated duck
presses flank the serving-room entrance, one of which props up the
Ten Commandment-size reservation book. A few years ago, Jerry
Berns personally delivered a sterling-silver duck press to Conrad
Hilton in California because he wanted one and the club had two.

Under a beamed ceiling and surrounded by rough cream-colored walls, dark wainscoting, and a collection of Georgian silver
plates, pewterware, urns, cups, samovars, plates, and tankards valued at $400,000, main-room diners eat in quieter surroundings: sil-
verware, white linen tablecloths and napkins in place before arrival;
tangerine carnations on the table, red and white ones in the corners;
a roomful of Marvin Davis straight-backed chairs. It is a more hab-
itable place for serious business talk, a sanctuary more suited for
stratagems than the livelier bar below. It is a room that brings to
mind Samuel Beckett's line "Something is taking its course." More
of the rouge-and-power set—Mrs. Douglas MacArthur, Ruth Nash
Bliss, Mrs. John Morris, Dr. Armand Hammer, Governor Brendan
Byrne—prefer this room, as did Nelson Rockefeller and Aristotle
Onassis. Compared with the babbling brook downstairs, it is a dawdling river along which elegant and weathered old boats temporarily
dock in safe ports.

Of course, this grand room has a preferred seating area that
corresponds to the bar's front, "21" section, the so-called celebrity
bay. Mrs. MacArthur and Dr. Hammer dined at the Rockefeller table, No. 123, in the far corner, while a longtime "21" regular who
could have his pick, William Stott, chose the Onassis table, No. 127,
in the opposite corner. The Tapestry and Bottle Rooms are generally regarded as venomous areas of oblivion, but more than a few
wheeler-dealers seeking obscurity settle affairs under the Balthazar
and Methuselah bottles or the wallpaper hunting scenes that replaced the valuable tapestry long ago.

Two young men dressed in expensive dark suits and white
shirts greeted Mr. Pete upstairs. They represented the new man-

agement generation at "21," "adopted cousins" brought in from outside the Kriendler-Berns-Tannen troika. The newest, Charles Wilfong, came directly from Cornell's School of Hotel Management three years ago. His blond colleague, Terry Dinan, was the only person ever to graduate from the kitchen staff to management ranks. The first outsider, however, was working downstairs with Walter Weiss. Bruce Snyder, a freshly scrubbed, boyish-looking Oklahoman with a phenomenal memory for names and occupations, joined "21" twelve years ago from the Marriott Corporation's in-flight-food-service operation. Working with Wilfong, Dinan, and Snyder was the family's new representative, Richard Tannen, in charge of banquets and private parties, about one-third of the restaurant's business. Today another 200 guests were being served in the club's four private dining rooms.

All four have proved vigorous and loyal guardians of the flame, working twelve-hour days to learn the complicated social rituals, the unalterable laws and those that bend: who receives the spray of flattery and who likes the formal approach; how to help a loyal "21" fatty about to expire, impaled on his own belt buckle, adhere to his diet; most important, table-geography etiquette. You can say no to anybody if you say it positively and nicely. You do it without negatives. If a man calls and says, "I asked for a table in the bar," and he is Tapestry Room material, you say, "We are holding something for you in the dining room." In a nice way make him feel you have a table somewhere. Don't fight him. Above all, it is not *they* have a table for you, but *we* are expecting you upstairs.

The outsider threesome also symbolize management's differing philosophies regarding the two floors. Mr. Sheldon and Bruce Snyder prefer the more glamorous see-and-be-seen bar, while Charles Wilfong and Terry Dinan fancy the upstairs sanctum sanctorum. "Why not put the beautiful people in this elegant room, where they can be displayed in proper surroundings, and assign the unattractive and insignificant to the darker, yammering bar?" they reason. "The man makes the table, not the table the man" is the official "21" line, which ranks in sincerity with "I am not a crook," once uttered by the diner at corner Table 10.

Model-handsome Terry Dinan checked reservations with headwaiter Tino Gavosto (35 years) near the only table outside the dining-room entrance, producer Jean Dalrymple's favorite. Charles Wilfong scolded a waiter for having added diced chicken to the

POWER POSITIONS IN THE BAR

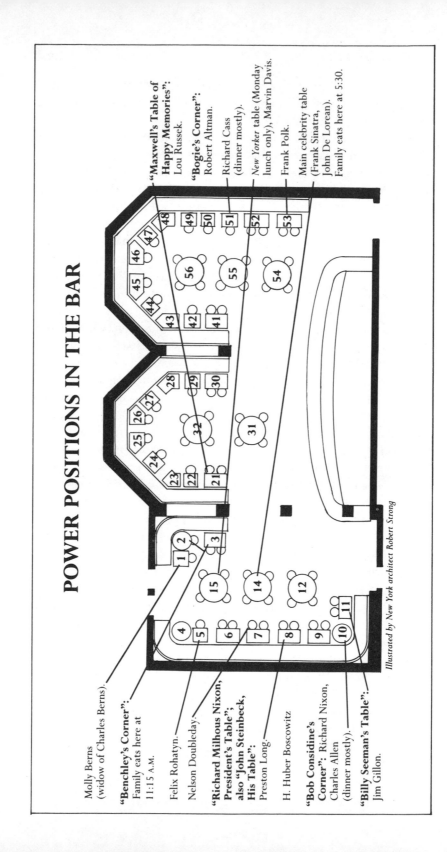

Molly Berns
(widow of Charles Berns).

"Benchley's Corner":
Family eats here at
11:15 A.M.

Felix Rohatyn.

Nelson Doubleday.

**"Richard Milhous Nixon,
President's Table";
also "John Steinbeck,
His Table":**
Preston Long.

H. Huber Boscowitz

**"Bob Considine's
Corner":** Richard Nixon,
Charles Allen
(dinner mostly).

"Billy Seeman's Table":
Jim Gillon.

**"Maxwell's Table of
Happy Memories":**
Lou Russek.

"Bogie's Corner":
Robert Altman.

Richard Cass
(dinner mostly).

New Yorker table (Monday
lunch only), Marvin Davis.

Frank Polk.

Main celebrity table
(Frank Sinatra,
John De Lorean).
Family eats here at 5:30.

Illustrated by New York architect Robert Strong

crème sénégalaise in the kitchen instead of at the table, then stood at the head of the stairs ready to receive guests. The waiter shrugged and popped a piece of parsley in his mouth as a breath freshener.

"Mr. Victor Potamkin, party of three," bawled Freddie the Escort, whose job was to precede the customer to the first landing to alert Charles or Terry. "Good afternoon, Mr. Potamkin. Glad to have you," greeted Charles in a perfect non-wheedling tone. "Your table is ready." New York's Cadillac king soon held a muted council with two associates two places down from the Onassis corner. Twenty feet away, Jack Paar, in matching lime-green shirt and tie, wearing smoke-tinted glasses, relaxed with his wife, Miriam. More names were announced as Charles, Terry, or Tino led the guests left to despair or right to honor and glory. As "21" has few ruthless seating creeds, Charles and Terry often confer in cryptic mumblings about table futures. Seldom is there any manic semaphore, and never any crude third-base coaching signals, such as Sherman Billingsley's finger alongside nose to indicate a guest of no consequence.

Striding up the stairs dressed in the preppie-emeritus mode (blazer, rep tie, gray slacks, Belgian loafers, no socks) came lanky Bill O'Shaughnessy, who bears a striking resemblance to the singer Jack Jones and who was talking about "21" as a way of life. "Rites of passage occur here, great events in your life. Years back, my son Matthew and I were downstairs, and the kid kept staring at one of the planes hanging from the ceiling. The late Bob Kriendler just reached up and gave it to him. Matthew never forgot that. Now my wife and I are splitting up, and the things we are fighting over most are the cups from '21.' " Not so long ago, the management presented silver cups to favorite families like the O'Shaughnessys (Bill's father-in-law is Walter Thayer, associate of Jock Whitney, publisher of the late *Herald Tribune*) with the newborn's name inscribed. The custom ceased with the rise of silver prices.

Pete Kriendler had prowled the room once and stopped near the entrance to chat with an old favorite, Rosser Reeves, who had inherited Joan Crawford's table, just inside the room on the left. The Electric Jackrabbit waved to habitué Roy Cohn, who was choosing his favorite cigars—104 Cabinettes—from a box sent from below, and spent time with the richest man in the building, Dr. Armand Hammer, who sat snug in the Rockefeller corner. Preppie-radio man O'Shaughnessy (president of big-band station

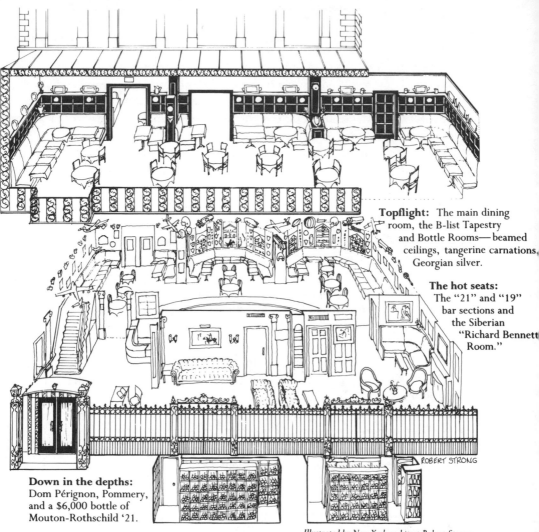

Topflight: The main dining room, the B-list Tapestry and Bottle Rooms— beamed ceilings, tangerine carnations, Georgian silver.

The hot seats: The "21" and "19" bar sections and the Siberian "Richard Bennett Room."

Down in the depths: Dom Pérignon, Pommery, and a $6,000 bottle of Mouton-Rothschild '21.

ROBERT STRONG

Illustrated by New York architect Robert Strong

WRTN) stood towering over the Izod-alligator czar, Vin Draddy. Mr. Pete left to check on the Bottle Room, where circumstances had beached a nice young couple named Anderson.

By 2:30 the dining room was empty, and only a few remained in the bar. A feeling of lassitude hung in the air as guests emerged onto the sidewalk, blinking at the bright sun, shaking off their semi-torpor, looking somewhat sad about the end of their self-indulgent hibernation. Inside, Ray Stark lingered over dessert. Morton Downey, 80, was a long way down the road from his *Camel Quarter-Hour* program and the days when the Stork Club was his hideout and he, Billingsley, and Arthur Godfrey owned a perfume company whose product Sherman used to give to favorites at Christmas. On this afternoon, Downey chatted with Jim Gillon and fired up the club's largest cigar, a $2 eleven-inch Jamaican Churchill. The bosses had retired to upstairs offices; Walter Weiss had started home to Long Island to nap and change his tux; the second shift in the kitchen had arrived, including the busboy who wraps the lemons in surgical gauze; only the bartenders, Phillip behind the tobacco counter, and Naini Shekhar, one of the ropes at the front door, were in place. The restaurant settled in for a brief siesta. Only in the early-morning hours between three and four, after the cleanup crew had left and before the arrival of the first kitchen mate, would there be another period of inactivity at 21 West 52nd Street.

The founders of "21" were not exactly like the polished, urbane hosts currently sitting down to lunch. Jack Kriendler's father, an Austrian immigrant from the Lower East Side, worked as a welder in the Brooklyn Navy Yard; his mother midwifed 3,000 Manhattan babies, including Jerry Berns. Charlie Bern's Austrian-immigrant parents lived on the West Side, above Hell's Kitchen. Both Charlie and Jack had worked part-time at Jack's uncle Sam Brenner's speak-easy while attending college. Jack, always the more adventurous, borrowed $1,000 from his sister and brother-in-law, the Tannen-baums, and opened "21"'s firstborn, the Red Head, on the west side of Sixth Avenue between 4th and Washington Place, the site today of McBell's, No. 359. The next year, on May 21, 1923, the most famous restaurant in America, Delmonico's, served its last dinner to 30 guests, just four years before its hundredth birthday.

There are fascinating parallels between that great American restaurant, the first to introduce haute cuisine to the country, and the "21" Club. Like Kriendler and Berns, Peter and John Delmonico had little previous restaurant experience. Realizing that New Yorkers had thrived on a meat diet since the seventeenth century, the Delmonicos loaded up the menu with beef, mutton, wild fowl, and game among the 346 entrées. Early on, "21" gained a reputation for fine game dishes such as mallard, pheasant, venison, and Scotch grouse. When the business prospered, the Delmonicos called in more family—Lorenzo, Siro, François, Constant—as "21" later summoned Kriendler's Bob, Mac, Pete, and nephew Sheldon Tannen. Delmonico's began psychological gambits still used at "21": writing menus in both English and French; raising prices above the competition's; paying employees well to ensure loyalty;

creating a relaxed, luxurious setting; attracting the rich and famous (Horace Greeley, Chester Arthur, August Belmont), the celebrity, after-theater crowd (Jenny Lind), the literary lions (Mark Twain, William Dean Howells, Bret Harte); building better restaurants as they followed the town's progress north; pampering favored clients; keeping it in the family.

In 1897, less than a year after Delmonico's made its last move uptown, to Fifth Avenue and 44th Street, Louis Sherry opened his Stanford White-designed Sherry's across the street and stole "the hectics," the fast crowd, from Del's. It forecast a dramatic change in American eating habits. With increased personal wealth—from more than 100 U.S. millionaires in 1880 to 4,000 in 1890 and 40,000 in 1916—people wanted spice and glitter, a faster style of life. The old standards of society—family background, bloodlines— had given way to money and a new urban population that wanted to spend and have a good time.

World War I and Prohibition changed the nation's nightlife habits once again. While the early 1920s brought bad times to New York restaurants because of the aid local police gave to the federal Volstead agents, a looser era came after 1924. New York had voted to abandon local enforcement; only a small federal force was left to monitor Manhattan. At the peak of Prohibition, over 32,000 "speaks" operated in New York, twice the number of saloons that had been padlocked in 1920.

One of these 32,000 was doing just fine. The Red Head had caught on with the sporty-newspaper-music-collegiate crowd, who enjoyed gregarious Jack Kriendler's slightly upper-crusty club atmosphere, a fraternity room of wise guys who could yell "Nerts to you" and practice their practical jokes and mock scares ("Iggers-jay, the ops-kay") in pig Latin. Three years later Berns and Kriendler bought a place across the street for $3,000 and changed the name to the Club Frontón. After a year, the city condemned the property to build a subway station. It was time to move uptown. They found a townhouse a few doors from where Bergdorf Goodman stood at the time, at Fifth and 49th, and purchased it for $15,000. The Puncheon Grotto opened at 42 West 49th in 1926. Three years later, condemnation proceedings—this time for Rockefeller Center— forced Kriendler and Berns to relocate again, to their best-known address, 21 West 52nd Street. On the snowy first of January of 1930, Jack and Charlie's "21" Club opened on the most famous speakeasy street in New York, neighbors with Tony's, Club 18, the

Yacht Club, Leon & Eddie's (with its sign, THROUGH THESE PORTALS THE MOST BEAUTIFUL GIRLS IN THE WORLD PASS OUT), and Frank & Jack's, where the technique of using a drunk to get rid of a drunk was perfected.

The club was a success from the beginning, attracting a wealthy and important clientele from café society, politics, and Wall Street who knew "21" or the Numbers or Three was immune from federal agents. It was raided only once. In 1932 ten federal cops spent twelve hours at the club looking for the 2,000 cases of liquor hidden behind the cellar door. The liquor out front had already disappeared, after the bartender pushed a button, which overturned shelves behind the bar and sent bottles crashing down an iron grating along a brick-lined chute and into the New York sewage system. In a decade of operating speaks, Jack and Charlie were convicted only once for liquor possession, and it proved good for business. Prosecutors analyzed the seized demon rum and declared under oath that it was first-class stuff. Newspaper editorials angrily wondered why "21" 's owners, rather than the salesmen of the rotgut, had to pay fines. (The restaurant's liquor supply is still well protected, though it no longer self-destructs. Wine-cellar attendant Mike Canales inserts a long metal wire into a tiny hole to release the catch that swings open the two-and-a-half-ton steel-and-brick door. Inside are 2,000 to 2,500 cases of wine and liquor, worth $155,325, including a $6,000 bottle of 1921 Mouton-Rothschild, Richard Nixon's Dom Pérignon 1959, Aristotle Onassis's 1962 Pommery, and the private stock of the famous—Henry Fonda, Burgess Meredith, Hugh Carey.)

By Repeal and the mid-thirties, the other family members had joined the booming enterprise: Pete Kriendler in 1939 after selling his seat on the New York Curb Exchange, now the American Stock Exchange, Mac in 1929 after leaving St. John's Law School, Bob after graduating from Rutgers in 1936, and Jerry Berns in 1938 after resigning from his post as drama critic of the Cincinnati *Enquirer*. Sheldon Tannen joined just before Jack's death, in 1947. In 1934, the first offshoot of "21" was formed, "21" Brands, a wholesale liquor business. It secured the exclusive U.S. distributorship of Ballantine's scotch and moved the company into a newly purchased brownstone. It was sold in 1970 to Foremost-McKesson.

As the years went by, the "21" traditions and trademarks developed. Jack began collecting the bric-a-brac and gimcracks, anything from Georgian silver to collegiate pennants to valuable

Remingtons. A friend of Bob's stuck a model airplane on the ceiling and thus began the bar-ceiling transportation-model craze. Robert Benchley had begun hanging out at the Puncheon Grotto and brought his Algonquin crowd over. Other writers followed: Steinbeck, Considine, O'Hara, Thurber; Hemingway ordered his "Papa Doble," four ounces of light rum and a squirt of grapefruit juice. For 40 years a Salvation Army band has played Christmas carols in the bar just before December 25 because Jack Kriendler and George Jean Nathan once invited the passing band inside to play and pass the hat. The Yale Glee Club serenades (without charge) before Thanksgiving.

After World War II, the expense-account crowd replaced the café-society revelers. Now there are publishers instead of writers, producers rather than actors, more team owners than players, more board chairmen than vice-presidents. No matter the cast of characters, "21" has continued to prosper. Restaurant receipts in 1967, $4.5 million; in 1980, $10 million. The cigar-and-gift distributorship, "21" Selected Items, which earned $750,000 in 1967, cleared $1 million last year. Income from Irongate Products, an importer of caviar, other specialty foods, and restaurant equipment, rose from $1.5 million in 1967 to about $4 million last year. The typical top-ranked New York restaurant does $16,000 worth of business per seat annually, according to Laventhol & Horwath, an accounting firm that conducts restaurant-industry studies. A seat at "21" averages $25,000.

The newest venture is more ambitious. In recent years, a newly formed "21" Management Company attempted to export its expertise by managing the Crickets restaurant in Chicago and the Jockey Club in Washington D.C. It withdrew from both operations after disagreements with owner John Coleman. Last year "21" signed an agreement to manage the Mansion on Turtle Creek in Dallas, a 145-room luxury hotel and restaurant financed by H. L. Hunt oil money. Another venture is planned for next year in Houston. Meanwhile, the late-afternoon naps are ending at 21 West 52nd Street, for there is a whole city of gold bracelets and pinstripes waiting to descend on this venerable old fortress of tradition.

Chef Anthony himself cooks for the family. Once again, at 5:30, the chieftains of "21" gather, this time at Table 14, underneath the USS *Intrepid* cap and the Pan Am 747 *Clipper Liberty Bell* jet for a pre-evening-crowd powwow. They have showered, rested, molted their dark suits for freshly pressed ones. Mr. Pete, however, bathes only in the morning. "When I visited Dr. Albert Schweitzer in Africa, he told me too many showers wash off essential body oils. In my lifetime he was the greatest man I have met, and I've known them all," mused The Boss while ordering fresh broccoli with lemon. "Churchill's next. Never met him but we used to send him sirloins and cigars during the war." Jerry Berns softly whispered to the captain in the politest voice, "Please ask the chef to send me a plate without old juice stains." Berns added with a wink, "Thank him for me." Like his brother before him, Jerry Berns is the cautious money man who carefully watches the profit-and-loss. He is also the club's representative to the restaurant industry, serving on the executive committee of the Culinary Institute of America, speaking to restaurant associations, managing the "21" scholarships. With the arrival of his clean plate, Berns talked about the visiting wine editor and the Louisiana honey given to him at noon by Tabasco magnate Edmund McIlhenny. After dipping in the silver finger bowls, the group adjourned to their posts to greet and work the crowd already filtering in from the street.

Mike Beamer, at the rope tonight, said hello to the CBS guys who like to come in just to relax in the fireplace lounge, ordering up the canapé plate and maybe a few South Sides (gin, lemon juice, fresh mint) before moving on. Mike checked over the reservations, separating the regulars and celebs from the unknowns. He welcomed a beautifully dressed old man named Richard Rimanoczy, who leaned on a cane, looking at the "21" paper plates in the display case, $3 a dozen. Mr. Rimanoczy announced to no one in particular that he had been walking down the "21" stairway on a Sunday morning when he heard the Japanese had attacked Pearl Harbor. Senator Abe Ribicoff and ex-mayor Robert Wagner and wives passed Mr. Rimanoczy on their way to Marvin Davis's table, No. 15, followed by Edgar Bronfman (Seagram's), who ordered his usual goujonettes of sole from the supper menu.

Headwaiter Peter Billia (35 years' service) had joined Walter Weiss for the evening. Walter would serve as captain and had already begun swordplay with a hunk of beef. The proud Billia showed his colleagues a letter announcing the promotion of one of his daughters to vice-president at Benton & Bowles. Billia's other daughter works as a chef at the Wine Press, and his son is a manager/headwaiter at Doubles. Billia smiled a hello to a big guy behind the bar wearing a marine pin over his nameplate, which read BRU.

Bru Mysak, 34 years at "21" with time out to pursue an acting career (subway killer in *Al Capone,* chauffeur in *The Notorious Landlady*), is the quintessential bartender: storyteller, patient listener—above all, mixologist. While he prepared one of his originals, a Foxy Lady (gin, Bailey's Irish Cream, and a cherry), created for Elizabeth Taylor's stage debut, Bru reminisced with a customer about watching Errol Flynn drink sixteen Jack Roses (applejack, lime juice, grenadine) before falling senseless to the floor.

In front of Bru in the "19" section, Mr. Pete sat with his guests, watercolorist Dong Kingman, just back from China, which Kriendler had visited earlier in the year, and the man who had arranged his trip, Yu Min-Sheng, chief U.N. correspondent for the Hsinhua News Agency. With Mr. Pete's blessing, Mr. Min-Sheng stood up and began bending the rules by snapping pictures of the guests. Something in the regal-roost "21" section, however, caught Mr. Pete's eye and made him very angry.

At Table 4, near the kitchen, Mrs. Bob Kriendler sat with a cute, pre-teen little nipper dressed in a blue blazer, rep tie, and gray slacks, quietly awaiting dinner. Children in the saloon! No one dared move the widow of Mr. Bob, but Pete chewed out Walter anyway and stomped around until his storm temper passed. The well-behaved child stared at the planes, trains, and trucks a lot while watching Robert Sarnoff, Anna Moffo, and Sonny Werblin eat. He perked up when actor Darren McGavin, all in white (including shoes and socks), passed through on his way to get a towel twirl and spiritual blessing from Otis in the Gents' Room. Jim Gillon ("Mr. G.") had returned, making him a "42," a twice-a-day "21" man.

Out front, Mr. Sheldon, Mr. Bruce, Mr. Jerry, and Mike the Rope all fluttered like butterflies around the important guest, a tiny woman dressed in red (like Bliss, De Lorean, Moffo), who had entered like royalty with her guests. Mrs. Douglas MacArthur had just returned from Washington, where she and President Reagan had dedicated a second-floor corridor in the Pentagon to her late husband. Smiling to all the enthralled lepidoptera, particularly Bruce Snyder, whose birthday (January 26) is the same as the general's, she carefully proceeded up the stairs to the Rockefeller table. Slipping past a couple of middle-aged jocks with Locust Valley lockjaw who were jangling change, slapping backs, and looking as if they were about to engage in butt slaps and break the huddle, strolled an attractive, overweight couple, Governor John Y. Brown and his wife,

Phyllis George, destined for the darkest penetralia of the celeb section.

Mr. Pete missed John Y (as everybody privately calls the Kentucky gov) but greeted the next man with open arms and a blunt, affectionate kiss. No one stands higher in the "21" Hall of Fame than Charles Allen (money), a regular since the clacking of Mah-Jongg tiles could be heard in the lounge. Always a night man, Allen owns Table 10—Nixon's favorite—in the corner. If Charlie Allen came in Monday night, the one night Yul Brynner dined at Table 10, on his night off from singing "Shall We Dance?" for the 10,000th time, the King of Siam moved over. Tonight Charlie was joined by his nephew, Herbert, president of Allen and Company, and Edgar Kaiser Jr. Once again the butterflies fluttered. Cigarettes were lit; the above air-conditioning vent tilted away; the phone was plugged in for Kaiser, its red umbilical cord snaking over his suit shoulder. Later, Edgar begged Mr. Pete to accept a ride in his new Grumman Gulfstream private jet to Alaska for the fishing trip. "Sure," Mr. Pete said, grinning his open, remembering smile. "Nobody lives better than I do. Nobody."

Was Mr. Sinatra coming or not? Table 14, vacated by Sarnoff's party, stood waiting. So did Frank's favorite wine (1969 Pétrus, $110, and 1970, $200) and his Sambuca Originale and the plate of hot peppers in olive oil he liked. All week, people had asked Walter and Peter Billia and others, "Ya got any Snotra tickets?" (for the singer's Carnegie Hall shows). Ol' Blue Eyes didn't show, but his wife, Barbara, did, with Dina Merrill and her husband, Cliff Robertson. They sat under the USS *Intrepid* cap and drank Frank's wines anyway. Martin Gabel and his wife, Arlene Francis, occupied the vacated Ribicoff-Wagner table, No. 15, next door.

While Bru fixed a Captain Blood (rum, cranberry and lime juice, and a dash of tequila in a champagne glass), the favorite of Earl Smalley, former part-owner of the Miami Dolphins (who never fails to say "What a way to go" after gulping a Captain Blood), a cheerfully inebriated friend of the house swayed through the front door, trying for a dead-stick landing. Mike the Rope coolly greeted the man, who began talking in more syllables than he was thinking in. "Here for dinner?" asked Mike. The man became nettled, belligerent. "F--- dinner. It's too expensive. I need a drink." Mike's eyes narrowed, his face still pleasant.

"Obviously, Bill, you've been overserved. I want you to walk over to the Gents' Room, wash your face, brush your hair a bit, make yourself presentable. If you make a misstep going into the bar, and I call you, that means 'Get lost.' There's a $7.95 buffet across the street at the Bombay Palace," Mike continued, still smiling pleasantly. The short speech stunned the man into compliance as if it had been his stern old granddad talking from the grave. He followed Mike's instructions, sheepishly returning from Otis's benediction and two towel twirls, realizing his punishment had been invited.

More trouble in the lobby. The last of the great oilmen, Michael Halbouty, with silver hair and mustache, had stormed past his book (*Wildcatter*), behind the tobacco stand, after complaining to Walter, and now he was giving Mike the Rope a what-for about everything. Walter had given the Texan one of the best tables in the house, Table 2, near the kitchen. Not good enough for Halbouty. His thin smile worked on the thermos-jug principle—containing heat without radiating it—and his attitude reflected what he expected in life, perfect obedience to his wishes as to a law of nature.

"Goddamn it, why did Walter give me that egomaniac table? Like 42nd and Broadway over there. Can't here a thang. Had to send back the salad. The service was terrible. Goddamn egomaniac table. Walter knows where I like to sit. S---." Mike, who had just been the tough guy, assumed a mock-affronted expression and turned into a positively radiant source of effusive blandishments. "Very sorry, Mr. Halbouty. Walter just doing his best. Very crowded tonight with the Snotra thing. Please accept our apologies. *Mea culpa,* Mr. Halbouty." The old wildcatter calmed down and asked his blond wife if she would like to go to the Rainbow Room. "Do the old one-two, eh, Mr. Halbouty," said Mike. "I don't think so, honey," said Mrs. H. "Probably get mugged walking over there anyway," grumbled Mr. H.

Toward midnight, the activity on both floors was winding down. The flood tide of theatergoers had descended on the place an hour and a half earlier (80 reservations were noted from 10:30 to 11), all looking for first-section bar tables like Oklahoma land grabbers. Most had settled into the silence of exile up in the Tapestry and Bottle Rooms or over in the Richard Bennett section. Mr. Pete had left hours ago, as he usually did. Mr. Sheldon had departed for a weekend in Westhampton. Of the chieftains, only Mr. Jerry remained.

All the young braves, however, still toiled at their posts. Charles Wilfong and Terry Dinan were grateful Bruce Snyder hadn't performed his "assume" number. "When you assume, you get in trouble," Bruce was fond of repeating. He would pull out a pad, write "ass/u/me," and say, "You make an ass out of you and me."

There have been other changes through the years besides the hiring of new blood and sturdier constitutions. In the early 1970s, the use of credit cards was permitted. Since tennis has become the rage, the club now opens on the Saturday of the U.S. Open matches rather than before the Marlboro Cup. With the closing of the stock exchange and banks on Saturdays, and with increased weekend traveling, Saturday's lunch crowd dwindled. Stock quotes traveled over TV screens instead of a ticker-tape machine. And the restaurant no longer employed a barber or masseur, although Mr. Pete stayed with his old employee Sven Erickson in West Palm Beach, where they fished together and got two rubdowns a day for old-time's sake.

In past years, there have been several serious attempts by strangers to buy "21." In 1969, the Ogden Corporation put up $10 million for the club and its subsidiaries, but the deal fell apart when Ogden's stock slipped below a stipulated minimum. And the collective consciousness of loyal "21"ers must have shivered on some inward seismograph when the principals agreed to sell 51 percent of the club and two adjoining buildings to Texas oil millionaire Baron Enrico di Portanova for over $13 million as a present for his wife, the Baroness Sandra. The deal remains in limbo, despite careful negotiations by the baron's attorney, Roy Cohn. Sheldon Tannen admits there are still serious suitors; that they need liquid capital for expansion plans; that, if sold, there will always be a clause guaranteeing management by the family; that he will never sell his shares of "21" stock. Until death separates them, Mr. Sheldon, Mr. Jerry, and Mr. Pete will be hanging around "the joint." Only one person has been there longer, Mrs. David Morse, who was born at 21 West 52nd Street and still comes around "the cradle," as she calls it.

The remaining male guests this night puffed on cigars; the women puckered stenciled mouths red as wine for perfunctory good-bye kisses, contorted their faces with stupendously suppressed yawns, took bird bites out of luscious, fattening desserts. Over at the bar, Mr. Jerry and his wife, Suzanne, discussed the merits of malt scotch. Both know their whiskeys. Suzanne, his wife of four years, works as a wine-sales representative for Knickerbocker Industries. Now Dewar's alternates with Ballantine's as "21" 's bar scotch. To Jerry, the Glenlivet twelve-year-old ranks just ahead of Dewar's White Label of the same year. But Suzanne's company sells Dewar's. Mr. Jerry sniffed his Glenlivet and beamed at his wife. "Hell, I don't drink it. I sell it."

Mark Singer

Joe Mitchell, A. J. Liebling and Lillian Ross found the street cultures of New York City fascinating subjects for their writing long before Mark Singer came along. But he has followed in their footsteps. His profile of Ben Shine, member of a quiet, law-abiding group of court buffs who have developed a taste for murder trials, could have been written about the regular spectators in courtrooms across the nation. Singer studied these court buffs for sixteen months before he was confident his portrait did justice to their lives.

Two years after Singer graduated from Yale University, he landed a job at *The New Yorker* magazine. At Yale, he had studied nonfiction writing with William Zinsser. For two years, Singer worked at the Yale alumni magazine, which Zinsser edited, and shopped for work in the New York publishing world. Eventually, the late Robert Bingham, a member of *The New Yorker* staff, introduced him to the editor, William Shawn.

When he arrived at the magazine as a "Talk of the Town" writer, in the fall of 1974, he was 23. "I came to *The New Yorker* without having any idea why I had been invited, and without really appreciating who William Shawn was," Singer said. "I meant to ask Bingham before he died why I was hired. There must have been some trace of humanity in my voice for Mr. Shawn to think I could come here and be a writer, but how did he *know?*"

Writing "Talk of the Town" stories—Singer estimates that he has written 200—eventually gave him the courage to try longer nonfiction pieces. Goodman Ace, old-time radio comedian; Gene Stipe, Oklahoma politician; Sam Cohn, motion picture and theatrical talent agent; Rubin Levine, street violinist; the five Brennan brothers, superintendents in luxury Manhattan apartment houses; and Benjamin Shine, court buff, all have been subjects of his profiles.

In 1983, Singer returned to his native Oklahoma to work on a book about the boom and bust in the Oklahoma oil and gas businesses during the early 1980s.

Court Buff

*I*n all sorts of circumstances, certain people in Brooklyn will commit murder. This fact fascinates Benjamin Shine more than it appalls him. Shine is a peaceable gentleman from Borough Park who would hate to be asked which he prefers—a sunny afternoon stroll alongside the Belt Parkway with his wife, Tillie, or a dukes-up double-murder trial. He is a self-taught student of the behavior of criminals, innocents, witnesses, lawyers, judges, and jurors. He is a court buff. As a sideline, he happens to be a student of the behavior of his fellow court buffs. Most weekdays, a dozen or more buffs show up at the State Supreme Court Building on Cadman Plaza, in downtown Brooklyn. Shine attends as regularly as any back-seat jurisconsult in the borough.

Although Shine has lived in Brooklyn for most of his seventy-three years, he is no provincial. He acknowledges that the other boroughs of New York City have bred their own miscreants. Having spent the past dozen years watching criminal trials—mainly murder trials—in Brooklyn, however, he has found it sensible and convenient to become a specialist. Consequently, he takes more interest in a corpse that has been deposited in an airshaft in Flatbush than in one that has turned up in the trunk of an automobile at La-Guardia Airport or in a vacant lot near Hunts Point. Shine realizes that in addition to murderers there are anti-social types out there who have the capacity for rape, theft, burglary, kidnapping, arson, or aimless mayhem—at times, of course, overlapping occurs—but he devotes most of his attention to homicides. He is not ghoulish, merely curious. "Where there's murder," he often says, quite accurately, "you know something's doing."

Anyone who regularly conducts business in the criminal courts of New York City grows accustomed to seeing buffs seated in the back of the room. Many shortsighted lawyers think of court buffs as part of the furniture, and ignore them. But enlightened and resourceful lawyers regard knowledgeable buffs as jurors' jurors. On occasion, during trial recesses, they seek the buffs' counsel. Attention of this sort pleases a buff. Just because one buff tells another that an inept lawyer is stinking up a courtroom with his performance, it doesn't mean that he wants the lawyer in question to know he thinks so. A lawyer who solicits a buff's opinion usually hears words of reassurance. It is in a buff's interest to massage a lawyer's ego. Lawyers call witnesses to testify, and courtroom testimony is often amazing. The way a buff sees it, lawyers deserve encouragement; they book a lot of free entertainment. "I'd pay a dollar to see a good trial, I really would," Shine has said—grateful, just the same, that he doesn't have to. "Some of these buffs, though, I think if you charged only fifty cents you'd lose quite a few."

The State Supreme Court in Brooklyn—"Supreme Kings," in the parlance of the legal community—is an eleven-story building that covers two square blocks. It has a talc-gray concrete exterior punctuated by rows of rectangular windows, and it sits on Cadman Plaza like a Second World War battleship in permanent drydock. Inside, it is made of durable materials—pink marble, oak, brushed aluminum. All felony proceedings that originate with indictments are heard in the State Supreme Court; there were four hundred and thirty-six murder indictments in Brooklyn last year. Between trials, the buffs of Kings County shuffle through the corridors of the Supreme Court Building with the luxurious confidence of warehouse owners at a bankruptcy auction. A man named Harry Takifman, a colleague of Shine's, once explained this attitude to me in pragmatic terms. "In this joint, you got your rape cases, you got your murders, your muggings, your narcotics," he said. "So if you don't like what you see in one courtroom you can always go shopping somewhere else."

Like his friend Harry Takifman, Shine is not prone to lofty pronouncements about the nature of mankind. He subscribes to all Ten Commandments but never moralizes. He enjoys exercising his critical faculties, and avails himself of the chance to do so on a daily basis. From time to time, I join him at Supreme Kings and take in a murder trial or two myself. I met Shine one winter morning while we were both devoting our attention to *People v. DiChiara*, a homicide trial that contained ample measures of novelty and poignancy. After years of listening to hundreds of variations on a limited number of themes—toll collector discovers wife and upstairs neighbor in flagrante, gun goes off six times; bongo player, father of four, dies

of stab wounds outside East New York social club on Saturday
night—Shine has come to resemble an uncommon sort of naturalist, the bird-watcher who studies flocks of starlings in the hope that
a green wood hoopoe will fly by. Eventually, one does. As I saw
more and more trials in Shine's company, I came to realize that People *v.* DiChiara, while not quite a green wood hoopoe, was still a
bird that had wandered away from its natural habitat. Shine is hap-
piest when a trial appeals to what he calls "the composite powers
of my mind." Shine has made up the verb "to composite"—or,
rather, has composited it. To composite, in his version, means to
embellish; to embroider reality; to transport the facts to the exurbs
of plausibility. A friend of Shine's, a buff named Leo Friedman, persuaded Shine to visit the Picasso exhibition at the Museum of Modern Art. Shine came away saying that while he wasn't crazy about a
lot of the artist's paintings he thought that "Picasso could composite—oh, and how."

People *v.* DiChiara had Shine compositing heavily. Frank
DiChiara was a Brooklyn clothing-factory owner who had been accused of stealing fourteen thousand dollars—the entire savings of
one of his employees, an Italian immigrant, and her husband—and,
while burglarizing their home, of shooting the couple's only child,
a thirteen-year-old girl, who, before dying, told the police, "My
mother's boss, Frank DiChiara, shot me." The first day I sat in on
the trial, I took a spot in the spectator gallery next to Shine. He nodded and smiled at me. A couple of minutes later, at the mention of
Frank DiChiara's name, he nudged me with an elbow and tilted his
head in the direction of the defense table.

"That's DiGennaro," he said softly, compositing with the pro-
nunciation of the defendant's name. Frank DiChiara wore a well-
cut suit and had dark hair, the physique of a stevedore, and a blank
expression.

"*That* guy?" I asked, aiming an index finger.

"Don't point," Shine warned. "Don't point in the courtroom,
and don't talk in the elevator if the other passengers have jurorly
appearances. Yeah. That one. And that's his family to your right."

After a discreet pause, I turned slowly and looked at two men
and a woman who shared the bench with us. She was pretty and
had black-dyed hair and wore a white wool coat with a white-dyed
fur collar. The men wore dark pin-striped suits and white shirts
with French cuffs and gold links. Each had a copy of *Il Progresso*
folded in his lap. In profile, both men distinctly resembled Frank

DiChiara. Someone in the group smelled of Juicy Fruit. My own mind began to composite.

The evidence in the case, as marshalled by Harold Rosenbaum, a district attorney who is as familiar to Brooklyn homicide buffs as Joe Torre is to Mets diehards, seemed conclusive. Rosenbaum is a journeyman who saw fit to introduce into evidence, apropos of nothing that I could figure out, a pair of heavy green cotton bloomers that the victim, Germania Zurlo, had customarily worn underneath her parochial-school uniform. Elena Zurlo, the victim's mother, a gray-haired woman in her early fifties, was on the witness stand at the time. Seeing the bloomers reduced Mrs. Zurlo to misery, and no doubt impressed the jurors. When the time came, they pronounced DiChiara guilty. Shine accepted the verdict as inevitable, but a seed of doubt lingered and germinated. "I was reluctant to go along with that jury in DiGennaro," he said weeks later. "You saw the guy in court. You saw how he looked. I didn't figure him to be the sort who steals fourteen thousand on a breaking-and-entering. He didn't look the part. Here he was with a factory in Williamsburg, a nice suit of clothes. I think he's more the type with a weekend house in the Poconos, maybe a limousine with a horn that honks out the theme from 'The Godfather.' A Poconos guy wouldn't be likely to try something like this." Shine paused and reshuffled the facts. "Don't get me wrong. I'm not saying fourteen thousand's not a good amount. Matter of fact, if you had a house in the Poconos already you could make some nice improvements with that much money." He paused again. "I don't think it would have happened if he hadn't panicked—this girl comes home from school and finds him there and he panics. And if the girl hadn't lived to say, 'My mother's boss shot me.' Now, there you have a classic example of a 'spontaneous declaration.' The victim knows she's gonna die, and she names her assailant. That's really something. Rosenbaum called this detective to the stand, and the detective said this girl said that DiGennaro shot her. Normally, hearsay they don't allow. But if it's a spontaneous declaration they allow the hearsay. It's an exception to the hearsay rule. She knows the end is near. So they allow it. On the other hand, you wonder about a guy who takes weekends in the Poconos. Of course, I'm only compositing."

When Shine wove this theory for me, it occurred to me that he might be an avid reader of mysteries and, perhaps, an underpaid literary critic. We had just eaten lunch and were taking a stroll. I asked him who his favorite compositors were.

"If I read too much anymore, my nerves fall asleep—which is what I want sometimes," he said. "I can listen to that guy Larry King on the radio and that puts me to sleep. I sleep the whole night through with the radio on. Reading—I used to like Maupassant and, yeah, Edgar Allan Poe and, whatsis, yeah, Arthur Conan Doyle. Poe I like a little less, because he gets too colorful before he gets to the point he's trying to make. Also, it's not compositing. It's fantasy. It's not close enough to the real thing. The only thing that's better than the real thing is maybe Arthur Conan Doyle. I classify Doyle's work as classic. After all, he's dead quite some time now."

It was a warm day, and we were walking across Cadman Plaza, moving between shade and light beneath a row of tall London plane trees, in no special hurry to find out what José Rotger and Miriam Acevedo had done with the shotgunned body of José Martinez after rolling it up in a rug on St. Marks Avenue.

"And not too much poetry," Shine added. "One poem I remember very well, though. You know this one?" He recited the first stanza of Shelley's "Love's Philosophy," applying a Brooklynese flourish to the lines:

> The fountains mingle with the river
> And the rivers with the Ocean,
> The winds of Heaven mix for ever
> With a sweet emotion;
> Nothing in the world is single;
> All things by a law divine
> In one another's being mingle.
> Why not I with thine?

"There's more than that, but I won't go on," he said.
"That was nice," I said. "When did you learn that?"
"Fifty years ago. That's what I recited to my wife when I first knew her. It gave me a lot of trouble. Since then, no more poetry."

Shine knows all about the uses of hyperbole. He also knows that Tillie Shine is a gracious lady. It doesn't bother her that her husband has taken an avocation and turned it into a fulltime occupation. She lets him go his way each day without any complaint and without any urge to tag along. "I'm not bloodthirsty," Mrs. Shine once told me. "Not that Ben really is, either. He likes a mystery. He always liked to read them. I remember from when we were first married, he always went to bed with a mystery."

One morning not long ago, I rode out to Brooklyn and met Shine on the steps of Supreme Kings. We walked through the lobby and took the elevator to the seventh floor. A guard there waved Shine past a metal-detector, and then they both watched as I emptied my pockets and submitted to being electronically frisked. Most of the courthouse personnel are familiar with Shine. They know his face, though they may not know his name. Someone new to the job could take a brief look at him and feel intuitively that he is not a man who would carry concealed weapons. He is myopic and, whether standing or sitting, seems always to lean slightly forward, as if in a perpetual state of aroused anticipation. The lenses of his eyeglasses are round, and the frames are thick and black. The eyeglasses suit his face, which is round and fleshy. He has peachy jowls, silky and plump, and they seem to have annexed the rest of him. From head to toe—a distance of five and a half feet—he looks like jowls with arms and legs. The top of his head is bald, but he has a fluffy fringe of white hair. Impressive salt-and-pepper tufts grow from his ears. Year round, he wears a hat. That day, it was a gray plaid snap-brim. It matched his gray plaid topcoat and gray vest, and managed not to clash with his blue plaid jacket, navy slacks, white shirt with blue stripes, and red-white-and-blue print bow tie. Before Shine became a court buff, he spent a quarter of a century as a travelling bow-tie salesman. During his career in bow ties, he travelled north as far as Buffalo, south to Richmond, east to Boston, and west to Chicago. Along the way, he always wore a nice piece of merchandise under his collar. Before he sold bow ties on the road, he owned a haberdashery. Each day now, he dresses with care. The act of selecting his daily wardrobe has a tonic effect. Shine believes that if he is going to spend a day in court he should make a businesslike appearance.

We walked down a corridor to Justice Edward Lentol's courtroom, where at that moment no business was being transacted. There were no jurors in the box, no lawyers or defendants in sight, no Justice Lentol seated on the bench beneath the engraved oak panelling ("The Welfare of the People Is the Supreme Law—Coke"). Two uniformed court officers sat in armchairs along one wall, making each other laugh. The bailiff stood nearby, reading the *Racing Form*. The clock on the wall above the spectators' section showed

that it was almost ten-fifteen. At ten o'clock, proceedings were supposed to have resumed in People *v.* Aviles and Aviles—a case in
which the charges included murder and attempted murder. When
possible, Shine tries to watch a trial from the ceremonial first pitch
and stay with it, for however long, until the jury departs to deliberate. The previous day, he had been in court for the opening in-
nings of People *v.* Aviles and Aviles. It had looked promising.

These were the facts: The brothers Aviles—Carlos and José—
were accused of the murder of Anthony Tinakos Goulias, who died
at the corner of Fifty-eighth Street and Third Avenue in Bay Ridge,
and the attempted murder of Nelson Ramos, who received a .22-
calibre-bullet wound in the neck but subsequently recovered. At the
time of the shootings, Carlos Aviles was the more or less constant
companion of Cookie Adorno, Ramos's sister. Two of the first witnesses called by the assistant district attorney on the case were Carmen Ramos, the mother of Nelson and Cookie, and Nelson himself.
Nelson, a lean, prematurely aging nineteen-year-old, told the court
that he and his late friend Anthony Tinakos Goulias had paid a visit
to Carlos Aviles one day after Cookie had complained that Carlos
was being especially unchivalrous. As Cookie and Goulias looked on,
Carlos and Nelson got annoyed with each other, Nelson struck Carlos, Carlos hit him back, Nelson struck Carlos again and headed for
the door, making threatening remarks on the way out—something
like that. A few hours later, on the street, someone shot Goulias and
Ramos. One died; the other lived to tell the judge about it. This all
happened on a Friday afternoon in July.

Near the start, the prosecution's case suffered because of these
assertions by the defense: that Goulias had a widely known pro-
pensity for carrying a gun in his pocket even while he was running
casual errands, and that Nelson, although he was still an adolescent,
had accumulated a criminal record. Carlos Aviles' lawyer, a tall,
gray-haired, crewcut man named Frederick D. Kranz, brought these
facts to light during his cross-examination of Nelson Ramos. The
state's case didn't improve at all when Carmen Ramos took the witness stand. The courtroom proceedings did not arouse Mrs. Ramos'
enthusiasm—that, at least, was the impression she conveyed. She
had orange hair, dark glasses, and a convincing scowl. Apparently,
she was still annoyed that someone had shot Nelson, whom she naturally loved like a son, and whom, she acknowledged under oath,
she "would lie to protect." During cross-examination, Kranz confronted her with an apparent discrepancy between her testimony at

the trial and her testimony during the grand-jury hearing that preceded it. A delay ensued while Mrs. Ramos' private attorney, who happened to be in the courtroom, approached the witness stand for a consultation with his client. After he retreated and Kranz's question was repeated, the court's Spanish interpreter announced that Mrs. Ramos wished to invoke her right against self-incrimination, as granted by the Fifth Amendment. Upon hearing this, the assistant district attorney rested his forehead against his palms.

Now, in court for the next installment, Shine reviewed the proceedings with far greater relish than Mrs. Ramos had brought to her task as a sworn witness. "She made a bad move up there," he said cheerily, the way a Yankees-hater might describe Reggie Jackson's fumbling of a line drive. "When Kranz asked whether she lied to the grand jury, she should've said, 'I don't lie. I was mistaken.' After all, everybody makes mistakes, right?" The question of Nelson's credibility suggested a different approach. "With him, I'm undecided. He's a Nelson and he sings, but he's no Nelson Eddy. Does he have a credibility problem? For this, I say, let's be Solomonic. I say let's cut him in half and see what's doing there."

Such a confection—the epigrammatic point of law layered between trenchant appraisals of human nature—is a specialty of Shine's. Although he does not aspire to become a walking version of Black's Law Dictionary, he does keep a generous supply of buzz-phrases at his disposal. He summons them regularly, alternating them with thoughts about, say, what jurors No. 4 and No. 9 might have eaten while watching television the previous evening. I have heard his explications of the rules regarding photographic evidence, the protection against incriminating testimony by a spouse, the evidentiary relevance of a witness's prior criminal record, and the admissibility of confessions. Upon request, he will do what he can to explain the distinctions between circumstantial evidence, direct evidence, technical evidence, and evidence-in-chief. He has memorized most of the exceptions to the hearsay rule. Shine, who is an adherent of the ours-is-not-a-perfect-system-but-it's-the-best-one-around school of thought, says that Roy Cohn is the most effective trial attorney he has ever seen. "He formulates sentences like a fresh-running brook," Shine says. "Very quick. It was a long time since I saw him. Two cases I saw, both in federal court. The one I remember, a guy hired out trucks. And one fellow didn't pay for the trucks, so he hired someone to break the fellow's legs. Roy Cohn lost, but he was very quick." In offering this compliment, Shine isn't comparing Cohn merely with the best in Brooklyn. Last winter, Shine happened to be in Miami for a couple of weeks at a time when F. Lee Bailey was defending a murder case there. "It was a nice case," Shine has recalled. "A guy accused of killing his mistress. A hung jury. Bailey was good, but he was only one of three lawyers on the defense team. I still say Roy Cohn has the sharpest mind."

To sit next to Shine in court and listen to his whispered running commentary often seems like watching a videotape with an out-of-sync play-by-play. He is adept at what amounts to simultaneous translation. As a lawyer rises from his chair to say "Objection, Your Honor," Shine mutters "Sustained" or "Overruled" before the judge ventures his opinion. Even more often, Shine raises a sotto-voce "Objection!" before the lawyer gets around to it. The lawyer, upon speaking, sounds like an amplified echo of Shine, who by then has ruled on his own objection. Instead of diminishing the suspense of the live action, this guessing game enhances the drama. Every now and then, Shine guesses wrong.

Many of Shine's jurisprudential ideas cannot be traced to any legal textbook. He enjoys speculating about how much certain lawyers earn, and he has opinions about how much their labor is actually worth. He gauges the degree to which a jury will be influenced by the similarity between a defense attorney's diction and a violin being played pizzicato. He knows intuitively when the wave in an accused man's pompadour amounts to a one-way ticket to prison. The crucial question in any criminal trial—superseding, ultimately, the absolute truth about guilt or innocence—is how the jury votes. Shine has heard a lot of perjury and feels confident that he can see a lie coming before the people in the jury box recognize it. Whenever he is asked to predict a verdict, he says, "I always say, 'With a jury, you never can tell.'" Then he proceeds to tell anyway. Shine tries to be soothing when he has to break bad news. "You're doing just great, just great," he is apt to tell a lawyer. "You're doing just great, but you aren't gonna win."

In certain circumstances, Shine will step forward to offer a lawyer an unsolicited opinion. A lawyer named John C. Corbett has been approached quite a few times with what Shine regards as a sound bit of strategic advice. Corbett, who is a former president of the Brooklyn Bar Association, is an imposing-looking man who usually wears a three-piece suit and a pocket watch and does his best to create the impression that neither he nor his client belongs in a criminal courtroom. During the past thirty-four years, he has defended two hundred and fifty accused murderers. Despite Corbett's efforts in their behalf, the vast majority of these people have gone on to become convicted murderers. It seems that one morning several years ago, Corbett and his pet dogs, dachshunds named Siegfried and Brünnhilde, were enjoying a walk along Avenue U, in Gravesend, when a city bus pulled over. The driver, who had once sat on a Corbett jury, emerged and began to tell the lawyer how skillfully he had defended the client. Recalling the case, Corbett pointed out that he must not have been skillful enough, because the accused man was sent away for twenty years. The bus driver was reassuring. "Oh, *him,*" he said. "No, I just didn't like the looks of that guy. The minute I laid eyes on him, I told myself he was guilty." This episode impressed Corbett so deeply that he decided to make it the centerpiece of his closing arguments in the future. Nowadays, he ritually recites the parable of the misguided bus driver and implores jurors to judge his clients strictly on the evidence that has been presented during the trial. He includes graphic details of his stroll with Siegfried and Brünnhilde. After twelve years in the courthouse, Shine has heard this anecdote more times than he cares to, and he now makes it a habit, whenever he sees Corbett, to say, "The Humane Society wants to know when you're going to stop abusing those dogs." Or, "Hey, Mr. Corbett, isn't it about time those dachshunds were put to sleep?" Corbett, of course, pays no heed. Shine, however, regards such helpful admonitions as being part of a serious buff's unwritten contract.

Some court buffs believe that a criminal trial should be, in effect, a morality play—as if reality could be scaled down to the level of a tabloid-headline-writer's imagination. Shine does not share this notion. Which is not to say that he underestimates the importance of theatricality in the courtroom. A courtroom bereft of shameless posturing and caterwauling holds no more charm than an insurance office. The expectant tingle that permeates the air just before the opening of a trial can be matched only in a Broadway playhouse five minutes before curtain time. There is this important difference, however, between Supreme Kings and the Shubert Theatre: court proceedings are frequently interrupted by unanticipated intermissions of unpredictable duration. The fact was that nothing was destined to happen on this particular morning in the matter of People *v.* Aviles and Aviles, even though certain evidence indicated otherwise. Kranz, the defense attorney, entered the room carrying a brown leather briefcase, which he put down on the defense table.

When Kranz's co-counsel, Harvey Greenberg, arrived, a few moments later, Shine said, "Good. We're in business." As the two lawyers conferred, Kranz fiddled, first idly and then intently, with the lock of the briefcase. Either he had forgotten the combination or the latches were stuck; nothing worked.

"Case closed," Shine observed.

"He should take it to Rikers Island," another buff said.

"These Aviles boys must be innocent," Shine concluded. "If Kranz had a decent clientele, one of them would know how to open that." Finally, Kranz gave up. It didn't matter. The presence of Kranz and Greenberg suggested that the defendants might be brought into the courtroom at any moment, that their handcuffs would be removed, that Justice Lentol's arrival would be heralded, that all would rise in his honor, that the assistant district attorney would set up shop, that the court stenographer would enter and poise himself expectantly at the keyboard of his instrument, that the judge would at last tell a court officer to summon the jurors, that the court officer would disappear, that he would return in the company of twelve voting, taxpaying citizens of Brooklyn, and that Shine and his colleagues would indeed be in business. None of this happened. The briefcase latches didn't spring open. No Justice Lentol. No action. The occupants of the spectator gallery sat. They waited.

As a rule, Shine takes a seat in the second of the four rows of the gallery. The first row is reserved for policemen, for attorneys who drop in to kill time or to study someone else's trial work, and for members of the press. When there are significant facts that Shine wishes to remember—the street address where the corpse was discovered, the distance away that the head was found from the torso—he takes notes. He reaches into his coat pocket and removes a blunt soft-lead pencil, a giveaway from Brooklyn Better Bleach, Inc. With this, he scribbles on whatever is handy—the margin of a newspaper, say, or the paper bag containing his lunch. At the end of the day, before he boards the RR train at the Borough Hall station and rides home to Borough Park, he tosses away the newspaper or the paper bag. If a trial attracts a lot of publicity, Shine may clip a few relevant news stories and carry them in a jacket pocket. After a couple of weeks, he throws them away as well. Shine cannot recall the names or the details of most of the trials he has observed or the nodding acquaintances he has made along the way, nor does he care to. Much of the testimony he has heard, he says, "the average man shouldn't want to know from." Still, he takes pride in his attention to details and strives for accuracy. If members of the press are available, Shine regularly confers with them to verify his notes. When none are around, he depends upon his fellow-buff Leo Friedman, who has perfect grammar and lovely penmanship. Friedman is a retired social-studies teacher from Sheepshead Bay. Once, when I had not been at the courthouse for a few weeks, I received a note from him that said:

> Ben and I have been wondering about your absence from the court scene. You've missed some interesting cases. The last one—before the Honorable Justice Sybil Kooper—a lesbian convicted for killing a guy whom she found sleeping with her girlfriend.
> The best to you and your family.
>
> LEO

Not long before Kranz arrived with his recalcitrant briefcase, Friedman had entered the courtroom in the company of several other buffs. Friedman is Shine's closest friend among the Brooklyn regulars. He has a trim build, gray hair, and a thin face creased by a perpetual half smile. Most of the year, his face is nicely suntanned. During the winter, it is nicely windburned. Friedman loves to fish, and he frequently takes day trips aboard Sheepshead Bay party boats. An inverse ratio exists between the flounder population in the bay and Freidman's passion for justice. In the event of sustained poor fishing, he rededicates himself to the pursuit of the truth, the whole truth, and nothing but. He always returns from a marine sabbatical in a refreshed frame of mind. Whenever Friedman makes a court appearance, he and Shine eat lunch together. From time to time, they are joined by Louis Entman, Sol Kenare, Moe Spector, Harry Takifman, Max Silverman, Charlie Rader, Charlie's sister Jean, and, on rarer occasions, Ann Lieberman, Sam Rosalsky, John Fulton, Anita Warrington, Murray Lauer, or R. C. Frank. These people make up the core of the Supreme Kings buffs.

Entman, Kenare, and Spector are a virtually inseparable triumvirate, who call each other by their nicknames—the Landlord, the Grocery Man, and Kissinger, respectively. The Landlord anointed the two others, and they, in turn, christened him. Louis Entman, the Landlord, is a slack-jawed man who once owned most of Flatbush—or, at the very least, four or five buildings. He still has some property there. The first days of each month, he tends to arrive in court late. Quite a few of his tenants need prodding. When he does manage to collect a nice lump of rent, he celebrates by taking a shave and changing into a relatively clean shirt. He owns a gray sharkskin suit, which has acquired a fine antique sheen, and a couple of neckties, which came into his possession around the time that Chief Justice Burger was studying for the bar exam. The Landlord has baggy eyes and looks somewhat like a bulldog who has just bitten into something unpleasant that was crawling in the garden. He blinks a lot. He is an enemy of dullness and a master of the one-sided conversation: "Can a wife testify against a husband? I don't know. Wait. I'll ask Kissinger. He'll know. He doesn't even know his own address. See him sitting over there smiling? He smiles because his underwear's too tight. I notice you don't work for a living. You must have a rich wife. I've got a rich wife, too. No fooling. I saw her bankbook. A hundred and fourteen dollars. Her mother left it to her. Yeah. She had a mother. My mother-in-law. Right. She finally learned how to write. I think she went to night school for a week. She took a vacation to Florida and sent me a postcard. It started out, 'Dear Lousy.' She knew me very well. What? This defendant needs a character witness? I'll be a character witness for him. Sure. Tell him I'll do it for twenty-five bucks. You want to know why the judge called a recess? I'll tell you. He has a date to play basketball. Look at that judge. I think he gets his clothes at the Fairchild funeral home. Hey, nice shirt you got on. You oughta buy it." When Entman is not talking, he pantomimes. His head bobs and his hands flutter. Every now and then, a bailiff who happens to be in a foul mood will throw the Landlord out of his courtroom. The Landlord can usually keep up his pantomime for as long as he has an audience. All buffs manage to catch up on their sleep at some point during a working day. Even Shine would not deny that at times he has rested his eyes in the courtroom. So have more than a few judges and jurors. Piping Muzak into the courthouse—up-tempo in the late morning and in midafternoon, or however the Muzak people do it—probably wouldn't help a bit. Whenever a puzzling technical question arises during a trial, the less attentive buffs consult first with Shine and then with the Landlord—unless these experts have briefly nodded off. The other buffs admire the Landlord's business acumen. He is one of the few members of the fraternity who are still engaged in a remunerative enterprise.

Kissinger is a retired tobacconist who faintly suggests an eighty-year-old version of the former Secretary of State. Like Henry Kissinger's parents, he has an intelligent son whose name appears in *Who's Who*. The Grocery Man, a widower in his eighties, used to run a mom-and-pop market in Coney Island. He now follows trends in the business by clipping discount coupons from the Wednesday newspapers. Most buffs are avid clippers of all sorts of coupons. More than once, Shine, reaching for his Brooklyn Better Bleach pencil, has instead come up with a handful of promises of cheaper mouthwash, say, or free French fries at Burger King. Once—this happened during the trial of two young men who were accused of robbing a laundromat owner named Oscar Biggs at gunpoint and then threatening to run him through a ten-minute cycle in an electric dryer—all the buffs came to court with green cash-register receipts. It seemed that a supermarket chain was redeeming small bales of these scraps for gift items, and Kissinger badly wanted a tote bag.

Perhaps more than any other buff, Kissinger has the ability to draw remarkable conclusions from apparently insignificant events and details. He does this despite a hearing problem that is advanced enough to disqualify him for jury duty. I was seated next to him one morning when a lawyer named Mario Marino appeared in the courtroom to argue a motion. Kissinger whispered to me, "That Marino used to shop in Sol's grocery store. During a summation, I saw him pull out a photograph of a herring and say, 'This is what the district attorney is trying to fool you with—a red herring.' I think he might have bought the herring from Sol." Later, when I asked Sol, the Grocery Man, to confirm or deny—I had learned early on that within the halls of justice, where life and death and the law are paramount, little things can count for a lot—he said he remembered that Marino had been a customer and he remembered selling herring, but he could not recall ever selling herring to an Italian.

Kissinger, a restless man, has adopted the role of scout. On an average day, he leaves the courtroom and returns in an excited state half a dozen times. After each constitutional, he reports his findings to the Grocery Man and the Landlord, and they pass the news along to the other buffs. The calendar clerk, whose office is on the seventh floor of the courthouse, maintains an up-to-date list of trials. Any buff who was inclined to consult with the clerk could avoid a lot of legwork. For their own reasons, however, buffs operate a private, word-of-mouth intelligence-gathering system. Kissinger, suddenly impatient, now said, "So what are we doing sitting here? We could go see the Mets. Anybody want to go to Aqueduct? I think there's a rape case down the hall. What are we waiting for?"

"We're waiting for the angel of death," Shine said as Kissinger headed for the door.

There was a brief silence after Kissinger left, and then Leo Friedman said, "This waiting in these state courts is a shame. You'd never find this in federal court."

"You know better than to compare federal and state courts," Shine replied. "In federal, it's all different."

"My point precisely," Friedman said. "And when a federal judge announces a lunch recess and says that court will resume at two o'clock you can be sure that court will be in session at two o'clock. Here, you sit around till two-twenty, two-thirty. Nothing happens. Nobody complains."

"But you can't compare federal and state," Shine insisted. "For one thing, they don't know from murders over there. Plus, in federal the calibre of the crime is on a much higher scale. You get a much higher-calibre judge, you get a higher-calibre lawyer, and you get a higher-calibre criminal. And a higher-calibre buff. Don't go comparing."

This observation disarmed Friedman, who seemed to turn his thoughts to less irritating topics, like whiting and fluke. Before long, Kissinger returned and announced, "There's a rape next door and a kidnapping down the hall."

The Grocery Man and the Landlord rose and departed with Kissinger, as did Harry Takifman and a couple of other buffs. Only Friedman and Shine remained, along with their fellow-buff Max Silverman.

"I saw that kidnapping," said Silverman. "A complete bust. If that was on television, I'd change the channel. All the time, the district attorney's saying, 'I object, I object.' So what? *I* object to the district attorney. The defense lawyer was a woman. Real heavyset. Strictly from hunger. If someone kidnapped her, after an hour they'd send her back."

"So what do you want to do?" Friedman asked Shine.

"You wanna go up to Davis?" Shine said. His tone sounded tentative.

Silverman smacked his lips—something he does often. He has a flat, rubbery face. A few years ago, Silverman had a job making deliveries for a dentist. Part of his compensation was in kind—a poorly fitted set of false teeth. On certain rare occasions, he wears the teeth. Otherwise, he leaves them at home and spends the day in court smacking his lips for effect. The name Davis provoked him. For a long stretch of time, a Brooklyn buff could say "You wanna go up to Davis?" and he might as well have said "You wanna go to the Statue of Liberty?" It was certainly worth seeing, but if you missed it today you could always catch it tomorrow. People *v.* Davis stood out as one of those expensive monuments to the Fifth and Fourteenth Amendments, with their guarantees of due process, and to the political clout of the Patrolmen's Benevolent Association of the City of New York. A former convict named Cleveland McKinley (Jomo) Davis, who had been a leader of the Attica prison rebellion in 1971, went through three long-running trials for the murder, in 1978, of Norman Cerullo and Christie Masone, two New York City police officers. Davis's first trial, in the spring of 1979, lasted eleven weeks and ended with a hung jury. The second one, which began later that year, lasted twelve weeks and ended the same way. A third trial began in April of 1980 and ended, after nine weeks, in acquittal. Justice John R. Starkey presided at the first trial, Justice Lentol at the second, and Justice Robert Kreindler at the third. Their respective courtrooms were on the ninth, seventh, and ninth floors, so it was usually a matter of "going up" to Davis. Going up to Davis did not appeal greatly to Shine, who likes a mystery to have a beginning, a middle, and a firm conclusion; still, People *v.* Davis was a murder, which Shine considers preferable to rape or kidnapping.

In the elevator on the way to the ninth floor, Friedman asked, "Ann the Blonde's there, right?"

Shine nodded and said, "She's taking it by the week. No meals."

Ann Lieberman is a skeptical woman who is drifting into her golden years with a head of pale-yellow-tinted hair. A buff could stay away from the Davis trial for days—despite its notoriety, it was a rather boring case—and all he had to do was track down Mrs. Lieberman and she would fill in the gaps. She had made People *v.* Davis her specialty. Because the defendant was an observant practitioner of Islam, the trial recessed on Fridays, the Muslim day of rest. She was "up to Davis" the four remaining weekdays, in a lathered state most of the time. Nothing she did could have concealed her contempt for the defendant, so she didn't bother trying. Not that Jomo Davis, if he noticed, should have taken this personally. It seems that Mrs. Lieberman has never seen a defendant who wasn't guilty—if not guilty of the crime in question, then of some other offense. This is a common buff point of view, although it is not one that Shine inclines to. Being literal-minded, he takes the Constitution at its word. Also, he loves suspense. Therefore, he sincerely presumes innocence.

"When I start a trial, I have an open mind," he says. "I divest myself of all prejudice. I put the district attorney on trial and let him put the defendant on trial. The defendant is presumed innocent all the way through. When the jury comes out and says he's guilty, then he's guilty."

Friedman used to share this sentiment, but then he was mugged one weekend afternoon while he was walking along Eastern Parkway. Four youthful offenders, none of whom, if they had been apprehended, would have been old enough to get their names printed in the newspaper, made off with Friedman's wristwatch, wallet, subway pass, library card, and good will.

"Oh, gee, Leo, I'm sorry," Shine had said when he heard the news.

"What do you mean, 'sorry'?" said Friedman. "Where were *you!*"

"What time was it?"

"Two o'clock."

"Two o'clock, I was by the Oceana Theatre," Shine recalled. "It was a double feature—'Hurricane' and 'Foul Play.' Two disasters for three dollars. I have a two-dollar pass, but you have to use that on a weekday."

"Anyway, they just lost an objective juror," Friedman concluded.

"Oh, don't take that attitude," Shine said, sounding genuinely dismayed. "Take their money. They're paying twelve dollars a day now, plus carfare. Don't tell them anything. If they ask were you ever mugged, say, 'I don't remember.' "

"And I'm a City College boy," Friedman said reflectively. "I didn't always feel this way."

"I'm a confirmed capitalist," Shine said. "I always have been."

A young woman with frizzy light-brown hair sat on the witness stand in the Davis courtroom. Her name was Laurie Weinman, and she was a witness for the defense. The buffs and I took seats in the row in which Mrs. Lieberman sat. An open spiral notebook rested in her lap. She saves all her voluminous jottings, and she doesn't mind homework. The courthouse doors are locked each evening at six o'clock. A jury that deliberates past that hour sometimes consigns Mrs. Lieberman to a phoneside vigil. Justice Sybil Hart Kooper, whose demeanor on the bench is more den-motherly than Portia-like, is a favorite with the Supreme Kings buffs. Justice Kooper remains in her chambers at the courthouse until a jury retires for the night, and during such waits she has received quite a few after-hours phone calls from Mrs. Lieberman. As a rule, Mrs. Lieberman speaks with the judge's law clerk, Mark Smith, and asks what's taking that jury so long to convict. At the end of the conversation, she says, "O.K., Mark. Tell Sybil I called." Mrs. Lieberman would have a hard time winning a smile contest even in her most buoyant moments. Now she looked as if she had just sucked on a lemon under duress. Laurie Weinman was describing her meetings with a man named Flaco, who had dropped out of sight after the gun battle in which Cerullo and Masone were killed—and in which Davis was wounded. Davis's attorneys contended that Flaco, and not the defendant, fired the murder weapon.

"The defense is calling its witnesses," Mrs. Lieberman said to me, in more of a stage whisper than I felt comfortable with. "A bunch of phonies. The prosecution had excellent witnesses. Beautiful witnesses."

Robert Bloom, one of Davis's attorneys, showed Prosecution Exhibit No. 7 to Miss Weinman and asked her to describe it. She identified it as a 9-mm. automatic pistol.

"Nice girl," Mrs. Lieberman said. "She didn't mind that this Flake-oh had guns. He went to her house. Nice kid. She went to college. A nice girl. Her parents sent her to college so she could learn about guns."

Mrs. Lieberman has the ability to contort her face in striking ways. Occasionally, she gets so emotionally wrapped up in a case that a judge or a defense attorney suggests that maybe everybody would feel better if she were to indulge this gift in a different courtroom. Now she was scribbling in her notebook, looking up to glance at the jury, and twitching around the eyes and mouth. When she saw me noticing this, she said, "I get involved. I talk to everybody. I talk to the assistant D.A.s. The judges. I've even talked to defense attorneys."

I looked at the inscription engraved in the wall above the judge's bench. It said, "Justice Is Truth in Action—Joubert." Then I looked at the back of the bench in front of us, where someone—

actually, several someones—had applied sharp objects that had eluded the metal detectors outside the courtroom. "ROSA + AL-FONSO" were in love, as were "SPEEDY + ALTHEA," "ANTHONY + PEACHES," "LIVINGSTON + AUDREY," "ANGEL + SARITA," and a few other lucky people. As Laurie Weinman testifed about her meetings with Flaco and her belief in Jomo Davis's innocence, Mrs. Lieberman clucked her tongue.

"I've got four children and eight grandchildren," she told me. "Two of my sons are C.P.A.s. My other son's in business with my husband. Two of my daughters-in-law are teachers. My son-in-law and daughter are teachers. They didn't live together before they got married. They didn't leave home. No guns. Knock on wood." She rapped "ANTHONY + PEACHES" with her knuckles. "It's a new age? Some age. Too good it isn't."

A few minutes later, Miss Weinman completed her testimony. On her way out of the courtroom, she smiled warmly at Davis and his lawyers. Mrs. Lieberman made a muffled gagging noise. When I turned to Shine and Friedman to see if they had any reaction, I realized that they weren't focusing intently on the proceedings.

"Ben, one of the jurors is eying you over," Friedman was saying.

"A man or a woman?" Shine asked.

"A woman."

"Oh, yeah? The one with the long dark hair?"

"No. The one who looks like Rocky Marciano."

From Shine's vantage point, the problem was that the Davis trial had political overtones. When Governor Hugh Carey announced his intention, in 1976, to finally "close the book" on the Attica rebellion, a report by the special prosecutor had recommended pardons for all but three of the inmates who had been charged with crimes stemming from the uprising; one of the three was Jomo Davis. Less than two years after Davis was paroled, he was arrested for the murders of the two policemen. During Davis's three trials, a cadre of sympathizers appeared each day in the courtroom. The spectators and the flavor of the trials seemed like ghostly anachronisms, throwbacks to recent history—Davis had become a sort of exhumed, junior-varsity Huey Newton—and Shine had no real appetite for that sort of history. Crime—Shine's kind of crime, anyway—has its roots in something less murky than politics. He feels at home with unadulterated motivations: passion, money, sin. People *v.* Davis featured complicated technical and forensic testimony—details that might have interested Shine if Davis's principal attorney, Robert Bloom, had been less plodding in his methods. Bloom's approach—halting diction, long pauses between questions, frequent short walks from the witness stand to the defense table to consult notes ("Excuse me, Your Honor, this will take just a moment"), then another pause—was more than a little soporific. Many years ago, Shine was spoiled by a Brooklyn district attorney named Benjamin Schmier.

"This Bloom's a real schlepper," Shine said. "Slow. I've never seen anything this slow. Maybe he figures if he goes slow it's that much longer before his client has to go to the penitentiary. Meanwhile, he's showing absolutely no respect for the buffs. I know that every lawyer has his own style, but I don't understand why somebody would want to have a *boring* style. He should have taken lessons from Ben Schmier. What a following he had. He's passed away. He loved to turn to a defendant during a closing argument and point his finger at him and shout, '*You are a murderer!*' It had a very good effect. Not so much with the defendant, but very good with the jury. Now, your best D.A. in Brooklyn today is Harold Rosenbaum, who did the DiGennaro case. He did a very good summation with that one."

"It was a masterpiece," Friedman agreed.

"Rosenbaum's coming here?" Max Silverman asked.

"No, not here," Shine said. "He was at Lentol."

"I thought so," Silverman said. "So who's this lawyer here? Rosenzweig?" He pointed at an assistant district attorney.

"No, that's someone else," Shine said. "No relation to Rosenbaum or Rosenzweig. Rosenbaum's I think on the fourth floor. He's an assistant district attorney. There's another assistant D.A. named Rosenzweig. There's a lawyer named Rosenblum. And a court clerk named Rosenberg. You gotta keep your Rosens straight, Max."

"What floor are we on?" Silverman asked.

"Nine."

"We move around so much sometimes I forget where I am."

"Stick with me, Max."

Because state governments, rather than the federal government, write the homicide laws, Shine spends only a modest amount of time on the upper floors of the United States District Courthouse, Eastern District of New York, which is two blocks north of Supreme Kings, on Cadman Plaza. For the sake of variety, he has

watched enough federal cases to have established diplomatic relations with many of the higher-calibre buffs of Brooklyn. Nevertheless, his appearances in the federal courtrooms are sporadic, and
when he does show up in one he is often obliged to endure a mild
form of hazing. The colloquy usually runs like this:

First federal buff: "What's the matter? You run out of murder
cases down the street?"

Second federal buff: "No. There was so much blood they ran
out of bandages."

Third federal buff: "How do you like the way these guys think
they can just show up here whenever they feel like it? They try to
sit in the front row. They don't pay dues. They never apply for
membership."

Shine: "Hoo, boy."

As the situation stands now, Shine takes a walk to the Emanuel
Celler Federal Building almost every day, but he spends most of his
time in the basement. The cafeteria there does a brisk lunch business
between noon and one-thirty. Shine enjoys passing an hour or so in
the dim fluorescent light, resting his elbows on a Formica tabletop,
munching a tuna on rye, and engaging in a measured and thoughtful
discussion of why someone would confess to having raped an
eighty-seven-year-old woman if he hadn't in fact done it. Most of
the other Supreme Kings buffs also make the daily pilgrimage to the
cafeteria, where they commingle with the buffs who keep office
hours upstairs. If the state courthouse had its own cafeteria, this trip
wouldn't be necessary. Some of the Supreme Kings buffs seem ill at
ease in the federal building. It strikes them as uncomfortably clean,
too austere. Confusing abstract art hangs in the lobby. The rest-
rooms have soap but no graffiti. When destiny guides certain buffs
to the upper floors of the federal building, they tend to sniff the air
suspiciously.

Shine's patience with the spectacle of the Jomo Davis trial began to diminish as his midday hunger pangs grew. He mentioned
this to Silverman, who, being toothless for the day, declined a
luncheon invitation. Shine and Friedman and I left Supreme Kings
together and walked across Cadman Plaza East. When we reached
the corner of Tillary Street, we encountered a friend of Shine's—a
federal-court buff called Bill Abramson.

"What's new?" Shine asked.

"Oh, a very good trial with Judge Nickerson," Abramson said.
"Drugs."

"Not again," Shine said.

"No, this is a nice one," Abramson said. "This morning, they had a witness—she's a concert pianist, she looks like a charwoman, but she's an anthropologist or something, she ran a travel agency, and I don't know what else. It's cocaine. There's money all over the place. It's conspiracy the government's trying to prove. Oh, they had about a hundred defendants, but a lot of them copped pleas already. Come up and watch."

Abramson walked off in a different direction, and we entered the federal building. As we went down a flight of stairs to the cafeteria, Shine said, "We should go see that one, Leo. I think they'll convict this woman."

"Why?"

"Normally, conspiracy's a tough charge to prove," Shine said. "But if she's a pianist, it's easy—'acting in concert.'"

Friedman said, "Ben. Please."

"Hey, I write 'em, kid. You want more? I got more."

"No. One a day is enough."

While Friedman and I waited in line to buy sandwiches, Shine found an empty table. When we had paid for our food, we saw him at the opposite end of the room, waving with both hands, like a signal corpsman coaxing in a distressed cargo plane. Bringing lunch in a brown paper bag means that Shine gains a makeshift note pad and a saving for the day of about three dollars. Though he has nothing against a bargain, this predilection is more of a habit than a necessity. He carries a typewritten list of his stocks and bonds in a clear-plastic envelope, which he keeps in his coat pocket, filed away with his grocery-discount coupons and the newspaper clippings from recent memorable trials. From time to time, he removes the list and reviews his portfolio, just to reassure himself. There is a brokerage house on Montague Street, not far from the courthouse, and he sometimes drops in to check the latest stock-market quotations. Shine has prudently diversified his holdings. Therefore, he didn't turn glum or get agitated when the accident occurred at the Three Mile Island nuclear power plant in 1979, even though he then held quite a few shares of General Public Utilities, the company that owns the plant. After almost four hundred murder trials, it would probably take a fully realized apocalypse—something on the order of the death of his automobile—to reduce Shine to grief. He drives a 1962 Mercury Meteor with eighty-five thousand miles on the odometer. Often, on Sundays, Shine and his wife take a pleasure trip along the Brooklyn shore. They park the Mercury in a convenient spot, walk a bit, rest a while, and then drive home. Shine is a skillful and dependable driver. Just that morning, he had awakened at four-thirty to drive to Kennedy Airport to pick up a niece who was flying in from Israel to visit her parents, in Flatbush.

"My wife's one of ten children, and I'm one of nine; I have twenty-seven nieces and nephews," Shine said, referring to his pre-dawn excursion. "One's a physicist, another's a psychiatrist, there's a rabbi, lawyers on both sides, one nephew works for I.B.M., an-other's an engineer who does calculations for rockets to the moon. I have one son, Lester, who lives on Long Island, in Ronkonkoma. He works for an electronics firm. My granddaughter Rhonda just graduated college and my granddaughter Caryn's in Hollywood, being an actress. Do my relatives know that I watch these trials every day? They know. I don't hide anything from them."

I asked Shine whether he had ever considered a career as a lawyer.

"It seems like an awful lot of work to me," he said. "I never gave it much thought. It wasn't practical, because you had to pay to work as a law clerk. Not like these young lawyers today. I know they make pretty nice salaries. I was born on Rutgers Street, on the lower East Side, and we moved to Brooklyn when I was still an infant. I was the seventh of the nine children. My father had a clothing com-pany, wholesale and retail, at East Broadway and Market Street, near Chinatown. The name of it was Strong Built. I worked there with him for quite a few years, until he moved to Israel. He moved there during the Depression, before the war, when it was still Pal-estine. During the Second World War, the government made me a uniform inspector for the Department of the Navy. I wanted to see combat, but I was too valuable as a uniform inspector. Yeah. They rated my work 'E' for excellent. When my father left for Israel, he gave the business to his sons. But, being there were five of us, I de-cided to go out on my own. I wanted to struggle all by myself. Yeah. When I still worked for my father, I'd go by the courthouse on Madison Street now and then to watch trials, but I didn't have that much time to do it. After the war, I opened my own place, Bentley Men's Shop, on West Twenty-third, near the Flatiron Building. How did I get the name Bentley? It was very simple. I took 'Ben' and 'Tillie' and put them together. Yeah. One day an immigrant came to me and said, 'You want to buy a lot of bow ties at a very low price?' I thought the price was good, so I bought. I bought so low I resold them both wholesale and retail. I had a haberdashery at street level and the wholesale business upstairs. Eventually, I went on the road with the bow ties—made it strictly wholesale. I went everywhere. I even went down in a coal mine—one hot summer day in Dickson City, Pennsylvania. I thought *my* business was bad, but you should try a coal mine sometime. When the bow-tie business tapered off, I went to long neckties. Then that tapered off, and I decided to retire. This was about twelve years ago, when a lot of these guys started with the open collars and no ties. Yeah. So I retired. I needed something else to do, so I started coming here every day to watch the trials. It's different from bow ties."

Shine's autobiographical discourse was interrupted by Charlie and Jean Rader, who stopped by to say hello. They are the only brother-sister buff team in Brooklyn. Jean, the elder, wears harlequin-framed tinted eyeglasses and warm clothing in every season and has the air of a woman of leisure on a cool day in Miami Beach. For Charlie, being a buff is like being on a permanent busman's holiday. In 1963, he retired from the New York Police Department, where he had risen to the rank of detective, second-grade, during a career that lasted thirty-one years. All that time spent in the company of lawbreakers had a peculiar effect on Charlie's interest in crime. As a courtroom bystander, he prefers not to get involved with anything really heinous. Instead, he and his sister spend most of their time on the third floor at Supreme Kings. This is where the big-money civil cases—often involving complaints of medical malpractice—go to trial.

"We've just been on three," Charlie told Shine and Friedman. "Malpractice. Paralyzed from the neck down. Two point seven million the jury awarded this young fellow. I'm telling you, they brought him into the courtroom on a stretcher and it was *very effective*. Twenty-nine years old. His wife divorced him after what happened to him. Two point seven million. There's more where that came from. You should come watch."

"Maybe we will," Shine said, and the Raders soon departed. When Friedman had finished his cigar, we rose and carried our plastic trays toward the cafeteria exit. There was a small window near the door, where we stacked the trays and silverware on an idle conveyor belt.

"Someday I'll take you to a place where judges eat lunch," Shine said, rubbing his palms together. "I have a cousin—my cousin Paul Widlitz—who's an administrative judge in Mineola, Long Island. I went to see my cousin Paul one day. I didn't tell him I was coming. I just walked into the courtroom while he was holding a divorce hearing. It was two deaf people—No, wait a minute, I'm mixing up. That was another time, in Judge DiGiovanna's courtroom, in Brooklyn. That was a case with two deaf people who wanted a divorce and they spent the whole time arguing in sign language. Afterward, I told Judge DiGiovanna, I said, 'You know why those two people are getting a divorce, Your Honor? They can't communicate with each other.' "

Friedman's face took on a pained expression. "Ben, I told you: one a day is enough."

We rode an elevator from the basement to street level—a silent ride—and when we hit the sidewalk Shine resumed talking. "Yeah, no, but by my cousin Paul, the judge, that was just a straight divorce. He saw me come in and he stopped the proceedings immediately and gave me a tour of the premises. Oh, that was a nice setup. A beautiful library, a place to eat, with the stoves and the Frigidaires. I told my cousin, 'Hey, Paul, you've got a real racket here.' It's nice to see how the other half lives."

"I don't hold with these buffs and judges being on a first-name basis," Friedman said. "For instance, I know that Judge Mishler, the federal judge, hardly ever goes downstairs to eat in the cafeteria."

"You're right," Shine said. "And Judge Barshay, at State Supreme—he's died, but he used to have a Frigidaire in his chambers, and he took lunch there."

Friedman lowered his voice and said, "I heard he kept it *very* well stocked with cream cheese and gefilte fish."

There is a row of wood-and-iron benches in the shade beneath the tall plane trees that line Cadman Plaza. Louis Entman, the Landlord, sat alone now on one of the benches. It was almost two o'clock—the hour when most trials are scheduled to resume after the lunch recess. A few yards ahead, Kissinger, the Grocery Man, and Charlie and Jean Rader were walking slowly toward Supreme Kings. When the Landlord noticed Shine and Friedman approaching, he called out, "You see Charlie Rader?"

"Yeah," Shine said. "Two point seven million dollars. That's hard work."

"Two point seven million," the Landlord repeated. "If I had that much money, I would have ordered the soup today."

"Where are you going now?" Shine asked.

"I sent the Grocery Man and Kissinger up to Davis," the Landlord said. "We're thinking of splitting up the business. I might end up there or I might go to Judge Lombardo. I hear he's supposed to have a new homicide. Where are you going?"

Shine looked up at the sky. It was cloudless, faintly breezy, an unspoilable afternoon. "There's a lot of possibilities," he said. "There's drugs at federal court. Charlie's got the malpractice. We saw some of Davis this morning. You say there's a murder at Lombardo. And that kidnapping down the hall from Lentol. That's it— Lentol. I'm going to Lentol. With those brothers. Aviles. Maybe that lawyer Kranz got his briefcase opened by now. I think I'll head back to Lentol. I want to see what's doing."

Barry Newman

Barry Newman has a wonderful job with horrible constraints. While others in this anthology write books and do pieces for magazines, Newman works for a newspaper and is bound more by the conventions of standard journalism. Yet he has found a way to write literary journalism, in spite of the constraints.

For eight years, Newman has traveled Europe and the Far East in search of stories for *The Wall Street Journal*. Based in Singapore for several years, he wrote pieces datelined Australia, India, Malaysia, Indonesia, and the islands of the South Pacific. Since 1981, he has been stationed in London with the freedom to range through most of Europe.

Newman, 37, cherishes the romance of his role as a roving foreign correspondent. *The Wall Street Journal* is, of course, a publication dedicated to economic and financial news, but it gives him remarkable freedom. "I can spend six weeks reporting a story," Newman said. "I can spend two or three weeks just writing it."

That's where the horrible constraints enter. "The damn thing still has to be two thousand words long." His editors resist his experiments with voice and point of view—he rarely uses the first person. Yet, because he stays on stories for weeks instead of hours, he learns what he needs to know. He concentrates on event and character, not on circumstance and "news value." He anticipates his readers will see the world differently than do his characters—which adds a touch of irony to his work. The two pieces reprinted here portray men who pursue symbols of dignity in order to soften the injuries inflicted upon them by class and age.

As with others who focus on singular lives, one of Newman's talents is his ability to find just the right person—someone whose life, although ordinary, suggests larger meaning. Resigned to the limits of space, he relies on readers who recognize the symbolic power in his stories.

"If the reader has the right sensibility, he'll see what you're doing without your having to spell it out. I like that better than being bludgeoned by these points, and I like being detached and letting the reader do part of the job." Perhaps because he writes about foreign people, Newman can create more of an ironic undertone than he could were he writing about Americans. The reader senses that he respects foreign values, but ultimately shares American feelings. Thus his values and opinions establish a culturally familiar voice for readers despite the restraints of brevity and newspaper style.

"Nobody could write stories like this without saying something about himself," Newman said. "I jiggle and juggle the formula at *The Wall Street Journal* as much as I can, and sometimes I go beyond the formula. The subtleties in my work, the underlying themes, are snuck in. Otherwise my editors might say I was editorializing."

He grew up in Rockaway Beach, across the bay from Brooklyn, and studied political science at Union College in Schenectady, New York. Newman may be the only *Wall Street Journal* reporter who flunked freshman economics. He worked his way up from copy boy on *The New York Times* to writing stories for the religion department before winning a job at *The Journal* in 1970. A collection of his dispatches from Asia and the South Pacific, *East of the Equator,* was published in 1980 in Hong Kong by the Dow Jones Publishing Company.

Fisherman

LEIGH, England—Kevin Ashurst's maggot farm—a cinder block shed attached to an air scrubber—is a mile outside this old mill town, in a field of pink wildflowers.

"Looking for work?" a tatooed man calls when a visitor drives up on a hot morning. In the yard, some dead sheep nourish a new generation of bluebottle flies. Two workers, bent over the carcasses, scoop the maggots into plastic tubs. The smell is about as bad as a smell can get.

Ashurst, a meaty man of 43, wipes his hand on his dungarees to clean off the offal, and extends the same hand in greeting. Then he reaches into a tub and brings up a sample of his finest produce—moist, white and writhing.

"See, that's the size of 'em, like," he says. "Them's good maggots, quality maggots. They'll keep like this for a week in the 'fridge."

Who keeps maggots in the 'fridge? Coarse fishermen do. Kevin Ashurst sells maggots to coarse fishermen. He's a coarse fisherman himself, and a good one. Coarse fishermen bait their hooks with maggots to catch coarse fish—like barble, dace, bleak and roach. Coarse fish live in murky waters, are mostly tiny and make awful eating. Game fishermen, who catch salmon and trout, think of them as vermin. Some think the same of coarse fishermen.

Until about ten years ago, British upper-class fishermen succeeded in keeping the upper-class fish to themselves. The working class had to fish in abandoned gravel pits and industrial canals. The sport wasn't refined, but it was diverting enough, once money got involved.

Fishermen pay to line up on a bank and vie for the weightiest total catch. The winner throws back his fish and takes home the kitty. The basic strategy hasn't changed much since the first competition in 1903: Catch tiddlers. Tiddlers add up, ounce by ounce.

This technique requires a hook the size of a mosquito's leg, a line as fine as a spider's web—and a rod that ought to be about thirty-six-feet long.

Coarse fishing is big in Britain, bigger than snooker. Almost four million people do it, and many others watch. Fishing matches get on television here, though fishing doesn't come across on the screen quite as well as darts does. Coarse fishing is big on the Continent, too, and in the Eastern Bloc. The world championship is held every year. Some have pulled in crowds of twenty thousand.

Last year's event took place on the Newry Canal in Northern Ireland. The winner was Kevin Ashurst, the maggot farmer from Leigh. In five hours of intensive fishing, he caught thirteen roach and one small bream, amassing the lowest winning weight on record: one pound, ten ounces.

"It came right for me," he told the announcer on national television. "It didn't come right for the other lads."

Ashurst quits work early this day and goes off to dig for gnat larvae, a variety of bait known around here as bloodworm. There's an evening match on the Bridgewater Canal. He has to prepare. Meanwhile, his wife serves tea to a visitor in their home on one of Leigh's back lanes, and shows off her husband's trophies: shelves full of brandy snifters, loving cups and statues of fish.

"I don't know what Kevin would do if he couldn't go fishing," Shirley Ashurst says. "Not that it relaxes him. If he isn't catching, he wants to know why. He racks his brain. He comes home and relives the match all over again." She takes an inscribed hunk of crystal from a shelf and wipes off a fingerprint. "It's a beauty, that," she says.

Shirley Ashurst's father mined coal. Kevin Ashurst used to fish with him, she remembers, and that's how Kevin and Shirley met. Ashurst's father was a coal miner, too. But after a bad accident, he quit to farm maggots. Kevin runs the farm now. He and Shirley have a twenty-one-year-old son. Someday, if he wants it, the maggot farm will be his.

"Do you hear something dripping?" Shirley Ashurst says. She puts down her teacup and dashes up the stairs. "He's got bloodworm in the bathtub."

After a while, Ashurst pulls up outside in a truck from the maggot farm and sets himself to sorting his new haul of worms in the garage. "See, that's come out of the muck, like," he says, displaying a squirming red mass in a bucket.

In T-shirt and baggy pants, he is redolent of maggot. His forehead is creased, his eyes tired. He has a Lancashire accent so thick an outsider can often make out only one word, transcribed here as "flipping," as in:

"I wish fishing were as popular as flipping darts. I'd be a flipping big star. I'd be riding around in a flipping limousine."

For the time being, Ashurst settles for a couple of maggot trucks and a station wagon. At 6 P.M., he loads the wagon with his rod (in ten sections) and his tackle box, which resembles a small refrigerator. He drives to the Royal Oak, a pub in Leigh, to draw a position on the banks of the canal for the three-hour competition.

The little pub is filled with coarse fishermen when he arrives. Pint glasses and bags of maggots line the bar. Ashurst pays the entrance fee and picks a number out of a box. He gets peg fifty-four. After thirty years of fishing the Bridgewater Canal, he knows it's a spot the fish don't fancy.

"You'll win anyway, Kevin," says the match official.

The canal runs right through Leigh and on through the countryside to the Liverpool docks. Its banks are flanked by the blackened brick remains of Victorian textile mills gone broke. The water, forty feet across and four-feet deep, is sluggish and green. For a mile along the towpath, hard by the old mills, coarse fishermen bait up.

Ashurst lugs his box to a piling and sits on it. He puts on his cap and assembles his rod, which is made of carbon fiber and costs $750. It doesn't have a reel; the line is tied to the tip. An angler has to take the whole thing apart again to bring in a fish, and he can do that often. Ashurst once caught 861 fish in five hours. They weighed a total of eighteen pounds, twelve ounces.

"Whatcha using?" shouts a man at the next peg.

"Worm," Ashurst shouts back.

For a maggot farmer, this seems extraordinary. But Kevin Ashurst senses a piscine appetite for bloodworm on the Bridgewater Canal tonight. Everyone else sticks to maggots. The next man skewers one on his hook and shoots a few more into the water with a slingshot. Ashurst rolls a wormball and lobs it into the murk.

"You have to remember where that landed," he says. "Then you lay your hook on the bottom. The fish congregate. You can overfeed them or underfeed them. Something's always wrong. There's a lot into this. Great anglers have to think."

Tenderly he threads one worm onto the hook. He swings the pole out and lowers the bait. And then he sits, concentrating on the peacock-quill float, holding the rod like a pole vaulter getting set for his next jump. "It strains the eyes," he says. "It's why I don't read much." For half an hour, as a gallery gathers behind him, Ashurst gets nary a nibble.

"Is that the lucky hat?" somebody says.

"Yeah," Ashurst mumbles. "Not much good, though."

"Should have had one by now, lad," says somebody else.

The quill twitches. Ashurst jerks the rod upward and out of the water comes a roach, battling for its life. It is two inches long and weighs about an ounce. Ashurst draws in the rod across his lap, twisting off section after section, and drops the fish into his keep net.

Now the worms are at work. Here comes another roach, and another, and a four-ounce bream. Ashurst hits stride: He can hook a fish, swing it to the bank, break down the rod, grab the fish, pluck out the hook, thread another worm, rebuild the rod, and be fishing again in twenty seconds. "If I maintain this, like, I'm gonna catch three pounds," he says.

Up and down the canal in the deepening twilight, anglers get fidgety. Nobody can match the world champion's pace. Desperate to win with one huge fish, they sling maggots with a fury. But Kevin Ashurst sticks to his worms and his strategy: Catch tiddlers. He sits on his box and stares stolidly at his quill until the official's final shout: "All out!"

"All out," Ashurst says softly to himself, and he pulls in his rod. A judge comes by to weigh the catch. Ashurst has sixteen fish. They tip the scales at three pounds, one ounce. "Well," Ashurst says, stepping briefly behind a bush, "that's flipping done with."

Back at the Royal Oak, coarse fishermen crush against the bar, ordering pints, noisily discussing the ones that got away. A thin voice rises at the far end of the bar to announce the winner. Conversation stops in a moment of shock. Somebody called I. Cunliffe caught a four-pound eel. He wins $94.95.

"It's a lie," somebody says.

"It were a good catch," says Kevin Ashurst.

But next morning at the maggot farm, Ashurst's eyes are even more tired than they were the day before.

"Couldn't sleep," he says, resting on his shovel. "Kept thinking I had a chance to win last night. Should have used a lighter float." He sprinkles some chicken heads into a box of dead fish. "Once you've had success," he says, "you can't let it stop. It isn't the money. It's prestige."

Banderillero

Just because your legs is dead don't mean your head is.

—Casey Stengel

VILLAMUELAS, Spain—Soldiers don't start out as generals nor politicians as presidents. In business, managers work their way up. Except for a lucky few, the realization slowly and steadily comes to just about everyone that the top is out of reach.

But bullfighting works the other way around. A bullfighter rockets to the top. From first blush, he is a matador—that bold and arrogant swordsman who artfully entices the bull to its moment of truth. A matador monopolizes the spotlight long enough to convince the world of his incompetence. Then his own moment of truth arrives: the shock of failure and the dawning knowledge that he will never be on top again.

The truth came to Ernesto Sabrino thirteen years ago.

"People stopped taking me seriously," he says, driving his old car through a rainstorm on a Sunday morning, heading out of Madrid and across the Castilian tableland to a bullfight in this little town. He is forty. His chestnut hair is all there, but he appears to have a small pillow under his worn blue sweater.

"Life as a matador became a life of pain," he says. "People made fun of me. Promises were never kept. When I was twenty-seven, I faced reality."

A bull gets dragged to the butcher's after its moment of truth. A matador, if he stays alive and retains some spunk, gets to be a banderillero. That's what Ernesto Sabrino is. So is his friend, Paco Dominguez, who is riding in the back seat. His hair is going, but he wears his jacket draped over his shoulders and carries his cigarette with his arm raised, as if acknowledging an ovation.

"The bullfight is a liberation," he says, blowing smoke into the front seat as the car circles the great stone bullring in Aranjuez. "We risk our lives with joy."

Sabrino pulls out a rag and wipes the condensation from the inside of the windshield. "Paco," he says, "you're a romantic. For me, everything is practical. Gambling with life and death is the way I make money. When you are a matador, you can dream. When you are a banderillero, you have to stop."

Banderilleros are the old men of the bullring. Suited up, these bull-fighters look like thick-waisted versions of young matadors. The crowd has a chance to take special note of them when they run at the bull with two barbed sticks and try to place them in its hump before the matador moves in for the kill. A hardy banderillero can keep at this until he is past fifty, although his run will inevitably seem longer every year.

Apart from those few seconds when he places the sticks, the old man's job is to make the matador look good. While the matador struts in front of the bull, taunting it, daring it to charge, the ban-derillero hovers in the background, an experienced eye on the an-imal's every twitch. When the matador fumbles, a flick of the banderillero's cape can, by distracting the bull, save the matador from a horn through the thigh and, occasionally, from humiliation. All the old man craves in return is some respect and a day's pay.

Villamuelas appears at the base of a slope: half a dozen streets of two-storied buildings. The bullring is just outside town. It is portable, made of corrugated tin and set up in a muddy field. Spain has fewer bullfights than it did before television and the family car. A banderillero takes what he can get.

"It's your legs and your head," Ernesto Sabrino says as he parks his car in front of the bar in the village square. "You need both. I jog. I don't drink or smoke. The crowd doesn't cheer for me. I'm beyond the point where I expect to be a star. But we are the pillars of the bullfight."

The rain has eased off. A woman is washing out a few things at the fountain. A man is selling fried dough. Strung between two balconies, a banner announces today's fiesta. The bar is packed, its floor littered with shrimp shells. The band sprawls on plastic chairs, drinking coffee. Men in berets lean on canes, wine glasses in hand. Sabrino works his way through, orders an anisette, then remembers he doesn't drink.

"Just a little," he says. "It warms my stomach. I haven't smoked for a week now." Paco Dominguez lights up. "Must you?" Sabrino says. But Dominguez ignores him—the matador is coming in: tall and svelte, chin held high, hair jet black, eyes hidden behind dark glasses. He is a novice, perhaps twenty-years old and, Sabrino confides, without promise.

"A rich kid," he says.

"He comes from a wealthy family," says Dominguez, turning back toward the bar. "His family is investing in him."

"I never had an investor in my life," Ernesto Sabrino says.

His story is the standard one for bullfighters. He was born in a town like this, left school at eleven, delivered groceries, studied the bullfight newspapers, worshipped Manolete. He walked all night to small-town *capeas*—illegal fights in rings built of boards and parked cars. At fourteen, he stood in front of a bull. At sixteen, he was gored. At eighteen, he was noticed. He dressed as a matador for the first time a year later, in 1961, and killed his first bull.

"I always thought I was good," he says, sitting down under the bar's television, which is showing a bicycle race. "There was one day in Rioja. I had a good bull that day. I mastered it. I was artistic. I cut two ears. For me, this was success. But I don't build sand castles; life proved me wrong."

He sips his anisette, and looks up at the bicycles.

In the bullfight business, the impresario pays the matador, sometimes well. The matador pays his banderilleros, though not always on time and rarely well. Fifty years ago, Ernest Hemingway wrote: "There is no man meaner about money with his inferiors than your matador." The banderilleros suffered on. Not until the start of this season did they finally vent their resentment. They walked out.

Their strike lasted a week in March. When it was over, they had won a pay raise of fourteen percent. Now a banderillero gets at least $400 for fighting in a first-class ring. In Villamuelas today, Sabrino should come away with $150. Crisscrossing Spain all summer, he might hit fifty towns and earn $10,000. The extra money will help. But when a bullfight is called off, a banderillero still gets no pay. Nor does he have much of a future, once those legs go.

"Money isn't all that important to me," Sabrino says as he drains his anisette. "I'm sincere about that. I'm talking about dignity."

Lunch is ready. The bullfighters and their entourage file past the bar into a bare hall at the rear. A movie screen hangs from the far wall, a stack of chairs in front of it. Two long tables have been set up in the middle of the hall. The matador and his family sit at one. The banderilleros and the picadors, who fight on horseback, sit at the other. So do a few of the impresario's functionaries, one of whom goes by the name of Cadenas.

Cadenas is getting old. He has a throaty voice and puffy skin. When Ernesto Sabrino was a matador, Cadenas was already a banderillero.

"For thirty-five years I was a bullfighter," he says, spitting out an olive pit. "Now I sell the tickets."

"When I'm through," Sabrino says, "I'd like to be a TV repairman." He takes a sip of wine and looks down at his plate. "The pork is tough," he says.

By late afternoon, when lunch is over, the crowd fills the square. The band plays the *Pasodoble Torero*. The loudspeaker crackles: "The greatest spectacle of bullfighting this afternoon in this wonderful city! Get your tickets now! A sensation!" The bullfighters begin to dress in the bedrooms on the other side of the bar. Then the rain comes down.

The impresario returns from the ring, his shoes muddied. "Impossible," he says. The mayor of Villamuelas steps out onto the balcony of the town hall, overlooking the square, and addresses the townspeople. The spectacular, he announces, is canceled.

Sabrino folds his cape. "A funeral," he says. "We don't get a peseta." He and Paco Dominguez drive back to Madrid to wait for the sun, stopping on the way for another anisette.

Two days later, the sun shines on the fiesta of another Castillian town, San Martin de la Vega. The bullring has been erected right in the square, and the cobbles covered with sand. This ring is dangerous. It has too few places for a bullfighter to hide. Looking less than lithe in his salmon-pink suit, Sabrino is keyed up, his face in a fixed grin.

"Sometimes I suffer so much fear in the ring I don't even see the women," he says, surveying the crowd from behind one of the barriers. As a banderillero, he has twice been seriously gored, both times in the groin. "Every time I get dressed for the fight," he says, "I know it can happen again." He takes a swig from a wineskin and shows his teeth to the fans.

The preliminaries soon end and the fight begins. As each bull charges into the ring, Sabrino hangs behind the barrier, letting the matador who employs him today show off his capework. On his first run, the banderillero plants the sticks perfectly, without the slightest attempt at pizzazz. On his second, the sticks go flying. The bull wheels and gives chase. Sabrino flees, stiff-legged, over the barrier, with a look on his face of crazed concentration.

It is the only moment all afternoon when the crowd pays him any heed. After his young matador gracefully dispatches the day's final bull, the coup de grace is left to Sabrino. He performs it with a sharp jab of a short knife, and cuts two ears for the youngster, just as two ears were cut for him on that day in Rioja. Flowers shower down. Sabrino stoops to collect them and presents a bouquet to another novice in his glory.

The bullfighters parade in triumph and disappear beneath the stands. As the crowd leaves, someone lets a spindly-horned calf run loose in the ring. The boys of San Martin de la Vega jump down onto the sand to dance circles around it, acting out their fantasies of becoming matadors someday.

Ron Rosenbaum

As a roving reporter for *Esquire* and *The Village Voice* during the 1970s, Ron Rosenbaum said he discovered that reporters were like traveling salesmen or confidence men.

"After you speak to thirty people about the same story," Rosenbaum wrote in the introduction to a collection of his articles, "this process of winning confidence inevitably becomes your pitch—you've seen which ways of presenting yourself and your mission work best with this particular constellation of people. Subtle adjustments are made in the way you identify yourself. You learn to tell the story of your story; anecdotes are picked up from earlier interviewees and trotted out; personal reminiscences and past stories are offered up, all in the effort to sell the notion that you, the reporter, are no ordinary traveling salesman but a merchant of truth, understanding, and empathy—in exchange for which commodities the innocent interviewees are asked to pay with pieces of their privacy."

His article, "The Subterranean World of the Bomb," written for *Harper's* in 1978, uses a voice that cuts through the confidence-man style of reporting. He reports on his encounters with others, but the article self-consciously drives the subject back into the private world of the author, rather than seeking to reveal the intimacies of his interviewees.

Rosenbaum, 38, graduated from Yale and now lives in New York. He has written a satirical novel, *Murder at Elaine's,* and is at work on another novel. His articles from *Esquire, The Village Voice, MORE, New York,* and *New Times* were collected in 1979 in a book, *Rebirth of the Salesman: Tales of the Song & Dance 70's.*

The Subterranean
World of the Bomb

Did anyone ever tell you about the last letter of Our Lady of Fatima? It's more than a dozen years since the night it was revealed to me, but I remember the circumstances exactly. I was in an all-night place called the Peter Pan Diner with a high school buddy of mine. It was 1964, I was 17, and we had been arguing for hours, as we often would, about such matters as the nature of Time before the creation of the universe and the mystery of the afterlife, when this guy hit me with the Fatima prophecy. He said he'd heard it from some seminarians who said they'd heard it from people in the church hierarchy, who said it was a hush-hush matter of intense concern to the Vatican, and to His Holiness himself.

Back in 1913, the story goes, a holy apparition appeared to three Portuguese children near the shrine to the Virgin at Fatima. The heavenly messenger handed the kids three sealed letters for transmittal to the Pope. Eyes only.

The first letter—marked for immediate unsealing—astonished Pope Pius X with a graphic description of a horrifying world war, this just months before the guns of August opened fire. The second letter, said to be marked "Do not open for twenty-five years," shocked Pius XI in 1938 with its vision of an even more terrible tragedy about to engulf civilization.

And then just last year—and here my friend's voice dropped, presumably to avoid frightening the people drinking coffee at the next table—just last year, he said, that wonderful man, the late Pope John, unsealed the third and last letter.

The last letter. The chill I felt creeping over me could not be ascribed to the Peter Pan Diner's creaky air conditioner.

"What was in it?" I asked.

"Nobody knows," my friend said.

"What do you mean nobody knows? They knew about the other ones."

"Yes," said my friend. "But this one is different. They say that when the Holy Father opened it and read what was inside he fainted on the spot. And that he never recovered. And that Pope Paul ordered the letter to be resealed and never opened again. Want to know why? Because the letter tells the exact date of when a total nuclear war that will destroy the entire human race will break out and the pope can't let it out because of the mass suicides and immorality if people were to learn exactly when they were going to die."

On January 13, 1975, the *New York Times* published a brief dispatch headed AIR FORCE PANEL RECOMMENDS DISCHARGE OF MAJOR WHO CHALLENGED "FAILSAFE" SYSTEM.

"What Major Hering has done," according to the lawyer for the ICBM launch officer, "is to ask what safeguards are in existence at the highest level of government to protect against an unlawful launch order . . . what checks and balances there are to assure that a launch order could not be affected by the President gone berserk or by some foreign penetration of the command system."

The major was not a hysterical peacenik. A combat veteran of Vietnam, he insisted he would have no moral scruples about killing 10 million or so people with his fleet of missiles. He just wanted to make sure that when he got the launch order it wasn't coming from an impostor or a madman.

Sorry, major, the Air Force replied, a missile crewman like you at the bottom of the chain of command has no "need to know" the answer to that question. In fact, you have no business asking it. When the *Times* story appeared, the Air Force already was on its way to hustling the major into suspension and early retirement.

Interesting, I thought to myself back in '75 as I tore out the story. But so many years after *Dr. Strangelove* and *Failsafe,* how was it possible that this question did not have a satisfying, reassuring answer, even if the Air Force did not want to disclose it to this troublesome major? And so I filed the clipping away in the semi-oblivion of my "possible stories" file.

Two years later I was prowling the corridors of the Pentagon with that now-tattered clipping and a need to know. I was trying to find someone who could give me a satisfactory, reassuring answer to Major Hering's question. I wasn't getting any answers. What I was getting, I realized, right there in the Pentagon, was an onset of

Armageddon fever unlike any since that night in the Peter Pan Diner when I heard about the Fatima prophecy.

I think it had something to do with seeing the man with the black briefcase face to face. It happened in a parking lot in Deerfield Beach, Florida, in January, 1976. I was traveling with and reporting on President Ford's Presidential primary campaign. The man with the black briefcase was traveling with President Ford, ready in case the President had to interrupt his Florida primary campaign to wage a nuclear war.

You know about the black briefcase, don't you? Inside are the Emergency War Order (EWO) authentification codes, which are changed frequently and are supposed to ensure that only the President, their possessor, can authorize a thermonuclear missile or bomber launch. When then-President Richard Nixon boasted to a group of congressmen shortly after the Saturday night massacre that "I could go into the next room, make a telephone call, and in twenty-five minutes seventy million people will be dead," he left out one detail: he would have to take the black briefcase into the room with him.

That day in Deerfield Beach, Commander in Chief Ford was making his way through throngs of suntanned senior citizens and pale Secret Servicemen out onto a fishing pier to pose with a prize marlin. Passing up a glimpse of the big fish, I was ambling back across a parking lot toward the press bus when suddenly I came upon the man with the black briefcase.

Somehow he seemed to have become separated from the Presidential party in the procession toward the pier, and now he stood fully and formally uniformed in the midst of baggy Bermuda shorts and tropical shirts. Peering about, looking for his lost Commander in Chief, the nuclear-briefcase man looked cut off, detached, uncertain how to respond. And in a different sense so was I. I felt a peculiar sense of dislocation staring at that briefcase. (In case you're interested it's a very slim and elegant one: supple black pebble-grained leather with a flap of soft leather fastened by four silver snaps.)

If you wanted to get technical you could say that if the word of a surprise attack on the way reached the President while he was posing with the prize fish, the fact that the man with the black briefcase was here with me and not out on the pier might delay our potential for nuclear retaliation by several, perhaps crucial, seconds.

On the other hand some half-a-billion citizens on the other side of the world might enjoy two or three more breaths before their lives were snuffed out by missiles sent by the black-briefcase code. Silly to make these calculations, but what is the proper response to the intimate presence of a key element of the doomsday trigger system? Scream bloody murder? Or should one take, as I did at the time, a detached, esthetic approach to the tableau—relish the piquant fris-son of irony at that artifact of instant apocalyptic death standing like a scarecrow amidst the sun-ripening age of the retirees?

Last year when I came upon the Major Hering clipping and read it again, that unsettling vision of the man with the black brief-case came to mind. And my response was different. This time *I* felt possessed by a "need to know," a compulsion that eventually led to a 4,000-mile tour of the nuclear trigger system, a pilgrimage that led me down into the Underground Command Post of the Strategic Air Command, up into B-52 bomb bays, down into missile silos, and deep into the heart of the hollowed-out mountain that houses our missile-attack warning screens.

My first stop was Washington, D.C., where, in the course of doing some preliminary research, I came upon a very unsettling document that has kept me up for many nights since. Entitled "First Use of Nuclear Weapons: Preserving Responsible Command and Control," it is the transcript of a little-noticed set of congressional hearings held in March, 1976. The transcripts represent a concerted effort by the International Security subcommittee of the House Committee on International Affairs to get the answers to Major Hering's question (indeed, it seems the Hering controversy in part provoked the hearings) and to questions about the curious behavior of then-Defense Secretary James Schlesinger in the last days of the Nixon Presidency.

As the impeachment process wore on and reports circulated about the President's potentially unstable temperament at the time, Schlesinger took an extraordinary action: he sent out orders to the various communications centers in the nuclear chain of command to report back to him, Schlesinger, any "unusual" orders from the President. The implication was that Schlesinger wanted to know about and, perhaps, veto, a potentially deranged Nixon whim to nuke Vladivostok or the House Judiciary Committee.

The brief flare-up over the Schlesinger order illuminated little more than the extent of consensus ignorance on just how we actually will do it when we do it. Like the facts of life to a bemused child, the facts of nuclear death, before it comes, are more like vague notions than actual clinical details.

We know there is no button wired into the Great Seal in the Oval Office. But that one phone call, the one that kills the seventy million—just where does it go? Who answers? Will the people who answer be loyal to the President or to the Secretary of Defense if the President's mental condition is suspect? If the Secretary of Defense could veto a launch by a mad President, could a Secretary of Defense *initiate* a launch if he felt the President was playing Hamlet and was mad *not* to launch?

The Command and Control hearings document reprints in its appendix a disturbing analysis of these questions by a professor of government at Cornell named Quester. Among other observations, Professor Quester suggests that it is the very precautions taken to thwart a madman general like *Strangelove's* Jack D. Ripper that have left us at the mercy of a madman President. Making sure that no one *below* the President can launch a nuclear war means giving to the President alone more unchecked power to do it himself on a whim and a single phone call. But the more power placed in the President's hands alone, the more vulnerable the entire U.S. nuclear arsenal is to being disarmed by simply knocking off the President. There must be some provision for a retaliatory threat to be credible in the event a "suitcase bomb," for instance, results in the death of the President, Vice-President, and most of the Cabinet, and no one can remember whether it's the Secretary of Agriculture or Commerce who is constitutionally mandated to decide whether we bomb Russia or China or both.

If such contingency plans—for physical rather than constitutional launch orders—exist, as Quester believes, then in effect we are almost back where we started. Because "Plan R," the linchpin of General Jack D. Ripper's surprise nuke attack plan in *Strangelove,* was just that sort of contingency plan—devised to ensure that our bombers would attack their targets even if the U.S. command authority were vaporized in a surprise attack.

Professor Quester's analysis opens up a dismaying number of disturbing paradoxes in "Command and Control" theory as well as practice. More disturbing than any one of these questions is the fact that these problems haven't been solved to everyone's satisfaction by this time. I felt a sinking feeling reading Quester and the other documentary analyses attached to the hearings: O God, did I really have to worry about this? Weren't people scared enough that it had been taken care of completely by now?

I went through the hearing testimony without much consolation. Some admirals and generals complained to the subcommittee that the new failsafe systems were too stringent—that, in fact, they were worried that they might not be able to launch their nukes when the time came because of all the red tape the bureaucrats had put betweeen them and their missiles. But when the committee tried to get the answers to questions such as those raised by Quester about the actual control of nuclear weapons at the top of the chain of command and the mechanics of the transfer of constitutional succession, they were told either that such information was classified and they had no "need to know," or that "no one was sure" what would obtain.

So I took my underlined and annotated copy of the Command and Control hearings transcript over to the Pentagon. Most questions were referred to the Strategic Air Command headquarters in Omaha, Nebraska, and that's when SAC gave me the big invitation.

Would I like, the SAC people asked, to visit the Underground Command Post buried beneath the Nebraska prairie? Would I like a tour through a Looking Glass Plane—one of the curiously named "airborne command posts" that would take over the launching of missiles if the SAC Underground Command Post suffered a direct 5-megaton hit? Would I like to go to a missile base in North Dakota and descend into an operational launch capsule and crawl into a B-52 bomb bay? Would I like to enter the hollowed-out mountain in Colorado that housed the headquarters of the North American Air Defense Command, the supersensitive safety-catch on the nuclear trigger?

Thermonuclear Porn Revisited

The nearest motel to the SAC Command Post is a Ramada Inn in a place called Bellevue, Nebraska. I stayed up late the night before my descent into the underground war room rereading *Failsafe,* spellbound once again by the scenes in the war room—half the book takes place there—the very underground war room to which I was to descend the next morning. Rereading *Failsafe* was one of the final assignments in the task of preparation I'd given myself in the month between my visit to the Pentagon and my actual departure for triggerworld. The overall task had been to recapitulate the ontogeny of the thermonuclear fever I suffered as an adolescent by rereading, in the order I'd originally devoured them, all the classics of a genre I've come to call thermonuclear pornography. Back when I was a kid I'd read it all.

I'd started with the soft-core stuff: the tear-jerking, postattack tristesse of the slowly expiring Australian survivors in *On the Beach,* spiced as it was with a memorable seduction ploy in which a doom-maddened woman goes so far as to unfasten her bikini top on a first date, a hint of the unleashed inhibitions the end of the world could engender. This only aroused my appetite for the more explicit stuff: such nuclear foreplay novels as *Red Alert* and *Failsafe* with their mounting urgencies as the stiffening finger on the atomic button brought the trembling world to the brink of "going all the way," to use a metaphor from another adolescent preoccupation whose urgencies may indeed have fueled this one. To a bored and repressed high school student, nuclear war novels were not about skin-searing blast-burns but were dramas of inhibition and release. In that sense the foreplay genre was somehow unsatisfying, ending, as most of them did, with some chastening and guilty retreats and vows of eternal nuclear chastity forevermore. Fruitlessly, I scoured the subgenres of post-World War III science fiction (mutants stalk humans in the rubble; wise aliens sift through ruins for clues to the extinction of life on Planet III) for at least a retrospective fantasy of what the actual outbreak of Armageddon would be like, but all they delivered were teasing references of the sort Woody Allen parodied in *Sleeper* ("We believe that the individual responsible for touching off the thermonuclear catastrophe was a man named Albert Shanker but . . . ").

It was not until I began reading the truly hard-core stuff—the strategists—that I found some measure of voyeuristic satisfaction. Reading Herman Kahn's *On Escalation* was like coming upon an illustrated marriage manual after trying to figure out sex from Doris Day movies. With what fierce joy and strange receptivity did I follow the exquisitely fine gradations on the forty-four-step escalation ladder erected by Herman Kahn, with its provocatively titled rungs like No. 4, "Hardening of Position"; No. 11, "Super Ready Status";

No. 37, "Provocative Counter Measures"; all the way up to the ultimate and total release of No. 44, "Spasm War."

That night in Bellevue I felt a renewed rush of that thermonuclear prurience when I reread the first big war-room scene in *Failsafe.*

Do you remember the war-room scenes in *Failsafe?* Do you remember *Failsafe?* That was the trembling-on-the-brink novel that wasn't funny like *Strangelove.* Or witty. But powerful. In *Failsafe,* a condenser burnout in a war-room machine fails to send a "recall message" to a nuclear-armed B-52 as it approaches its "failsafe point," and the bomber heads toward target Moscow as men in the White House and the SAC war room try to defuse the fateful, final explosion.*

Back to the war-room scenes in *Failsafe.* Here's something you might *not* remember about those scenes, something I recalled only on rereading the novel. When the big crisis occurs, the war room is sealed off and two civilian visitors touring the place, just as I will be, are trapped inside as the greatest drama in history unfolds before them.

Before falling asleep that night in my Ramada Inn room, I must admit I entertained myself with some old-fashioned nuke-porn fantasies. After all the SALT talks had broken down, détente was crumbling into recriminations about human rights. Jimmy Carter was flying around in his nuclear emergency command plane and running nuclear-alert escape drills at the White House. Did he know some-

---

Failsafe and *Dr. Strangelove* are based on mistaken premises, as Sidney Hook pointed out in his contemporaneous polemic *The Failsafe Fallacy.* The Air Force never had a policy of ordering planes to strike their targets unless recalled at a certain point. Bombers would fly to designated points outside Soviet airspace during alerts, but the policy, now known as "positive control" rather than the tainted "failsafe," required that a bomber turn around and head back unless it received a direct voice-communication order to strike. A mechanical failure might cause a plane to turn back by mistake but not to head for Moscow. Unfortunately Hook falls victim to a fallacy of his own in *The Failsafe Fallacy,* assuming that by discrediting a key assumption in a speculative novel he has somehow discredited the notion that we have *any* reason to fear a nuclear war caused by mechanical failure. In fact, warnings of possible surprise attacks have been triggered on NORAD radar screens by flights of Canada geese and the reflection of the moon under peculiar atmospheric conditions. Under certain contemplated alert postures—the hair-trigger, or launch-on-warning, stance, for instance—such mechanical errors could be enough to launch our entire arsenal mistakenly.

thing we didn't? Alarmist articles with ominous titles such as "Why
the Soviet Union Thinks It Can Fight and Win a Nuclear War" were
appearing in sober journals. A Soviet surprise attack could happen
at any time, warned retired Colonel Richard Pipes in *Commentary.*
What if it were to happen tomorrow? I fantasized. What if, as in
Failsafe, I was to find myself trapped on the Command Balcony
when the real thing began and the footprints of incoming missiles
began stalking across the big war-room screens?

What an exciting prospect—that memorable phrase of John Dean's
on the White House tapes leaped to mind. I wouldn't mind it one
bit; I realized that in some small way I might be hoping for it. That
I could entertain such shameful speculation indicates not only that
nuclear annihilation appeals to infantile fantasies of grandiosity but
also that it is almost impossible to take the idea of nuclear annihilation to heart, so that it can be felt the way other deaths are feared
and felt. What sane human could be excited at the prospect of his
friends and loved ones dying on the morrow? Yet there is something
in the totality of the way we think of nuclear death that not only
insulates but appeals. I think it has to do with some early extreme
ways of phrasing and thinking about it.
    When early strategists began to talk about the totality of nu-
clear war, they used phrases like "the death of consciousness" on
the planet. Kissinger used the only slightly more modest phrase "an
end to history." Without consciousness not only is there no history,
there is no sorrow, no pain, no remorse. No one is missing or
missed. There is nothing to feel bad about because nothing exists to
feel. A death so total becomes almost communal. The holocaust of
the European Jews left behind millions to feel horror, bitterness,
and loss. When people began applying the word "holocaust" to nuclear war they meant a holocaust with no survivors, or one in which,
to use the well-known phrase, "the survivors would envy the dead."
Even now when a much-disputed scientific report argues the probability for long-term post-holocaust survival, at least in the southern
hemisphere, one does not, if one is an American, think of surviving
a total nuclear war. One thinks of dying in a flash before there's time
to feel the pain. Could that be the attraction, if that word may be
used, of nuclear war? Is there some Keatsian element "half in love
with easeful death" in our fantasies of the end?
    Back in 1957 Norman Mailer wrote in *The White Negro* that the
absoluteness of the idea of nuclear annihilation will liberate the psy-

chopath within us, and indeed, Charles Manson wrote of the welcome cleansing prospect of atomic war. In a curiously similar passage in a letter home from Korea, David (alleged "Son of Sam") Berkowitz wrote of his desire for release from atomic fear.

Such theories perhaps account for the perverse fantasy "attractions" of Armageddon, but how to account for the desensitization to the reality? As the demons of nuke-porn fantasies gathered about me in my Bellevue room that night I began to wonder if the very structure of the nuke-porn genre I'd been rereading that had been so stimulating in my adolescence—that thrilling sense of the imminence of release it created—might contribute to the problem of response I felt as an adult. The cumulative effect of pornography, particularly on a virginal sensibility, is to arouse expectations of intensity that reality sometimes fails to deliver. Back in junior high and high school saturation with nuke porn led me to a preoccupation with the dates and deadlines, with that familiar adolescent question, "When will it finally happen?"

Of course there was always an erotic component to the original thermonuclear fever. According to one study of the premillennial fevers that have swept religious communities (from the early Christians, who castrated themselves to avoid the heightened temptation to sin in the little time remaining before the Second Coming, to the wave of ark-building that swept the Rhine when a noted sixteenth-century astrologer predicted a Second Flood), in almost every instance the terror at the prospect of the end of the world was mingled with "fierce joy, sexual orgies, and a kind of strange receptivity."

Back in October, 1962, when it seemed at last it *would* happen, it was with thrilled anticipation and fevered fantasies that my (male) high school cronies and I regarded the Soviet ships approaching the imaginary line in the Atlantic Ocean, breach of which could shortly trigger all-out war. The chief fantasy engendered in the giddiness of the lunchrooms and locker rooms was this: As soon as the Absolute Final Warning came over the P.A. we'd steal a car and approach one of the girls at the other lunch table with the following proposition: The bombs are gonna fall in twenty-four hours. You don't want to die a virgin, do you?

But the October crisis passed and we were all still virgins. There still remained homework to do before graduation. The famous *Bulletin of the Atomic Scientists* doomsday clock has hovered close to the witching hour for three decades and we still haven't heard the chimes of midnight. The Fatima prophecy still had power to chill me when I heard it in 1964—after all, hadn't C.P. Snow declared in 1960 that nuclear war was a "mathematical certainty" by the end of the decade? But by 1970, when the C.P. Snow dead-line passed, I'd forgotten there was something special to celebrate.

It's not that these people were false prophets—indeed, at worst they may have been merely premature, at best they may have issued self-*un*fulfilling prophecies; by arousing enough concern they helped prevent or postpone that which they predicted. But what-ever processes of internalizing, eroticizing, or numbing were re-sponsible, there is no question that the Seventies have been a decade almost totally desensitized to the continued imminence of doom that caused hysteria fifteen years ago.

What happened to the superheated apocalyptic fever that pervaded the national consciousness from the mid-Fifties to the early Sixties? The bombs are still there, and the Threat, but when was the last time you had an opinion on the morality of massive retaliation? Can you even recall having an opinion on the gun-in-the-fallout-shelter question? Ban-the-bomb marches? The better-Red-than-Dead de-bate? Does anyone live his life as if the End were really twenty-five minutes away? Why did we say Good-bye to All That? Or did we?

In his study of Sabbatai Sevi, the fabulous false messiah of sev-enteenth-century Palestine, scholar Gershom Scholem distinguishes between two strains of eschatological (end of the world) sensibili-ties: the apocalyptic and the mystical. In the apocalyptic mode, the various revelations of cataclysmic messianic advents, and, to shift to a Christian example, the visions of the titanic last battle at Arma-geddon (an actual place in the disputed West Bank, by the way), are taken to represent actual physical upheavals, literal military battles that will be waged on the surface of the earth. In the mystical mode, on the other hand, these climactic wars between the forces of God and His Adversary, and similar upheavals described in sacred books, are said to be waged *internally*—within the mystical body (*corpus mysteriosum*) of the believer—for possession, not of the world, but of the soul.

After reading the literature of nuclear annihilation it seems clear to me that what happened in the mid-Sixties was an internal-ization of the apocalyptic fevers and their transformation into myst-ical symptoms.

When the test-ban treaty drove the visible mushroom clouds underground in 1963, it was not long before there sprang up among post-Hiroshima progeny the impulse to ingest magic mushrooms and their psychedelic cognates. The experience of "blowing the mind" from within was an eroticized replication of the no-longer-visible explosion. The once-feared death of consciousness on earth threatened by nuclear annihilation was replaced by the desire for the annihilation of the ego. It's possible that the concept of "bad vibes" can be seen as a cognate of invisible radiation. A generation that grew up with the fear of the ineradicable contamination of its mother's milk by fallout has developed a mystical obsession with the purity of all it ingests, and it can be argued that Jack D. Ripper, the nuke-mad commander in *Strangelove* obsessed with the purity of his "precious bodily fluids," is the spiritual godfather of the health-food movement. The guru who offers a short circuit to "the clear light" is particularly seductive to a generation that expected to be short-circuited to heaven by the "light brighter than a thousand suns."

That short-circuiting of time had long-term characterological effects that are only now being revealed: a belief that one would never live to be a grown-up discouraged any patience for the acceptance of the need to grow up. Indeed, like Peter Pan (not the diner), the bomb allowed the transformation of the present into a never-never land in which no gratification need be postponed and one could celebrate here what Tom Wolfe aptly called the "happiness explosion" instead of the unhappy one we once feared.

In a similar way the antiwar movement, which grew in part out of the ban-the-bomb fervor, found part of itself seduced into a mystical fascination with making bombs. One of the women survivors of the Weather Underground townhouse-bomb-factory explosion wrote a poem called "How It Feels to Be Inside an Explosion"—perhaps the ultimate internalization.

The persistence of the explosive word "blow" in the slang of the late Sixties and early Seventies may in itself be a residue of the internalization of the apocalyptic. Why else do we describe ourselves as feeling blown away, and getting blown over, blown out, getting the mind blown, getting blown (sexually). And is it an accident that the moving epitaph Ken Kesey spoke for the climactic failure of his attempt at a mystical group-mind fusion that failed to transcend fission was, as Tom Wolfe records it, "We blew it."

There is an undeniable but puzzling erotic element in the

mystical symptomology. As I was trying to explain my theory of nuclear pornography to a onetime SDS activist, now a feminist, she did a double take and said that the transformation I was talking about paralleled an explanation she had been developing for the persistence of rape motifs in the sexual fantasies of purportedly liberated women. Rape, she said, in the imagination of many women is an analogue of the unthinkable in nuclear terms, a traumatic, disarming surprise attack that leaves the consciousness devastated. Since there is no certain defense, and constant fear of psychic annihilation is impossible to live with, a transformation occurs in which the constantly terrifying specter of the external rapist is internalized and transformed into an erotic actor in sexual fantasies.

Tomorrow morning at last I would be able to stop fantasizing about the nuclear trigger. I was going to put my finger on it.

Alone with the Sanest Men in America

They call it the "Command Balcony" of the war room, and it was to be, after two preparatory briefings, my first vision of triggerland. The Command Balcony—I loved the lofty theatricality of the name—was where the President's phone call would be answered when he decided the time had come to unleash the missiles.

Uneasy is the descent into the war room. One is led down steel corridors where hard-nosed security-detachment men wearing blue berets and conspicuously displayed pearl-handled pistols guard the blast-proof doors which are marked NO LONE ZONE. The doors, my guide reassures me, are also gas-and radiation-proof and able to withstand a direct hit with a five-megaton warhead. This is not totally reassuring. In order to take my mission to the command post with proper seriousness, I had absorbed a full-scale "Briefing on Soviet Strategic Capabilities," which emphasized the growing threat from larger Soviet missiles able to deliver a "throwweight" up to twenty megatons with increasing accuracy. But no matter. Provisions have been made against the sudden vaporization of these underground premises. The instant the circuits begin to melt, all command-post functions will instantly revert to "The Looking Glass Plane." This curious code name is given to the "airborne command post," one of a rotating fleet of planes that have been circling the Midwest since February 1961 ready to take over the running of the war from above the blasts.

At first I thought the code name "Looking Glass" must refer to the postattack function—reflecting messages back and forth to surviving authorities at various points on the ground, or perhaps to the mirror-bright aluminum bottom half of the plane designed to deflect the glare of the nuclear blasts from the battle below. I couldn't believe the Air Force would deliberately advert to that dark Carrollian fantasy of hallucinatory chess. But when I asked my guide, an Air Force major, about the origin of "Looking Glass" he told me, "Sir, I can't say for sure but I assume they had that Lewis Carroll book in mind." Later that day I would be taken through an actual Looking Glass Plane on standby for an eight-hour shift aloft, but that morning when I went through the blast-proof doors and out onto the Command Balcony, then I was truly through the looking glass—although, as I would soon find out, not the side I thought.

The Command Balcony is a glassed-in mezzanine of the small two-story theater that is the war room of the Strategic Air Command. In the orchestra pit below, the "battle staff" works away at computer terminals and radar displays complete with all the glowing dials of dimly lit, melodramatic movies. Looming over all, of course, is the fourth wall of the theater—the "big board." Its six two-story-high panels dominate the view from the Command Balcony. Above the open panel closest to me the alert-status indicator reads 1 on a scale of 5. During the October War of 1973 it read 3. A whirling red light flashed above the big board and a message flashed on ordering the battle staff to cease all unnecessary tasks and stand by for orders.

This morning as I walked in the big board was blanked out. For security purposes, I was told. It was not until some moments later that I was to look up and see that fateful sign on the big board. First I wanted to sit in the command swivel chair. There it was ahead of me, a big black swivel chair in the central well of the Command Balcony. The chair is reserved, in time of nuclear war, for the commander in chief of the Strategic Air Command, or CINCSAC as he's known on the Command Balcony. It's from this chair that CINCSAC will gaze at the big board and make his moves in the decisive first minutes of nuclear war. On a panel in front of the CINC-SAC swivel chair are the red phone and the gold phone. The

President and the Joint Chiefs call in the orders on the gold phone. CINCSAC executes them on the red phone.

"The President can make you a General," observed onetime CINCSAC General Curtis Lemay, who sat in this chair for many years, "but only communications can make you a commander."

I seated myself in the swivel chair. I picked up the gold phone. I picked up the red phone. The battle staff was humming away beneath me. And for a moment, sitting there in the CINCSAC swivel chair, indulging myself in the seductive grandiosity of this position in the last synapse between command and execution of that awesome final order, for a moment I felt like a commander.

I also felt like a child, let loose with the war toy I'd always wanted. And I also felt like a potential war criminal. Will some tribunal in the rubble see this article and condemn me posthumously for failing to rip both gold and red phones out of their sockets?

But suddenly, when I looked up from my command-chair reverie to the big board, I felt foolish. A three-line message had flashed onto the big board. Could this be It? Not quite. When I read it I cringed. All my fantasies fled in embarrassment. This is what the message said:

> WELCOME MR. RON ROSENBAUM
> FROM HARPER [*sic*] MAGAZINE
> TO COMMAND BALCONY SAC HEADQUARTERS

Then an Air Force photographer stepped forward to take my picture in the command chair as a memento, and then a whole dog-and-pony show of a briefing began, featuring a call on the red phone from the Looking Glass Plane airborne with a preprogrammed "Greetings from the captain and crew to Mr. Rosenbaum, distinguished visitor to SAC's command post."

I could go on. It was in many ways a fascinating briefing but from the moment I saw that first WELCOME sign on the big board I had the sinking feeling they had turned this place, this focal point of nuke-porn fantasies, into a tourist trap. It might as well have been Disneyworld or some bankrupt and bogus "astronaut-land" in some bypassed south Florida subdivision for all the magic that remained. Suddenly all that had seemed forbidden, awesome about the stage upon which civilization's final drama may be played appeared like cheap stage tricks. Even the dimmed lights, "the pools of darkness" that in *Failsafe* "gave the sense of immensity of almost limitless reach," were dimmed only for the duration of my stay on the Command Balcony. They were dimmed to make a slide show, complete with flashlight pointer, more visible as it was projected on the screen. I felt cheated, teased with the illusion of command, then brought down to earth feeling like a cranky, disappointed tourist. A thermonuclear crisis would just not seem at home here on the Command Balcony any more than on a high school auditorium stage.

And that perhaps was the point. The Strategic Air Command is proud of its command-and-control system, does not think of it as an exotic, thrilling Strangelovian mechanism. It's *just* a mechanism, a sophisticated one, but a neutral mechanism they administer, certainly not an evil one—it hasn't done any evil, it hasn't really done anything except be there so long it's become routine.

That moment on the Command Balcony, I later realized, was the point at which I passed through to the other side, a Looking Glass of sorts. I was the one who had been living in a fever of Carrollian nightmares. The world I'd stepped into was relentlessly sane, its people very well adjusted. The paradoxical metaphysic of deterrence theory had become part of their ground of being. No one gave it a second thought, seldom a first. They spent little time in reflection of any kind, much less a Looking Glass sensibility. They were not there to shoot missiles and kill people. They were there *to act as if they would* shoot missiles and kill people because by so doing they'd never have to actually do it. They were content that their role was ceaselessly to rehearse, never perform that one final act.

They could have fooled me. I was fascinated by the aplomb of the missile crewmen I met. These are the guys who will actually pull the trigger for us. Of course they don't pull a trigger, they twist a key. Each two-man crew of "launch control officers" must twist their respective keys simultaneously to generate a "launch vote" from their capsule, and the two-man "launch vote" of another capsule is required before the four twisted keys can together send from ten to fifty Minutemen with MIRVed warheads irrevocably on their way to their targets.

These men will not be voting alone of course. When we pay our income taxes we are casting our absentee ballot in favor of a launch vote, and, should the time ever come, in favor of the mass murder of tens of millions of innocents. Morally, metaphorically, our finger is on the trigger too. But theirs are on it physically day in and day out for years.

I tried to get them to talk about it. Up at Minot AFB the Fifty-fifth Missile Wing helicoptered me out to an operational Minuteman-missile launch capsule nestled in the midst of vast fields of winter wheat. Fifty feet below the topsoil in the capsule I tried to edge into larger subjects—does it make a difference being able to know your target?—but there seemed to be nervousness on both sides, perhaps because of the presence of a senior officer and a tape recorder. Fortunately at the last minute I was able to arrange, as the final unofficial stop in my tour of the nuclear fortifications, a different kind of meeting with missile crewmen.

Let me tell you about that last stop. Because it was there that I finally got the feel of those brass launch keys—I actually got to twist them and get the feel of launching a nuke—and it was there that I first discussed such issues as nuclear surrender and the Judo—yes, Judo—Christian ethic, and it was there that I first learned the secret of the spoon and the string.

I can't tell you exactly where it was—I agreed to keep the name of the base and the names of the missile men I spoke to out of the story. But I can tell you it was a Minuteman base and the men I spoke to were all launch-control officers. And these are no ordinary missile crewmen. Even among the highly skilled Minutemen men these are the crème de la crème I'm visiting with this Saturday morning. These six guys in their blue Air Force fatigues and brightly colored ascots are a special crack crew of missile men culled from capsules all over the base into a kind of all-star team. This morning they are practicing in a launch-capsule "problem simulator" for the upcoming "Olympic Arena" missile-crew competition out at Vandenberg AFB, where they will represent the honor of their base in a kind of World Series of missile-base teams.

You see, the Air Force goes to some length to imbue the men in its missile squadrons with a military esprit—a task rendered difficult by the sedentary and clerical nature of military-capsule duty. Missile men never need learn to fly a plane and most don't. The romantic flyboy spirit is something of a handicap for men condemned to spend twenty-four hours in a twenty-by-nine-by-ten-foot capsule. There's no need to develop that special brand of nerve and confidence Tom Wolfe, in his study of astronauts, called "the right stuff." The right stuff for a missile crewman is a disposition far more phlegmatic and stolid. So the typical missile crewman of the sample I met was often a pudgy bespectacled graduate of a Southern technical school with a low-key, good-ol'-boy sense of humor, who volunteered for missile duty because the Air Force would pay for the accounting degree he could earn in his spare time in the launch capsule. The Air Force is still run by flyboys who tend to treat the missile crewmen as junior partners. Still the Air Force tries to incorporate the missile men into its traditional gung-ho spirit. It gives them all dashing ascots to wear, as if they were units of some Australian Ranger battalion trained to kill men with their bare hands, when all they actually are expected to do with their bare hands is twist a key. (One almost suspects some deadpan tongue-in-cheek flyboy parody in the ascot touch.) And there are all sorts of patches and merit badges for the annual "Olympic Arena" competition, which is strenuously promoted and prepped for all year round.

This morning these missile men have been practicing for "Olympic Arena" in a special glass-walled launch-control capsule "simulator" that replicates the conditions of the big missile Olympic games. These are not as dramatic as they might sound—no jousting between Titans and Minutemen, no target shooting, no actual launchings at all, in fact. Instead the competition consists of "problems" computer-fed into the capsule simulators, and the crews go through the checklists in their capsule operations manuals to solve the problems. Problems thrown at them can be anything from retargeting half their missiles from Leningrad to Moscow to putting out a fire in the capsule trash bin. For every possible problem it seems there is a checklist to follow, and the activity I watch in the capsule consists mainly of finding the right checklist in the right briefing book and following the instructions. Victory goes to those who follow their checklists most attentively. More like a CPA competition than an Arthurian tournament.

During a break in the problem-solving I am invited into the capsule simulator to look around. It is exactly like the working missile capsule I had been permitted access to a few days ago in every respect but one. The keys. In the working missile capsule the keys are locked securely in a fire-engine-red box that is to be opened only in time of high-level nuclear alert. But as soon as I walked into the simulator that morning I caught sight of the now-familiar bright red box with its little red door wide open. And then I saw the keys. They gleamed brassily, each of them inserted into their slots in the two launch consoles, just as they will be in the last seconds before launch. Apparently the keys had been left there from a launch-procedure problem. I looked at the key closest to me. It had a round brass head, and looked like an old fashioned apartment key. It was stuck into a slot with these positions marked upon it: SET on top, and LAUNCH to the right. This particular key was turned to OFF.

I asked one of the crewmen if I could get a feel of what it would be like to turn the key.

"Sure," he said. "Only that one there, the deputy commander's, the spring-lock mechanism is a little worn out. Come over here and try the commander's key." First I tried the deputy's key all the way to the right from OFF to LAUNCH. Almost no resistance whatsoever. Very little tension.

"Come over and try the other one," one of the crewmen suggested. "That'll give you the real feel of a launch."

To launch a missile, both launch-control officers in the capsule must twist their respective keys to the right within two seconds of each other and hold them there for a full two seconds. The key slots are separated by twelve feet so no one man can either reach over or run over from one key to another and singlehandedly send in a "launch vote." Even if this were to happen, a two-key-twist, two-man "launch vote" from a second capsule in the squadron is still required to send any one missile off.

I sat down in the commander's chair—it's not unlike an economy-class airline seat, complete with seat belt. I turned the key to LAUNCH. This time it took some healthy thumb pressure to make the twist, and some forearm muscular tension to hold it in LAUNCH. Not a teeth-clenching muscular contraction—the closest thing I can compare it to is the feeling you get from twisting the key in one of the twenty-five-cent lockers at Grand Central Station. Nothing special, but the spring-lock resistance to the launch twist is enough to require a sustained effort of will from the person doing the twisting. For two seconds that person and at least three other people must consciously believe they are doing the right thing killing that many millions of people. Two seconds is perhaps time for reflection, even doubt.

Later, outside the simulator, I asked the missile crewmen if they'd ever imagined themselves having a doubt about their grip on the keys when the time came for that final twist of the wrist. What made them so sure they'd actually be able to do it, or did they just not think of the consequences?

"No," one of the crewmen said. "During training out at Vandenberg they'd show the whole class films of the effects of nuclear blasts, Hiroshima and all that, just so we wouldn't have any mistake as to what we're getting into. It's true that they ask you if you will carry out a properly authenticated launch order, and they check your psychological reaction, and the checking doesn't stop there. We're constantly required to check each other for some signs of unusual behavior. But you have to understand that when the launch order comes it won't come as a sudden new trauma. We get practice alerts and retargeting procedures all the time, and the launch will just be a few more items on a procedural checklist we've gone through thousands of times."

By this time we'd adjourned to a small, concrete-floored room containing vending machines for Coke and candy and a few scratched metal folding chairs. Being in a room with the sanest men in America can be disconcerting. And these men were—officially—extremely sane. That constant psychological checking of each other they spoke about is part of the Air Force's Human Reliability Program, which is supposed to be a kind of mental early-warning system to catch people with access to nuclear warheads who are going insane, before their madness turns violent or, worse, cunning.

Of course the Air Force definition of sanity might seem a bit narrow to some, involving as it does the willingness to take direct part in the killing of, say, 10 million people by twisting a key when the proper order is given, while insanity means trying to kill them without proper orders or refusing to kill them despite orders. Nonetheless it is fascinating to read through Air Force Regulation 35-99, Chapter 7, "Psychiatric Considerations of Human Reliability," which is the missile-base commander's guide to early detection of "Concealed Mental Disorders." Regulation 35-99 divides these hidden threats into four categories: "The Suspicious," "The Impulsive," "The Depressed," and "Those with Disturbances of Consciousness." Regulation 35-99 then details "the early signs in observable behavior that strongly suggest the possibility of present or emerging mental disorder" in each category.

Now the trickiest category, according to Regulation 35-99, is "The Suspicious" (don't ask me what school of psychopathology this taxonomy comes from), which enumerates thirteen "clues to paranoid traits." Tricky, because as the Air Force points out "the following clues are sometimes seen in normal everyday behavior." Indeed, it is difficult to read the description of the thirteen clues without thinking of the "normal everyday behavior" of nuclear powers.

There is, for instance: "a. Arrogance—wherein the individual assumes or presumes the possession of superior, unique, or bizarre abilities, ideas, or theories."

Now, one would think that a man able to participate in the launch of up to thirty separate nuclear warheads and help extinguish human civilization with a twist of his key would be a bull goose loony not to "presume the possession of superior, unique, or bizarre abilities." The implication here is that sanity in a launch means *not* thinking about this reality, sanity means the kind of studied insanity or fugue state that ignores one's true relation to the world. Then there is: "b. Lack of humor—especially the inability to laugh at oneself, one's mistakes or weaknesses." Now that is pretty funny. When you think about all the occasions for merriment there must be down there at the controls of an ICBM launch capsule, it's hard to believe anyone would be crazy enough not to see the humor in it all. It's good to know that Regulation 35-99 will keep an eye out to yank the occasional gloomy gus right out of there, so we can be assured that when we go we'll die laughing.

Now clue "l."—"legal or quasilegal controversy about pay, time, accidents, unsatisfactory purchases, or matter of authority"— is an interesting one for a couple of reasons. This "paranoid trait," according to the regulation, "is often seen in conjunction with 'letters to the editor,' 'to the president of the company,' or 'to senior commanders.' " One can immediately see the appeal of this definition to the senior commanders who administer the regulation. But it raises interesting questions. One does not want the launch capsules filled with teeth-gnashing irritable cranks, yet the presumption of irrationality that attaches to any question about "matters of authority" assumes that all authority is rational, an assumption that was implicitly challenged by Secretary of Defense Schlesinger when he tried to ensure that if President Nixon went batty and decided to launch a few nukes during the impeachment crisis, someone would question his authority.

But for the moment let us leave Regulation 35-99 behind with a parting glance at the Air Force's official characterization of the Mad Bomber. He comes under subsection 7-14, which cites "Some Specific Cases of the Paranoid Schizophrenic" for the missile-base commander to have in mind when he's checking out his men. The only other "specific case" mentioned in this subsection is an unnamed "would-be assassin of President Roosevelt [who] came to Washington to shoot the President and thus to draw public attention to the buzzing sensation in his head."

"To the Mad Bomber of New York," according to the regulation, "the need for revenge seemed paramount, dating back to an ancient grudge against a public utility company."

And yet isn't our nuclear retaliatory policy based on our belief in revenge—that any strike against us must be avenged with nuclear warheads even if it means destroying the rest of human society? Just as planting bombs in public places did not restore the Mad Bomber his pension rights (apparently the source of his grudge against Con Ed), neither would a retaliatory nuclear strike restore the lives or freedom lost from the strike we suffered first. Could this analysis of the Mad Bomber have been a sly comment on the sanity of the nuclear balance of terror slipped into the Air Force insanity definitions by some military shrink with a sense of irony?

In any case let us return to that vending-machine room off the launch-capsule simulator, where indeed a discussion ensues with the sanest men in America, which gets into the basic question of revenge by way of Las Vegas and leads us to the secret of the spoon and string.

I don't want you to get the wrong idea about these missile crewmen. I soon discovered that the Human Reliability Program in practice does not necessarily eliminate all but docile automatons. The missile men have lively responsive intelligences and very upbeat personalities. And despite their devotion to pure professionalism, even they are not entirely unconscious of the ironies of their particular profession. They, too, occasionally get that sense of dislocation at the awesomeness of their position and the ordinariness of their life. I got that sense from listening to one of the crewmen tell me a story about a curiously dislocating encounter he had in a Las Vegas hotel.

He'd accumulated some leave time from the long hours of vigils he had spent down in his launch-control capsule, and he'd decided to spend it in the gambling palaces of Vegas.

"I went alone and one night I wanted to get into one of the big floor shows they have," he told me. "Well, when I asked for a ringside table they told me that as I was by myself, would I mind sharing with another couple. I say okay and these two people introduce themselves. The guy says they're from North Carolina where he's a dentist. Then he asks me what I do."

Introductions can sometimes be awkward for a Minuteman launch-control officer. A stranger will casually ask him his line of work and if he just comes out and says "I'm a Minuteman-missile launch-control officer," well, it's not as if everyone will stare into his eyes for signs of incipient missile-shooting madness, but there is, sometimes, a feeling of wary scrutiny. People don't know exactly how to respond to the unprepossessing presence of a man who is the most powerful and deadly warrior in human history.

"But not this dentist." He displayed none of the usual fears about Strangeloves in disguise, no suppressed whiff of awe at the personified presence of the end of the world.

"Hell no," the missile crewman was telling me. "The only thing this guy was worrying about was whether the thing would actually take off when it came time for wartime launch. He kept saying, 'I just want that bird to fly when the time comes.' He kept saying, 'I want that bird to fly.' "

The crewman shook his head. "It was funny because when the bird flies that means he and his family are probably vaporized. I couldn't figure it. It used to be people you'd run into would worry we'd go off half-cocked and start a war. Now this guy was all excited like he couldn't wait to see it."

"Fact is," said another missile crewman, "most of us have never even launched even a test down at the Vandenberg range. And nothing's ever been test-launched from an operational silo. Once they had a program that was going to let us launch from one of our silos. No warhead of course. From here into the Pacific. But some Indian tribe objected to missiles flying over their sacred burial ground or something and they canceled it. I can maybe see what that dentist was getting at. You sit down there and you know you've got launch capability and you know when you and your buddy turn the keys she'll fly all right but you sure would feel more comfortable if you had it happen once. I tell you I've spent a year and a half underground and I'm halfway to my M.S., but for all those hours down there, when I get out I sure would like to be able to say 'I launched a missile.' "

Again I asked these sanest of all men how they could be sure they'd be able to launch when they knew it was for real.

"One thing you have to remember," one of the crewmen told me, "is that when I get an authenticated launch order I have to figure my wife and kids'd be dead already up above. The base is ground zero. Why shouldn't I launch? The only thing I'd have to look forward to if I ever got up to the surface would be romping around with huge mutant bunny rabbits." We all laughed. It seemed funny at the time.

"Okay, then, put it this way," I said. "If you assume that when you get the launch order everyone on our side has been devastated by a Soviet first strike, is there any purpose served by destroying what's left of humanity by retaliating purely for revenge?"

"What it all comes down to," said one of the older crewmen, "is the Judo-Christian ethic."

"You mean Judeo-Christian," one of the others murmured.

"Right, like I said, the *Judo*-Christian ethic teaches that you never strike first but if someone hits you, you can strike back."

"Wait a minute," I said. "Isn't it Christian to forgive, turn the other cheek, rather than seek revenge? Say you're Jimmy Carter, a serious Christian, and you're President when the whole deterrence thing fails and for some reason the Soviets are tempted to strike or preempt our strike. You see those missiles coming in on the radar screen and know mass murder is about to happen to your people and nothing you can do will stop it. Is there any point in committing another act of mass murder?"

"You think he should surrender?" one of the crewmen asked me.

"I don't know," I said, taken aback by the abruptness of his question.

"That's the thing, you know," another crewman said. "Once you start thinking all that your head starts going in circles. You got to change the subject. There's a point where you gotta stop asking questions and go to work. You've just got to have faith that you're doing the right thing. It all comes down to professionalism. We know our presence here helps deter war and . . ."

"Course we thought about the problem if we get a launch order if one of us in a capsule crew suddenly turns peacenik at the last minute," one of the crewmen interrupted to say. "And we came up with a solution. We figured out that the whole two-key thing is really bullshit when you get down to it because we figured out how to get a launch with just one man and a spoon and a string."

"Spoon and a string?"

"Well," the crewman continued, "what you do is rig up a thing where you tie a string to one end of a spoon and tie the other end to the guy's key. Then you can sit in your chair and twist your key with one hand while you yank on the spoon with the other hand to twist the other key over." Now this guy was talking about using some old-fashioned ingenuity to carry out an authorized "execution order." It could of course be used in the service of an unauthorized launch conspiracy. Since launching an ICBM still requires a launch vote from two separate launch-control capsules, it would require two men in cahoots with two spoons and two strings—and probably two pistols—to carry out such an unlikely caper; however, since the two-key system is at the heart of the credibility of the entire command-and-control system, someone in the Air Force just might want to get out a spoon and string, go down into a capsule, and see whether someone might have overlooked a little safeguard.

Nevertheless, I actually found myself more reassured by the missile crewmen's willingness to tell me about the spoon-and-string trick than I was frightened by its possible application. The kind of person who'd cheerfully volunteer the spoon-and-string story is not the kind of person who'd be likely to conspire to use it to try to provoke World War III.

In fact I was quite impressed with the robust psychological health of the missile crewmen. If they didn't engage in rigorous analysis of the moral consequences of their triggerman role, none of them seemed at all the type to want to conspire to start a nuclear war. They put in a lot of idle hours down in the capsule studying for accounting and law degrees, and a nuclear war would seriously disrupt their professional prospects when they got out. Meeting the missile men was the most reassuring part of my trip.

Major Hering, you'll recall, was likewise not the least concerned with the mental health of his fellow crewmen. He was worried about the upper links in the chain of command. And unhappily, as one studies those upper reaches more closely, the chain of command seems less like a chain than a concatenation of spoons and strings.

How will Vice-President Mondale, off in Hawaii when a suitcase bomb blows up the White House, wage nuclear war from Waikiki with no black-briefcase man at his side. And don't think President Carter, notified of what looks on the radar screens like a surprise attack, will be able to dip into Russian literature to help him decide whether to retaliate against Moscow and Leningrad, or Leningrad and Kiev. If, in fact, the Joint Chiefs do decide to consult the Constitutional Commander in Chief on the nature of a retaliatory response (faced with a 'use it or lose it' situation military commanders tend to shoot first and consult the Supreme Court later; the Joint Chiefs have no need of the President to launch the missiles physically if they feel he's wavering when the time has come to strike back), the consultation will consist of presenting the Commander in Chief with comprehensive preprogrammed attack options generated by our chief nuclear war-gaming computer, the SIOP machine.

SIOP, I should explain, stands for "Single Integrated Operating Plan." It is *the* basic nuclear war plan for all U.S. forces and details exactly which missiles and which bombers will blow up which targets in case of nuclear attack. The SIOP machine is a vast computer complex in a subbasement of the Underground Command Post that generates the Emergency War Orders for transmittal to each element of the SIOP attack. In addition, the SIOP machine is constantly war-gaming its own war plan against its own estimate of the Russian war plan, which SIOP calls RISOP, and updating itself after it counts the computerized death score.

What this means in practice is that the key decisions about how we will respond *in every conceivable nuclear crisis* have already been made by the SIOP machine. Most of us may not think of nuclear war at all these days. The SIOP machine thinks about nuclear war for us twenty-four hours a day. The SIOP will run our nuclear war for us.

In fact, the only moment in my entire sentimental journey I felt genuinely "in touch" with nuclear war was the time I felt the SIOP machine. I don't think it's on the regular tourist trail in triggerworld but I made a special request to see the SIOP machine after reading so much about its awesome capabilities. Even in sophisticated strategic literature the SIOP is spoken of with reverential, almost Delphic, awe, and its pronouncements are surrounded with Delphic mystery. No one even knows how many targets are on the SIOP hit list. One scholarly study of recent nuclear targeting strategy devoted a long footnote to examining whether a fragmentary declassified report which declared that there were 25,000 targets in the SIOP really might have been a misprint, perhaps deliberate, for 2,500 targets.

The secrets inside the SIOP machine, our actual war plans, are perhaps the most secret secrets in America. According to a two-part report by Seymour Hersh in the *New York Times* (December, 1973), a story whose implications were lost in the Watergate deluge, the Nixon Administration's hysterical and ultimately self-destructive reaction to the Ellsberg affair may have been triggered not by his release of the Pentagon Papers but by the possibility—explored secretly in the highest councils of the Nixon White House—that Ellsberg might also release some of the sacred SIOP secrets. In 1961, in the days when he was an eager young Rand Corporation analyst, a fledgling Strangelove who had already made a highly respected debut with a pamphlet on the "Art of Nuclear Blackmail," Ellsberg had been summoned by the Pentagon to review the existing system for the command and control of the nuclear trigger weapons. As part of that work Ellsberg was permitted to review the SIOP and the Joint Strategic Target List. In a recent talk on "the nature of modern evil" at the *Catholic Worker,* Ellsberg, now repentant, described his first look at the primitive SIOP. It shocked him, he said, to learn we had only one nuclear war targeting plan: hit 400 targets in Russia and China. Estimated casualties 325 million. Whether Ellsberg went on to help redesign the SIOP he would not say, and whether he had any significant knowledge of the SIOP secrets as it evolved into a sophisticated computerized targeting system Ellsberg would not say. But according to Hersh's unnamed source (who sounds like Ehrlichman), the very possibility that Ellsberg would reveal sacred SIOP secrets the way he revealed the Pentagon Papers—the possibility that he would thereby show the Russians our hand in the bluffing game that is deterrence strategy—was enough to drive Nixon and Kissinger up the wall. According to this theory all the seamy things done to Ellsberg and the Watergate cover-up that was necessary to even *them* up can be traced to fear for the sanctity of the SIOP.

Well, you might say, doesn't everyone know what we'll do when attacked? What difference does it make which missiles go where when they all go boom and make everyone dead? It makes a difference to the strategists. For them the game of deterrence, the delicate balance of terror, is not a stalemate but an ongoing poker game in which the dynamics of bluff, ambiguity, and esoteric as opposed to declaratory policies are constantly shifting. As Bernard Brodie, the elegant grand master of civilian nuclear strategists, notes, "Good military planning should distinguish between what the President says he'll do and what he's likely to do." Kissinger, an unreconstructed Machiavellian among strategists, called the latter—our real plans as opposed to what we say we'll do—the esoteric strategy.

Inside the SIOP machine are not only the secret war plans of our esoteric strategy but, in addition, a wide array of targeting options based on computerized war-gaming of possible Soviet responses to our responses to their responses. One missile crewman I spoke to, overwhelmed by the majesty and complexity of the SIOP, burst into a veritable ode to its chivalric, jousting-like possibilities. "Just think," he said, "we're engaged in a test of wills with the Soviets somewhere and they push us too hard and push comes to shove, we don't have to choose between incinerating the planet and giving up. With the new SIOP options we can pinpoint a shot across the Kamchatka Peninsula and if they don't start listening to reason just walk those Nudets [Air Force word for nuclear detonation] across Siberia till they start to feel the heat in Moscow. Course they'll probably start on the Gulf of Mexico with theirs, walk 'em across to Houston, and start to head north, but we'll have our response to that all programmed in the SIOP. You know something else? I understand that before Carter took office he was given a detailed SIOP briefing and the guy was so shaken by it, that's why he suddenly comes out and says we got to abolish all nuclear weapons. The SIOP was too much for him. He just couldn't handle it."

So what actually goes on within the SIOP machine? Many nuclear wars: "practice" wars between SIOP and RISOP. After each battle a computer program counts the dead, estimates the damages, and looks for a way to improve the score in our favor in the next nuclear war. The predictive value of the nuclear wars waged within the SIOP machine is handicapped since it has to match itself against its own estimate of RISOP, which, like SIOP, consists of preplanned reactions that can be changed or rejected by national leaders in the heat of crisis. So the wars within SIOP can become a tenuous solipsistic affair, like a computer playing chess with itself. Still it is awesome being in a room in which the world has ended so many possible ways, perhaps even the precise way it will.

Toward the end of my tour of the SIOP machine I asked the colonel guiding me through the warrens of computers in the SIOP subbasement if I could touch the machine. He looked at the captain accompanying me and shrugged. Not far from me was a first-generation computer element of the SIOP machine. On top of its stacked magnetic tapes was a red "Top Secret" sign, but there was nothing secret for me to see. Only to feel. So I put my hand on its gray alloyed surface and felt in my palm the residual hum and tremor of the thousands of nuclear wars waged by SIOP and RISOP, those ceaselessly clashing computer programs, locked like Gog and Magog in endless Armaggedons within its ghostly circuitry.

That was the closest I came to the answers. The answers to Major Hering's question. To my questions about the nitty-gritty details of our actual as opposed to our declared or bluffed targeting strategy. All the answers but one. What happens if we lose?

It was at the very end of my tour of the SIOP machine that I happened to ask an innocuous question that led me down the road into the swamp of "surrender studies."

"In all these wars between SIOP and RISOP," I asked the colonel in charge of the SIOP room, "do we always win?"

The colonel seemed taken aback. He said something about "programming optimum outcomes" or something like that.

"Well, does SIOP ever admit defeat to RISOP or surrender to it?"

"I should hope not," he said.

I had heard whispers about forbidden "surrender studies" when I was down in Washington, whispers about people who have been hounded out of government for daring to suggest that, despite our endless contingency planning and war-gaming, we wouldn't know how to surrender if forced to because we're not permitted to consider the possibility of a loss. It sounded silly, and until that brief exchange in the SIOP room I'd assumed—as I had when I first read of Major Hering's question—that someone somewhere had the answers. But now I was told that even the SIOP machine was not programmed to consider surrender. And so when I returned from my pilgrimage I decide to track down these "surrender studies" I'd heard about.

What I discovered was that in the entire exotic garden of nuclear-war-fighting strategy theory, surrender is the one forbidden fruit. A subject more unthinkable than The Unthinkable itself. In fact, thinking about it has actually been declared illegal in some cases.

Indeed, the short, sad history of surrender studies in the nuclear age reveals that the few intrepid theoreticians who have ventured into that *terra incognita* have come back scarred by the charge that just talking about it can cause it. Back in 1958 a Rand Corporation analyst by the name of Paul Kecskemeti published a modest scholarly monograph entitled *Strategic Surrender.* Beginning with the premise that surrender, like war, is an extension of politics by other means, Kecskemeti explored the various strategies of twentieth-century surrenders—what each party to a surrender was able to win and lose (yes, a loser can "win" a surrender by getting more concessions than his actual strength should command). High marks go to the Vichy French and Germans for their eminently professional disposition of the surrender of France in 1940; a pathetic failing grade to the Americans and Italians who botched the surrender of Italy in 1943. Though his is largely a historical study Kecskemeti did append to the work a section on "Surrender in Future Strategy," with a subsection on "Surrender in Nuclear War"—the latter slightly more than one page long. That was enough. When his book appeared, the great post-Sputnik, Red-or-Dead debate still raged across the land and Kecskemeti had been gracious enough in his preface to acknowledge that "this study was prepared as part of the research program undertaken for the United States Air Force by the Rand Corporation." Swift and massive retaliation fell upon the book. You could call it overkill. There were outcries from the warlords of Congress that taxpayer money was being used to pave the way for capitulation to the Soviets. President Eisenhower was described as upset and horrified as he demanded an immediate explanation from the Pentagon. "I've never seen Ike more mad," said one aide. Everything at the Pentagon stopped for two hours while they tried to get to the bottom of the surrender-study flap. The *New York Times* reported a "tumultuous session" of Congress, and "the most heated debate of the year" brought forth near unanimous passage of one of the strangest resolutions ever to issue from that body. This one, attached as a rider to an appropriations bill and passed in August, 1958, specifically forbade the use of any federal funds to finance the study of surrender.

On the inside cover of the library-battered copy of *Strategic Surrender* I have in my hands, some outraged reader has scrawled: "Americans would rather die on their feet than live on their knees." It's an attitude that has made even the boldest nuclear strategists a bit gun-shy about discussing surrender. In what seems like a characteristically black-humored recognition of the delicacy of using the forbidden word, the index to the second edition of Henry Kissinger's early study of *Nuclear Weapons and Foreign Policy* contains the following laconic citation: "Unconditional Surrender. See Victory, Total."

Even the fearless Herman Kahn, forever urging us to call a

spade a spade and a grave a grave in matters of nuclear war, prefers
to discuss "responses to postattack blackmail" rather than "surrender negotiations." In his treatise *On Thermonuclear War*, Kahn grum-
bles that "the investigation of the feasibility of various [postattack]
blackmail tactics is not only a difficult technical question, but seems
contrary to public policy as set forth in recent legislation forbidding
use of federal funds for the study of 'surrender.' " But the master
strategist is something less than his usual crusading self when he
quits the subject with the terse comment that "such research is important." When he publishes research on surrender problems, Kahn
talks of "conflict termination." He talks of "crisis resolution," and,
most ingenuous of all, "de-escalation." None, not even he, dares call
it surrender.

Officially anyway. Inconclusive inquiries to the Defense Department failed to turn up any indication that the surrender-study
ban had ever been repealed, although no one there seemed to know
of its existence or was prepared to believe its existence, even after
I read them several front-page *New York Times* stories on the controversy.

Kecskemeti remembers. I spoke to him last summer, almost
two decades after the big fuss, and it sounded to me as if in his
scholarly way he was still steamed up about what happened to his
book. He blamed it on "a stupid article in the *St. Louis Post*," leaked,
he said, by Missouri Senator Symington, the former Secretary of the
Air Force, who was preparing to run for President on a Strengthen-
America's-Defenses platform.

Kecskemeti described the Senate debate on surrender. "Sen-
sational, demagogic—and silly," he says. "My book was totally mis-
understood. The question is whether great powers are able to end
a war short of total annihilation. If this is to be done it must be
thought about ahead of time."

The Seductions of Strategy

My pursuit of what might seem like the arcana of surrender studies
led me next to a question, another one of those Carrollian rabbit
holes in the landscape of nuclear strategy, that is even more fundamental and immediate: Will we respond to a Soviet nuclear attack
at all? Is it possible in some circumstances, despite our declarations,
that we just won't retaliate?

I first came upon this notion in an elegant analysis of "War Termination" by Fred Ikle, the hawkish former head of the Arms Control and Disarmament Agency. (Ikle took over after the doves there were purged in exchange for Henry Jackson's support of the original SALT agreement.) In the conclusion of his analysis Ikle argues that deterrence—the threat of nuclear retaliation if we are attacked—commits us to a morally abhorrent, genocidal, retaliatory vengeance if the threat fails and we *are* attacked. The logical implication is that in the aftermath of a Soviet surprise attack, we might surrender without firing a shot.

Turn the other cheek and give in.

No less a person than Richard Nixon acknowledged the possible wisdom of such a course of action. Consider the situation I'd be in, Nixon said, "if the Soviet Union, in a surprise attack, were able to destroy all of America's fixed land-based missile force and would confront the U.S. with a choice of doing nothing or launching air- and sea-based nuclear forces only to see the U.S.S.R. inflict even more damage upon us in return." The implication is that Nixon would have surrendered in such circumstances.

I used to have long arguments on this point back in high school. What good would pure vengeance do you if you're dead, I'd ask. Ridiculous, my friends would say: if they knew someone like you was running things and bluffing they'd be more likely to attack. So don't tell them, I'd say, make them think we will strike back but if it does happen, don't. What is to be gained by killing off the rest of the human race?

I had long dismissed this as a naive adolescent hobbyhorse of mine until I tried the question out on the missile crewmen that morning and found it provoked an interesting discussion about the Judeo-Christian ethic. I was even more surprised to find, when I plunged back into the literature of nuclear strategy upon return from my tour, that "Deterrence as a Great Big Bluff" is discussed by some of the most sophisticated nuclear strategists as a very real possibility.

The most rational deterrence policy, writes Bernard Brodie, perhaps the most authoritative and rational of the first generation of strategists, involves convincing an enemy that we are utterly inflexible, vindictive, and even irrationally committed to retaliation against a potential attack, no matter what.

But, argues Brodie, that most rational deterrence policy "involves commitment to a strategy of response which, if we ever had to execute it, might then look foolish." In other words, a rational person may decide it's foolish to retaliate. "It remains questionable," Fred Ikle tells us, "whether the execution of a retaliatory strike can serve the national interests once it has failed as a threat." And there it is again, in the most graphic terms possible, in, of all places, *Strategic Review,* one of the most militantly—albeit scholarly— hawkish nuclear-strategy journals. In the February 1976 issue of *Strategic Review* military strategy writer R.J. Rummel asks, "If deterrence fails would a President push the button? Of course not."

What does this mean? Is Jimmy Carter, who pledged never to lie to the American people, bluffing us along with the Russians? Is that part of the esoteric strategy? Has he secretly decided he won't push the button in that situation? Do the Joint Chiefs know? Would they let him get away with it? Do we want him to tell us, and thus the Russians, making an attack at least marginally more likely?

As you can see, once you get into the Looking Glass world of esoteric strategy, answers become elusive as the questions develop elaborate mirror images: What do we think they think we think they think about what we plan to do? Nuclear war is waged these days not with missiles but with conceptions of missile strategies, with manipulations of perceptions and metaphysical flanking maneuvers. Mental nuclear war (after Blake's Milton: "I shall not cease from mental flight . . .") goes on all the time, often in obscure and veiled forms.

Consider the esoteric implications behind the appearance and disappearance of a single footnote from the prepared text of a speech Henry Kissinger delivered to the Commonwealth Club of San Francisco on February 3, 1976. Appended to his otherwise unremarkable address on "The Permanent Challenge of Peace: U.S. Policy Toward the Soviet Union" was an eight-line footnote—appended, that is, to some printed versions of the speech and not to others. The official version delivered to the Soviet embassy by the State Department did have the footnote, and there was a message for the Soviets in that footnote, a veiled threat of great consequence between these lines:

> To be sure, there exist scenarios in planning papers which seek to demonstrate
> how one side could use its strategic forces and how in some presumed circum-
> stance it would prevail. But these confuse what a technician can calculate with
> what a responsible statesman can decide. They are invariably based on as-

sumptions such as that one side would permit its missile silos to be destroyed without launching its missiles before they are actually hit—on which no aggressor could rely where forces such as those possessed by either the U.S. or the U.S.S.R. now and in the years ahead are involved.

Now the real subject of this footnote is a declared U.S. nuclear strategy known as the "ride out" doctrine. Under it, we have committed ourselves not to respond immediately to a Soviet missile attack we see developing on our radar screens. Instead, incredible as it may sound at first, we are pledged to just sit back and track the incoming missiles, presumably aimed at our missile silos, watch as they blast holes in the Great Plains, ride out the attack, count up the number of missiles we still have left in working order, and *then,* and only then, strike back.

There are several strategic considerations behind what sounds like very odd behavior. First, we have confidence that our silos, for now at least, are sufficiently "hardened" so that the Soviets could not confidently expect to knock enough of them out to cripple our ability to retaliate. Second, confidence in our ability to ride out an initial attack allows us the luxury of not having to fire off our missiles merely on the basis of a radar warning that our silos are under attack; which means that we are less likely to be put in the "use it or lose it" dilemma, as the strategists call it, and precipitously launch our missile force on the basis of perhaps mistaken warnings or small accidental or unintended Soviet launches. Finally, declaring that we'll keep our missiles in their silos during a first strike against us almost compels the Soviets to target on them rather than on our large cities. They are bait of a sort.

Between the lines of that footnote there was an explicit message for Soviet nuclear strategists: a warning to them that if they attempted to develop a silo-busting missile capability—warheads accurate and powerful enough to destroy our Minutemen *inside* their hardened silos—they'd be making a big mistake and wasting billions of dollars. Because if they did develop that capacity we could simply renounce our "ride out" policy and shift to a "launch on warning" stance. This would make them look silly because under that posture, at the first sign of attack our missiles would let fly and the billions of dollars the Soviets had spent on a silo-busting capacity would be wasted busting empty silos.

Of course there are grave dangers to a launch-on-warning policy. Critics call it a "hair trigger" posture. And indeed if the Soviets thought we had shifted to it, they would, in the event of an accidental launch on their part, feel compelled to launch the rest of their arsenal because they'd know our hair trigger would be sending ours their way before we'd have time to verify whether it was an accident.

When the footnote set off a controversy over a possible U.S. "hair trigger" stance, and the footnote was dropped and then restored again, the State Department blandly denied there had been any change in U.S. policy. And officially there had not been. But Kissinger was playing what his former aide, Morton Halperin, calls the game of "the clever briefer." The footnote was designed to frustrate the ambitions of a hypothetical wily Kremlin advocate making a brief for a silo-busting capacity. "You want us to spend billions for this," a Soviet leader would reply to "the clever briefer." "But Kissinger has declared they will go to launch-on-warning if we do it and we will have gained nothing for our billions. What do you say to that?"

There is no good answer. Even though the footnote was deleted and the veiled warning shrouded in ambiguity, raising the possibility should be enough to defeat the arguments of "the clever briefer." That doesn't mean that the feint worked, that we won the War of Kissinger's Footnote. Indeed some military critics argue that Kissinger's subtle Machiavellianism was no match for the Soviets' mushrooming megatonnage. But that, in any event, gives you an idea how the game is played.

By this time, several months after my return from the nuclear shrines, several months of immersion in the literature of nuclear strategy, pursuing the paradoxes of esoteric and declaratory strategy ostensibly to write about the state of the art, I realized something was happening to me. I was becoming obsessed by the art, hooked again as I was as an adolescent by the piquant intellectual seductiveness of nuclear strategy. Finally, last August, I felt compelled to make a second pilgrimage. I was looking for some way to escape from the accumulation of nuclear esoterica I had submerged myself in and all of which seemed to be insulating me further from rather than bringing me more "in touch" with nuclear war, whatever that meant—I was sure I would know it if I felt it.

So I flew up to Boston on Hiroshima Day. A small item in Boston's *Real Paper* had attracted my attention: someone was actually going to hold an old-fashioned ban-the-bomb-type demonstration up there to commemorate the Hiroshima and Nagasaki bombings. I'm not talking about one of those anti-nuclear-power demonstrations. These have become very fashionable of late after the organizational success of the Clamshell Alliance's mass civil disobedience on the site of the proposed Seabrook nuclear reactor. There's no shortage of anti-nuclear-power demonstrations.

But a demonstration against nuclear weapons. How odd. As a sometime chronicler of the antiwar demonstrations of the late '60s and early '70s I knew that the only people who still did that were the small and aging band of the pacifist faithful, the War Resisters League, and other, smaller, old-fashioned peace groups; and I couldn't recall the last time I'd heard of them doing anything. This demonstration, part of a series of Hiroshima Day actions, seemed to have been engendered by many of the old peace-movement people hoping to rebuild the kind of mass movement that had disappeared after the test-ban treaty was approved. Apparently this was causing some ruffled feathers among the anti-nuclear-power partisans. According to a friend of mine in Boston, the Clamshell Alliance had refused to give its support to the Hiroshima Day demonstration because "some of them think it's just these old peace-movement people trying to take advantage of the energy the Clamshell people have established. The Clamshell people believe it's important to organize a base in the community rather than just to demonstrate." This snooty attitude confirmed a theory I'd had that the anti-nuclear-power movement was a way for activists to sublimate their feelings of impotence in the face of the massive nuclear-weapons establishment. You can prevent a reactor from being built, you can even shut it down if it's unsafe, but the nuclear warheads are already there, they are extremely unsafe, and no one believes they'll ever go away.

I remember how far gone into the swamp of strategic thinking I was by the time I arrived at Faneuil Hall for the opening speeches of the Hiroshima-Nagasaki ban-the-bomb demo-commemoration. I can remember because my first few pages of notes on that event are devoted to a four-line joke I found written on a wall of the men's room at Faneuil Hall and an analysis of the way that particular joke illuminated the dilemma of just-war theologians who employ the principle of "double effect" (developed in the thirteenth century to justify the use of the catapult as a siege weapon) to justify the "un-intentional" slaughter of innocents contemplated by certain nuclear retaliatory strategies.

The joke on the men's-room wall was unusual only in that it was not really dirty, just mildly "sick."

"How did you get that flat tire?" it began.

"I ran over a milk bottle."

"Didn't you see it?"

"No, the damn kid was carrying it under his coat."

Get it? Now let me explain what this has to do with nuclear war. The late '50s and early '60s were full of heady debate for theologians with almost everyone wrestling with the problem of whether conduct of thermonuclear war could, or should, be guided by the same moral principles that were used to define a "just war" or whether thermonuclear war must be considered beyond the bounds of anything justifiable under any circumstances. Even thornier was the question of whether possession of nuclear weapons for deterrent purposes without use, but with the threat of potential use, could be moral if use was immoral. And were some kinds of use, some kinds of threatened use, better than other kinds of threats? No one wrestled more heroically with these problems than Protestant theologian Paul Ramsey. No one tried more strenuously to demonstrate that the application of complex Judeo-Christian moral principles to the most esoteric elements of nuclear strategy was a possible, indeed important, enterprise. Differing with Christian pacifists and "international realists," both of which schools insisted that no moral distinctions could apply to such an essentially immoral or amoral (respectively) enterprise, Ramsey plunged into the thicket of targeting strategy. For my money his finest or most ridiculous hour is his attempt to synthesize an acceptably Christian deterrent posture: he calls for a declared policy of massive counter-city retaliation that will really be a bluff.

Here the milk-bottle joke is instructive. According to Ramsey's just-war reasoning (and assuming the milk bottle is some deadly weapon), it is okay to run over the boy as long as you *intend* to run over only the milk bottle. Or to apply it now to nuclear targeting, it is okay to respond to a nuclear strike by hitting an enemy's military targets (counterforce targeting) and killing tens of millions of people who happen to live within radiation range—it is okay so long as you *intend* to knock out only the military installations and the killing of innocent civilians is "unintentional" collateral damage resulting from the "double effect" of an ICBM on both combatant and noncombatant elements of the population.

This rationalization was developed to justify the use of the catapult as a siege weapon since it was impossible to see over the besieged walls to make sure the catapulted projectile hit only the combatants within a city. Ramsey also endorses a modified "bluff of deterrence" position: he believes that an *efficacious* deterrent threat requires that we declare we will wreak retaliation on cities, but that when the moment for retaliation comes we should adhere to counterforce military targeting or none at all.

Ramsey's efforts are a heroic act of rational apologetics, but one can't help but wonder if they don't serve to legitimize all forms of nuclear response since only a few scholastic quibbles seem to separate the sanctified from the unsanctified bomb blast.

I have been staring at blast wounds and radiation burns on and off for two days. The organizers of the three-day demonstration had assembled every major Hiroshima documentary film and they were running them over and over in various church basements around Boston. In addition, there was a round-the-clock three-day vigil in memory of the victims of Hiroshima and Nagasaki. At first, rather than standing in public I preferred to sit in anonymity and watch the wound films. I felt that after all the intellectualizing over the metaphysics of deterrence theory I might have lost a sense of compassion and that a good dose of Hiroshima horrors might bring me back to my humanity.

I was wrong. Too many pictures of wounds end up blurring the distinctions between the agony left behind by *any* war and the potential for utter annihilation to be feared from the next one. After all, the missile crewmen told me they had been shown graphic films of Hiroshima before being asked if they'd be willing to twist those keys. And still they'd said yes.

At last, driven by shame, perhaps at my lack of response to the wound watch, I headed for the plaza outside Faneuil Hall, where I resolved to spend the hours until dawn standing silently in the memorial vigil for victims of Hiroshima and Nagasaki. The vigil—a semicircle of people standing still around a mushroom-shaped memorial—had been going on round the clock since the anniversary hour of the Hiroshima bombing, and would continue until eleven the next morning, the time the bomb hit Nagasaki. I had actually resolved to stay up all night in the vigil on each of the previous two nights, but it was raining one night and there were some friends to see the second night and I never quite made it out onto the plaza. But this time I was determined to make it nonstop through to the dawn, hoping to do some quiet thinking about the whole matter. Instead of running around looking for another esoteric document, another trigger icon to touch, another fantasy to explore, I needed to stand still and think for a while.

The sociable sounds of a late-night singles-bar complex and the aromas of an all-night flower market wafted over to that part of the plaza where memories of mass death were being memorialized in defiance of the summer merriment. The semicircle around the mushroom-cloud memorial was manned mainly by members of the old peace-movement crowd sprinkled with some young Boston Brahmin pacifist types. On a nearby bench, apparently keeping an intermittent vigil on the vigil, were two shopping-bag ladies. They spent most of their time endeavoring to fix the mechanism of a rusty, skeletal umbrella someone must have discarded many rains ago. There was a rambling discussion in some obscure mode of com-munication in which I could make out references to cancer of the thyroid, which one or both of them thought she was getting. About 2 or 3 A.M., a wino tried to challenge the silent vigilants to argument on nuclear strategy but he tired of the lack of response. The singles bar closed up and until dawn there was little but silence to disturb the thinking I wanted to do.

For the first three hours I tried my best to think about the vic-tims of Hiroshima and Nagasaki, but I was thinking mainly about my feet. Should I shift my weight from the right to the left and back again, or divide it between the soles of both. Which strategy was more likely to get me through the morning with the least discom-fort? (Ever since high school days working in a supermarket job I've had trouble standing up for prolonged periods. I have high arches, you see, and . . .)

God, how inhumane, you must be thinking to yourself. This guy is at a memorial for 180,000 people blasted and burned and he's talking about his high arches. In my defense I would say I was aware of the absurdity of it—the emblematic absurdity at least. By spend-ing an inordinate amount of time thinking about my physical stance I was avoiding what I felt was my duty in this story, in life, to find a comfortable stance, *the* correct strategic stance, or at least a moral position, on the subtleties and the stark crudities of nuclear war.

As I shifted about for a stance I recalled my final phone conversation with Major Hering. It had taken me some time to track him down. He's an ex-major now and he and his family have had to shift location more than once as he looks for the right position, readjusts to the civilian job market. In the meantime he'd been doing some long-haul trucking in order to make ends meet.

At first the Air Force had tried to disqualify him for missile-crewman service under the provisions of the human-reliability regulation: because he wanted to be reassured a launch he executed was constitutional, he was, they tried to say, unreliable. When that failed the Air Force removed him from missile-crewman service and tried to transfer him to other duties. The major appealed that decision all the way up to the Secretary of the Air Force, lost, and then took an early retirement. He really had *wanted* to be a missile crewman and he fought his appeal fiercely with copious research into command-and-control problems to support his thesis. He told me he had a number of filing cabinets filled with documents that supported his position and revealed new unanswered questions, and he felt I should read through the files and the transcript of his hearings and appeals before I spoke to him. "It'll take you about a week or more of reading," the ex-major told me. I'd have to wait until after his next truck run, and after his new job was resolved. Then he'd be prepared to get back into it with me. "This whole thing has taken a lot out of me, as you can imagine, so I'd want to know you're serious before getting back into it all again," he said. The next time I called his number he'd moved to another city and I decided to pass up the filing cabinets.

I had a feeling that Major Hering's question had cost him a lot, cost him a comfortable couple of years down in the cozy launch-control capsules, years in which as it turned out he never would have had to face the constitutional command question his stringent conscience compelled him to ask. Cost him a promising military career and a couple of years of his life trying to extract from fragmentary unclassified sources what were the contingency plans for constitutional succession problems at the top of the chain of command and control. Finding himself alone among all missile crewmen in thinking independently on such questions must have been a burden.

Should We Call Our Own Bluff?

Kecskemeti, Ramsey, all those who try to think about nuclear war as more than the three-dimensional chess of the strategists suffer for their efforts.

There are two kinds of "unthinkables" in the thinking on this subject. There is the fashionable "unthinkable" of Kahn and company (how many million casualties are "acceptable" in a nuclear war: twenty? forty?), which in fact was never unthinkable at all to the Defense Department and defense contractors who funded this self-proclaimed daring intellectual adventure. And then there are unfashionable unthinkable questions. Major Hering's question. Unilateral disarmament. Remember that? While Herman Kahn's unthinkables have bankrolled him into a comfortable existence giving posh seminars on the shape of centuries to come, a man like David McReynolds, the War Resisters League organizer who helped lead the big ban-the-bomb demonstrations in the Sixties, sits in a drafty old room near the Bowery and speaks to an audience of five. He's raising again the question of unilateral disarmament at an anarchist-sponsored "Freespace University." In addition to the moderator and me, there are two men off the Bowery with shopping bags who seem mainly interested in getting out of the rain. There's an unreconstructed Stalinist who keeps changing the subject to a long-winded defense of the legitimacy of Soviet intervention in Czechoslovakia (counterrevolutionary provocation, he says) and an ex-Marine who begins all his questions with long quotations from Marcus Aurelius.

Despite it all, McReynolds delivers a brilliant polemical analysis of deterrence theory, in which he argues that unilateral disarmament is the only moral alternative to the mass murder for vengeance our declared retaliating policy calls for. Despite Air Force Regulation 35-99, McReynolds may be the sanest man in America on this subject, yet he has me and a Marcus Aurelius freak to listen to him, if you don't count the shopping-bag men.

Speaking of shopping-bag people, it's getting close to dawn now at this vigil we've drifted away from. I've drifted into a trance after settling into a more or less comfortable stance, but the shopping-bag women bring me out of it with a vociferous discussion of the skeletal umbrella and more talk of thyroid cancer. I recall a groggy illumination at this point: here, before me, was a perfect emblem of what I'd been trying to think about—how the shopping-bag ladies were not unlike sophisticated nuclear strategists, arguing in their peculiar language over the operation of that rickety contraption of an umbrella which, like the contrivance of deterrence theory, provides only symbolic protection for the two powers who seek shelter beneath its empty framework. Suddenly, I realized that the fact that these women had been talking about cancer of the thyroid as they watched the vigil was no accident. An increased incidence of thyroid cancer was a much-feared consequence of strontium 90 in the fallout-scare days of the late '50s and early '60s. They were *thinking* about it. Maybe, unlike the rest of us, they never stopped thinking about it. Maybe that's what drove them to the streets and shopping bags. Maybe they were among the unfortunate few who have not been afflicted by that mass repression we've used to submerge nuclear arousal in our consciousness.

Who else do you know who talks about it?

Well I figured it all out after dawn. My stance.

The illumination I finally received that morning came in the notion of a simple modest proposal. Open up the SIOP. The most frustrating barrier to intelligent thinking about the strategic and moral consequences of our nuclear policy is our continued preoccupation with esoteric strategy—with bluff, ambiguity, and mirror-image metaphysics.

Every targeting strategy, every targeting option the SIOP machine presents to the National Command Authority, represents a profound moral choice. An eye for an eye. Or two eyes. Two cities or one. Total vindictive retribution. Symbolic response or none at all. It's impossible to calculate the moral consequences we as individuals bear for such choices made in our name if the actual content of the choice is hidden behind the sleight of hand of esoteric strategy.

Should we resign ourselves and allow the SIOP machine and its think-tank tenders to make perhaps the most important decisions ever made, to churn out "optimum outcomes" according to definitions of "optimum" values that remain hermetically sealed in its program? We have no way to engage the machine or those who program it in debate over those values or the options they generate. If we were to move toward a democratically determined SIOP, we would have to reveal our bluffs, lay our cards on the table. Games of bluff are inevitably incompatible with democratic decision-making since an electorate can't vote to bluff by policy without, of course, betraying any possible success to an adversary.

Well, let them know. Let us know. Let us no longer be insu-
lated from the master target list, from the master targeting strategy,
from the moral options. We are all missile crewmen—all of us who
pay taxes pay for the twin brass keys, even if we won't twist them
ourselves when the time comes. But in one way or another we all
have our finger on the trigger, and it's about time we knew where
we're aiming, who's really giving the orders to fire, and whether we
ought to obey.

Bill Barich

Bill Barich had reason enough to escape. His wife had suffered two miscarriages and then her doctors discovered a brain tumor. The tumor, it turned out, was nothing more than a dark spot on an X-ray plate. Three novels sat unpublished in their battered mobile home seventy miles north of San Francisco.

Twice before, during periods of lingering sadness, Barich had left home. As a student at Colgate, he escaped to Florence and spent his junior year exploring the galleries of the Uffizi and studying the humanist scholars of the Italian Renaissance. And while his mother lay dying, Barich discovered a favorite pastime of the Florentines, horse racing.

At age thirty-five, Barich left home for Golden Gate Fields with $500, nearly his entire savings. Its builders had situated the track on San Francisco Bay in an elegant northern California setting. But wealthy bettors were attracted to the lush southern California tracks during the 1960s, and Golden Gate Fields had trouble drawing prime thoroughbred racing stock. Barich spent ten weeks at the track in 1978, living at the Terrace Motel, keeping a journal, learning to handicap, studying trainers and jockeys and horseflesh, and gradually understanding the mysteries of gambling which had amused his beloved Florentine philosophers.

He published his first book, *Laughing in the Hills*, from which this excerpt is drawn, in 1980. Barich's short story, "Hard To Be Good," appeared in the 1983 *Best American Short Stories*. His articles on horse racing, English pubs, fishing and other subjects have appeared in *The New Yorker*, and were collected in a book, *Traveling Light*.

Magic

*T*he cripples always amazed me, there were so many of them. They arrived early, well before the first race, and were wheeled or otherwise assisted across the parking lot and then past the three hucksters selling mimeographed sucker sheets. A tall radish-cheeked man sold Bob's card, and a man whose skin was almost cream-colored sold Bull's, but they were generally ignored in favor of the unsavory man in a trench coat who was stationed closest to the door. "*Hoymet!*" the man cried, picking at his chin, "Hoymet heah, five winnahs yestahday, Hoymet has da double for ya," and the cripples reached into their pockets and donated a dollar for the Hermit's daily words of wisdom. They were plentiful, these words, because the hermit usually offered two selections in every race and threw in five combinations for the daily double, as well as a smattering of exacta numbers and exacta suggestions and long-shot exactas, below which, in bold block letters, the following cautionary sentence was printed: TANFORAN RACING ASSN. DOESN'T SPONSOR THESE SELECTIONS.

Inside, the cripples stationed themselves along the clubhouse rail, their wheelchairs lined up near the finish line, and began quietly sorting through their materials: *Forms,* programs, suggestions clipped from the daily papers, and the sucker sheets. They had a dignity about them, a stillness that remained undisturbed even as the action around them increased. While watching them assemble I thought of their ranks, of all our ranks, being duplicated at racetracks across the land. Every day twenty-six thousand of us descended on Santa Anita, ten thousand more stopped in at Calder in Florida, and another twenty-one thousand made their deposits at Oak Lawn Park. Even the poorest tracks had a following—four thousand a day at Latonia in Kentucky and a thousand at tiny Rilito Downs in New Mexico. Many greenbacks made the rounds; four million dollars would be handled at Santa Anita alone. In a given year we'd watch some sixty-nine thousand races, in which sixty-two thousand horses would start a total of six hundred thousand times for purses totaling three hundred thirty-six million.

A short fat man breezed by, on his way to cash in a winning ticket from the previous day. "You see that race?" he asked. "Our Star Chuck? The one who paid a hundred fifty? I had that horse." He showed me the ticket, grasping it protectively between his thumb and index finger, "I rode in with this guy, he's not even a friend of mine, really, but his name's Chuck, so for the hell of it when he bought a ticket on the horse I bought one, too. Then the horse comes in. I couldn't believe it. The horse came in. Twenty-seven years I'm handicapping, I never once hit a big winner. Not once. Then the horse comes in. I couldn't believe it. So that's how it happens, I said. I think my hair was standing up. I couldn't believe it. Hell with this, I said, went out, sat in the car the rest of the afternoon."

In the men's room the stalls were all occupied by students, clipboards balanced on their knees, and an old guy with ratbreath was washing his dentures in the sink. "I was born in Wichita," he said. "My mother was a Cree. She never touched alcohol. It made her crazy. I love racing but if I ever win any money I'm going back to Kansas. If you don't believe me you can ask Don."

Riding down the elevator I studied the toupees on display, the worst I'd ever seen, worse even than those in burlesque houses or on the TV weathermen in small towns. They inspired disbelief. These were clown rugs, the kind of mustard-colored mats that were plastered to heads, then whisked away by fishing hooks or blown sky-high by studio wind machines. Stunning polyester and doubleknit ensembles were also on parade, the Spiegel catalog come to life. A young man with a wolfman pompadour and an expensive but tasteless suit was putting the make on a classically cheap-speed blonde. "I went to Vegas over the weekend," he said. "You know Wayne Newton? The singer? I hang out with his bodyguard's brother-in-law."

Turnstiles were clicking briskly down on the ground level, where people strode determinedly off buses from Oakland, Richmond, and San Francisco as though they'd been promised a big slice of Transformation Pie and couldn't wait to bite into it. "I dreamed the numbers last night," said a balding lady in a heavy fur coat and mittens. "Four and six, clear as could be, only I never did dream what race they was in. Going to cost me twenty dollar to find out. Be worth it, though. Last week, one exacta, it paid a thousand dollar. A thousand dollar. I said *a thousand dollar!* You know how long it take me to make that kind of money?"

Upstairs members of special groups were being led to their tables in the special groups' section near the Turf Club. Most of them had never been to the track before, or maybe just once during the Second World War when Uncle George rolled into town and dragged everybody to Bay Meadows, and as they picked their seats they seemed openly thrilled by the excitement at hand, the *raciness* of racing. They lived in bedroom communities and were dressed simply unless they belonged to a group that believed in funny hats or badges or other emblematic attire, and they would spend the afternoon eating and drinking and betting on pretty horses and long shots. One of them—it was impossible to say at the outset *which* one—would win a hundred dollars and become an addict. "It started at Golden Gate," he would say later, "over creamed chicken on toast." Management took good care of special groups and named a purse in honor of each of them: Rotary Club of Piedmont Purse, Nomads of Santa Rosa Purse, Women in Construction Purse, R.J.'s Cocktail Lounge Purse, Fashionettes Social Club Purse, Standard Oil Wives Purse, NARF Fun Groupe Purse, and Mary and Bob Franchetto's Fortieth Birthday Party Purse.

Right after the national anthem, the black kids who seemed to live under the paddock got ready to work. There were three or four of them, streetwise jivey kids with hair done in cornrows and dreadlocks, and each day they staked out a square of macadam directly below the runway leading from the Jockeys' Room to the paddock. When jockeys strolled down the runway before a race, the kids were *on their case* immediately, hooking fingers through the chain-link fence and pulling themselves onto the concrete ledge and beginning their interrogation.

"Hey, Mahoney," they yelled at Bill Mahoney, who walked the runway like a condemned man, as though a thirty-pound weight had been embedded between his shoulder blades, "you gonna give that horse a ride today? You gonna ride him right? What about that horse, Mahoney? He sound? He feelin' all right? Last time out he was limpin', Mahoney. C'mon, tell the truth, don't be lyin' to me now." Most jockeys stared off into space, but a few seemed to enjoy the exchange. " 'Rique, my man, hey there, Muñoz, hey, *'Rique* my *man,* you gonna get that horse out of the gate this time? I'm askin' now, 'Rique, you dig? 'Cause if you don't get him out, that sucker don't stand a chance. Aw, don't be makin' faces, 'Rique, you can talk to *me.*" Every once in a while they charmed a jockey, one who knew what it was like, and the jockey winked or muttered a few syllables out of the corner of his mouth and the kids ran off to bet. We were all pilgrims in our way.

II

I sat by the Terrace swimming pool, reading about magic. A salesman from an educational publishing company sat in the chair next to mine. I'd met him earlier when he'd caught me staring into his car, a late-model Pontiac with a back seat full of globes, spheres of reinforced cardboard, blue, green, and brown, spilled into a tangle of equatorial seat belts. The sight was marvelous, and not a little unexpected, and I lingered, staring, until the salesman came out of his room and asked me what the hell I was doing. The globes had overwhelmed me, I said, and then showed him my room key to prove I wasn't a thief. This made him feel guilty. Minor judgmental errors tend to unhinge men who've been drinking alone in motel rooms since two in the afternoon. He opened the trunk of his car and insisted on giving me an outdated model he'd collected from a Berkeley retailer. "Keep it, keep it," he said. "I already credited the guy's account. Company can't use it." He tapped the globe with a finger. "Africa's all screwed up. They keep changing the names over there."

I put the globe on my dresser and as a fair-trade gesture gave the man—Ted—a warm beer from my stash on the windowsill, which was a mistake. When I went to sit by the pool Ted joined me, bringing along an ice bucket, two sani-sealed glasses, and a half-bottle of Old Stasis bourbon. He wanted to get a little snockered and then go looking for "nookie," but I was after the magic and couldn't explain. So we sat together and listened to the ice melt. It melted slowly, with no audible variation. Finally Ted got to his feet and pulled up his trousers, which seemed to contain thousands of pennies, and said, "Well, I better turn in. Got to be in Palo Alto early tomorrow." We shook hands and he made me write my name and

address on the back of his business card so he could send me an atlas, *gratis,* when he got home to Citrus Heights, some horrible
planned community near Sacramento. The atlas has yet to arrive.

III

In 1460 a Macedonian monk brought Cosimo de' Medici a manuscript reputed to be an incomplete copy of the secret, magical *Corpus
Hermeticum,* a book supposedly written by Thoth, the Egyptian god
of wisdom, who was known to the Florentines by his Greek name,
Hermes Trismegistus. Hermes was held in high regard for his powers and valued, as were many things during the Renaissance, for his
antiquity. He predated Plato, for whom Cosimo had forsaken Aristotle, and hence was considered *prima materia,* closer to the flame.
Cosimo was old and sick and wanted to read the *Corpus,* even in
fragmentary form, before he died, so he repaired to his villa above
Florence and summoned court scholar Marsilio Ficino.

"I arrived here at Careggi yesterday," he wrote Ficino in his
letter of instruction, "not in order to till my fields, but to cultivate
my soul."

Ficino came at once. He was a short serious melancholy man
who'd established his reputation as a translator early in life, while
still at school. Cosimo had made him a ward of the Medici so he
could translate, for Cosimo's delectation, Plato's work from Greek
into Latin without being subjected to the usual distractions of pen-
urious scholars. For Ficino the arrangement was a windfall. Since his
youth he'd been devoted to Plato and to the notion that love in its
idealized Platonic form was the universe's glue, its sustaining principle; Cosimo's patronage gave him the freedom to try to reconcile
such doctrines with those of the Church. Religion and philosophy
were both spiritual pursuits, he believed, and it was his desire to
fuse his own mystical Platonism with the conceptual core of Christianity. To this end he labored on in a villa near Cosimo's, under the
blank marble stare of a bust of Plato that Cosimo had given him.
Once a year, on Plato's birthday, Ficino held a banquet for leading
statesmen, artists, writers, and students, the nucleus of his informal
"Academy." Arriving guests, tired from the long journey on horseback, up from the city into hills leavened with vines and olive trees,
were instructed to take note of the motto Ficino had inscribed (per-

haps as a caution against the weight of his own humors) on a wall
of the villa: FREE TROUBLES, BE HAPPY IN THE PRESENT.

At Cosimo's request, Ficino set aside his other work and took
up the fragments of the *Corpus*. He recognized the importance of the
find; only Zoroaster came before Hermes in the genealogy of wisdom. By 1463, Ficino had finished a translation, Greek to Latin. This
he presented to Cosimo, who was almost on his deathbed. The *Corpus* was something of a disappointment, though, at least in its phil-
osophical sections, which only echoed the longings and aspirations
of Humanism. In one characteristic passage, Pimander, an aspect of
the Divine Mind, floats down to earth to give dozing Hermes advice
on conducting his life. Man's doubleness complicates existence, Pimander says; your flesh is mortal, but you are immortal by connection to essential man. Unlike other creatures, man can grow and
change and perhaps become one with the Divine Mind. "You are
light and life, like God the Father of whom Man was born. If therefore you know yourself as made of light and life . . . you will return
to life." This was familiar stuff, but the magical elements in the *Corpus* excited Ficino and his friends and helped to liberate the
figure of the magus from the granite and doxology of the medieval
church.

Before the advent of Christianity, and through the period of
its inception and diaspora, magicians had flourished in and around
Florence. They were consulted not only for potions and abracada-
bras, but for the medicinal herbs, roots, and barks that formed the
substance of the early pharmacy. But priests were afraid of them and
believed that they practiced a form of black magic designed to top-
ple the Church, so a campaign against them was mounted and they
were forced underground. The *Corpus* helped to redefine magic and
broaden the scope of its praxis. There were really *two* categories of
magic, black and white, malevolent and benevolent, and Hermes ad-
vocated the use of a variety of the latter, called *sympathetic.*

According to the scholar Francis Yates, this magic worked by
simpatia, sympathy, by "knowing the mutual reports running
through all nature, the secret charms by which one thing can be
drawn to another." It explored affinities and relationships and tried
to attract celestial energy, *spiritus,* and then deploy it in the service
of benign goals. Pico pushed this distinction even further. He described sympathetic magic as "the utter perfection of natural philosophy," hardly magical at all, and certainly separate from that

other magic "which depends entirely on the work and authority of demons, a thing to be abhorred, so help me the God of truth, and a monstrous thing." Even the word *magus* had been misconstrued, Pico wrote. In fact it derived from Persian and "expresses the same idea as 'interpreter' and 'worshipper of the divine' with us." Pico's naive reformulation, sure to appeal to academics, did much to enhance magic's reputation, and soon magical texts of all sorts, translations as well as newly written materials, were in great demand. Ficino contributed a volume called *On Capturing the Life of the Stars.* It was an eclectic compendium, somewhat like an herbal, full of imaginative prescriptions for healing body and soul.

An Arabian manual, *Picatrix,* had influenced Ficino's work and portions of it were quoted in the book I was reading. There was a long description of a city Hermes/Thoth had built in Egypt and controlled by manipulating images.

> On the eastern gate he placed the form of an Eagle; on the western gate, the form of a Bull; on the southern gate the form of a Lion, and on the northern gate the form of a Dog. Into these images he introduced spirits which spoke with voices, nor could anyone enter the gates of the City except by their permission. There he planted trees in the midst of which was a great tree which bore the fruit of all generation. On the summit of the castle he caused to be raised a tower thirty cubits high on the top of which he ordered to be placed a light-house the colour of which changed every day until the seventh day after which it returned to the first colour, and so the City was illuminated with these colours. Near the City there was an abundance of waters in which dwelt many kinds of fish. Around the circumference of the City he placed engraved images and ordered them in such a manner that by virtue of it the inhabitants were made virtuous and withdrawn from all wickedness and harm. The name of the City was Adocentyn.

The description had a fairy-tale piquancy, and that night I dreamed of Adocentyn. It was still with me in the morning when I went to the track.

IV

The race was for two-year-olds, a five-furlong sprint, and I looked over the stock in the paddock before making my wager. The horses had run only once or twice before, or not at all, and they were still green and had the alert playful look of the ranch about them. They weren't aware of resistances, opposition, the gradual wearing down of tissue and desire, and some of them had a bafflement in their eyes when they surveyed the grandstand and the unfamiliar faces reading their limbs. I liked to bet two-year-olds because they were so young and guileless. Older horses, the *Form's* "hard-hitting veterans," were often deceptive before a race, drag-assing around, shuffling, their backs swayed and noses dappling the dust, and more than once I'd lost money when just such an animal rose into himself a hundred yards from the gate, suddenly pumped up on thoroughbred afflatus, and led the field from wire to wire.

Two horses in the present field attracted me, Pass Completion, the favorite, and an outsider, Flight Message. Both looked honest, and I was standing in front of a toteboard, trying to decide between them, when an old man came up and asked if he could look at my *Form.* He was very polite, with clean pink cheeks, and he smelled of cologne and a dash of clubhouse whiskey and wore gold-rimmed specs and a traditional senior citizen's shirt, white nylon and short-sleeved, with a strapped T-shirt beneath it.

"Haven't read one of these for years," he mumbled, running the spine of his comb under lines of type. "Say, this horse *has* been working well. Raindrop Kid. Raindrop Kid. What're the odds?" he asked, squinting.

"Eighteen to one."

"Eighteen to one? Eighteen to one?" His eyes were gleaming now and a bit of froth appeared on his lips. "That's an overlay if ever I saw one," he said before vanishing into the six-dollar-combination line.

Around me people were suddenly moving, prodded into action by the five-minute-warning buzzer, and I was arrested by the swarming colors and shapes, nests of teased hair, lime-green trousers, dark skin. I wondered if the old man knew what he was talking about or if he was just another trailer-park baron on holiday. It occurred to me that he might be a manifestation, some emissary from the outposts of my consciousness. I looked around. He wasn't there. Time was passing, so I stepped into the flow to play Pass Completion, but when I reached for my money, I pulled out something along with it, a small antique medal my brother had given me years ago. I'd used it as a key chain until the hook at the top had broken, and now I carried it for sentimental reasons. It pictured a knickered boy in a golf cap rolling up his sleeves and preparing to flick a marble at other marbles arranged in a cruciform at the center of a circle. Above the boy's head were the words, "United States Marble Shooting Championship Tournament." His feet rested on laurel leaves. There was no illustration on the other side, only text: "Malden Championship Awarded to Emil Lawrence by *The Boston Traveler,*" it read. Nowhere did it mention Adocentyn, but I still bet Raindrop Kid to win.

Sometimes a race unfolds exactly as you've envisioned it, with the horses cleaving to a pattern in your brain, and this seemed to be happening now. Raindrop Kid broke slowly, as I thought he would, and was seventh at the three-sixteenths pole, but I expected him to begin moving soon and he did, on the outside. By the stretch he was in striking distance. His legs were fully extended and he moved along in an effortless coltish glide. He trailed My Golly, whom I hadn't even considered, and as he drew up to challenge I waited for the next phase of the pattern to develop, horses hooked and matching stride for stride, and then the final phase, the Kid's slick expenditure of energy he'd held in reserve, his head thrown forward just far enough to nip My Golly at the wire. But it was My Golly who began to accelerate, drawing away, and I watched him pass the finish line and felt the pattern dissolve, soup draining into my shoes.

Then the "Inquiry" sign appeared on the toteboard. The stewards were going to review a videotape of the race because my jockey, Rogelio Gomez, had lodged a complaint against Enrique Muñoz on My Golly, claiming Muñoz had bumped him in the stretch. The sign had a strange effect on me. It was one turnaround too many and I felt unpleasantly suspended. I turned away and looked up and saw a sparrow trying to pin a moth against the windbreak of the grandstand. The ongoing business of biology made me aware of the sound of my heart and the blood circulating through my body. I took a deep breath, but the air was warm and settled miasmatically in my lungs. Somebody had spilled popcorn down the steps in front of me, and for a while I counted kernels. The waiting was bad, as it always is, and I tried thinking about other things. The man next to me had a digital watch strapped to his wrist and I wondered how such instruments would affect our sense of time, extracting numbers from some bottomless well instead of graphing them, as clock hands did, across a recognizable globe. Computers with their miniaturized functions had a tendency to destroy space by making it seem equivalent to time, of the same invisible substance, when in fact the opposite was true: space was real, was grass, trees, rivers, and earth, real as horses are and so of greater validity than human constructs like time.

A sudden explosion of bulbs, brilliant flashes on the toteboard, interrupted my cogitation, and then John Gibson, the track announcer, announced in that grand theatrical manner he had, full of hesitations, that after examining the videotape . . . the stewards . . . had decided . . . to *disqualify* My Golly and award the race to Raindrop Kid. The Kid paid thirty-eight dollars and twenty cents for every two dollars wagered to win, and when I collected my money I could feel the heat in my hands, all through me, and I knew how hot I was going to get.

V

All week long I kept winning. It had nothing to do with systems, I was just *in touch*. When I walked through the grandstand I projected the winner's aura, blue and enticing. Women smiled openly as I passed. I drank good whiskey and ate well. One night I went to a Japanese restaurant and sat at a table opposite Country Joe Macdonald, the singer who'd been a fixture at rallies in the sixties. Joe had a new wife with him, and a new baby who refused to sit still and instead bawled and threw an order of *sushi* around the room. A chunk of tuna flew past my ear. Even this seemed revelatory, the domestic roundness of a star's life, his interrupted meal, carrying the baby crying into the night, and I knew that someday soon Tuna or Seaweed or Riceball would appear on the menu at Golden Gate and I'd play the horse and win. Things fleshed themselves out before my eyes. In a liquor store I bought two bottles of Sapporo Black and went to sit on the Terrace steps and listen to my upstairs neighbor's piano exercises, the dusky fastnesses of ivory. This tune, I thought, will never end.

VI

One morning as I stood by the rail I saw Debbie Thomas galloping Bushel Ruler. He looked good coming through the fog, the edges of his body softened by mist, the contours hidden in smoke, Leonardo's *sfumato*. Debbie was standing in the stirrups, holding him. Her hair billowed out from under her pink and red cap, and she seemed as she rode to be centered in him, her balance absolute. I was waiting for her back at the barn. She took off her cap and asked me to hold Bushel's reins. He didn't like it. He started moving toward me, shaking his head and rolling back his lips to exhibit his awful teeth. They were stained various shades of brown from hay, oat husks, bran, and mash and reminded me of the eroded, unbrushed nubbins dentists showed you when they were trying to coerce you to *floss*. Debbie yanked on the reins. "He's just feeling good," she said. Grooms always said this when their horses were acting rowdy and appeared ready to kick. I remained on guard. Horses always got you when you weren't looking. The other day, Debbie said, she'd been walking down the shedrow, minding her own business, when *clunk,* this new colt of Dick Leavitt's stuck his head out of his stall and wrapped his mouth around her arm. She showed me the purple bruise.

"What'd you do?"

"Went and got a rake and hit him with it."

She squirted liquid soap into a bucket and filled it with water. The solution smelled minty. I led Bushel to a spot near the hot-walker and Debbie started bathing him, working a sponge over his withers. He didn't like this either, not in the chilly fog, and he snorted a few times and backed away. Again Debbie yanked on the reins. "You cut that out," she said, bringing her face close to his, "or I'll go get the shank," a piece of leather rope used for teaching manners. She gave me the sponge and I washed Bushel's right side. It was like washing a car, involving similar motions, sponge to bucket, and sloppy suds, but horse felt better under my hand than chrome had ever done. There was something sensual in the washing, feeling Bushel's bunched muscles and his coat slick with water, and experiencing at the same time the reticulated nature of the back-stretch, my eye drawn to other grooms washing other horses all down the shedrow. They seemed to recede into space like the figures reflected in the background bulbs and mirrors of Flemish paintings. Debbie passed me an aluminum sweat scraper, a thin curved blade about a foot long, and I used it to scrape off the excess soap. Then she took bushel and hooked him to the hotwalker. He felt the pull and began to circle. Midway through the second go-round he let out a whinny, flexed his quarters, and shot both rear legs into the air.

"*Still* feeling good," Debbie said.

I stepped back a few steps, thinking of skulls busted like pumpkins, coils of brains.

Debbie could still remember the day she fell in love with horses. It happened in Virginia when she was a little girl. Her father took her to a horse show and she pressed her nose to the auditorium rail and looked down at the floor of the arena where Morgans and high-stepping Tennessee Walkers were on parade. The pageantry of the event stuck in her mind, and when she was nine she got a pony of her own and won titles all over the state. After graduating a year early from high school, she was offered several jobs but turned them down (the scene was too "political," she says) and instead went to work for a famous trainer of show horses in Massachusetts. She wasn't happy there. The trainer was tough, a stickler for detail. Debbie's day began at six and ended at dusk; she earned next to nothing. In the barn there was a large clock overhead, and every task the grooms had to perform was apportioned by it. Each horse received exactly forty minutes' grooming, then forty minutes' brushing with a currycomb. When the grooms finished, they had to sweep the barn, muck out the stalls, and arrange the dirty straw in a precise checkerboard pattern outside. Debbie lasted about three months. She left after the first frost, slipping away with a friend and boarding a plane for the friend's house in San Rafael, California.

Once she'd settled in Debbie went looking for a job at Bay Meadows. She got some work galloping horses and slowly built up her clientele, handling twelve to thirteen head every morning at three or four dollars a ride. Eventually she left California to work for a man who ran his horses at tracks in the East and Midwest, and made the Grooms' Grand Tour of Major Racing Installations in the United States. Every groom seemed to have made the tour at least once and they returned from it with copious mental notes on the various facilities available—backstretch accommodations, the quality of cafeteria food, the night life nearby. In Delaware Debbie got her trainer's license. The oral exam was difficult, she said, and to illustrate she told me about a man who tried to take it without bothering to study. "What does 'stifle' mean?" the examiners asked him.

The man shrugged "Means I don't get no trainer's license," he said. Debbie was glad she'd made the tour. "Now I know the grass *isn't* greener," she liked to say. She liked working for Glen Nolan. He paid her well and had recently advanced her twenty-five hundred dollars so she could claim an ancient router named Benson, a hard-hitting vet if ever there was one. Benson was stabled at Nolan's farm, burning hay, and rode in by van on days when he was scheduled to race. He was the fourth horse Debbie had owned and she'd made money on all of them. She was shrewd in money matters. Her own wagers, carefully placed, supplemented her income and allowed her to rent a small apartment in El Sobrante. She thought of herself as a homebody who spent quiet evenings among her cats, dogs, books, and friends. Perhaps she needed to make this distinction between her racetrack persona, brisk and efficient, and the more feminine self she was forced to keep hidden. Even though she discouraged them, backstretch Lotharios pursued her avidly. On Saturdays, she worked in pari-mutuels and from its pool of eligible bachelors she drew her suitors. When a young pari-mutuel clerk came by the barn one morning to say hello, dressed to the macho nines in patterned body shirt and aviator glasses, I saw Debbie flustered for the first time, trying to balance herself as she'd done so successfully on Bushel Ruler.

VII

Everybody had a theory about why so many young women came to the track looking for work, but I discarded them in favor of a very simple equation best put by little Liz Taylor in *National Velvet*. "I can't help it, father," Lizzie whined, "I'd rather have that horse happy than go to heaven!" What I saw in the shedrows was an ongoing love affair. For the most part, it revolved around service, and also the aesthetic pleasure to be derived from handling horses, but there was a randy underside to it as well, which could be seen in the smiles of certain ponygirls as they rode off the track after a good gallop, and in the dreamy-eyed look some grooms got as they stroked the flank of a colt. Most women hadn't read D. H. Lawrence, but a few of them raved to me about the books of Walter Farley, which they'd read in adolescence. Farley had written a series of juveniles starring the Black Stallion, who is described as follows when he makes his first appearance on a ships' landing in a small Arabian port:

> White lather ran from the horse's body; his mouth was open, his teeth bared. He was a giant of a horse, glistening black—too big to be pure Arabian. His mane was like a crest, mounting, then falling low. His neck was long and slender, and arched to the small, savagely beautiful head. The head was that of the wildest of all wild creatures—a stallion born wild—and it was beautiful, savage, splendid. A stallion with a wonderful physical perfection that matched his savage, ruthless spirit.

Once a young woman got a job, she was assigned tacitly to one of two prevailing social roles, princess or tramp. Princesses came to work at six in the morning, often with makeup on, lipstick, blusher, even eyeshadow. They were friendly but aloof, smiled but seldom laughed, worked hard, accepted no invitations, and remained untouchable except within the confines of a monogamous relationship. Tramps, it was understood, were fair game. They chewed gum, went braless, liked to party, and screwed around. If a woman slept with a man once, and only once, in healthy abandon, without any thought of the future, she ran the risk of being consigned forever to trampdom and hit upon by every lackluster dooley in manure-stained jeans.

"That girl who works for so-and-so," said one clucking male groom to another, "I hear she does the trick." Because women were permitted to do "men's work," the backstretch was supposed to be a liberated place, but I saw little evidence of this. More often I felt as if I were back in high school, observing the same tedious sexual constraints.

A few women at Golden Gate seemed suspended momentarily between roles. I saw the slim blonde from the Home Stretch every now and then, wandering around as though shopping for permanence. She'd picked up a friend along the way, a tall girl with pale blue eyes and ice-blond Nordic hair, and together they cruised the backstretch and grandstand waiting for something to happen. There was another woman around whom I thought of as a fallen princess not quite ready to become a tramp. I'd heard that she'd worked once for a trainer, but now she was unemployed. One morning I saw her alone on the infield grass, dressed in a flowing Hawaiian shirt and trousers. While jockeys bundled in rubber suits jogged around her, sweating off pounds, she did handstands and cartwheels, bouncing barefooted off the trunks of palms. Another morning, cold and foggy, she stood next to me during workouts. She wore a watch cap and a navy-blue greatcoat that touched the top of her shoes. Across the shoulders of the coat, thrown there like a fur piece, was a white cat. Every time the cat moved, the fallen princess caught it and returned it to her shoulders. When the sun came out she took off her cap, and long brown hair fell in tangles to her waist.

VIII

When Pico fell in love he did so with abandon. He became enamored of a grocer's wife in Arezzo who was married to a relative of Lorenzo de' Medici's. Presumably Pico could have carried on an affair, as did so many of his contemporaries, but he wanted all or nothing. So he mounted a night raid, taking along his secretary and twenty other men on horseback, then snatched his mistress from her donjon of commerce and spirited her away to a town nearby, barely escaping with his life. Fifteen men were killed in the skirmish following the kidnap. The siege came to an unhappy conclusion when Pico was arrested. Only Lorenzo's intervention saved him from the gallows. It was impossible for the wife of someone related to the Medici to be unfaithful, he said, and the kidnapped woman was returned to her husband a little the worse for wear. As for Pico, he wasn't capable of concocting such a plan. Certainly his secretary had misled him, said Lorenzo, turning the poor secretary over to the constables.

IX

From my grandstand seat I looked down at the paddock and there was Debbie Thomas leading Bushel Ruler around, both of them groomed and promising, her blond hair setting off the dark rippling of his coat. This was Bushel's debut. He looked strong and full of purpose, and Debbie had told me he was ready to win. At any moment I expected to feel the sensation that always accompanied the magic. I experienced it most vividly in my body, where I felt a sudden slackening of tensions, and then a lightness all over, as though

I'd just lost twenty pounds. When I was in this state I never doubted that my horse would win. Sometimes the race itself seemed anti-climactic. Nothing was happening, though, nothing at all. I tried to remember how it had felt to wash Bushel, the water and soap, the feel of his muscles, but the details remained fixed in their arc, useless to me now. In spite of my doubts I bet the horse as heavily as I'd ever bet any horse, knowing even as I laid my money down that I was in violation of some important principle.

I had ten long minutes to wait, and the couple sitting in front of me were making things worse with their constant chatter. They were from Cleveland, visiting an Albany relative, a bald old coot with a flame-red crown, and they kept talking about the Boy Mayor. "Kucinich's honest as all get out," the Cleveland man would say, "he just won't do what the crooks tell him to do." The Cleveland lady would respond by rolling up the sleeves of her dress a little higher and pitching in *her* two cents. "It's not just because he's Polish we like him," she'd say, "he means to do right by everybody, even the coloreds." I was perversely fascinated by the conversation, which went on and on, disrupting handicappers left and right, but at the same time I wished I had a manual of racetrack etiquette to present to these visitors from Ohio, one with as much bite as Giovanni della Casa's. "When you have blown your nose," della Casa advised his ill-mannered Florentine compatriots, "you should not open your handkerchief and inspect it, as if pearls or rubies had dropped out of your skull."

"Who do you like in this race, Ralph?" the coot asked his guest.

Before he could answer his wife extracted two dollars from her purse and waved them around.

"I don't care who *he* likes," she said, "you go bet that pretty number-two horse for me. That Bushel Whatzisname."

This cut me to the quick. I hated to be in line at a window and hear the person in front of me play the horse I intended to play. Such occurrences hurt my chances, stuffing too many expectations under a single saddle, and the Cleveland woman's commitment would be even worse, weightier, more fraught with neurosis. She was gross, she was stupid, she loved the Boy Mayor, and I knew I was sunk. Before my eyes the city of Adocentyn rose in reprimand. Dogs barked, lions roared, bulls lowered their heads and rammed into the walls, and from the eastern gate eagles took flight, their talons festooned with losing tickets. The magic could not be forced. It was instead a matter of being receptive, of sitting still, of recognizing the moment and then seizing it as Pico had seized his inamorata.

I had a few seconds' worth of elation when Bushel broke well and moved into second place, and I got another jolt when he was still second on the turn, and my heart was beating but good when he was *still* second going into the stretch, but then he began to fade, shortening his stride and sinking back into the commonplace, his ears drooping, his tail sagging, his body unable to sustain the effort just as I'd been unable to sustain the illusion. Together we watched as the other horses disappeared into the distance, dust in our eyes, space stretching out before us, and Sunday's Best, neat as a new suit, spitclean as a barbered head, receding from sight, galloping through the pinhole of victory.

I stopped at Nolan's barn to see Debbie, but she was talking to Gardell, the trainer, and neither of them looked ready for company. Debbie's checks were flushed and she was collecting tack with a fury. Bushel was already on the hotwalker. Some people say that horses know when they've lost, but I didn't notice any change in him. Maybe it would show next race, when he had less pride on which to draw. For now he was just circling. The next morning I learned why Debbie had seemed so angry. Bushel had been claimed by Mel Eisen, who trained for Dallas Black. Apparently Eisen had been tipped off to Bushel's potential when he saw him in a training race, running well against much more expensive stock. Debbie was disconsolate. She told me she'd cried for two straight hours after the race. Later that night, though she wasn't supposed to, she'd snuck over to Eisen's barn to check on Bushel. When he saw her coming, he stuck his head out of his stall and whinnied and nickered, just as he'd always done in the past.

XIV

I watched the Kentucky Derby in the press box. The race was a pure and emotional thing, and it brought us back to the essence of the sport and bleached our bones of caring. I came away from it feeling refreshed, and I thought how nice it would be actually to go to Kentucky someday and watch the race from that crackerjack grandstand and drink overpriced mint juleps and smell the ripe perfume of southern girls. This was the start of something, hope.

That night I went on a minor-league celebration with Arnold

Walker, who'd finished the day ahead and couldn't tolerate all that extra cash in his pockets. We had a big dinner at Spenger's and Arnold spilled some cabernet on his good gray vest. Next he dragged me into the room where they have the oyster bar and wall-size TV. "It's not so bad," he said. "Here, have a seat. I think you'll like it." He forced me to drink another bottle of wine and watch a beauty pageant. The semifinalists walked onstage through an arch formed by the crossed sabers of some cadets from the Citadel while the Citadel choir sang "You Light Up My Life." "I love it," Arnold said. "I absolutely love it." The Question Period followed the parade. Leroy Neiman, the Famous Artist, was a judge and he tried to trick one of the girls into revealing something out of the ordinary. "If you could pick one woman," Leroy said, winding up, ready to toss a spitball, "*other than your mother,* as your model, who would it be and why?" Miss Massachusetts thought it over. "My grandmother," she said. Miss Florida told what a bad driver she was, having accidents all the time and once driving right onto a porch where some old lady was eating breakfast. "I'll bet she takes drugs," said Arnold. "What'll you give me?" I wouldn't give him anything. We watched the coronation and the tears and then I went back to the Terrace and fell asleep in my clothes. When I woke in the morning the first thing I saw was the globe Ted had given me. I spun it around, looking for Italy.

About the Editor

Norman Sims teaches journalism history and writing classes at the University of Massachusetts at Amherst. He has a Ph.D. in communications from the University of Illinois, and his articles and reviews have appeared in *Journalism History, The Quill,* and other publications. In the early 1970s he worked as a reporter for United Press International. Since 1981 he has been a trustee and advisor to *Salt,* a magazine in Maine devoted to cultural journalism.